Lecture Notes in Computer Science　　　8337

Commenced Publication in 1973
Founding and Former Series Editors:
Gerhard Goos, Juris Hartmanis, and Jan van Leeuwen

Raja Natarajan (Ed.)

Distributed Computing and Internet Technology

10th International Conference, ICDCIT 2014
Bhubaneswar, India, February 6-9, 2014
Proceedings

 Springer

Volume Editor

Raja Natarajan
Tata Institute of Fundamental Research
School of Technology & Computer Science
Homi Bhabha Road, Colaba, Mumbai 400005, India
E-mail: raja@tifr.res.in

ISSN 0302-9743   e-ISSN 1611-3349
ISBN 978-3-319-04482-8   e-ISBN 978-3-319-04483-5
DOI 10.1007/978-3-319-04483-5
Springer Cham Heidelberg New York Dordrecht London

Library of Congress Control Number: 2013957425

CR Subject Classification (1998): C.2.0-2, C.2.4-5, F.2.2, H.3.3-5, H.4.1, H.5.3,
H.2.7-8, I.2.6, E.3, K.6.5, H.2.4

LNCS Sublibrary: SL 3 – Information Systems and Application,
incl. Internet/Web and HCI

Typesetting: Camera-ready by author, data conversion by Scientific Publishing Services, Chennai, India

Printed on acid-free paper

Springer is part of Springer Science+Business Media (www.springer.com)

Preface

Welcome to the proceedings of the 10th International Conference on Distributed Computing and Internet Technology (ICDCIT) held during February 6–9, 2014, at the Kalinga Institute of Information Technology (KIIT) University in Bhubaneshwar, India. The ICDCIT 2014 conference was sponsored by KIIT University. ICDCIT is an international forum for the discussion of contemporary research in distributed computing, Internet technologies, and related areas. Proceedings of all the past nine ICDCIT conferences have been published in the Springer LNCS series – volume 3347 (year 2004), 3816 (2005), 4317 (2006), 4882 (2007), 5375 (2008), 5966 (2010), 6536 (2011), 7154 (2012), and 7753 (2013).

ICDCIT 2014 received 205 abstracts, of which 197 (from nine countries) were followed by their full versions. The Program Committee consisted of 44 members from 15 countries. Each submission was reviewed by at least two Program Committee members, and on average by three Program Committee members, with the help of 62 external reviewers. The Program Committee meeting was conducted electronically over a period of two weeks in October 2013. The Program Committee decided to accept 29 papers (15%) for presentation and publication in the LNCS proceedings. The accepted papers fall into two disjoint categories, viz., regular papers and short papers. Among the 29 accepted papers, 18 are regular papers with a maximum length of 12 pages each, and 11 are short papers with a maximum length of six pages each. The Program Committee decided to introduce the category of short papers in order to make the conference more inclusive, and to provide greater scope for interesting conference presentations and discussions. We would like to thank all the Program Committee members for their hard work dedicated to reviews and discussions, and all the external reviewers for their invaluable contributions.

This volume also contains the full papers of six distinguished invited speakers: Gérard Berry (Collège de France, France), Bud Mishra (Courant Institute, USA), Elizabeth Buchanan (University of Wisconsin-Stout, USA), Anupam Datta (CMU, USA), Vivek Borkar (IIT Bombay, India), and François Fages (INRIA Paris-Rocquencourt, France). We would like to thank all the invited speakers for readily accepting our invitations to speak and also for sending their papers.

Our thanks to Achyuta Samanta (Founder KIIT), for his support of ICDCIT 2014 and for providing the infrastructure of KIIT to organize the conference. We are grateful to KIIT for sponsoring ICDCIT 2014. Our thanks to P.P. Mathur (Vice-Chancellor, KIIT) for the sponsorship. We are grateful to Maurice Herlihy (General Chair) and the Advisory Committee for their invaluable support and guidance. We are indebted to Arup Abhinna Acharya (Organizing Chair), D.N. Dwivedy, and Hrushikesha Mohanty for their tireless efforts that made ICDCIT 2014 in Bhubaneshwar possible.

Our thanks to all the authors whose scholarly submissions offered an interesting technical program. EasyChair made the handling of submissions and the production of the proceedings extremely smooth and efficient. For the publishing process at Springer, we would like to thank Alfred Hofmann and Anna Kramer for their constant help and cooperation. We acknowledge the Tata Institute of Fundamental Research (TIFR) for providing the infrastructural support to carry out this editorial work.

Our thanks to all the participants for the lively interactions that made ICD-CIT 2014 enjoyable.

February 2014   Raja Natarajan

Organization

Program Committee

Shivali Agarwal	IBM - IRL, India
Natasha Alechina	University of Nottingham, UK
Sowmya Arcot	UNSW, Australia
Gautam Barua	IIT Guwahati, India
Suman Bhattacharya	Tata Consultancy Services, India
Nikolaj Bjorner	Microsoft Research, USA
Meenakshi D'Souza	IIIT Bangalore, India
Van Hung Dang	Vietnam National University, Vietnam
Anwitaman Datta	NTU, Singapore
Elsa Estevez	UNU - IIST, China
Pablo Fillottrani	Universidad Nacional del Sur, Argentina
Michele G. Pinna	Università di Cagliari, Italy
Manoj Gore	MNNIT, India
Diganta Goswami	IIT Guwahati, India
Chittaranjan Hota	BITS-Pilani Hyderabad, India
Devesh Jinwala	SVNIT, India
Sanjeev K. Aggarwal	IIT Kanpur, India
Ajay K. Bisoi	KIIT University, India
Rushikesh K. Joshi	IIT Bombay, India
Jukka K. Nurminen	Aalto University, Finland
Salil Kanhere	UNSW, Australia
Deepak Kapur	University of New Mexico, USA
Delia Kesner	Université Paris 7, France
Simon Kramer	University of Lausanne, Switzerland
Paddy Krishnan	Oracle Labs, Australia
Valli Kumari Vatsavayi	Andhra University, India
Shyamanta M. Hazarika	Tezpur University, India
Sanjay Madria	Missouri S&T, USA
Sudhir Mudur	Concordia University, Canada
Krishnendu Mukhopadhyaya	ISI, India
Parimala N.	JNU, India
Ankur Narang	IBM - IRL, India
Raja Natarajan	TIFR, India (Program Chair)
Rajdeep Niyogi	IIT Roorkee, India
Adegboyega Ojo	UNU - IIST, China
Radha Krishna P.	SET Labs Infosys, India

Dana Petcu   West University of Timisoara, Romania
Krithi Ramamritham   IIT Bombay, India
Srini Ramaswamy   ABB Corporate Research, India
Manas Ranjan Patra   Berhampur University, India
Bhawani Sankar Panda   IIT Delhi, India
Manoj Saxena   University of Delhi, India
Hardeep Singh   GNDU, India
Hideyuki Takahashi   Tohoku University, Japan

Additional Reviewers

Amintoosi, Haleh   Karmakar, Arindam
Banik, Aritra   Larrea, Martín
Bapat, Jyotsna   Li, Kai
Bartoletti, Massimo   Li, Zhidong
Bengtson, Jesper   Lucas, Stephen
Biswas, Santosh   Maali, Fadi
Bondale, Nandini   Mandal, Partha Sarathi
Boratto, Ludovico   Martha, Venkata Swamy
Borisaniya, Bhavesh   Mohanty, Hrushikesha
Boro, Debojit   Nayak, Deveeshree
Cai, Xiongcai   Nitti, Marco
Casu, Giovanni   Parmar, Keyur
Cenci, Karina   Patel, Sankita
Channapayya, Sumohana   Paul, Himadri Sekhar
Chazelle, Bernard   Pazokifard, Banafsheh
Cimoli, Tiziana   Porwol, Lukasz
Contractor, Dipen   Prabhakaran, Vinod
Das, Gautam K.   Reinhardt, Andreas
Das, Nabanita   Sai Deepak, Krishnamurty
Das, Sandip   Sathish, V.
Di Ruberto, Cecilia   Sau, Buddhadeb
Doshi, Nishant   Scalas, Alceste
Epps, Julien   Semenovich, Dimitri
Ganugula, Uma Devi   Seshadhri, S.
Ghosh, Sanjay   Shah, Deven
Ghosh, Sasthi   Sudarsan, Sithu
Gunetti, Daniele   Sundaravaradan, Jithendrian
Gupta, Anupam   Sur, Arijit
Hüttel, Hans   Venkatesh, T.
Jariwala, Vivaksha   Yu, Liguo
Joshi, Hemant   Zhang, Jin

Table of Contents

Section 1: Invited Talks

Hop and HipHop: Multitier Web Orchestration 1
  Gérard Berry and Manuel Serrano

Reinforcement Learning for Matrix Computations: PageRank as an
Example 14
  Vivek S. Borkar and Adwaitvedant S. Mathkar

The New Normal? Revisiting Ethical Issues in Internet Research 25
  Elizabeth A. Buchanan

Cyber Security via Signaling Games: Toward a Science of Cyber
Security 34
  William Casey, Jose A. Morales, Thomson Nguyen,
  Jonathan Spring, Rhiannon Weaver, Evan Wright, and
  Bud Mishra

Privacy through Accountability: A Computer Science Perspective 43
  Anupam Datta

Cells as Machines: Towards Deciphering Biochemical Programs in the
Cell 50
  François Fages

Section 2: Distributed Computing

A Spatial Web Crawler for Discovering Geo-servers and Semantic
Referencing with Spatial Features 68
  Sonal Patil, Shrutilipi Bhattacharjee, and Soumya K. Ghosh

Software Transactional Memory Friendly Slot Schedulers 79
  Pooja Aggarwal and Smruti R. Sarangi

An Improved Approach of Decoupling in Mobile Cloud Computing 86
  Sohini De, Alok Misra, and Suddhasil De

Value Added Services on Stationary Vehicular Cloud 92
  Narayanan Vignesh, Rengaraj Shankar,
  Sundararajan Sathyamoorthy, and V. Mary Anita Rajam

FTM²: Fault Tolerant Batch Mode Heuristics in Computational Grid ... 98
  Sanjaya Kumar Panda, Pabitra Mohan Khilar, and
  Durga Prasad Mohapatra

SNAPWebD and SNAPSync: A Web Desktop and Transparent *sync*
of NFS and Standalone System Logical Volumes 105
  Anupama Potluri, Krishna Vutukuri, and Garvit Sharma

Section 3: Sensor Networks

Energy-Aware Multi-level Routing Algorithm for Two-Tier Wireless
Sensor Networks 111
  Tarachand Amgoth, Nabin Ghosh, and Prasanta K. Jana

Minimum Range Assignment Problem for Two Connectivity in Wireless
Sensor Networks 122
  Bhawani Sankar Panda and D. Pushparaj Shetty

A Digital-Geometric Approach for Computing Area Coverage
in Wireless Sensor Networks 134
  Dibakar Saha, Nabanita Das, and Shyamosree Pal

Effect of Choice of Discretization Methods on Context Extraction
from Sensor Data – An Empirical Evaluation 146
  Sangeeta Mittal, Krishna Gopal, and Shankar Lall Maskara

Section 4: Internet Technologies and Applications

Discrete Krill Herd Algorithm – A Bio-Inspired Meta-Heuristics
for Graph Based Network Route Optimization 152
  Chiranjib Sur and Anupam Shukla

A New Number System Using Alternate Fibonacci Numbers as the
Positional Weights with Some Engineering Applications 164
  Koushik Sinha, Rabindranath Ghosh, and Bhabani Prasad Sinha

User Profiling Based on Keyword Clusters for Improved
Recommendations 176
  Deepa Anand and Bonson Sebastian Mampilli

Equilibrium Balking Strategy in an Unobservable $GI/M/c$ Queue
with Customers' Impatience 188
  *Dibyajyoti Guha, Abhijit Datta Banik, Veena Goswami, and
  Souvik Ghosh*

Energy-Aware H.264 Decoding 200
  Arani Bhattacharya, Ansuman Banerjee, and Susmita Sur-Kolay

A Cost Effective Approach for Analyzing Software Product Lines 212
  *Ganesh Khandu Narwane, Shankara Narayanan Krishna, and
  Anup Kumar Bhattacharjee*

Fuzzy Logic Based Similarity Measure for Information Retrieval System
Performance Improvement 224
    Yogesh Gupta, Ashish Saini, A.K. Saxena, and Aditi Sharan

Maximizing Information or Influence Spread Using Flow Authority
Model in Social Networks 233
    Mohamed Mustafa Faisan and S. Durga Bhavani

Section 5: Security

A Second View on SecureString 2.0 239
    Günter Fahrnberger

Friend or Foe: Twitter Users under Magnification 251
    *Arjun Datt Sharma, Ansuya Ahluwalia, Shaleen Deep, and
    Divya Bansal*

Game Theoretic Attack Response Framework for Enterprise
Networks 263
    Arkadeep Kundu and Soumya K. Ghosh

Dynamic Ciphertext-Policy Attribute-Based Encryption for Expressive
Access Policy 275
    Y. Sreenivasa Rao and Ratna Dutta

Improvisation of Biometrics Authentication and Identification
through Keystrokes Pattern Analysis 287
    Dwijen Rudrapal, Smita Das, and Swapan Debbarma

Enhancing Privacy in Online Social Communities: Can Trust Help
Mitigate Privacy Risks? 293
    Venkata Swamy Martha, Nitin Agarwal, and Srini Ramaswamy

Section 6: Multimedia

Detection and Reduction of Impulse Noise in RGB Color Image Using
Fuzzy Technique 299
    Debashis Mishra, Isita Bose, Madhabananda Das, and B.S.P. Mishra

An Efficient Method for Speckle Reduction in Ultrasound Liver Images
for e-Health Applications 311
    *Suganya Ramamoorthy, Rajaram Siva Subramanian, and
    Deebika Gandhi*

Comparative Improvement of Image Segmentation Performance
with Graph Based Method over Watershed Transform Image
Segmentation 322
    Suman Deb and Subarna Sinha

Modeling Diffusion of Tabletop for Collaborative Learning Using
Interactive Science Lab Simulations 333
    Raghu Raman, Prema Nedungadi, and Maneesha Ramesh

A Binarization Feature Extraction Approach to OCR: MLP vs. RBF ... 341
    Amit Choudhary, Savita Ahlawat, and Rahul Rishi

Author Index 347

Hop and HipHop: Multitier Web Orchestration

Gérard Berry[1] and Manuel Serrano[2]

[1] Collège de France, 11 place Marcelin Berthelot, 75231 Paris Cedex 05, France
Gerard.Berry@college-de-france.fr
[2] Inria Sophia Méditerranée, 2004 route des Lucioles, 06902 Sophia Antipolis, France
Manuel.Serrano@inria.fr

Abstract. Rich applications merge classical computing, client-server concurrency, web-based interfaces, and the complex time- and event-based reactive programming found in embedded systems. To handle them, we extend the Hop web programming platform by HipHop, a domain-specific language dedicated to event-based process orchestration. Borrowing the synchronous reactive model of Esterel, HipHop is based on synchronous concurrency and preemption primitives that are known to be key components for the modular design of complex reactive behaviors. HipHop departs from Esterel by its ability to handle the dynamicity of Web applications, thanks to the reflexivity of Hop. Using a music player example, we show how to modularly build a non-trivial Hop application using HipHop orchestration code.

1 Introduction

Our aim is to help programming rich applications driven by computers, smart-phones or tablets; since they interact with various external services and devices, such applications require orchestration techniques that merge classical computing, client-server concurrency, web-based interfaces, and event-based programming. To achieve this, we extend the Hop multitier web programming platform [8] by the new HipHop domain specific language (DSL), which is based on the synchronous language Esterel [1]. HipHop orchestrates and synchronizes internal and external activities according to timers, events generated by the network, GUIs, sensors and devices, or internally computed conditions.

Like Esterel, Hiphop is a concurrent language based on the perfect synchrony hypothesis: a HipHop program repeatedly reacts in conceptual zero-delay to input events by generating output events; synchronization and communication between parallel statements is also performed in conceptual zero-delay. Perfect synchrony makes concurrent programs deterministic and deadlock-free, the only non-determinism left being that of the application environment. Its implementation is cycle-based, execution consisting of repeated atomic cycles "read inputs / compute reaction / generate outputs" in coroutine with the main Hop code. Concurrency is compiled away by static or dynamic sequential scheduling of code fragments. Cyclic execution atomicity avoids interference between computation and input-output, which is the usual source of unexpected non-determinism and synchronization problems for classical event-handler based programming.

R. Natarajan (Ed.): ICDCIT 2014, LNCS 8337, pp. 1–13, 2014.

While Esterel is limited to static applications, HipHop is designed for dynamicity. Its implementation on top of Hop makes it possible to dynamically build and run orchestration programs at any time using Hop's reflexivity facilities. It even makes it possible to modify a HipHop program between two execution cycles (not detailed here). It also simplifies the language by importing Hop's data definition facilities, expressions, modular structure, and higher-order programming features. It relies on the Web asynchronous concurrency and messaging already supported by Hop.

Section 2 briefly presents the Hop language. Section 3 describes HipHop and its relation with Hop. Section 4 presents a music application. Section 5 briefly overviews related work. We conclude in Section 6.

2   Hop

Hop has been presented in several publications [9,8]. We only remind its essential aspects and show some examples that should be sufficient to understand the rest of the paper.

Hop is a Scheme-based multitier functional language. The application server-side and client-side are both implemented within a single Hop program. Client code is distinguished from server code by prefixing it with the syntactic annotation '~'. Server-side values can be injected inside a client-side expression using a second syntactic annotation: the '$' mark. On the server, the client-side code is extracted, compiled on-the-fly into standard JavaScript, and shipped to the client. This enables Hop clients to be executed by unmodified Web browsers.

Except for its new multitier programming style, Hop uses the standard Web programming model. A server-side Hop program builds an HTML tree that creates the GUI and embeds client-side code into scripts, then ships it to the client. AJAX-like service-based programming is made available by service definitions, a service being a server-side function associated with a URL. The with-hop Hop form triggers execution of a service. Communication between clients and servers is automatically performed by the Hop runtime system, with no additional user code needed.

The Hop Web application fib-html below illustrates multitier programming. It consists of a server-built Web page displaying a three-rows table whose cells enumerate positive integers. When a cell is clicked, the corresponding Fibonacci value is computed on the client and displayed in a popup window. Note the '~' signs used lines 3,6, 7, and 8 which mark client-side expressions.

```
1: (define-service (fib-html)
2:    (<HTML>
3:       ~(define (fib x) ;; client-side code since prefixed by ~
4:           (if (< x 2) 1 (+ (fib (- x 1)) (fib (- x 2)))))
5:       (<TABLE>
6:           (<TR> (<TD> "fib(1)" :onclick ~(alert (fib 1))))
7:           (<TR> (<TD> "fib(2)" :onclick ~(alert (fib 2))))
8:           (<TR> (<TD> "fib(3)" :onclick ~(alert (fib 3)))))))
```

Let us modify the example to illustrate some Hop niceties. Instead of building the rows by hand, we let Hop compute them. The new Hop program uses the (iota 3) expression (line *9*) that evaluates to the list (1, 2, 3) and the map functional operator that applies a function to all the elements of a list. The $i expression (line *8*) denotes the value of i on the server at HTML document elaboration time, seamlessly exported to the client code:

```
1: (define-service (fib-html)
2:    (<HTML>
3:       ~(define (fib x) ...)
4:       (<TABLE>
5:          (map (lambda (i)
6:                  (<TR>
7:                     (<TD> "fib(" i ")"
8:                        :onclick ~(alert (fib $i)))))
9:             (iota 3)))))
```

Before delivery to a client, the server-side document is compiled on the server into regular HTML and JavaScript. It can then be executed by all standard browsers.

3 The HipHop Programming Language

HipHop embeds the reactive primitives of Esterel [1] within Hop while making maximal usage of Hop's expressive power. By convention, the '&' suffix is associated with HipHop code. Technically speaking, a HipHop form should be seen in two ways. First, it is a Hop constructor that builds a Hop value that represents a HipHop abstract syntax node. This makes it possible to dynamically build and run HipHop programs from within Hop. Second, it is a temporal statement executed by a *reactive machine* that communicates with Hop using logical HipHop events built by Hop out of physical or programmed events.

The reactive machine is triggered by Hop and perform conceptually instantaneous and deterministic *reactions* to its input HipHop events, generating output HipHop events.

3.1 HipHop Events

HipHop logical events are abstract Hop values of class HipHopEvent. They can be inputs and outputs of the reactive machine or local to the HipHop program, then helping synchronization and communication between its concurrent parts. HipHop events have an optional boolean presence/absence *status* and an optional *data value*. The status and value of each event are unique in each reaction and broadcast to the parallel components of the HipHop program.

The status of an event is *absent* by defaut. Input events are set *present* from Hop prior to the reaction using the hiphop-input! Hop form; this determines the *input context*. Local and output events are set present from within the

HipHop program by executing the `emit&` statement. The status of an event e is not memorized between successive reactions. It is read using the (`now&` e) form, while the status at the previous reaction is read using the (`pre&` e) form.

The data value of an event is defined when setting the status, either from Hop using `hiphop-input!` for an input or by `emit&` for an output or local. Contrarily to the status, the value is memorized between reactions. The current value of e is returned by the (`val&` e) form, while the value at the previous reaction is read using the (`preval&` e) form. As for Esterel, several emissions can occur for the same event in the same reaction; they are said to be *simultaneous*. In that case, the final value of the event is obtained by combining the individually emitted values using a combination function specified in the event Hop object declaration.

3.2 Reactive Machines and Their Reactions

Reactive machines interface Hop and HipHop. A machine M is defined by its HipHop input/output logical event interface and its HipHop program.

Hop delivers an input event `A` with value v to a reactive machine M using the form (`hiphop-input!` M `A` v). Any number of inputs can be delivered before a reaction; they are only valid for this reaction. A reaction is triggered from within Hop by (`hiphop-react!` M). Determining when a machine should react is solely Hop's responsibility. However, to simplify a common case, it is possible to write (`hiphop-input-and-react!` M `A` v) to pass an input and trigger a reaction right away.

A reaction may trigger output events, the actual output action being performed by associated Hop listeners associated with the events and stored in the reactive machine. To handle data, a reaction may also trigger the evaluation of Hop expressions using the `atom&` HipHop statement, see Section 3.4.

Seen from Hop, a HipHop reaction is simply a standard function call. Seen from HipHop, the execution of the reaction is conceptually performed in zero-delay, the HipHop program sleeping between two successive reactions and remembering its control state from one reaction to the next. This coroutine execution scheme avoids interference between input event registering and reactions, which is a common cause of unwanted non-determinism and deadlocks with classical threading techniques.

A reactive machine can be executed on the server or shipped to and executed on a client, because it is a standard Hop object. Several reactive machines can coexist in the same application, making it possible to use a GALS programming model (Globally Asynchronous, Locally Synchronous) without extra overhead. This will not be detailed here.

3.3 HipHop Intuitive Execution Semantics

The reactive code is based on deterministic sequencing, concurrency, and temporal statements inspired from Esterel [1]. Control positions are memorized from one reaction to the next. To illustrate sequencing, consider the following sequence:

```
(seq&
  (await& A)
  (await& B)
  (emit& O)
```

where A and B (resp. O) are input (resp. output) HipHop events. Intuitively, the code waits for A and then B to be present, before emitting O and terminating synchronously: O is emitted within the reaction triggered by B. Technically, at first reaction, the HipHop control flow stops on (await& A), and yields back control to Hop. HipHop control stays there at each subsequent reaction until the first reaction where A is present. In this reaction, control immediately moves to (await& B) and stays there until the next reaction where B is present. During this reaction, and without further delay, it outputs O and terminates.

To illustrate concurrency, consider now the following HipHop code:

```
(seq&
  (par& (await& A) (await& B))
  (emit& O)
```

Here, A and B are waited for in parallel, not in sequence. The par& statement terminates when all its arms are terminated. Thus, O is emitted exactly when the last of A and B occurs (note that A and B may be both present in the same reaction if they have been both input into the reactive machine before the reaction is triggered). In HipHop, concurrency and sequencing can be mixed arbitrarily, and the same holds for all other instructions.

We say that a statement that starts and terminates in the same reaction is *instantaneous* or *immediate*; this is the case for emit&. Otherwise, we say that the statement *pauses*, waiting for the next reaction, and we call it a *delay statement*; this is the case for await&. Things that happen in the same reaction are called *simultaneous*. This is of course a conceptual notion in terms of abstract reactions, not a physical one.

3.4 HipHop Core Statements

As for Esterel, statements are divided into *core statements*, which are primitives and handy *derived statements*. Thanks to Hop's reflexivity, derived statements can be trivially defined from core statements using Hop. We first detail the core statements.

The nothing& statement does nothing and terminates instantaneously. It is the HipHop no-op. The (emit& e [v]) statement emits its event e with value determined by optional v. It terminates instantaneously. The (atom& expr) statement calls Hop to executes the expr Hop expression; it is instantaneous, which means that its Hop argument execution time should be kept negligible in practice.

The `pause&` statement delays execution by one reaction: it pauses for the reaction and terminates at the next reaction.

The (`if&` *test then else*) statement instantaneously evaluates *test*. If the result is true, it immediately starts *then* and behaves as it from then on; otherwise, it does the same with *else*. These can be arbitrary HipHop statements. Termination of the `if&` statement is instantaneously triggered by termination of the selected branch. The `seq&` statement executes its arguments in order: the first one starts immediately when the sequence starts; when it terminates, be it immediately or in a delayed way, the second argument is immediately started, etc. For instance, (`seq&` (`emit&` A) (`emit&` B)) immediately emits A and B, which are seen as simultaneous within the reaction, while (`seq&` (`emit&` A) (`pause&`) (`emit&` B)) emits A and B in two successive reactions.

The `loop&` statement is a loop-forever, equivalent to the infinite sequential repetition of its argument statements, themselves implicitly evaluated in sequence. For instance, (`loop&` (`pause&`) (`emit&` A)) waits for the next reaction and then keeps emitting A at each reaction. Exiting a `loop&` can only be done by using the `trap&`/`exit&`, `abort&`, and `until&` statements, see below.

The `par&` statement starts its arguments concurrently and terminates when the last of them terminates. Therefore, (`par&` (`await&` A) (`await&` B)) immediately terminates when both A and B have been received. Remember that all arms of a `par&` statement see all statuses and values of all (visible) events in exactly the same way.

The `suspend&` statement immediately starts its body. At all following instants, it suspends (freezes) the execution of its body for the reaction when its condition is true. The `suspend&` statement terminates if its body is executed and terminates. For instance,

```
(suspend& (now& A)
   (loop&
      (emit& B)
      (pause&)))
```

emits B at first instant and at all subsequent instants where A is absent.

The `trap&` statement defines a named exit point for its body. The `exit&` statement provokes immediate termination of the corresponding `trap&` statement, as well as immediate termination of all concurrent statements within the `trap&` body, which do normally receive the control at that instant.

The `local&` statement declares local events in the first argument list. Their scope is the body, which is the implicitly `seq&` list of the remaining HipHop arguments. The declared events are not visible from Hop. A `local&` statement terminates when its body does.

3.5   HipHop Derived Statements

The derived statements can be easily defined from the kernel ones using Hop. The `halt&` statement pauses forever; it is defined as (`loop&` (`pause&`)). The

sustain& statement keeps emitting its event at each reaction. The await& statement pauses and waits for its expression to become true and terminates:

```
(define (await& evt)
   (trap& (done)
      (loop&
         (pause&)
         (if& (now& evt) (exit& done)))))
```

The abort& statement instantaneously kills its sequential body when its condition becomes true, not passing the control to its body in this reaction; this is
what we call *strong abortion*:

```
(define (abort& evt . stmt-list)
   (trap& (done)
      (par&
         (suspend& (now& evt) stmt-list)
         (await& evt (exit& done)))))
```

The until& statement instantaneously kills its body when its condition becomes
true, but only at the end of the reaction, passing the control to its body for the
last time at that reaction as for an exited trap&; this is what we call *weak abortion*. The loop-each& statement immediately starts its body, and then stongly
kills it and restarts it immediately whenever its condition becomes true. The
every& statement is similar but starts by waiting for the condition instead of
immediately starting its body (see [7]).

Once defined, these statements can be freely used in HipHop programs. Note
that this makes the language fully user-extensible. One can also build dynamically statements from dynamic values computed during Hop execution, and even
dynamically modify the program between two reactions, for instance to use and
orchestrate services dynamically detected at runtime. Note also that there is no
need to redefine the basic arithmetic, list, and string expressions since Hop's
ones can be reused (with some care however, no details given here).

4   An Application Example

We build a Lastfm-like smart music player called HopFM that orchestrates musical content and related information available on third party Web sites. It plays
music continuously, switching from one artist to another according to musical
similarities. It automatically fetches and displays information about music and
authors.

The user first selects a musical genre in a dynamically discovered list. This
activates the Hop control screen of Figure 1. The top of screen is used to adjust
the volume, pause the music, switch to the next track, etc. Below stands the
Start button (zone 2, Figure 1) that starts HopFM when clicked. HopFM then
searches the internet for a random artist of the selected genre, downloads a limited number of tracks of this artist, and starts playing. When a new track starts,

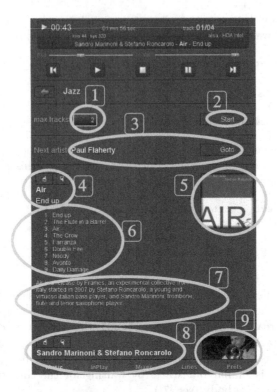

Fig. 1. The smartphone screenshot of HopFM. Ellipses show active zones managed by Hiphop. Zone 1 sets the number of tracks to play per artist. Zone 2 initiates the music play by starting the reactive machine. Zone 3 displays the name of the next artist and the button to switch to his music. Zone 4 reports the current track name and the album name; the two top buttons enable the user to emit positive or negative recommendations. Zone 5 displays the album image, zone 6 the album's track list, zone 7 comments about the album. Zone 8 displays the artist name and two buttons to emit positive or negative recommendations. Zone 9 displays an image of the artist.

HopFM looks for related information on the internet: the associated album, its image, its track list, and reviews. In parallel, HopFM searches and displays information about the played artist: his biography, his discography, some news, and some blogs and reviews.

Also in parallel, the application searches the Web for similar artists to be played later on, either when the currently downloaded tracks are over or when the user clicks the ⎡Goto⎤ button (zone 3). If no similar artist is found, or if all the known similar artists have been played, HopFM randomly chooses a new random artist of the genre and starts again. HopFM keeps running until the user clicks the top stop button.

The music player uses the following third-party services to retrieve musical contents and information about the tracks and artists: *Free Music Archive*[1] (FMA), which provides mp3 music and informations about the tracks, albums, and artists; *EchoNest*[2], a database about tracks, artists, images, artist similarities, and alignment information between other databases; *MusicBrainz*[3], an open music encyclopedia that collects music metadata.

HipHop orchestrates the requests to these remote services. For instance, to search for an artist image, several requests to several sites are emitted simultaneously. As soon as the first one completes, the other ones are aborted and the GUI is updated. If the artist changes before any request completes, all current requests are aborted.

HipHop also handles user interactions and signals raised by the actual hardware music player. Web services returns or errors, user interaction, and music player events are the three sources of external asynchrony. They are all managed uniformly by HipHop, local synchronous parallelism and communication being essential to regulate and orchestrate external asynchrony.

4.1 HopFM Implementation

Clicking $\boxed{\text{Start}}$ invokes the Hop client-side `hopfm-play` function, which constructs a reactive HipHop machine, creates various events, binds the external Hop events to the HipHop interface events, creates a HipHop reactive program, loads it into the machine, and eventually triggers the first reaction:

```
(define (hopfm-play catalog genre::genre)

   (define musicstate (instantiate::HipHopEvent))
   (define track (instantiate::HipHopEvent))
   (define artist (instantiate::HipHopEvent))
   (define playlist (instantiate::HipHopEvent))
   ...

   (define (hopfm&) ...)

   (let ((M (instantiate::HopHifiMachine
               (program (hopfm&)))))
     ;; bind the machine to external HopHifi events
     (add-event-listeners! M musicstate track artist)
     ;; trigger first HipHop reaction
     (hiphop-react! M)))
```

The Hop function `add-event-listeners!` connects the actual hardware player to the HipHop program. It binds Hop listeners that forward the events to HipHop.

---

[1] http://freemusicarchive.org
[2] http://echonest.com
[3] http://musicbrainz.org

```
(define (add-event-listeners! M musicstate track artist)
   (add-event-listener! server "hophifi-state"
      ;; listener called when the music player state changes
      (lambda (e)
         ;; forward the Hop event to HipHop
         (hiphop-input-and-react! M musicstate (event-value e))))
   (add-event-listener! server "hophifi-track"
      ;; listener is called when a new track starts
      ;; or when the playlist changes
      (lambda (e)
         (let* ((ev (event-value e))
                (tk (list-ref ev.playlist ev.song)))
            ;; forward the track and artist to HipHop
            (hiphop-input! M track tk)
            (hiphop-input! M artist (track-artist tk))
            (hiphop-react! M)))))
```

The HipHop program hopfm& runs a number of components in synchronous
deterministic parallel, each in charge of a specific task. These components synchronize each other by communicating synchronously using the HipHop events
defined above: track, artist, playlist, album, etc. The random-playlist&
component looks for random playlists, each playlist being associated with an
artist; playlist& waits for playlist changes and starts searching for the next
artist; track& waits for the hardware player to start a new track, checks if it
belongs to a different album or to a different artist and, in this case, emits the
HipHop events album and artist towards the other components; artist-info&
waits for a new artist event, searches the internet for information about that
artist, and emits an event that lets the gui& component update the screen. The
HipHop program stops when the user clicks the main ⎡stop⎤ button, which raises
the musicstate HipHop event with value stop; the enclosing until& statement
then generates a global preemption that kills all internal activities and terminates; termination can also occur if no artist is found (musicstate value ended).

```
(define (hopfm&)
   (until& (memq (val& musicstate) '(stop ended))
      (par& ;; running all the components in synchronous parallel
         ;; peek a random playlist
         (random-playlist& catalog genre playlist)
         ;; playlist manager
         (playlist& playlist)
         ;; deal with new tracks
         (track& track album artist)
         ;; manage new artists
         (artist-info& catalog genre artist bio discog similar playlist)
         ;; update the gui
         (gui& musicstate track album artist bio discog similar))))
```

Let us detail `random-playlist&`. Its operation requires two steps: calling FMA for a random artist of the desired genre and checking that this artist has published music. The FMA request is proxied via the Hop server using the HipHop `with-hop&` statement that takes as parameter a service call and a HipHop event to emit if the request completes successfully; `with-hop&` simply terminates silently otherwise. Note that the artist found is kept local, since the global artist handled by other modules is the one currently played.

```
(define (random-playlist& catalog genre playlist)
   (trap& found
      ;; start looping
      (loop&
         ;; creates two local events
         (local& ((local-artist (instantiate::HipHopEvent))
                  (local-playlist (instantiate::HipHopEvent)))
            ;; get a random artist from FMA
            (with-hop& ($hopfm/genre/artist/random genre catalog)
               local-artist)
            ;; get the tracks of that artist
            (with-hop& ($hopfm/artist/tracks (val& local-artist))
               local-playlist)
            (if& (pair? (val& local-playlist))
               ;; an artist with music is found
               (seq&
                  (emit& playlist (val& playlist))
                  (exit& found)))))))
```

The `artist-info&` component searches in parallel an image of the current artist, information about that artist, and a similar artist with a playlist. it outputs `bio`, `discog`, `similar`, and `playlist` towards the other components as soon as the corresponding information has been found.

```
(define (artist-info& catalog genre artist bio discog similar playlist)
   (every& (now& artist) ;; we have a playlist for that artist
      (par&
         ;; request a similar artist list
         (similar-artist& catalog genre playlist artist similar)
         ;; fetch artist biography and discography
         (artist/bio& artist bio discog)
         ;; fetch the artist images
         (artist/image& artist))))
```

The `artist/image&` subcomponent of `artist&` calls FMA and EchoNest in paralle to find an artist image. As soon as one server responds, the other request is aborted using a `trap&` statement with `exit&` triggered when the `img` local signal is received. If no image is found, the currently displayed image is hidden:

```
(define (artist/image& artist)
   ;; find the first image out of two services
   (let ((el (dom-get-element-by-id "hophifi-internet-artist-image")))
      (local& ((img (instantiate::HipHopEvent (name "image"))))
         ;; try to find one image on two different servers
         ;; abort the pending request as soon as one returns
         (trap& (done)
            (par&
               (seq&
                  (with-hop& ($hopfm/artist/image (val& artist)) img)
                  (if& (now& img) (exit& done)))
               (seq&
                  (with-hop& ($hopfm/artist/image/echonest (val& artist))
                     img)
                  (if& (now& img) (exit& done)))))
         (if& (now& img)
            ;; update the GUI with the new image
            (atom&
               (node-style-set! el :visibility "visible")
               (set! el.src (val& img)))
            ;; no image was found, hides the current one
            (atom& (node-style-set! el :visibility "hidden"))))))
```

Note the architectural power of nested preemption. In `artist&` above, when the `artist` signal event is received, the `every&` preemption loop kills is body, aborting `artist/image&` and by transitivity its spawned `with-hop&` requests that might still be pending. Furthermore, the enclosing `until& musicstate` statement of `hopfm&` has an even greater preemption power since it kill all activities in the program: external preemptions dominate internal ones.

The other HopFM HipHop components are omitted here because their implementation is similar.

5 Related Work

We presented a preliminary version of HipHop at the Plastic'11 workshop [2]. While the core language has been kept stable, the integration with HOP has been entirely redesigned and the former version should be considered as obsolete.

Orc [3] addresses the service coordination issue by proposing a combinator-based process calculus The temporal algebra of HipHop is richer than that of Orc. However HipHop does not yet offer the flexibility of the Orc data-stream pipeline $f > x > g$ operator for large-scale data processing. Flapjax [5] provided a unified framework for client-side event-based programming, based on implicit control defined by data streams instead of explicit control in Hiphop. Jolie [6] is a framework to write and orchestrate Web Services using a service-oriented programming language inspired by the π-calculus. However, contrarily to HipHop, Jolie is limited to server-only orchestration.

6   Conclusion

We have presented HipHop, a new domain-specific synchronous language geared to the orchestration of services and user intreaction within Hop on server and client sides. HipHop deals with logical events exposed by Hop. Its statements are imported from Esterel. They are based on temporal sequentiality, concurrency and preemption, which make it possible to replace the traditional asynchronous thread / event-handler spaghetti [4] by a well-understood synchronous programming style imported from embedded systems programming. The reflexivity of Hop makes it possible to build HipHop programs, ship them to clients or other servers, and run them.

With our LastFM example, we have sketched how to orchestrate Web services and GUI events with HipHop, using its reactive statements as key architectural tools.

Our current implementation is an interpreter directly based on Esterel's constructive semantics [1]. More efficient implementations will certainly be needed for large-scale applications, see [7].

Acknowledgements. We thank Cyprien Nicolas, who implemented HipHop in Hop and participated in the PLASTIC'11 first paper about HipHop.

References

1. Berry, G.: The foundations of Esterel. In: Proof, Language and Interaction: Essays in Honour of Robin Milner. MIT Press (2000)
2. Berry, G., Nicolas, C., Serrano, M.: HipHop: A Synchronous Reactive Extension for Hop. In: Proceedings of the PLASTIC 2011 Workshop, Portland, USA (October 2011)
3. Kitchin, D., Cook, W.R., Misra, J.: A language for task orchestration and its semantic properties. In: Baier, C., Hermanns, H. (eds.) CONCUR 2006. LNCS, vol. 4137, pp. 477–491. Springer, Heidelberg (2006)
4. Lee, E.A.: The Problem with Threads. IEEE Computer 39(5), 33–42 (2006)
5. Meyerovich, L.A., Guha, A., Baskin, J., Cooper, G.H., Greenberg, M., Bromfield, A., Krishnamurthi, S.: Flapjax: a programming language for ajax applications. In: Proceeding of the 24th ACM SIGPLAN Conference on Object Oriented Programming Systems Languages and Applications, OOPSLA 2009, pp. 1–20. ACM, New York (2009)
6. Montesi, F., Guidi, C., Lucchi, R., Zavattaro, G.: Jolie: a java orchestration language interpreter engine. Electr. Notes Theor. Comput. Sci. 181, 19–33 (2007)
7. Potop-Butucaru, D., Edwards, S.A., Berry, G.: Compiling Esterel. Springer (2007)
8. Serrano, M., Berry, G.: Multitier Programming in Hop - a first step toward programming 21st-century applications. Communications of the ACM 55(8), 53–59 (2012)
9. Serrano, M., Gallesio, E., Loitsch, F.: HOP, a language for programming the Web 2.0. In: Proceedings of the First Dynamic Languages Symposium, Portland, Oregon, USA (October 2006)

Reinforcement Learning for Matrix Computations: PageRank as an Example

Vivek S. Borkar and Adwaitvedant S. Mathkar

Department of Electrical Engineering,
Indian Institute of Technology,
Powai, Mumbai 400076, India
{borkar.vs,mathkar.adwaitvedant}@gmail.com

Abstract. Reinforcement learning has gained wide popularity as a technique for simulation-driven approximate dynamic programming. A less known aspect is that the very reasons that make it effective in dynamic programming can also be leveraged for using it for distributed schemes for certain matrix computations involving non-negative matrices. In this spirit, we propose a reinforcement learning algorithm for PageRank computation that is fashioned after analogous schemes for approximate dynamic programming. The algorithm has the advantage of ease of distributed implementation and more importantly, of being model-free, i.e., not dependent on any specific assumptions about the transition probabilities in the random web-surfer model. We analyze its convergence and finite time behavior and present some supporting numerical experiments.

Keywords: Reinforcement Learning, PageRank, Stochastic Approximation, Sample Complexity.

1 Introduction

Reinforcement learning has its roots in models of animal behavior [1] and mathematical psychology [2], [3]. The recent resurgence of interest in the field, however, is propelled by applications to artificial intelligence and control engineering. By now there are several textbook accounts of this development [4] (Chapter 16), [5], [6], [7], [8], [9]. To put things in context, recall that methodologically, reinforcement learning sits somewhere in between supervised learning, which works with a reasonably accurate information regarding the performance gradient or something analogous (e.g., parameter tuning of neural networks), and unsupervised learning, which works without such explicit information (e.g., clustering). To be specific, supervised learning is usually based upon an optimization formulation such as minimizing an error measure, which calls for a higher quantum of information per iterate. Reinforcement learning on the other hand has to manage with signals somehow correlated with performance, but which fall short of the kind of information required for a typical supervised learning scheme. It then makes simple incremental corrections based on these 'suggestive though inexact'

R. Natarajan (Ed.): ICDCIT 2014, LNCS 8337, pp. 14–24, 2014.

signals, usually with low per iterate computation. The latter aspect has also made it a popular framework for models of bounded rationality in economics [10].

Our interest is in its recent avatar as a scheme for simulation-based methodology for approximate dynamic programming for Markov decision processes which has found applications, among other things, in robotics [11]. These can be viewed as stochastic approximation counterparts of the classical iterative methods for solving dynamic programming equations, such as value and policy iteration. Stochastic approximation, introduced by Robbins and Monro [12] as an iterative scheme for finding the roots of a nonlinear function given its noisy measurements, is the basis of most adaptive schemes in control and signal processing. What it does in the present context is to replace a conditional average appearing on the right hand side of the classical iterative schemes (or their variants) by an actual evaluation at a simulated transition according to the conditional distribution in question. It then makes an incremental move towards the resulting random quantity. That is, it takes a convex combination of the current value and the random right hand side, with a slowly decreasing weight on the latter. The averaging properties of stochastic approximation then ensure that asymptotically you see the same limiting behavior as the original scheme.

But there are other situations wherein one encounters iterations involving conditional averages. In fact, by pulling out row sums of a non-negative matrix into a diagonal matrix pre-multiplier, we can write it as a product of a diagonal matrix and a stochastic matrix. This allows us to cast iterations involving non-negative matrices as iterations involving averaging with respect to stochastic matrices, making them amenable to the above methodology. This opens up the possibility of using reinforcement learning schemes for distributed matrix computations of certain kind. Important instances are plain vanilla averaging and estimation of the Perron-Frobenius eigenvectors [13]. Reinforcement learning literature is replete with means of curtailing the curse of dimensionality, a hazard only too common in dynamic programming applications. This machinery then becomes available for such matrix computations. An important special case is the case of linear function approximation, wherein one approximates the desired vector by a weighted combination of a moderate number of basis vectors, and then updates these weights instead of the entire vector [14].

In the present article, we illustrate this methodology in the context of Google's PageRank, an eigenvector-based ranking scheme. It is primarily based on the stationary distribution π of the 'random web-surfer' Markov chain, equivalently, the normalized left Perron-Frobenius eigenvector of its transition probability matrix. This chain is defined on a directed graph wherein each node i is a web page. Let $\mathcal{N}(i) :=$ the set of nodes to which i points. Let $d(i) := |\mathcal{N}(i)|$ and $N :=$ the total number of nodes. The chain moves from i to $j \in \mathcal{N}(i)$ with a probability $(1 - c)\frac{1}{d(i)} + \frac{c}{N}$, and to any other node in the graph with probability $\frac{c}{N}$ where $c > 0$ is the 'Google constant'. The latter renders it irreducible, ensuring a unique stationary distribution. An excellent account of the numerical techniques for computing π, essentially based on the 'power method' and its variants, appears in [15], along with a brief historical account. See also [16]. While a bulk of the work in this direction has been on efficient computations for the power method, there have also been alternative approaches, such as Markov Chain Monte Carlo [17], [18], optimization based methods [19], and schemes based on stochastic approximation and/or gossip [20], [21], [22].

Such 'spectral ranking' techniques, made popular by the success of PageRank, are in fact quite old. See [23] for a historical survey. Evaluative exercises of this kind occur in other applications as well, such as reputation systems or popularity measures on social networks. In such applications (for that matter, in search), it is unclear whether the assumption that each $j \in \mathcal{N}(i)$ is equally important to i is reasonable. Motivated by this, we propose a model-free scheme based on ideas from reinforcement learning. This idea has also been discussed in [13]. The present scheme, however, differs in an essential way from [13] in that whereas [13] views PageRank as a special instance of the general problem of eigenvector estimation, we exploit the special structure of the random web-surfer model to simplify the problem to a simple linear scheme. This is very much in tune with some of the works cited above (notably [20], [22]), but with a non-standard sample and update rule. The outcome is an algorithm that can run on accumulated traces of node-to-node interactions without requiring us to explicitly estimate the probabilities associated with these.

The next section describes our algorithm and its convergence analysis. Section 3 describes finite time analysis and a variant of the basic scheme. Section 4 presents some numerical experiments. Section 5 concludes with some general observations.

2 The Algorithm

Let P be an $N \times N$ stochastic matrix. Define $\hat{P} := cP + \frac{1-c}{N} \begin{bmatrix} 1 & \cdots & 1 \\ \vdots & \ddots & \vdots \\ 1 & \cdots & 1 \end{bmatrix}$. Let π denote the unique stationary probability distribution of $\hat{P}$. That is, for $\mathbf{1} := [1, 1, \cdots, 1]^T$,

$$\pi = \pi \hat{P}$$

$$= \pi cP + \pi \frac{1-c}{N} \begin{bmatrix} 1 & \cdots & 1 \\ \vdots & \ddots & \vdots \\ 1 & \cdots & 1 \end{bmatrix}$$

$$= c\pi P + \frac{1-c}{N} \mathbf{1}^T$$

$$\Rightarrow \pi(I - cP) = \frac{1-c}{N} \mathbf{1}^T$$

$$\Rightarrow \pi = \frac{1-c}{N} \mathbf{1}^T (I - cP)^{-1}.$$

Here π is a row vector and every other vector is a column vector. Since we are only interested in ranking we can neglect the factor $\frac{1-c}{N}$. Thus by abuse of terminology,

$$\pi^T = 1 + cP^T\pi^T.$$

To estimate π, we run the following N dimensional stochastic iteration. Sample (X_n, Y_n) as follows: Sample X_n uniformly and independently from $\{1, 2, ..., N\}$. Sample Y_n with $P(Y_n = j|X_n = i) = p(i,j)$, independent of all other random variables realized before n. Update z_n as follows:

$$z_{n+1}(i) = z_n(i) + a(n)(I\{X_{n+1} = i\}(1 - z(n)) + cz_n(X_{n+1})I\{Y_{n+1} = i\}), \quad (1)$$

where the step-sizes $a(n) > 0$ satisfy $\sum_{n=0}^{\infty} a(n) = \infty$ and $\sum_{n=0}^{\infty} a(n)^2 < \infty$. Hence $z_n(i)$ is updated only if X_{n+1}, Y_{n+1} or both are i. We can write (1) as follows:

$$z_{n+1}(i)$$
$$= z_n(i) + a(n)(I\{X_{n+1} = i\}(1 - z(n)) + cz_n(X_{n+1})p(X_{n+1}, i) + M_{n+1}(i)),$$

where $M_{n+1} := cz_n(X_{n+1})I\{Y_{n+1} = i\} - cz_n(X_{n+1})p(X_{n+1}, i)$ is a martingale difference sequence w.r.t. $\sigma(X_m, Y_m, m \leq n; X_{n+1})$. By Theorem 2, p. 81, [24], the ODE corresponding to the iteration is

$$\dot{z}(i) = \frac{1}{N}(1 + \sum_{j=1}^{N} cz(j)p(j,i) - z(i)).$$

In vector form,

$$\dot{z} = \frac{1}{N}(1 + cP^T z - z).$$

Since the constant $1/N$ doesn't affect the asymptotic behavior, we consider

$$\dot{z} = (1 + cP^T z - z) =: h(z). \quad (2)$$

Define $h_\infty(z) := \lim_{a\uparrow\infty} \frac{h(az)}{a} = cP^T z - z$. It is easy to see that $\frac{h(az)}{a} \to h_\infty(z)$ uniformly on R^N.

Theorem 1. Under the above assumptions, $z(t) \to z^*$ a.s., where z^* is the unique solution to $h(z^*) = 0$.

Proof: Define $V_p(z(t)) := \|z(t) - z^*\|_p$, $p \in [1, \infty)$. As in the proof of Theorem 2, p. 126, [24], for $1 < p < \infty$,

$$\dot{V}_p(z(t)) \leq \|cP^T(z(t) - z^*)\|_p - \|z(t) - z^*\|_p.$$

Integrating,

$$V_p(z(t)) - V_p(z(s)) \leq \int_s^t \left(\|cP^T(z(r) - z^*)\|_p - \|z(r) - z^*\|_p \right) dr.$$

Letting $p \downarrow 1$,

$$V_1(z(t)) - V_1(z(s)) \leq \int_s^t \|cP^T(z(r) - z^*)\|_1 - \|z(r) - z^*\|_1 dr,$$

$$\leq - \int_s^t (1 - c)\|z(r) - z^*\|_1 dr,$$

$$\leq 0,$$

with equality iff $z(t) = z^*$. We similarly get that $V_1(z(t)) := \|z(t)\|_1$ is a Lyapunov function for the scaled o.d.e $\dot{z}(t) = h_\infty(z(t))$ which has the origin as its globally asymptotically stable asymptotic equilibrium. By Theorem 9, p. 75, [24], $\sup_n \|z(n)\| < \infty$ a.s. In turn (2) has z^* as its globally stable asymptotic equilibrium with $V(z(t)) = \|z(t) - z^*\|_1$ as its Lyapunov function. The claim follows from Theorem 7 and Corollary 8, p. 74, [24]. $\qquad\square$

3   Remarks

1. We first look at sample complexity of the stochastic iteration. We mainly use section 4.2 of [24] to derive sample complexity estimates.

   Let $1 \leq m < M < N$. Let z^* denote the stationary distribution. Without loss of generality (by relabeling if necessary), let $z_1^* \geq z_2^* \geq \dots \geq z_N^*$, i.e., the components of z^* are numbered in accordance with their ranking. We shall consider as our objective the event that the top m ranks of z^* fall within the top M ranks of the output of our algorithm when stopped, for a prescribed pair $m < M$. This is a natural criterion for ranking problems, which are an instance of 'ordinal optimization' [25]. To avoid pathologies, we assume that $z_m^* > z_M^*$. We shall derive an estimate for the number of iterates needed to achieve our aim with 'high' probability. Let $C := \{z \in \Delta^N : \text{ if } z_{l_1} \geq z_{l_2} \geq \dots \geq z_{l_N} \text{ then } z_i \geq z_{l_M}, 1 \leq i \leq m\}$, where $\frac{N}{1-c}\Delta^N$ is the N-dimensional probability simplex. Thus C consists of all distributions such that the top m indices of z^* are in the top M indices of the given distribution.

   Let Φ_T be the time-T flow-map associated with the differential equation, where $T > 0$. Thus,

   $$\Phi_T(z) = e^{\frac{cP^T - I}{N}T}(z - (cP^T - I)^{-1}\mathbf{1}) - (cP^T - I)^{-1}\mathbf{1},$$

   with $\Phi_T(z^*) = z^*$. Define

   $$C^* := \{z \in C : \|z - z^*\|_1 \leq \min_{z' \in \partial C} \|z' - z^*\|_1\},$$

and for $\epsilon > 0$,

$$C^\epsilon := \{x : \inf_{y \in C} \|x - y\|_1 < \epsilon\}.$$

Then

$$\min_{z \in \Delta^N - C} \left[\|z - z^*\|_1 - \|\Phi_T(z) - z^*\|_1\right]$$

$$= \min_{z \in \Delta^N - C} \left[\|z - z^*\|_1 - \|e^{\frac{cP^T - I}{N}T}(z - z^*)\|_1\right]$$

$$\geq \min_{z \in \Delta^N - C} \left[\|z - z^*\|_1 - \|e^{\frac{cP^T - I}{N}T}\|_1 \|(z - z^*)\|_1\right]$$

$$= (1 - \|e^{\frac{cP^T - I}{N}T}\|_1) \min_{z \in \Delta^N - C} \|z - z^*\|_1$$

$$= (1 - \|e^{\frac{cP^T - I}{N}T}\|_1)\kappa$$

where $\kappa := \min_{z \in \Delta^N - C} \|z - z^*\|_1$ and $\|A\|_1$ for a matrix A is its induced matrix norm. We argue that $\|e^{\frac{cP^T - I}{N}T}\|_1 < 1$. To see this, view $Q = cP - I$ as the rate matrix of a continuous time Markov chain killed at rate $1 - c$. Then $e^{\frac{cP - I}{N}T}$ is its transition probability matrix after time $\frac{T}{N}$, whose row sums will be uniformly bounded away from 1. The claim follows. Let $\gamma > 0$ and pick $T > 0$ such that

$$\gamma \geq \min_{z \in \Delta^N - C} [\|z - z^*\|_1 - \|\Phi_T(z) - z^*\|_1].$$

Since $\max_{z \in \Delta^N} \|z - z^*\|_1 = 2$,

$$\frac{\max_{z \in \Delta^N} \|z - z^*\|_1}{\gamma/2} \times (T + 1) \leq \tau := \frac{4}{(1 - \|e^{\frac{cP^T - I}{N}T}\|_1)\kappa} \times (T + 1).$$

Let $n_0 := \min\{n \geq 0 : \sum_{m=0}^{n} a(m) \geq \tau\}$. Also, let $\mathcal{N}_\eta(S) := \{z : \inf_{y \in S} \|z - y\|_2 < \eta\}$ denote the open η-neighborhood w.r.t. $\|\cdot\|_2$ norm of a generic set S. Set $\delta := \frac{\gamma}{2\sqrt{N}}$. Then $\|x - y\|_2 < \delta \implies \|x - y\|_1 < \frac{\gamma}{2}$. Arguing as in Corollary 14, p. 43 of [24], we have

$$P(z_n \in N_\delta(C^{\frac{\gamma}{2}}) \, \forall n \geq n_0 + k) \geq 1 - 2Ne^{-\frac{K\delta^2}{N \sum_{m=k}^{\infty} a(m)^2}} = 1 - o(\sum_{m=k}^{\infty} a(m)^2),$$

where $K > 0$ is a suitable constant. (In *ibid.*, replace H^ϵ by C^* and Δ by γ.)

2. Note that at each time n, we can generate more than one, say m pairs $(X_n^i, Y_n^i), 1 \leq i \leq m$, which are independent, each distributed as (X_n, Y_n) above, and change the iteration to:

$$z_{n+1}(i) = z_n(i) + a(n)(I\{i \in \{X_{n+1}^j, 1 \leq j \leq m\}\}(1 - z(n))$$

$$+ c \sum_{j=1}^{m} z_n(X_{n+1}^j) I\{Y_{n+1}^j = i\}).$$

That is, we update several components at once. This will speed up convergence at the expense of increased per iterate computation.

4   Numerical Experiments

In this section we simulate the algorithm for different number of nodes. The results for the cases when the number of nodes are 50, 200 and 500 are plotted in Figure 1, Figure 2 and Figure 3 resectively. The dotted line indicates the distance between z^* and z_n w.r.t. n. The solid line indicates the percentage of top 5 indices of z^* that do not feature in the top 10 indices of z_n. Figure 4, Figure 5 and Figure 6 further show (for 200 nodes) that the number of iterations required to achieve this objective varies inversely with variance of z^*.

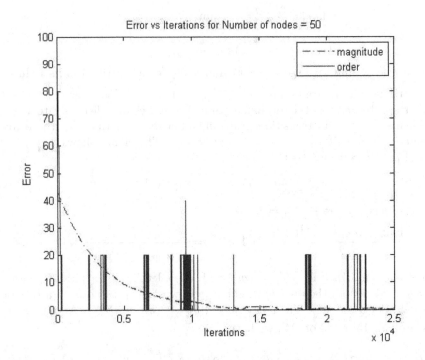

Fig. 1. Varaince of z^*=47.1641

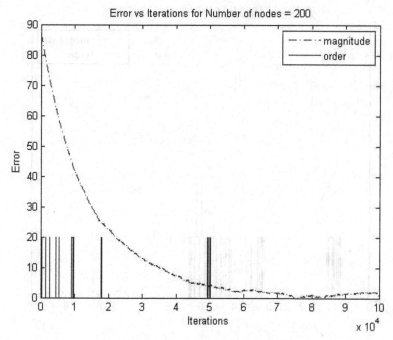

Fig. 2. Variance of $z^* = 277.3392$

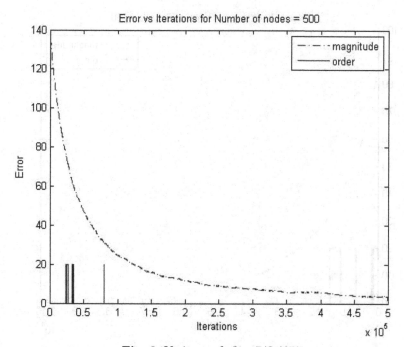

Fig. 3. Variance of $z^* = 743.4651$

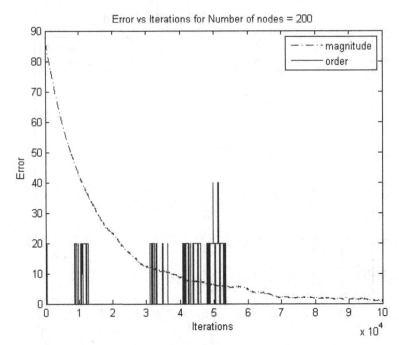

Fig. 4. Varaince of z^*=259.6187

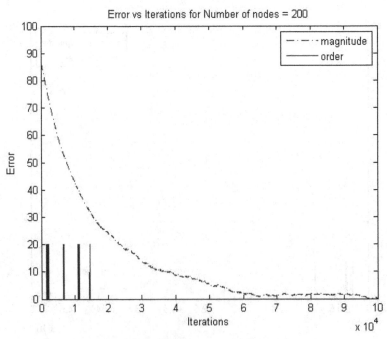

Fig. 5. Variance of z^*=335.6385

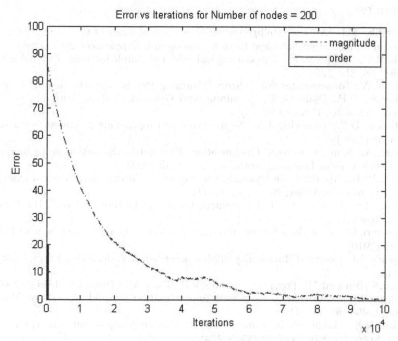

Fig. 6. Variance of $z^* = 365.0774$

5   Conclusions

In conclusion, we highlight some of the important features of the above scheme, which are facilitated by the reinforcement learning framework.

1. As already mentioned, the scheme does not depend on an a priori model for transition probabilities, but is completely data-driven in this aspect.
2. We use 'split sampling' introduced in [14] for reinforcement learning, sampling pairs (X_n, Y_n) with the desired conditional law for Y_n given X_n, but with uniform sampling for $\{X_n\}$. This is a departure from classical reinforcement learning, where one runs a single Markov chain $\{X_n\}$ according to $\hat{P}$ and $Y_n = X_{n+1}$.
3. Since we are iterating over probability vectors as they evolve under a transition matrix, the scheme requires *left-multiplication* by row vectors thereof. This is different from usual reinforcement learning schemes, which involve averaging with respect to the transition probabilities, i.e., *right-multiplication* by a column vector. We have worked around this difficulty by modifying the update rule. In classical reinforcement learning algorithms based on a simulated Markov chain $\{X_n\}$, one updates the X_nth component at time n, i.e., the ith component gets updated only when $X_n = i$. In the above scheme, the ith component gets updated both when $X_{n+1} = i$ and when $Y_{n+1} = i$, albeit in different ways. This is another novel feature of the present scheme.

References

1. Thorndike, E.L.: Animal intelligence: an experimental study of the associative processes in animals. Psychological Review, Monograph Supplement 2(8) (1998)
2. Bush, R.R., Mosteller, F.: A mathematical model of simple learning. Psychological Review 58, 313–323
3. Estes, K.W.: Towards a statistical theory of learning. Psychological Review 57, 94–107
4. Bertsekas, D.P.: Dynamic Programming and Optimal Control, 4th edn., vol. 2. Athena Scientific, Belmont (2007)
5. Bertsekas, D.P., Tsitsiklis, J.N.: Neuro-dynamic Programming. Athena Scientific, Belmont (1996)
6. Gosavi, A.: Simulation-based Optimization, Parametric Optimization Techniques and Reinforcement Learning. Springer, New York (2003)
7. Powell, W.B.: Approximate Dynamic Programming: Solving the Curses of Dimensionality, 2nd edn. Wiley, New York (2011)
8. Sutton, R.S., Barto, A.G.: Reinforcement Learning: An Introduction. MIT Press, Cambridge (1998)
9. Szepesvari, C.: Algorithms for Reinforcement Learning. Morgan and Claypool Publishers (2010)
10. Sargent, T.J.: Bounded Rationality in Macroeconomics. Oxford Uni. Press, Oxford (1994)
11. Thrun, S., Burgard, W., Fox, D.: Probabilistic Robotics. MIT Press, Cambridge (2005)
12. Robbins, H., Monro, J.: A stochastic approximation method. Annals of Math. Stat. 22, 400–407 (1951)
13. Borkar, V.S., Makhijani, R., Sundaresan, R.: How to gossip if you must (preprint, 2013), http://arxiv.org/abs/1309.7841
14. Borkar, V.: Reinforcement Learning - A Bridge between Numerical Methods and Markov Chain Monte Carlo. In: Sastry, N.S.N., Rajeev, B., Delampady, M., Rao, T.S.S.R.K. (eds.) Perspectives in Mathematical Sciences. World Scientific (2008)
15. Langville, A.N., Meyer, C.D.: Google's PageRank and Beyond: The Science of Search Engine Rankings. Princeton Uni. Press, Princeton (2006)
16. Langville, A.N., Meyer, C.D.: Deeper inside PageRank. Internet Mathematics 1(3), 335–380 (2004)
17. Avrachenkov, K., Litvak, N., Nemirovsky, D., Osipova, N.: Monte Carlo methods in PageRank computation: when one iteration is sufficient. SIAM J. Numer. Anal. 45(2), 890–904 (2007)
18. Avrachenkov, K., Litvak, N., Nemirovsky, D., Smirnova, E., Sokol, M.: Quick detection of top-k personalized PageRank lists. In: Frieze, A., Horn, P., Prałat, P. (eds.) WAW 2011. LNCS, vol. 6732, pp. 50–61. Springer, Heidelberg (2011)
19. Polyak, B.T., Timonina, A.V.: PageRank: new regularizations and simulation models. In: Proc. of 11th IFAC World Congress, Milano, August 28-September, pp. 11202–11207 (2011)
20. Ishii, H.: Distributed randomized algorithms for PageRank computation. IEEE Trans. Auto. Control 55(9), 1987–2002 (2010)
21. Nazin, A.V., Polyak, B.T.: The randomized algorithm for finding an eigenvector of the stochastic matrix with application to PageRank. Doklady Mathematics 79(3), 424–427 (2009)
22. Zhao, W., Chen, H-F. and Fang, H-T.: Convergence of distributed randomized PageRank algorithms. arXiv:1305.3178 [cs.SY] (2013)
23. Vigna, S.: Spectral ranking, http://arxiv.org/abs/0912.0238
24. Borkar, V.S.: Stochastic Approximation: A Dynamical Systems Viewpoint. Hindustan Publ. Agency, Cambridge Uni. Press, New Delhi, Cambridge (2008)
25. Ho, Y.-C.: An explanation of ordinal optimization: Soft computing for hard problems. Information Sciences 113(3-4), 169–192 (1999)

The New Normal?

Revisiting Ethical Issues in Internet Research

Elizabeth A. Buchanan

Endowed Chair and Director
Center for Applied Ethics
University of Wisconsin-Stout
buchanane@uwstout.edu

Abstract. The use of the Internet as a research tool or venue has grown exponentially, and with such growth, continued attention to an array of ethical issues is necessary. One of the long-standing ethical issues in Internet research revolves around privacy and identifiability. This paper will contextualize the current state of Internet research and its ongoing ethical considerations with attention to a new "default of identifiability." It describes issues related to Internet-related human subjects research, though it is not intended to align with regulatory guidance. Instead, the paper seeks to stimulate further discussion across disciplines about the ethics of contemporary Internet research.

Keywords: Internet research, social media, ethics, research practice, identifiability, privacy, data management, ethics review boards.

1   Introduction

With over 2 billion Internet users across the world [1], individuals' every day realities involving and expectations of technologies and their affordances have shifted, and shifted rapidly over the past twelve years. Between 2000 and 2012, the world has seen over 566% growth of Internet users, with some regions, including Africa, the Middle East, and Latin America/Caribbean reporting growth upwards of 1000 to 3000% [1]. Daily life is technologically mediated in nearly every sphere, from work to leisure to personal health and medicine and beyond. With the growth and development in both scope and size of the Internet, the practicalities of daily life now include pervasive and ubiquitous computerization, surveillance, data sharing, and vast data harvesting. Continuous data flows and mediated realities are the norm.

Data have become the new currency, and more data exist at the interface of, or intersection between "public" and "private" zones or spheres. Individual and collective rights and responsibilities are again points for interrogation in public policy, including research ethics policies. It is a truism that technologies continually lap law and regulations, challenging them, pushing their boundaries, contorting their applications. The Internet, in its most broadly conceived ways, simply confounds traditional jurisprudence, and in its stead, emerging models of Internet governance have emerged [2]. Tensions exist between technical standards, legal precedent, and social norms:

R. Natarajan (Ed.): ICDCIT 2014, LNCS 8337, pp. 25–33, 2014.

The original and early Internet architectures, as Lawrence Lessig once described, defied "regulability" [3]. Regulations, traditionally speaking, maintain control over individuals and collective social spaces: "To regulate well, you need to know (1) who someone is, (2), where they are, and (3), what they're doing" [3]. The early Internet was unregulable, Lessig contends, but a change from a "default of anonymity to a default of identification" is upon us [3] and has significant implications for the research enterprise. This shift to an architecture of identifiability and its attendant regulability has been seamless, swift, and purposeful. Commercial interests—the market—present at least as much control as government, and more and more, the two are inextricably linked in their architecture of control: Think of the vast incestuous interrelationships between and among governments, telecoms, Internet companies, and the "data industry" as a whole. Data are international currency, bought, sold, and traded at individuals' wills.

In the time of the great boom in Internet users, the predominance of the social media terrain has expanded; social media rely heavily on vast knowledge about an individual, the interconnectedness of his or her reality, identity, locality, networks of connections, and much more. Using Lessig's concept of regulability in its simplest sense, anyone using the Internet of 2013 passively conforms to, and increasingly more common, contributes actively to new norms of identification and prediction. Data flows continually track the individual, where she is, and what she's doing, all the while creating distinct algorithms of patterns and prediction. Patterns are established as individuals concede to regulability, and algorithms are rarely surprising in today's Internet. Not unexpectedly, the ethics of algorithms are now a topic of keen interest.

With these concepts of regulability as context, this paper will contextualize the current state of Internet research and its ongoing ethical considerations with attention to a new default of identifiability. It describes issues related to Internet-related human subjects research, though it is not intended to align with regulatory guidance but uses key regulatory principles from the United States. Instead, the paper seeks to stimulate further discussion across disciplines about the ethics of contemporary Internet research.

2   Internet Research Circa 2013: The New Normal?

In March 2013, a federal advisory board to the United States Secretary of Health and Human Services defined Internet research with the following [4]:

• Research studying information that is already available on or via the Internet without direct interaction with human subjects (harvesting, mining, profiling, scraping—observation or recording of otherwise-existing data sets, chat room interactions, blogs, social media postings, etc.)

• Research that uses the Internet as a vehicle for recruiting or interacting, directly or indirectly, with subjects (Self-testing websites, survey tools, Amazon Mechanical Turk, etc.)

• Research about the Internet itself and its effects (use patterns or effects of social media, search engines, email, etc.; evolution of privacy issues; information contagion; etc.)

• Research about Internet users—what they do, and how the Internet affects individuals and their behaviors

• Research that utilizes the Internet as an interventional tool, for example, interventions that influence subjects' behavior

• Others (emerging and cross-platform types of research and methods, including m-research (mobile))

• Recruitment in or through Internet locales or tools, for example social media, push technologies.

Today, Internet-based or Internet-enabled research activities are conducted by a wide-range of disciplines. Social science research and market research, in the forms of online surveys and inventories, observations and online interviewing have increasingly moved towards online tools, for myriad reasons: costs, efficiency, subject access, and advanced logic models within online tools. Online ethnography, once a domain unique to researchers in universities and lab settings, is now an accessible and engaging methodology: "New modalities, new actors (social and technical), and new configurations have emerged" for online ethnographies of virtual worlds [5]. Trend analysis, crowd-sourcing, and large scale epidemiological mapping are conducted with Twitter and Google data [6, 7]. Medical research utilizes social media fora such as MySpace and Facebook [8] for the recruitment of subjects and conduct of research, while stand-alone online research platforms are developed to study such topics as HIV [9] and illicit drug use [10]. Deception research within psychological research to computer security research is particularly rich in online environments [11, 12]; and, clinical research trials are now conducted in fully online spheres [13]. One pioneering example, Pfizer's REMOTE trial, paved the way forward, and while the trial was suspended due to low enrollment, officials at the pharmaceutical giant believe that "virtual trials will shape the future of the industry" [14].

Internet research circa 2013 involves a great deal of geo-locational and geo-intentional data. Large-scale surveillance networks collect and share past, present, and future locational data. "Beyond location awareness, it is far more important to know where a person is headed and his *(sic)* needs and wants at the destination" [16]. Human rights and community-based participatory research makes use of participatory sensing research which involves "always-on, always-present devices carried by billions can capture and transmit users' location, images, motion, and user input. Mobile technologies are becoming a platform to document community needs and advocate for civic change, to understand personal habits and routines, and to document health problems and manage chronic illness. These new forms of data collection software utilize techniques traditionally employed by tools of surveillance: granular data gathering, sophisticated modeling, and inferences about personal behavior and attributes" [17]. These highly dense data are desirable to many stakeholders and end users including of course, researchers across disciplines.

Internet research circa 2013 is undeniably rich and complex, and nowhere has the complexity been more profound in the research enterprise than in the domain of "human subjects" research. As evidenced by the definitions offered above, as well as typified in those few examples, the situatedness of individuals within Internet research and the extent of their data differ across the variety of Internet research experiences. It is seemingly much easier to conceptualize the human subject in a virtual trial over the individual in an ethnography of an avatar-based chat room, for example. Traditional research ethics principles such as respect for persons, beneficence, and justice may "not address many issues raised by the unique characteristics of Internet research" [4]. The unique characteristics of Internet research include such qualities as "*greased*" and "*malleable*," which James Moor attributed to computer data in the 1980s [15]; "*trackbackability*" or "*mineability*," qualities emerging from the increased power of search engines and algorithms which feed into the identifiably and locality of Internet data; the concept of "*mashability*"—the combination of unique and discrete data sources into a surprising new whole; *scale, access,* and *variety,* qualities often attributed to the concept of "big data; and "*interoperability*, and *interconnectedness:*" data that travel across platforms in the collapse of "the Internet" and cell/mobile/grid data. With each of these characteristics, the potential for identifiability emerges more readily; identifiable information is valuable, and of course, further value is created in the intermingling of data. It is also in those intersections of data where potential ethical lapses may occur. The misappropriation of data, or the combination of certain discrete data may lead to unintended consequences. Large-scale data now exist across borders and domains, across platforms and venues, and across time. As researchers we must ask, "how much and what kinds of data can we use, if they are all available to us?" Where is the ethical line, which, when crossed, puts research subjects in a new form of danger, as a result of identifiability? Are there "downstream" harms created by persistent data flows, and if so, how significant are the ethical concerns for researchers? Ultimately, the architecture and infrastructure of the Internet places researchers in a position of unfamiliarity: Future interoperabilities and interconnectedness between data, coupled with identifiability and use of data contributes to a future unknown. A researcher realistically does not know how data will exist in emergent platforms, and thus, cannot practically foresee how research data of today will be repurposed or reconstituted in the not too far off future. This reality, too, holds the potential for innovative research and discovery, but cautions are necessary. Research conventions for managing research data in stream are not yet well established, thus, reflections on the ethics of the research data life cycle are important.

Considering these qualities of Internet research and its data patterns, there are more readily collapsible boundaries between individuals and researchers, subjects and third parties interested in their data, and between public and private interests. The reality of today's ubiquitous data collection, logging, and surveillance has fed into a mindset of nonconsensual access to data and a default position which assumes Internet data public. Taken together, these default positions of "identifiability" and "public" present both challenges and opportunities for researchers as a new normal of research and concomitantly, research ethics has emerged. Research regulations across the world are specific and prescribed and do not account for the complexities of Internet architecture and its data, its forms of transmission and its life cycle. Internet researchers today have available to them thick, rich data in multiple forms and media, readily available for analysis. In today's Internet, studying one isolated issue or variable is challenging, as Internet data bleeds over boundaries and interconnects with seemingly innumerable other data. The ethics of use and the ethics of the research frame must be critical considerations for researchers given the new norm of identifiability and spread of data.

These ethical considerations of use affect others in the increasingly visible and expansive research frame. Research ethics refers to these *other* individuals in different ways: "Secondary subjects," "bystanders," 'third parties," or "collateral subjects." These other individuals are implicated or made visible and identifiable by virtue of another's data. When considering secondary subjects, a typical example includes family members. For example, when private information is obtained from a subject about another family member's physical or mental health, and that person is identified, the family member may be considered a secondary subject. A third party in research is an individual (or organization or institution) who is not a researcher or a subject, but who is affected by the relationship between those persons [18]. Collateral subjects are exposed by their proximity to other subjects. Communal norms and the "collective" provide a research space with meaning that may only exist in that whole. In the context of Internet research, these "others" in the research frame or stream of data are critical experiential contributors—and as such, could be construed as subjects. A social media page develops rich meaning in context, and others create that context and contribute to the ways in which researchers engage in their studies.   The new normal of research relates to the socialability of data: Does a tweet or a post matter if no one is there to read it? Meaning is made in the interconnectedness and identifiability of data, where ethical complexities also reside.

This paper now turns to some brief commentary on particular concepts and constructs from human subjects regulations in the United States in order to tease out areas of contestation.

3   Are We Our Data?

In the United States, human subjections protections were first published in 1974 [19], and across the world, varying regulations and policies for human subjects protections exist [20]. For research subjects to be protected in the US and many other countries, a series of considerations (Is it research? Is it research involving human subjects? [19]) are used to ascertain the applicability of federal research regulations. This paper is less concerned with those specific processes and determination points, and nuanced thinking around regulations vis-à-vis Internet research is the topic for another day.

To date, no discrete regulatory guidance or policy governs the conduct of Internet research specifically, and instead, those forms of research that are conducted on or through the Internet is reviewed or evaluated analogously to any other form of research. Debates over the specificity of Internet research are long-standing, and consensus around this specificity or "specialty" remains elusive [21, 22], and such debates occur across research ethics boards, with anecdotal data suggesting some boards are more cautious when reviewing Internet-based research than other non-Internet based research [22]. Such cautions emerge, quite possibly, from the novel ways in which Internet users are, by choice or not, identifiable and exposed in myriad ways. Cautions are also borne from the absence of applicable guidance: For example, in the US regulatory model, those research "others," the bystanders or collateral participants, are not protected as such. They are, strictly speaking, either subjects or they are not. There is no in between, and the binarism of this approach is not suitable to the realities of today's Internet research. Moreover, within human subjects research regulations in the United States, such concepts as "private," "identifiable," "reasonable expectation of privacy," and "readily ascertainable" were used to describe conditions in research well before the Internet of today. These terms now fail to adequately or appropriately conform to the realities experienced by Internet researchers, particularly, and Internet users, generally. To further explicate this, consider the original definitions from the US Code of Regulations, §46.102,

(f) *Human subject* means a living individual about whom an investigator (whether professional or student) conducting research obtains

(1) Data through intervention or interaction with the individual, or
(2) Identifiable private information.

Intervention includes both physical procedures by which data are gathered (for example, venipuncture) and manipulations of the subject or the subject's environment that are performed for research purposes. Interaction includes communication or interpersonal contact between investigator and subject. *Private information* includes information about behavior that occurs in a context in which an individual can reasonably expect that no observation or recording is taking place, and information which has been provided for specific purposes by an individual and which the individual can reasonably expect will not be made public (for example, a medical record). Private information must be individually identifiable (i.e., the identity of the subject is or may readily be ascertained by the investigator or associated with the information) in order for obtaining the information to constitute research involving human subjects [19].

From that definition, there are at least three main concepts from a Internet research ethics perspective deserving of ongoing discussion and ethical reflection: The most obvious and most discussed issue for researchers and ethics boards in the literature has been *private information*; second, the *expectation that no recording or observation is taking place*; and third, *information that is expected to not be made public*. It is important to remember that these considerations are part of a larger set of decisional points, and may seem taken out of context or logical application. The purpose in doing so is to explicate these concepts vis-à-vis Internet research, circa 2013 and be mindful of ethics over compliance.

Today's Internet, recall from Lessig, is highly regulable: regulability requires identifiability. Private information is that which is individually identifiable. Social media only works—only thrives—with such information: Databases of the future, Birkin commented in 2012, are increasingly reliant on personal data; that future is now. One only need consider genetic databases [24]. Those databases enable mining and matching, raising the potential for partial identifiers to be combined and individuals fully recognized [4]. Privacy advocates and security experts have much to say about today's default positions of identifiability [25, 26], and research ethics boards may need to find themselves in greater alignment with institutional security infrastructures. The new normal for research ethics boards includes robust and rigorous data protections, as individuals are increasingly identifiable through their data.

And, if we accept that Internet users and by extension, subjects expect and accept surveillance and data sharing on a daily basis, no reasonable expectation of privacy may exist. Or, given the default architecture of identifiability, it may be now "unreasonable" to have any expectation of privacy. If an Internet user contributes information to a particular forum for a specific purpose, knowing that it is being logged and archived, he or she may have no future reasonable expectations that those data will not be utilized for another purpose, including a research purpose. There may no longer be a context in which recording or observation does not occur. Active and passive surveillance are always contributing to data flows across networks, data are continually in transit and being harvested, aggregated, personalized, and fed out to others entities on the network. (For example, see Figure 1, of the big data enterprise to conceptualize data in the network [27]). In this confluence of data, noise, and other forces of the network, isolating the individual subject and specifically what ethical concerns exist becomes more challenging for both the researcher, as noted earlier, and for the research ethics board which still seeks to protect that individual subject. "Clean and unfettered" research is becoming harder to conduct in and on Internet spaces and tools due to the noise and intermingling of data, venues, and algorithmic processing from multiple sources. This also means that research ethics boards are forced to sort through the noise to determine what ethical concerns are paramount, and this includes a more nuanced approach to the entirety of the research frame and the scale of use.

© Matt Turck (@mattturck) and ShivonZilis (@shivonz) Bloomberg Ventures

Fig. 1.

4   Concluding Remarks

Today's Internet enables research of unprecedented scope, scale, and dimension. Innovation abounds, as new modeling, new forms of representations, and new methodologies emerge, and individuals, including and especially researchers, grow to accept the new normal of identifiability and its attendant consequences and benefits. The ethics of use and the ethics of the data life cycle are at the center of broad scale research ethics considerations. This paper has worked around the edges of extant regulation, and instead, has offered ways of conceptualizing elements of Internet research ethics, circa 2013. Certain assumptions are here to be challenged: is the new normal of identifiability fundamentally problematic from a research perspective? Are researchers, those who are accountable to research ethics boards, operating under an increasingly difficult set of standards, when it comes to privacy and identifiability protections? If the market, and indeed governments, are privy to the benefits of big data research, and the modeling and prediction it enables, will academic researchers remain relevant? Or, will the research enterprise continue along a path combining public and private interests, governments, and their citizens? And, will there be a concomitant rise of privacy technologies used en masse to change the current mode of regulability? Ultimately, Internet users, whether actively or knowingly involved in research or not, are all data sources. Let us, as researchers, remember why, when, and where the individual matters.

References

[1] Internet Usage Statistics,
    http://www.internetworldstats.com/stats.htm
[2] The Center for International Governance Innovation,
    http://www.cigionline.org/series/
    governing-internet-chaos-control-or-consensus
[3] Lessig, L.: Code Version 2.0. Perseus Books Group, New York (2006)
[4] Secretary's Advisory Committee to the Office for Human Research Protections,
    http://www.hhs.gov/ohrp/sachrp/mtgings/2013%20March%20Mtg/i
    nternet_research.pdf
[5] Boellstorff, T., Nardi, B., Pearce, C., Taylor, T.L.: Ethnography and Virtual Worlds. Princeton University Press, Princeton (2012)
[6] Scanfield, D., Scanfield, V., Larson, E.: Dissemination of Health Information Through Social Networks: Twitter and Antibiotics. Am. Jrn. of Infectious Control 38(3), 182–188 (2010)
[7] Goodchild, M., Glennon, A.: Crowdsourcing Geographic Information for Disaster Response: A Research Frontier. Intl. Jrn. of Digital Earth 3(3), 231–241 (2010)
[8] Bull, S., Levine, D., Schmiege, S., Santelli, J.: Recruitment and Retention of Youth for Research Using Social Media: Experiences from the Just/Us Study. Vulnerable Children and Youth Studies 8(2), 171–181 (2013)
[9] Rosser, B.R., Miner, M., Bockting, W., Ross, M., Konstan, J., Gurak, L., Stanton, J., Edwards, W., Jacoby, S., Carballo-Diéguez, M.R., Coleman, E.: HIV Risk and the Internet. AIDS Behav. 13(4), 746–756 (2009)

[10] Barrett, M., Lenton, S.: Beyond Recruitment? Participatory Online Research with People Who Use Drugs. Intl. Jrn. of Internet Research Ethics 3(2), 69–86 (2009)

[11] The Ethical Research Project,
http://www.ethicalresearchproject.org

[12] The National Institute of Standards and Technology's Computer Security Division,
http://csrc.nist.gov/

[13] Roehr, B.: Pfizer Launches Virtual Clinical Trial. BMJ 342, d3722 (2011)

[14] Outsourcing   Pharma.com,   http://www.outsourcing-pharma.com/
Clinical-Development/Pfizer-could-re-launch-virtual-trial-
programme-as-soon-as-2013

[15] Moor, J.: What is Computer Ethics. Metaphilosophy 16(4), 266–275 (1985)

[16] StreetFight, http://streetfightmag.com/2013/09/04/
geo-intent-going-to-where-the-puck-will-be/

[17] University of Illinois, http://nationalethicscenter.org/content/
article/177

[18] Resnick, D., Sharp, B.: Protecting third parties in human subjects research. IRB 4, 1–7 (2006)

[19] United States Code of Federal Regulations.Title 45 Public Welfare Department of Health and   Human   Services   Part46   Protection   of   Human   Subjects   (2009),
http://www.hhs.gov/ohrp/humansubjects/guidance/
45cfr46.html

[20] Buchanan, E.: Internet Research Ethics: Past, Present, Future. The Blackwell Handbook of Internet Studies. Wiley-Blackwell, Oxford (2010)

[21] Elgesem, D.: What is special about the ethical issues in online research? CEPE Proceedings   (2001),   http://www.nyu.edu/projects/nissenbaum/
ethics_elgesem.html

[22] Konstan, J., Rosser, S., Cohen, J.: Internet Research: Is it Different? Is It Special? Inb: PRIM&R Advancing Ethical Research Conference (2013)

[23] Buchanan, E., Odwazny, L.: Ethical Internet Research. PRIM&R Webinar (2012)

[24] Birkin, M.: Big Data Challenges for Geoinformatics. GeoinforGeostat: An Overview 1:1 (2012), doi:10.4172/2327-4581.1000e101

[25] Sweeny, L.: Who Controls Your Data? (forthcoming)

[26] Sweeney, L.: Navigating Computer Science Research Through Waves of Privacy Concerns: Discussions among Computer Scientists at Carnegie Mellon University. ACM Computers and Society 34 (2004)

[27] Turck, M., Zillis, S.: Big Data Landscape (2013), http://mattturck.com/2012/
10/15/a-chart-of-the-big-data-ecosystem-take-2/

Cyber Security via Signaling Games: Toward a Science of Cyber Security

William Casey[1,2], Jose A. Morales[1,2], Thomson Nguyen[1,2], Jonathan Spring[1,2], Rhiannon Weaver[1,2], Evan Wright[1,2], Leigh Metcalf[3], and Bud Mishra[1,2]

[1] Courant Institute, NYU, New York
[2] Software Engineering Institute, CMU, Pittsburgh
[3] Software Engineering Institute, CMU, United States
{mishra,tvn210}@nyu.edu,
{wcasey,jamorales,jspring,rweaver,ewright}@cert.sei.edu,
lbmetcalf@cert.org
http://cs.nyu.edu/mishra/

Abstract. In March of 2013, what started as a minor dispute between SPAMHAUS and CYBERBUNKER quickly escalated to a distributed denial of service (DDoS) attack that was so massive, it was claimed to have slowed internet speeds around the globe. The attack clogged servers with dummy internet traffic at a rate of about 300 gigabits per second. By comparison, the largest observed DDoS attacks typically against banks had thus far registered only 50 gigabits per second. The record breaking SPAMHAUS/CYBERBUNKER CONFLICT arose 13 years after the publication of best practices on preventing DDoS attacks, and it was not an isolated event.

Recently, NYU's Courant Institute and Carnegie Mellon Software Engineering Institute have collaboratively devised a game-theoretic approaches to address various cyber security problems involving exchange of information (asymmetrically). This research aims to discover and understand complex structures of malicious use cases within the context of secure systems with the goal of developing an incentives-based measurement system that ensures a high level of resilience to attack.

1 Introduction

In the 2010 JASON report [Mitre, 2010], the authors wrote "The need to secure computational infrastructure has become significant in all areas including those of relevance to the DoD and the intelligence community. Owing to the level of interconnection and interdependency of modern computing systems, the possibility exists that critical functions can be seriously degraded by exploiting security flaws." However, they also lamented, "While the level of effort expended in securing networks and computers is significant, current approaches in this area overly rely on empiricism and are viewed to have had only limited success." The following rationale was offered: *"The challenge in defining a science of cyber-security derives from the peculiar aspects of the field. The "universe" of cyber-security is an artificially constructed environment that is only weakly tied to the physical universe."*

R. Natarajan (Ed.): ICDCIT 2014, LNCS 8337, pp. 34–42, 2014.
© Springer International Publishing Switzerland 2014

Thus the difficulty in developing a *science of cyber security* (SCS) is thought to stem from its inherent Manicheanness [Mitre, 2010], where the adversary is strategic and utilitarian as opposed to being oblivious and stochastic (i.e. Augustine). However, it must also be noted that a significant fragment of a science of cyber security (SCS) has to be built upon a complex computational infrastructure that is amenable to reasoning and re-engineering based on logical models such as Kripke structures. Thus, it appears that a successful approach to the cyber security problem may come from an amalgamation of a dualistic approach, which are partly based on techniques from game theory (inspired and validated with the tools of systems biology, e.g. analysis of immune systems) and partly based on model building (e.g., machine learning and statistical inference) and model checking. In light of this discussion, it may be worth re-examining the strategic choices that entities such as SPAMHAUS and CYBER-BUNKER made [Williams, 2013,Gallagher, 2013,Lee, 2013,Schwartz, 2013], despite the obvious fact that both parties must have been well-informed about the accepted norms and best practices that were incorporated in the hardware, software and protocol architectures; divorced from a model of the humans and the utilities they wished to derive from their strategic choices, the protocols, practices and norms [Saint-Andre, 2009] achieved precious little.

We propose a novel approach, in which we model cyber security in terms of classical Information-Asymmetry Games (also called Signaling Games) [Casey, 2013], where the players (i.e., agents) assume either a role of a sender (S) or that of a receiver (T). The sender has a certain type, t, for instance: *beneficent* (C for cooperator) or *malicious* (D for defector), which could be assumed to be given by nature. The sender observes his own type while the receiver does not know the type of the sender. Based on his knowledge of his own type, the sender chooses to send a message from a set of possible messages $M = \{m_1, m_2, m_3, \ldots, m_j\}$; these messages are allowed to be complex: for instance, an offer of a mobile app with certain advertised utility and a price. The receiver observes the message but not the type of the sender or the ability to fully verify the message. Then the receiver chooses an action from a set of feasible actions $A = \{a_1, a_2, a_3, \ldots, a_k\}$; the receiver may be *oblivious/trusting* (C for cooperator) or *vigilant/mistrustful* (D for defector) – for instance, the offer of a mobile app may be ignored, accepted, verified or rejected (with a possibility of a reputation-labeling of the app, the sender or the app-store, etc.). The two players receive payoffs dependent on the sender's type, the message chosen by the sender and the action chosen by the receiver. Examples of various modes of attacks and how they map to such abstract games will appear in the full paper. In this paper, we focus only on a simple model of transaction involving transfer of an app from a sender (an app store) to a receiver (an app user).

Because of the informational asymmetry, it is possible for a sender to be *deceptive*, as is often the case in the cyber context. Traditional techniques such as making the signaling somewhat "costly" for the sender can help, but must be engineered carefully, since otherwise the very information-sharing capabilities of the cyber system can be seriously compromised. There have been proposals for new internet architecture, new internet protocols and "bandwidth-as-price" mechanisms [See [Walfish *et al.*, 2010], [Yau *et al.*, 2005], [Beitollahi and Deconinck, 2012], [Lee *et al.*, 2007], [Doron and Wool, 2011], [Fu *et al.*, 2011], [Kargl *et al.*, 2001], [Xie and Yu, 2009], [Bhatia *et al.*, 2012], and [Huang *et al.*, 2007]], but any such approach can burden the normal transactions with an unwelcome and unacceptably heavy overhead.

We, instead propose a system based on an explicit pricing, using *M-coins*[1]. The other key ingredient is based on mechanisms for credible deterrence. However, the focus of this paper will be on two topics: (1) a simplified model for a repeated game that results from our analysis and (2) the empirical results obtained from an agent based simulation.

2   The Game Theoretic Models

Below (in Table 1) we describe a parameterized payoff matrix associated with a single transaction, where a sender may act in the "*cooperate*" behavior mode by sending a useful app honestly or the "*defect*" behavior mode by sending a malicious app deceptively, and where a receiver may act in the "*cooperate*" behavior mode by accepting trusted or the "*defect*" behavior mode by responding with a challenge. The payoff-parameters in the table are as follows: $a =$ the *cost*

Table 1. Row player is the sender, column player is the receiver

Sender,Receiver	receive trusted	receive challenge
send clean	$(a, -a+b)$	$(a-c, -a-g)$
send malware	$(a+d, -a-d)$	$(a-c-e, -a+f-g)$

of app, $b =$ the *value of app*, $c =$ the *cost of verification*, $d =$ the *benefit of hack*, $e =$ the *cost of getting caught*, $f =$ the *benefit of catching malicious user*, and $g =$ the *cost of challenging a sender*.

Table 2 simplifies the payoff matrix for the joint strategy considering both roles of sending and receiving per user in repetition of a single transaction:

3   The Results from Simulation

To examine the details of the potential dynamics of the resulting repeated game, we consider a reproducing population model where reproduction of a given strategy depends on its performance. Strategy mutation is possible in order to explore all possible finite strategies with mutation rates determined by a parameter μ. We include the population structure parameters δ and α, similar to how they

---

[1] M-coins have some resemblance to bit-coins and share many of the properties of bit-coins, but also differ significantly in the way they are acquired, in how the number in circulation is controlled and how they expire.

Table 2. Row player is the sender, column player is the receiver

receiver → sender ↓	CC	CD	DC	DD
CC	b b	$b-c$ $-g$	$-d$ $b+d$	$-c-d$ $d-g$
CD	$-g$ $b-c$	$-c-g$ $-c-g$	$f-g$ $b-c-e$	$-c+f-g$ $-c-e-g$
DC	$b+d$ $-d$	$b-c-e$ $f-g$	0 0	$-c-d-e$ $d+f-g$
DD	$d-g$ $-c-d$	$-c-e-g$ $-c+f-g$	$d+f-g$ $-c-d-e$	$-c-e+f-g$ $-c-e+f-g$

are used in [Traulsen and Nowak, 2007,van Veelen *et al.*, 2012] to explore reciprocity, and provide observations over a unit-square in $\delta \times \alpha$. Note that when $\delta = \alpha = 0$ the sender-receiver-pairs for each game are randomly chosen regardless of their types and change in every round; whereas when $\delta = \alpha = 1$ the sender-receiver-pairs remain constrained to similar types and unchanged from round to round. In general $(\delta, \alpha) \in [0, 1]^2 \setminus \{(0, 0), (1, 1)\}$, the pairing is done with similar or dissimilar types for a round and remain fixed for a random number of rounds of the game.

The simulation model is as follows:

Initialization: Create a random population of N users who choose a repeated-game strategy randomly over a set of seed-strategies. This set of agents provides the population at time $k = 0$.

The simulation model is constructed with the following update-cycle:

Pairing: Using the population at time $(k - 1)$ we create $N/2$ random pairings. *Population Structure parameter*: For each pair with probability α one strategy is selected with the other removed and replaced with a copy of the selected strategy. Therefore for a given strategy s within the population its probability of playing itself is $\alpha + (1 - \alpha)p_s$ where p_s is the frequency of strategy s's occurrences in the population at time $(k - 1)$. Parameter α allows for an investigation into a spectrum of possible population structures from $\alpha = 0$ (random pairing), to $\alpha = 1$ (stronger and general forms of kinship and spatial/network-connectivity-based closeness for $\alpha > 0$).

Strategize: Each selected pair will play a repeated game with a number of plays dependent on a geometric distribution with continuation parameter δ. The expected number of plays per game is $1/(1 - \delta)$, for example $\delta = 0$ reduces to single shot games.

Determine Payoff: Strategy payoff is determined using automata and payoff matrix; a multiplicative discount factor for payoff may be introduced (omitted here).

Next Round: A population of size N is re-created by sampling the strategies at time $(k-1)$ using a distribution whose density is computed as proportional to population normalized performances. This set of agents constitutes the population at time k.

Mutate: Each user-agent is subject to the possibility of mutation with mutation rate μ; a mutation creates a strategy one-mutation step from its previously selected strategy determined in the preceding step. Mutation steps may add or delete a state, re-label a state or re-assign an edge destination. Mutation rates are performed in-situ on the population and update the population at time k.

3.1   Behavior Modes (dependent on parameters d, e, f, g)

We summarize the results from our simulation as shown below:

3.2   Strategies

See Figure 1, for a list of strategies whose fitness is studied during the simulation. We list in Figures 1(a), 1(b), 1(c) and 1(d) strategy-profiles with single state. In the rows below these figures, we list in Figures 1(e), 1(f), 1(g), 1(h), 1(i), 1(j), 1(k) and 1(l) several more strategy-profiles with two states.

3.3   Equilibrium Strategies at a Glance

Figure 2 shows the asymptotic structures of the strategic behavior of the population.

3.4   Limiting Measures of Send Cooperate and Receive Cooperatively

Figure 3 examines the nature of cooperative behavior[2] as a function of the parameters δ and α that jointly determine "correlation of encounters."

---

[2] Note that, when the cost of checking g is sufficiently large (in particular compared to the other which provide benefit or shifting burden to the attacker) the population will simply penalize any strategy that does so to such an extent that survival of a checking strategy among competing non-checking strategies is extremely rare. The data includes a few thousand runs for which challenging strategies are eliminated from the population (because of the high cost, without a commensurate benefits for doing so): see Fig3(b) [1118], where since the values are constant and zero they are all mapped to the mean of the jet color map (green). Note further that the act of challenging must have a price that coincides with a benefit for doing so (for example when $g = f$) or a means of shifting the cost burden to the attacker (for example when $g = e$).

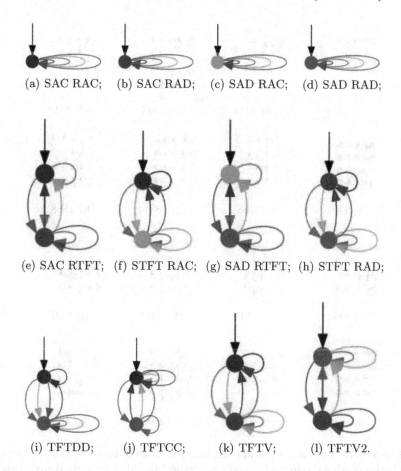

Fig. 1. Repeated game strategy encoded as *finite state automata*. Black arrows indicate initial state. Blue indicates a play of sending cooperatively and receiving trusted. Purple indicates a play of sending cooperatively and receiving untrusted (defect action may challenge reputation of sender). Green indicates a play of sending defect (attacks) and receiving trusted. Finally red indicates a play of sending defect and receiving untrusted. Arrows indicate the transition taken depending on an opponent's previous play. A repeated game may occur for any pairs of agents; the number of plays determined by a geometric distribution continuation parameter δ. Above: twelve seed strategies for population dynamics with evolution pressures for strategy fitness.

4 Discussion

In the JASON report, the committee addressed the following question ($Q2$ on page 4): *Are there "laws of nature" in cyber space that can form the basis of scientific inquiry in the field of cyber security? Are there mathematical abstractions or theoretical constructs that should be considered?* The answer they provided

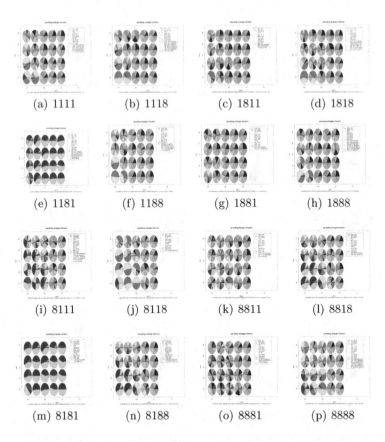

Fig. 2. Infrequent mutation rates applied to populations of twelve seed strategies provide a notion of what strategies have advantages and are culled for various environments or settings of payoff matrix values. Exploration of d, e, f, g are shown above. Each chart provides a view of which strategy fixate in the population at various values of d, e, f, g, pie charts are organized over the unit square of α, δ.

is rather pessimistic: "There are no intrinsic "laws of nature" for cyber-security as there are, for example, in physics, chemistry or biology. Cyber-security is essentially an applied science that is informed by the mathematical constructs of computer science such as theory of automata, complexity, and mathematical logic." In contrast, we show that by suitably modeling the agents of a system and the utilities they wish to achieve in cyber space, and under the standard assumptions of "common knowledge of rationality," a suitable law can be imposed on the system, which can evolve to a desirable equilibrium.

We believe that, although our work is preliminary and require further research, it is promising and could prove to be immensely useful, especially to policy makers in the security community.

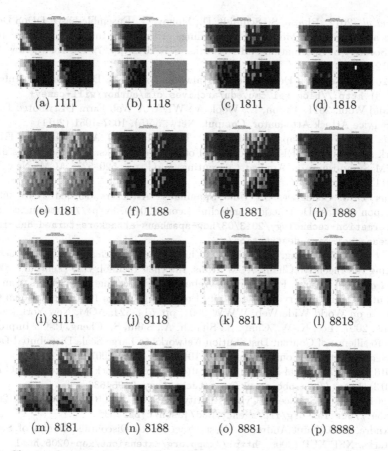

Fig. 3. Charts of aggregate population behavior at various values of d, e, f, g showing overall percentage of time a population sends cooperatively and receives trusted. Each chart has four sub charts with average percentage send cooperatively plays shown in the upper left, average percentage of receive cooperatively plays shown in the upper right and standard deviation for each percentage shown below. Each quadrant provides a view for simulations over the α, δ parameter unit square.

Acknowledgements. We would like to thank members of the Software Engineering Institute, and in particular two colleagues: Bill Scherlis and Dean Sutherland, for creating the opportunities for this collaboration. The research reported here was supported by a joint CMU-SEI-NYU grant.

References

Beitollahi and Deconinck, 2012. Beitollahi, H., Deconinck, G.: Review: Analyzing Well-known Countermeasures Against Distributed Denial of Service Attacks. Comput. Commun. 35(11), 1312–1332 (2012)

Bhatia *et al.*, 2012. Bhatia, S., Schmidt, D., Mohay, G.: Ensemble-based DDoS Detection and Mitigation Model. In: Proceedings of the Fifth International Conference on Security of Information and Networks, SIN 2012, pp. 79–86. ACM, New York (2012)

Casey, 2013. Casey, W.: Deterrence for Malware: Towards a Deception-Free Internet (2013), http://blog.sei.cmu.edu/archives.cfm/author/will-casey+

Doron and Wool, 2011. Doron, E., Wool, A.: WDA: A Web Farm Distributed Denial of Service Attack Attenuator. Comput. Netw. 55(5), 1037–1051 (2011)

Fu *et al.*, 2011. Fu, Z., Papatriantafilou, M., Tsigas, P.: CluB: A Cluster Based Framework for Mitigating Distributed Denial of Service Attacks. In: Proceedings of the ACM Symposium on Applied Computing, SAC, pp. 520–527. ACM, New York (2011)

Gallagher, 2013. Gallagher, S.: How Spamhaus' Attackers Turned DNS into a Weapon of Mass Destruction. arstechnica.com (2013), http://arstechnica.com/information-technology/2013/03/how-spamhaus-attackers-turned-dns-into-a-weapon-of-mass-destruction/

Huang *et al.*, 2007. Huang, Y., Geng, X., Whinston, A.B.: Defeating DDoS Attacks by Fixing the Incentive Chain. ACM Trans. Internet Technol. 7(1) (February 2007)

Kargl *et al.*, 2001. Kargl, F., Maier, J., Weber, M.: Protecting Web Servers from Distributed Denial of Service Attacks. In: Proceedings of the 10th International Conference on World Wide Web, WWW 2001, pp. 514–524. ACM, New York (2001)

Lee *et al.*, 2007. Lee, K.-W., Chari, S., Shaikh, A., Sahu, S., Cheng, P.-C.: Improving the Resilience of Content Distribution Networks to Large Scale Distributed Denial of Service Attacks. Comput. Netw. 51(10), 2753–2770 (2007)

Lee, 2013. Lee, D.: Global Internet Slows after Biggest Attack in History. BBC news (2013), http://www.bbc.co.uk/news/technology-21954636

Mitre, 2010. Mitre. Science of Cyber-security. JASON, MITRE Corporation (2010), https://www.fas.org/irp/agency/dod/jason/cyber.pdf

Saint-Andre, 2009. Saint-Andre, P.: Best Practices to Discourage Denial of Service Attacks. XSF XEP (2009), http://xmpp.org/extensions/xep-0205.html

Schwartz, 2013. Schwartz, M.J.: DDoS Spam Feud Backfires: Bulletproof Cyberbunker Busted. Informationweek.com (2013), https://www.informationweek.com+/security/attacks/ddos-spam-+feud-backfires-+bulletproof-cyb/240151895

Traulsen and Nowak, 2007. Traulsen, A., Nowak, M.A.: Chromodynamics of Cooperation in Finite Populations. PLoS One 2(3), e270 (2007)

van Veelen *et al.*, 2012. van Veelen, M., García, J., Rand, D.G., Nowak, M.A.: Direct Reciprocity in Structured Populations. Proceedings of the National Academy of Sciences 109(25), 9929–9934 (2012)

Walfish *et al.*, 2010. Walfish, M., Vutukuru, M., Balakrishnan, H., Karger, D., Shenker, S.: DDoS Defense by Offense. ACM Trans. Comput. Syst. 28(1), 3:1–3:54 (2010)

Williams, 2013. Williams, R.: DDoS Attack Against spamhaus Exposes Huge Security Threat on DNS Servers. hothardware.com (2013), http://hothardware.com/News/DDoS-Attack-Against-Spamhaus-Exposes-Huge-Security-Threat-On-DNS-Servers/

Xie and Yu, 2009. Xie, Y., Yu, S.-Z.: Monitoring the Application-layer DDoS Attacks for Popular Websites. IEEE/ACM Trans. Netw. 17(1), 15–25 (2009)

Yau *et al.*, 2005. Yau, D.K.Y., Lui, J.C.S., Liang, F., Yam, Y.: Defending Against Distributed Denial-of-Service Attacks with Max-Min Fair Server-Centric Router Throttles. IEEE/ACM Trans. Netw. 13(1), 29–42 (2005)

Privacy through Accountability:
A Computer Science Perspective*

Anupam Datta

Computer Science Department
Electrical and Computer Engineering Department
CyLab
Carnegie Mellon University
danupam@cmu.edu

Abstract. Privacy has become a significant concern in modern society as personal information about individuals is increasingly collected, used, and shared, often using digital technologies, by a wide range of organizations. To mitigate privacy concerns, organizations are required to respect privacy laws in regulated sectors (e.g., HIPAA in healthcare, GLBA in financial sector) and to adhere to self-declared privacy policies in self-regulated sectors (e.g., privacy policies of companies such as Google and Facebook in Web services). This article provides an overview of a body of work on formalizing and enforcing privacy policies. We formalize privacy policies that prescribe and proscribe *flows* of personal information as well as those that place restrictions on the *purposes* for which a governed entity may use personal information. Recognizing that traditional preventive access control and information flow control mechanisms are inadequate for enforcing such privacy policies, we develop principled *accountability* mechanisms that seek to encourage policy-compliant behavior by detecting policy violations, assigning blame, and punishing violators. We apply these techniques to several U.S. privacy laws and organizational privacy policies, in particular, producing the first complete logical specification and audit of all disclosure-related clauses of the HIPAA Privacy Rule.

1   Introduction

Privacy has become a significant concern in modern society as personal information about individuals is increasingly collected, used, and shared, often using digital technologies, by a wide range of organizations. Certain information handling practices of organizations that monitor individuals' activities on the Web,

---

* This work was partially supported by the NSF Science and Technology Center TRUST, the NSF Trustworthy Computing grant "Privacy Policy Specification and Enforcement: Information Use and Purpose," and HHS Grant no. HHS 90TR0003/01. The views and conclusions contained in this document are those of the authors and should not be interpreted as representing the official policies, either expressed or implied, of any sponsoring institution, the U.S. government or any other entity.

R. Natarajan (Ed.): ICDCIT 2014, LNCS 8337, pp. 43–49, 2014.

data aggregation companies that compile massive databases of personal information, cell phone companies that collect and use location data about individuals, online social networks and search engines—while enabling useful services—have aroused much indignation and protest in the name of privacy (see, for example, a series of articles in the Wall Street Journal [1]). Similarly, as healthcare organizations are embracing electronic health record systems and patient portals to enable patients, employees, and business affiliates more efficient access to personal health information, there is trepidation that the privacy of patients may not be adequately protected if information handling practices are not carefully designed and enforced [2–4]. To mitigate privacy concerns, organizations are required to respect privacy laws in regulated sectors (e.g., HIPAA in healthcare, GLBA in financial sector) and to adhere to self-declared privacy policies in self-regulated sectors (e.g., privacy policies of companies such as Google and Facebook in Web services).

This article provides an overview of a body of work on formalizing and enforcing practical privacy policies using computational techniques [5–15] conducted jointly with my students, postdoctoral researchers, and colleagues at Carnegie Mellon, Stanford, and New York University. We find that one significant difference from traditional security settings is that the enforcement mechanisms in privacy settings often have only *black-box access* to the programs and people who operate on personal information. For example, a class of privacy threats in hospitals arises from authorized insiders (e.g., doctors, nurses, administrative staff) who have a legitimate right to access personal information, but may abuse that right to inappropriately share and use that information; an enforcement mechanism employed by the hospital can observe the behavior of authorized insiders as recorded on audit logs, but does not have access to the programs (algorithms) running inside their minds. Similarly, a Web user or privacy advocacy group interested in checking if Google is using sensitive information, such as race, for advertising can interact with Google's program over the Web by supplying different kinds of information to it and observing the displayed ads, but will typically not have access to the code for Google's advertising program. Thus, my research program has focused on principled audit and accountability mechanisms for enforcing privacy properties by detecting policy violations, assigning blame and optimally managing risks stemming from privacy violations. These mechanisms operate with black-box models of the systems (programs and people) that operate over personal information.

The rest of the paper is organized as follows. Section 2 provides an overview of contextual integrity—a normative theory of privacy—and a logic of privacy that we developed informed by this theory. We used this logic to produce the first complete formalization of the HIPAA Privacy Rule and the Gramm-Leach-Bliley Act. Section 3 provides an overview of our algorithm for checking incomplete audit logs for compliance with policies expressed in the logic. This algorithm automatically checks some parts of privacy policies (e.g., pertaining to temporal conditions) and outputs other parts (e.g., pertaining to purposes and beliefs) in a residual policy that has to be checked by other means. Section 4 describes our work on formalizing and enforcing purpose restrictions in privacy policies. Finally, Section 5 describes our work on audit algorithms that prescribe effective resource allocation strategies for auditors interacting with byzantine and strategic adversaries.

2 Contextual Integrity and Logic of Privacy

The central thesis of contextual integrity is that *privacy is a right to appropriate flow of personal information* [16]. The building blocks of this theory are *social contexts* and *context-relative informational norms*. A context captures the idea that people act and transact in society not simply as individuals in an undifferentiated social world, but as individuals in certain capacities (roles) in distinctive social contexts, such as healthcare, education, friendship and employment. Norms prescribe the flow of personal information in a given context, e.g., in a healthcare context a norm might prescribe flow of personal health information from a patient to a doctor and proscribe flows from the doctor to other parties who are not involved in providing treatment. Norms are a function of the following parameters: the respective roles of the sender, the subject, and the recipient of the information, the type of information, and the principle under which the information is sent to the recipient. Examples of transmission principles include confidentiality (prohibiting agents receiving the information from sharing it with others), reciprocity (requiring bi-directional information flow, e.g., in a friendship context), consent (requiring permission from the information subject before transmission), and notice (informing the information subject that a transmission has occured). When norms are contravened, people experience a violation of privacy. This theory has been used to explain why a number of technology-based systems and practices threaten privacy by violating entrenched informational norms. In addition, it provides a prescriptive method for determining appropriate norms for a context (see [16]). This theory is now well known in the privacy community and has influenced privacy policy in the US (for example, 'respect for context' was included in the Consumer Privacy Bill of Rights released by the White House in 2012 [17]).

The idea that privacy expectations can be stated using context-relative informational norms is formalized in a *semantic model* and *logic of privacy* proposed with colleagues at Stanford and New York University [5] and developed further in follow-up work with my students and postdoctoral researchers [7]. At a high-level, the model consists of a set of interacting agents in roles who perform actions involving personal information in a given context. For example, Alice (a patient) may send her personal health information to Bob (her doctor). Following the structure of context-relative informational norms, each transmission action is characterized by the roles of the sender, subject, recipient and the type of the information sent. Interactions among agents give rise to *traces* where each trace is an alternating sequence of states (capturing roles and knowledge of agents) and actions performed by agents that update state (e.g., an agent's knowledge may increase upon receiving a message or his role might change).

Transmission principles prescribe which traces respect privacy and which traces don't. While contextual integrity talks about transmission principles in the abstract, we require a precise logic for expressing them since our goal is to use information processing systems to check for violation of such principles. We were guided by two considerations in designing the logic: (a) *expressivity*—the logic should be able to represent practical privacy policies; and (b) *enforceability*—it should be possible to provide automated support for checking whether traces satisfy policies expressed in the logic.

A logic of privacy that meets these goals is presented in our recent work [8]. We arrive at this enforceable logic by restricting the syntax of the expressive first-order logic we used in our earlier work to develop the first complete formalization of two US privacy laws—the HIPAA Privacy Rule for healthcare organizations and the Gramm-Leach-Bliley Act for financial institutions [7][1]. These comprehensive case studies shed light on common concepts that arise in transmission principles in practice—data attributes, dynamic roles, notice and consent (formalized as temporal properties), purposes of uses and disclosures, and principals' beliefs—as well as how individual transmission principles are composed in privacy policies[2].

3   Policy Auditing over Incomplete Logs

We observe that traditional preventive access control and information flow control mechanisms are not sufficient for enforcing all privacy policies because at run-time there may not be sufficient information to decide whether certain policy concepts (e.g., future obligations, purposes of uses and disclosures, and principals' beliefs) are satisfied or not. We therefore take the position that audit mechanisms are essential for privacy policy enforcement. The importance of audits has been recognized in the computer security literature. For example, Lampson [18] takes the position that audit logs that record relevant evidence during system execution can be used to detect violations of policy, establish accountability and punish the violators. More recently, Weitzner et al. [19] also recognize the importance of audit and accountability, and the inadequacy of preventive access control mechanisms as the sole basis for privacy protection in today's open information environment. However, while the principles of access control and information flow control have been extensively studied, there is comparatively little work on the principles of audit. Our work is aimed at filling this gap.

Our first insight is that *incomplete audit logs* provide a suitable abstraction to model situations (commonly encountered in practice) in which the log does not contain sufficient information to determine whether a policy is satisfied or violated, e.g., because of the policy concepts alluded to earlier—future obligations,

---

[1] This logic, in turn, generalizes the enforceable propositional temporal logic in [5].

[2] The model and logic supports information use actions in addition to transmission actions, so, strictly speaking, it can express policies that are more general than transmission principles.

purposes of uses and disclosures, and principals' beliefs. We formalize incomplete logs as partial structures that map each atomic formula to true, false or unknown. We design an algorithm, which we name reduce, to operate iteratively over such incomplete logs that evolve over time. In each iteration, reduce provably checks as much of the policy as possible over the current log and outputs a residual policy that can only be checked when the log is extended with additional information. We implement reduce and use it to check simulated audit logs for compliance with the entire HIPAA Privacy Rule. Our experimental results demonstrate that the algorithm scales to realistic audit logs. This technical result is reported in a joint paper with my then postdoctoral researchers D. Garg and L. Jia [8].

4 Formalizing and Enforcing Purpose Restrictions

In recent work, we developed the first formal semantics for privacy policies that place restrictions on the purposes for which a governed entity may use personal information—an important and pervasive class of policies in practice (PhD thesis of M. C. Tschantz co-advised with J. M. Wing) [10, 11]. Purpose occupies a central place in numerous influential privacy guidelines and regulations, including OECDs Privacy Guidelines, the EU Privacy Directive, US privacy laws and organizational privacy policies in sectors as diverse as healthcare, finance, Web services, insurance, education, and government. For example, HIPAA requires that hospital employees use personal health information only for certain purposes (e.g. treatment). We argue that (a) an action is for a purpose if it is part of a plan for achieving that purpose and (b) a piece of information is used for a purpose if it affects the planning process. We model planning using (Partially Observable) Markov Decision Processes and design algorithms for auditing actions of agents by building on algorithms for plan recognition. The algorithms compare logged actions to a model of how an agent attempting to achieve the allowed purpose would plan to do so. If the logged actions differ from the model, the algorithm reports a potential violation.

5 Audit Games

Recognizing that audit mechanisms are constrained by available resources (it may not be possible to inspect every potential violation) and adversaries may adapt to beat them, I have also initiated a formal study of audit games (jointly with my students J. Blocki and A. Sinha, and colleagues N. Christin and A. Procaccia at Carnegie Mellon) that model the interaction between the auditor and auditees as a game. We have developed algorithms for computing optimal audit strategies that prescribe resource allocation for auditing Byzantine [9, 15] and rational auditees [13, 14]. The algorithms advance the state-of-the-art in online learning and algorithmic game theory to address these problems.

Let me highlight one result in this line of work. In [14], we model the audit process as a game between a defender (e.g, a hospital) and an adversary (e.g., an employee). The defender audits a given set of targets (e.g., health record accesses) and the adversary chooses a target to attack. The defender's action space in the audit game includes two components. First, the allocation of its inspection resources to targets; this component also exists in a standard model of physical security games [20]. Second, we introduce a continuous punishment rate parameter that the defender employs to deter the adversary from committing violations. However, punishments are not free and the defender incurs a cost for choosing a high punishment level. For instance, a negative work environment in a hospital with high fines for violations can lead to a loss of productivity (see [21] for a similar account of the cost of punishment). The adversary's utility includes the benefit from committing violations and the loss from being punished if caught by the defender. Our model is parametric in the utility functions. Thus, depending on the application, we can instantiate the model to either allocate resources for detecting violations or preventing them. This generality implies that our model can be used to study all the applications previously described in the security games literature [20]. To analyze the audit game, we use the Stackelberg equilibrium solution concept [22] in which the defender commits to a strategy, and the adversary plays an optimal response to that strategy. This concept captures situations in which the adversary learns the defender's audit strategy through surveillance or the defender publishes its audit algorithm. In addition to yielding a better payoff for the defender than any Nash equilibrium, the Stackelberg equilibrium makes the choice for the adversary simple, which leads to a more predictable outcome of the game. Furthermore, this equilibrium concept respects the computer security principle of avoiding "security through obscurity"— audit mechanisms like cryptographic algorithms should provide security despite being publicly known. We view this work as a first step toward a computationally feasible model of audit games.

References

[1] Wall Street Journal: What they know, http://online.wsj.com/public/page/what-they-know-digital-privacy.html (accessed on September 24, 2013)
[2] Hulme, G.: Steady Bleed: State of HealthCare Data Breaches. InformationWeek (September 2010), http://www.informationweek.com/blog/healthcare/229200720
[3] US Health and Human Services: HIPAA enforcement, http://www.hhs.gov/ocr/privacy/hipaa/enforcement/index.html (accessed September 24, 2013)
[4] Robertson, J.: New data spill shows risk of online health records. Yahoo News (August 2011), http://news.yahoo.com/data-spill-shows-risk-online-health-records-120743449.html
[5] Barth, A., Datta, A., Mitchell, J.C., Nissenbaum, H.: Privacy and contextual integrity: Framework and applications. In: Proceedings of the 27th IEEE Symposium on Security and Privacy, Oakland, pp. 184–198 (2006)
[6] Barth, A., Datta, A., Mitchell, J.C., Sundaram, S.: Privacy and utility in business processes. In: Proceedings of the 20th IEEE Computer Security Foundations Symposium (CSF), pp. 279–294 (2007)

[7] DeYoung, H., Garg, D., Jia, L., Kaynar, D., Datta, A.: Experiences in the logical specification of the HIPAA and GLBA privacy laws. In: Proceedings of the 9th Annual ACM Workshop on Privacy in the Electronic Society, WPES. Full version: Carnegie Mellon University Technical Report CMU-CyLab-10-007 (2010)

[8] Garg, D., Jia, L., Datta, A.: Policy auditing over incomplete logs: Theory, implementation and applications. In: Proceedings of the 18th ACM Conference on Computer and Communications Security, CCS (2011)

[9] Blocki, J., Christin, N., Datta, A., Sinha, A.: Regret minimizing audits: A learning-theoretic basis for privacy protection. In: Proceedings of the 24th IEEE Computer Security Foundations Symposium (CSF), pp. 312–327 (2011)

[10] Tschantz, M.C., Datta, A., Wing, J.M.: Formalizing and enforcing purpose restrictions in privacy policies. In: IEEE Symposium on Security and Privacy, pp. 176–190 (2012)

[11] Tschantz, M.C., Datta, A., Wing, J.M.: Purpose restrictions on information use. In: Crampton, J., Jajodia, S., Mayes, K. (eds.) ESORICS 2013. LNCS, vol. 8134, pp. 610–627. Springer, Heidelberg (2013)

[12] Tschantz, M.C., Datta, A., Wing, J.M.: Information flow investigations. Technical report cmu-cs-13-118, Carnegie Mellon University (2013)

[13] Blocki, J., Christin, N., Datta, A., Sinha, A.: Audit mechanisms for provable risk management and accountable data governance. In: GameSec, pp. 38–59 (2012)

[14] Blocki, J., Christin, N., Datta, A., Procaccia, A.D., Sinha, A.: Audit games. In: IJCAI (2013)

[15] Blocki, J., Christin, N., Datta, A., Sinha, A.: Adaptive regret minimization in bounded-memory games. In: GameSec (to appear, 2013)

[16] Nissenbaum, H.: Privacy in Context: Technology, Policy, and the Integrity of Social Life. Stanford University Press (2010)

[17] House, T.W.: Consumer data privacy in a networked world: A framework for protecting privacy and promoting innovation in the global digital economy (February 2012)

[18] Lampson, B.W.: Computer security in the real world. IEEE Computer 37(6), 37–46 (2004)

[19] Weitzner, D.J., Abelson, H., Berners-Lee, T., Feigenbaum, J., Hendler, J.A., Sussman, G.J.: Information accountability. Commun. ACM 51(6), 82–87 (2008)

[20] Tambe, M.: Security and Game Theory: Algorithms, Deployed Systems, Lessons Learned. Cambridge University Press (2011)

[21] Becker, G.S.: Crime and punishment: An economic approach. Journal of Political Economy 76, 169 (1968)

[22] von Stackelberg, H.: Marktform und Gleichgewicht. Springer, Wien & Berlin (1934); VI, 138 S. 8. J. Springer (1934)

Cells as Machines: Towards Deciphering Biochemical Programs in the Cell

François Fages

Inria Paris-Rocquencourt, EPI Contraintes, France

Abstract. Systems biology aims at understanding complex biological processes in terms of their basic mechanisms at the molecular level in cells. The bet of applying theoretical computer science concepts and software engineering methods to the analysis of distributed biochemical reaction systems in the cell, designed by natural evolution, has led to interesting challenges in computer science, and new model-based insights in biology. In this paper, we review the development over the last decade of the biochemical abstract machine (Biocham) software environment for modeling cell biology molecular reaction systems, reasoning about them at different levels of abstraction, formalizing biological behaviors in temporal logic with numerical constraints, and using them to infer non-measurable kinetic parameter values, evaluate robustness, decipher natural biochemical processes and implement new programs in synthetic biology.

1 Introduction

At the end of the 90s, with the end of the human genome project, research in bioinformatics started to evolve, passing from the analysis of the genomic sequence and structural biology problems, to the analysis of complex post-genomic interaction networks: expression of RNA and proteins, protein-protein interactions, transport, signal transduction, cell cycle, etc. Systems biology [31] is the name given to a new pluridisciplinary research field, involving biologists, computer scientists, mathematicians, physicists, to promote a change of focus towards system-level understanding of high-level functions of living organisms, from their biochemical bases at the molecular level. The main outcome of this effort has been the creation of, and easy access to,

- databases and ontologies of cell components [2];
- repositories of models of cell processes [11], through the definition of common exchange formats such as the Systems Biology Markup Language (SBML) [28,27];
- model editors [33,19] and simulation tools [24,37], making it possible to reproduce *in silico* analyses in articles, with models published as supplementary material;
- and the construction of a whole cell predictive computational model of the bacterium *Mycoplasma genitalium* including its 525 genes by Karr et al.[29].

R. Natarajan (Ed.): ICDCIT 2014, LNCS 8337, pp. 50–67, 2014.

Formal methods from theoretical computer science have been successfully applied in systems biology to master the complexity of biological networks and decipher biological processes, mostly at the molecular and cellular levels. The distinction between syntax and semantics is particularly fruitful for designing modeling languages and for reasoning about biological systems at different levels of abstraction. While interaction diagrams are the key for interacting with biologists, their transcription in formal graphs or formal languages compels the modeler to eliminate any ambiguity, and enables the use of a wide variety of structural or dynamic analysis tools. In these approaches, the mathematical formalisms of ordinary differential equations (ODE) and partial derivate equations (PDE) appear as low-level languages on top of which high-level languages can be designed to directly reflect the structure of the interactions, and apply novel static analysis methods.

The use of Petri nets to model chemical processes was proposed in [39] together with standard Petri net tools for static analyses. The notion of T-invariant is a key tool for analyzing extreme fluxes and optimizing metabolic networks [50], and provides a definition of modules in biochemical networks [21]. P-invariants provide structural conservation laws that can be directly used to eliminate variables in mathematical models based on ordinary differential equation models [47]. The notion of siphons and traps provide sufficient conditions for persistence and accumulation of molecular species in a network of reactions [1,36]. Petri nets have also been generalized to handle continuous dynamics [34,35,44] and to model gene regulatory networks [10]. The use of process calculi from concurrency theory was also proposed in [41] and inspired subsequent work in several directions including stochastic modeling [38,40], space and membrane dynamics [8], and molecular biology combinatorics [15].

In this paper, we review the development over the last decade of the biochemical abstract machine (Biocham, http://contraintes.inria.fr/biocham) software environment for modeling cell biology molecular reaction systems, reasoning about them at different levels of abstraction, formalizing biological behaviors in temporal logic with numerical constraints, and using them to infer non-measurable kinetic parameter values, evaluate robustness, decipher natural biochemical processes and design new biochemical programs in synthetic biology.

2   Biochemical Reaction Systems

Let S be a finite set of s molecular species. A reaction is a triple (s, s', f), noted $s \xrightarrow{f} s'$, where $s, s' : S \to \mathbb{N}$ are multisets over S (stoichiometric coefficients), and $f : \mathbb{R}^s \to \mathbb{R}$ is a mathematical function over molecule quantities, called the rate function. Multisets are used for representing reactants and products in reactions, and a reaction is fundamentally a multiset rewriting rule. The chemical metaphor based on multiset rewriting has been proposed in computer science to program concurrent processes [4,5] and to reason about concurrent programs [7]. However in biochemistry, the reaction rates of the reactions may differ by several orders of magnitude, and it is crucial for many properties to consider the continuous-time dynamics of the reactions. Each reaction is thus supposed to be given with a rate function.

A limited number of reaction schemas occurs in biochemical reaction networks. *Binding* reactions of the form

$$A, B \xrightarrow{kAB} C$$

bind two molecular compounds together, such as the *complexation* of two proteins or complexes to form a bigger complex, or the binding of a promotion factor (resp. an inhibitor) on a gene to activate (resp. inhibit) its transcription. The mass action law kinetics used in that reaction states that the rate of the reaction is proportional to the number of its reactants. The rate constant k represents the affinity of the two molecules to bind together. The inverse unbinding reaction is of the form

$$C \xrightarrow{k.C} A, B$$

with again a mass action law kinetics, where the rate constant characterizes the stability of the complex.

A molecular species like a protein can also be modified under the action of an enzyme, such as a kinase for a *phosphorylation* reaction, or a phosphatase for a dephosphorylation reaction. This is represented by a reaction of the form

$$A \xrightarrow{v.A/(k+A)} B$$

with a Michaelis-Menten kinetics. That rate function for enzymatic reactions results in fact from the reduction of the three elementary reactions with mass action law kinetics,

$$A, E \underset{k_2 C}{\overset{k_1.A.E}{\rightleftarrows}} C \xrightarrow{k_3.C} B, E$$

by quasi-steady state approximation [45]. The same reaction schema can also be used to model the active *transport* of a molecule A from one compartment, to another compartment where A is denoted by B.

Synthesis reaction, such as the synthesis of an RNA by a gene activated by its promotion factor, are of the form

$$A \xrightarrow{v.A^n/(k+A)^n} A, B$$

with a Hill kinetics of order n. That rate function provides a sigmoidal response, i.e. a switch-like behavior to the synthesis process, and comes from the reduction of a system of n cooperative reactions.

Degradation reactions of the form

$$A \xrightarrow{k.A} \_$$

have the empty multiset as product, and either a mass action law kinetics in the case of spontaneous degradation, or a Michaelis-Menten or Hill kinetics in the case of an active degradation process under the action of other molecules.

These formal systems of reactions can be interpreted at different level of abstraction in a hierarchy of semantics. The most concrete interpretation is provided by the *Chemical Master Equation* (CME), which defines the probability of being in a state x at time t as

$$\frac{d}{dt}p^{(t)}(x) = \sum_{j:x-r_j\geq 0} f_j(x-v_j).p^{(t)}(x-v_j) - \sum_{j=1}^{n} f_j(x-v_j).p^{(t)}(x)$$

where v_j is the change vector $s'_j - s_j$ of reaction j and $f_j(x)$ is the propensity of reaction j in state x defined by the rate function.

The *differential semantics* of a reaction system is a deterministic interpretation, which describes the time evolution of the mean $E[X(t)]$ by an ODE. The ODE derives from the CME by a first-order approximation. We have

$$\frac{d}{dt}E[X(t)] = \sum_{x}\frac{d}{dt}p^{(t)}(x) = \sum_{j=1}^{n} v_j.E[f(X(t))]$$

which gives, by first-order approximation of the Taylor series about the mean,

$$\frac{d}{dt}\mu = \sum_{j=1}^{n} v_j.f(\mu).$$

Given initial concentrations for species, such an ODE can be simulated by standard numerical methods for stiff systems.

For instance, the ODE associated to the reaction system

$$S, E \xrightarrow{10.S.E} C \xrightarrow{10.C} P, E, \quad P \xrightarrow{P} S$$

is $dS/dt = k3.P - k1.E.S$, $dE/dt = k2.C - k1.E.S$, $dC/dt = k1.E.S - k2.C$, $dP/dt = k2.C - k3.P$. Figure 1 shows the amplification of the input E in the output P, in a simulation of that ODE with initial concentration 10 for S and a cosine function of time for the input E.

The *stochastic semantics* of a reaction system is defined by a Continuous Time Markov Chain (CTMC) over integer numbers of molecules (discrete concentration levels). The rate functions of the reactions lead to state transition probabilities after normalization by the sum of the propensities of each reaction in each state. The Stochastic Simulation Algorithm of Gillespie [20] provides a simulation method which computes numerical traces, most often similar to the ODE simulation for large numbers of molecules, but may exhibit qualitatively different behaviors in the case of small numbers of molecules, for instance in the case of gene expression as a gene usually is in one single copy in a cell.

The abstraction of the stochastic semantics by simply forgetting the probabilities, gives the non-deterministic *Petri net semantics* of the reactions, where the discrete states define the number of tokens in each place, and the transitions consume the reactant tokens and produce the product tokens [39].

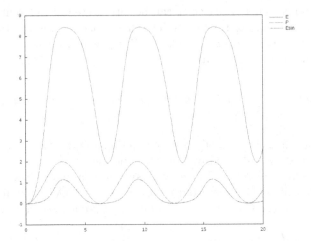

Fig. 1. Simulation of the time evolution of the concentration of output P in the differential semantics of the reaction system $S, E \xrightarrow{10.S.E} C \xrightarrow{10.C} P, E, P \xrightarrow{P} S$, with initial concentration 10 for S, and a cosine function of time (depicted by E_{sin}) for input E

The abstraction of the Petri net semantics in the *Boolean semantics* defined by the Boolean abstraction function over integers, $\beta : \mathbb{N} \longrightarrow \{0, 1\}$ with $\beta(0) = 0$ and $\beta(x) = 1$ if $x > 0$, is a non-deterministic asynchronous Boolean transition system suitable for reasoning on the presence/absence of molecules. In Biocham, the Boolean semantics of the reactions associates several Boolean transitions to one reaction. For instance, a complexation reaction like $A, B \longrightarrow B$, is interpreted by 4 Boolean transitions, one for each possible complete consumption of the 2 reactants: $A \wedge B \longrightarrow C \wedge \pm A \wedge \pm B$. This is necessary for the abstraction result to hold with respect to the Petri net or stochastic semantics. It is worth noticing that with a Boolean abstraction defined by a threshold value θ, i.e. $\beta_\theta(x) = 0$ if $x < \theta$ and $\beta_\theta(x) = 1$ if $x \geq \theta$, several Boolean transitions must be introduced for the products as well, for instance the complexation reaction gives rise to 16 Boolean transitions for taking into account the possible production of the 2 products, either below or above the threshold value.

In [18], all these discrete and stochastic trace semantics of reactions systems have been related by formal abstraction relationships (Galois connections) in the framework of abstract interpretation [14]. This shows that if a behavior is not possible in the Boolean semantics for instance, then it is not realizable in the Petri net or stochastic semantics for any kinetic laws and kinetic parameter values. This is a strong motivation for reasoning at a high level of abstraction in the Boolean semantics of reaction systems, which may be sufficient to answer questions about large interaction maps.

3 Symbolic Model-Checking of Biochemical Systems

Regulatory, signaling and metabolic networks are very complex mechanisms which are far from being understood on a global scale. Data on the kinetics of the individual reactions is also rare and unreliable, making the building of quantitative models particularly challenging in many cases. In those situations, qualitative analyses can however be conducted in the Boolean semantics of the reactions, using the powerful model-checking tools developed for circuit and program verification [13].

A Boolean state specifies the presence or absence of each molecule in the system at a given time, and any set of states can be represented by a Boolean constraint over the molecule variables. The *Computation Tree Logic* CTL* is a modal logic that extends propositional logic with two path quantifiers, $\mathbf{A}$ and $\mathbf{E}$ ($\mathbf{A}\phi$ meaning that ϕ is true on all computation paths, and $\mathbf{E}\phi$ that it is true on at least one path), and several temporal operators, $\mathbf{X}\phi$ (meaning that ϕ is true on the next state on a path), $\mathbf{F}\phi$ (meaning that ϕ is finally true on some state on a path), $\mathbf{G}\phi$ (globally true on all states on a path), $\phi\mathbf{U}\psi$ (until, meaning that ψ is finally true and ϕ is always true before), and $\phi\mathbf{R}\psi$ (release, meaning that ψ is either globally true or always true up to the first occurrence of ψ included). In this logic, $F\phi$ is equivalent to $true\mathbf{U}\phi$, $G\phi$ to $\phi\mathbf{R}false$, and we have the following duality properties: $\neg\mathbf{X}\phi = \mathbf{X}\neg\phi$, $\neg\mathbf{E}\phi = \mathbf{A}\neg\phi$, $\neg\mathbf{F}\phi = \mathbf{G}\neg\phi$, $\neg(\phi\mathbf{U}\psi) = \neg\psi\mathbf{R}\neg\phi$.

The fragment CTL of CTL* imposes that a temporal opertor must immediately follow a path quantifier. This logic CTL can express a wide variety of properties of biochemical networks [9] like state *reachability* of ϕ ($\mathbf{EF}\phi$), *steadyness* of ϕ ($\mathbf{EG}\phi$), *stability* ($\mathbf{AG}\phi$), reachability of a stable state ($\mathbf{EFAG}\phi$), ϕ *checkpoint* for ψ ($\neg\psi\mathbf{R}\phi$), *oscillations* ($\mathbf{EG}(\mathbf{F}\neg\phi \wedge \mathbf{F}\phi)$ over-approximated in CTL by $\mathbf{EG}(\mathbf{EF}\neg\phi \wedge \mathbf{EF}\phi)$) etc.

Figure 2 reproduces Kohn's map of the mammalian cell cycle [32] using some graphical conventions introduced by K. Kohn to represent the different types of interactions (complexation, binding, phosphorylations, modifications, synthesis, etc.). This map has been transcribed in a reaction model of 732 reaction rules over 165 proteins and genes, and 532 variables taking into account the different forms of the molecular species [9]. The astronomical number of Boolean states in this system, 2^{532}, prevents the explicit representation of the state graph, however, a set of states in this space can nevertheless be represented symbolically by a Boolean formula over 532 variables, and the transition relation by a Boolean formula over twice that number of variables. For instance the formula *false* represents the empty set, *true* the universe of all states, x the set of 2^{531} states where x is present, etc. Our first result in [9] was to show the performance of the state-of-the-art symbolic model checker NuSMV [12] using the representation of Boolean formulae by ordered binary decision diagrams (OBDD), on this non standard transition system from biology. Table 1 shows that the compilation of the whole 732 reactions into Boolean formulae took 29 seconds, and simple

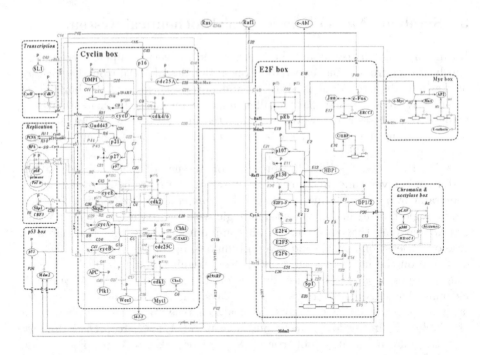

Fig. 2. Kohn's map of the mammalian cell cycle control [32]

reachability and oscillations properties could be checked in a few seconds. The negative answer to the query concerning the oscillation of cyclin B revealed the omission of the synthesis of cyclin B in Kohn's map.

The encoding of biological properties in temporal logics provides a *logical paradigm for systems biology* that makes a bridge between theoretical models and biological experiments, through the following identifications:

$$biological\ model = transition\ system,$$
$$biological\ property = temporal\ logic\ formula,$$
$$model\ validation = model\text{-}checking,$$
$$model\ inference = constraint\ solving.$$

A formula ϕ, learned from biological experiments, can be tested in a model $\mathcal{M}$ by model-checking techniques to determine whether $\mathcal{M} \models \phi$. Furthermore, a model-checker can also compute the set of initial states for which a formula is true, and suggest biological experiments to verify a CTL property predicted by the model, on the real biological object [6]. In particular, the checkpoints proved in a model of the cell cycle, or of a signaling network, provide possible drug targets to block the cell cycle, or a signaling cascade.

Table 1. Runtime in seconds obtained on Kohn's map with NuSMV in 2002 on a Pentium 3 at 600MHz, for checking simple CTL reachability and oscillation properties in a state corresponding to phase G2 of the cell cycle. The absence of possibility of oscillation for cycB corresponds to the omission of a reaction in Kohn's map, for the synthesis of cyclin B.

CTL query	Answer	CPU time	whitness time
compilation of the reactions	-	29	-
reachable SL1(p)	yes	29	124
reachable cycE	yes	2	22
reachable cycD	yes	1.9	11.5
reachable pcna-cycD	yes	1.7	48.7
cdc25C(Nterm) checkpoint cdk1-cycB(Thr161))	no	2.2	49.22
oscillation cycA	yes	31.8	-
oscillation cycB	no	6	-

4   Quantitative Temporal Logic Constraints

4.1   Threshold and Timing Constraints

The temporal logic approach to the specification of imprecise dynamical properties of biological systems can also be made quantitative and applied to quantitative models over concentrations. The idea is to lift it to a first-order setting with numerical (linear) constraints over the reals, in order to express threshold or more complex constraints on the concentrations of the molecular compounds and time.

For instance, the reachability of a threshold concentration for a molecule A can be expressed with the formula $\mathbf{F}(A > v)$ for some value or free variable v. Such formulae can then be interpreted on a finite numerical trace (extended with a loop on the last state) obtained either from a biological experiment, or from the numerical simulation of an ODE model, giving the concentrations of the molecules at discrete time points, e.g. Figure 3.

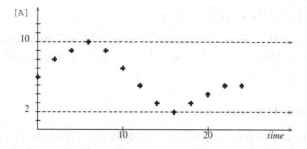

Fig. 3. Numerical trace depicting the time evolution of a protein concentration

In Biocham, we use the First-Order Linear Time Logic with linear constraints over the reals (FO-LTL($\mathbb{R}_{\text{lin}}$)) to specify semi-qualitative semi-quantitative properties of a biological dynamical system. LTL is the fragment of CTL* without any path quantifier and only time operators interpreted on a trace. The grammar of FO-LTL($\mathbb{R}_{\text{lin}}$) formulae is summarized in Table 2.

Table 2. Grammar of FO-LTL($\mathbb{R}_{\text{lin}}$) formulae where c denotes linear constraints over molecular concentrations, their first derivative, free variables and the time variable.

$$\phi ::= c \mid \phi \Rightarrow \psi \mid \phi \wedge \phi \mid \phi \vee \phi \mid \mathbf{X}\phi \mid \mathbf{F}\phi \mid \mathbf{G}\phi \mid \phi\mathbf{U}\phi \mid \phi\mathbf{R}\phi$$

Timing constraints can be expressed with the time variable and free variables to relate the time of differents events. For instance, the formula $\mathbf{G}(Time \leq t_1 \Rightarrow [A] < 1 \wedge Time \geq t_2 \Rightarrow [A] > 10) \wedge (t_2 - t_1 < 60)$ expresses that the concentration of molecule A is always less than 1 up to some time t_1, always greater than 10 after time t_2, and the switching time between t_1 and t_2 is less than 60 units of time.

A local maximum for molecule concentration A can be defined with the formula $\mathbf{F}(A \leq x \wedge \mathbf{X}(A = x \wedge \mathbf{X}A \leq x))$. This formula can be used to define oscillation properties, with period constraints defined as time separation constraints between the local maxima of the molecule, as well as phase constraints between different molecules.

In [43,17], it is shown how the *validity domain* $\mathcal{D}_{(s_0,...,s_n),\phi}$ of the free variables of an FO-LTL($\mathbb{R}_{\text{lin}}$) formula ϕ on a finite trace $(s_0, ..., s_n)$, can be computed by finite unions and intersections of polyhedra, by a simple extension of the model-checking algorithm, as follows:

- $\mathcal{D}_{(s_0,...,s_n),\phi} = \mathcal{D}_{s_0,\phi}$,
- $\mathcal{D}_{s_i,c(\boldsymbol{x})} = \{\boldsymbol{v} \in \mathbb{R}^k \mid s_i \models c[\boldsymbol{v}/\boldsymbol{x}]\}$ for a constraint $c(\boldsymbol{x})$,
- $\mathcal{D}_{s_i,\phi\wedge\psi} = \mathcal{D}_{s_i,\phi} \cap \mathcal{D}_{s_i,\psi}$,
- $\mathcal{D}_{s_i,\phi\vee\psi} = \mathcal{D}_{s_i,\phi} \cup \mathcal{D}_{s_i,\psi}$,
- $\mathcal{D}_{s_i,\mathbf{X}\phi} = \mathcal{D}_{s_{i+1},\phi}$,
- $\mathcal{D}_{s_i,\mathbf{F}\phi} = \bigcup_{j=i}^{n} \mathcal{D}_{s_j,\phi}$,
- $\mathcal{D}_{s_i,\mathbf{G}\phi} = \bigcap_{j=i}^{n} \mathcal{D}_{s_j,\phi}$,
- $\mathcal{D}_{s_i,\phi\mathbf{U}\psi} = \bigcup_{j=i}^{n}(\mathcal{D}_{s_j,\psi} \cap \bigcap_{k=i}^{j-1} \mathcal{D}_{s_k,\phi})$.

For instance, on the numerical trace of Figure 3, the validity domain, depicted in Figure 4, of the formula $\mathbf{F}(A \geq y_1 \wedge \mathbf{F}(A \leq y_2))$, where y_1 and y_2 are free variables, is $y_1 \leq 10 \wedge y_2 \geq 2$.

4.2   Parameter Optimization

One major difficulty in quantitative systems biology, is that the kinetic parameter values of the biochemical reactions are usually unknown, and must be infered from the observable behavior of the system under various conditions (differences

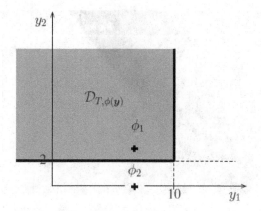

Fig. 4. Validity domain of the formula $\mathbf{F}(A \geq y_1 \wedge \mathbf{F}(A \leq y_2))$ on the trace of Figure 3. The two points correspond to the formulae $\phi_1 = \mathbf{F}(A \geq 7 \wedge \mathbf{F}(A \leq 3))$ (true) and $\phi_2 = \mathbf{F}(A \geq 7 \wedge \mathbf{F}(A \leq 0))$ (false) respectively.

of milieu, drugs, gene knock-outs or knock downs, etc.). In our quantitative temporal logic setting, this problem amounts to solve the inverse problem of finding parameter values for an ODE model such that an FO-LTL($\mathbb{R}_{\text{lin}}$) specification is true.

However, the classical true/false valuation of a logical formula is not well suited to guide the search. State-of-the-art continuous optimization algorithms such as evolutionary algorithms, require a fitness function to measure progress towards satisfiability. Such a continuous satisfaction degree in the interval $[0, 1]$ can be defined for FO-LTL($\mathbb{R}_{\text{lin}}$) formulae, by replacing constants by variables, which was in fact our original motivation for considering formulae with free variables.

Indeed, a specification of the expected behavior given by a closed formula, for instance

$$\phi_2 = \mathbf{F}(A \geq 7 \wedge \mathbf{F}(A \leq 0)),$$

can first be abstracted in a formula with free variables by replacing constants with free variables, e.g.

$$\phi = \mathbf{F}(A \geq y_1 \wedge \mathbf{F}(A \leq y_2))$$

with the objective values 7 for y_1 and 0 for y_2. Then, the validity domain $\mathcal{D}_{T,\phi}$ of the formula ϕ on a trace T obtained by simulation for some parameter values, makes it possible to define the *violation degree* $vd(T, \phi, o)$ of the formula on T with objective o, simply as the distance between the validity domain and the objective point o, i.e. 2 in our example (see Figure 4). A *continuous satisfaction degree* in the interval $[0, 1]$ can then be defined by normalization as the inverse of the violation degree d plus one,

$$sd(T, \phi, o) = \frac{1}{1 + vd(T, \phi, o)}$$

i.e. $1/3$ in our example.

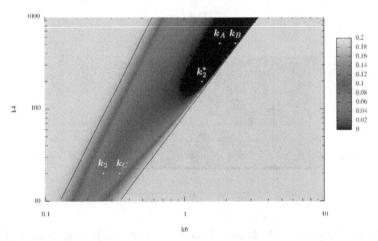

Fig. 5. Landscape of the satisfaction degree of an oscillation property with amplitude constraint, on a color scale from yellow to black, as a function of two parameters in a quantitative model of the yeast cell cycle from [48]. The parameter sets k_A, k_B and k_2^* satisfy the specification. The parameter sets k_c and k_2 violate the amplitude constraint. CMA-ES iteratively samples the landscape to find a path in a random walk from k_2 to k_2^* for instance.

In Biocham, we use the Covariance Matrix Adaptation Evolution Strategy (CMA-ES) of N. Hansen [22] as a black-box optimization algorithm, with the satisfaction degree of an FO-LTL($\mathbb{R}_{\text{lin}}$) specification as fitness function, and unknown kinetic parameter values (initial concentrations and control parameters) as variables. On a quantitative model of the cell cycle [48], Figure 5 depicts the landscape of the satisfaction degree of an oscillation property with amplitude constraint, as a function of two parameters of the model. The landscape is iteratively sampled by CMA-ES to find a path towards satisfaction, and optimize the model parameter values, for instance going from k_2 to k_2^* in a few steps.

The FO-LTL($\mathbb{R}_{\text{lin}}$) satisfaction problem generalizes the classical curve fitting problem, by providing a powerful language to express significant properties of the dynamics, instead of requiring a complete curve that could over-specify the behavior. This is particularly useful in biology where experimental data may be imprecise in nature, with important cell-to-cell variability, irregular oscillation periods and phases, and should not be taken as exact specification.

This strategy for optimizing parameters with respect to an FO-LTL($\mathbb{R}_{\text{lin}}$) specification allowed us to solve a wide variety of problems in systems biology, for fitting models to experimental data in high dimension (up to 100 parameters), revisiting the structure of the reaction network in case of failure, making new biological hypotheses based on simulation, and verifying them by new experiments, for instance for deciphering the complex dynamics of a cell signaling network in [23]. The same strategy for parameter optimization can also be used to compute control parameters to achieve a desired behavior at the single cell of cell population levels. This has been used for the model-based real-time control of gene expression in yeast cells using a microfluidic device in [49], and at the whole body scale, to couple models of cell cycle, circadian clock, drug effects, DNA repair system, and optimize anti-cancer drug chronotherapeutics in [16,3].

4.3   Robustness Measure

In [30], Kitano gives a general definition of the robustness of a property ϕ of a system S with respect to a set P of perturbations given with their probability distribution, as the mean functionality of the system with respect to ϕ under the perturbations, with the system's functionality defined in an *ad hoc* way for each property.

In our framework, this definition can be instanciated to a complete definition for FO-LTL($\mathbb{R}_{\text{lin}}$) properties, simply by taking their continuous satisfaction degree as functionality measure, as follows [42]:

$$\mathcal{R}_{S,\phi,P} = \int_{p \in P} prob(p) \; sd(T_p, \phi) \; dp.$$

In a model, this definition of robustness can be evaluated by

1. sampling the perturbations according to their distribution;
2. measuring the satisfaction degree of the property for each simulation of the perturbed model;
3. and returning the average satisfaction degree.

This methodology has been used in [42] to design and implement in synthetic biology using a cascade of gene inhibitions, a robust switch satisfying some timing constraints. Moreover, continuous parameter sensitivity indices can be computed in this approach to determine the most important parameters for improving the robustness of the design.

On the quantitative model of the yeast cell cycle [48] and the oscillation with amplitude constraint depicted in Figure 5, the estimated degree of robustness for parameters k_A, k_B and k_C are respectively 0.991, 0.917 and 0.932. This is consistent with the location of points k_A, k_B and k_C. Perturbations around point k_A have high probabilities of staying in the region satisfying the specification whereas perturbations around point k_B have high probabilities of moving the system to the region with no oscillation. k_C is more robust than k_B even though, as opposed to k_B, its violation degree is non null. This is explained by the abrupt transition between oscillating and non oscillating regions near k_B compared to the smoother transition near k_C.

5   Biochemical Programming

Synthetic biology prolongs systems biology with the aim of designing biological systems that perform novel, useful tasks, and implementing them *in vivo* by reengineering and optimizing existing natural organisms. This is achieved by modifying the genes or integrating DNA constructs in living cells, or by creating cell-free vesicles, using bioengineering techniques. Synthetic biology keeps modeling and the characterization of components as central methodology to achieve its goals. Some successes of this nascent field include: the constitution of registries of standard biological parts and the organization of the iGEM competition at MIT; the creation by Craig Venter of a cell with a synthetic genome; the production by Sanofi of artemisinin, an antimalarial drug, by a biosynthetic pathway in a yeast chassis.

However, in order to design robust interaction networks and to be reliable in a clinical context, synthetic circuits must progress in their biochemical implementation of logical tasks and simple operations.

One way to attack this problem is to study the compilation of imperative programs in biochemical reaction systems over proteins. In [46], Senum and Riedel have shown how Boolean and arithmetic operations can be robustly implemented with biochemical reactions using mass action law kinetics, and only two kinetic rate constants s and f, for fast and slow reactions respectively. These transformations use an intermediate language of *conditional reactions* with preconditions. The preconditions are logical expressions over Boolean variables associated to each molecular species. The Boolean truth values are defined from the concentrations with a threshold function β_θ as in Section 2.

For instance, a reaction with precondition A is simply transformed by adding A as catalyst (i.e. both reactant and product). For a disjunctive precondition, $A \lor B$, two reactions are created, one with A and one with B as catalyst. A negation in a precondition amounts to test the absence of a molecular species which cannot be directly done in a biochemical reaction. The idea is to introduce a witness molecule A' for the absence of A without affecting A, using the following slow and fast mass action law kinetic reactions: $\_ \xrightarrow{s} A'$, $A, A' \xrightarrow{f.A.A'} A$, $2 * A' \xrightarrow{f.A'^2} A$.

For the copy instruction, B:=A, compiling it with just one reaction $A \longrightarrow B$ would destroy A. On the other hand, the reaction $A \longrightarrow A, B$ would increase B at each increment of A. In order to localize the computation for the copy, the following conditional reactions are used

$$
\begin{array}{ll}
A \longrightarrow C & \text{precondition } G \\
G \longrightarrow \_ & \text{precondition } \neg A \\
C \longrightarrow A, B & \text{precondition } \neg G
\end{array}
$$

where G is a start signal molecule for executing the instruction and which is consumed in the process. This is the basic idea to implement arithmetic operations and comparisons thourhg asynchronuous biochemical computation.

In [25], the authors further extend this approach to the compilation of program control flows. For instance, the following program for the Euclidean division of A by B, is compiled, first in a conditional reaction program where initially Q is zero and C is initially of a unit amount:

```
Q:=0                    A, B ⟶ D
while A>=B do           C ⟶ Q, E   precondition ¬B
begin                   D ⟶ F      precondition ¬C
    A:=A-B;             E ⟶ G      precondition ¬D
    Q:=Q+1;             F ⟶ B      precondition ¬E
end;                    G ⟶ C      precondition ¬F
R:=A                    D ⟶ R      precondition B ∧ ¬A
```

and then into a system of biochemical reactions with only two fast and slow mass action law kinetics. The execution with initial concentrations $[A] = 20$ and $[B] = 3$ produces the result $[Q] = 6$, $[R] = 2$ as follows:

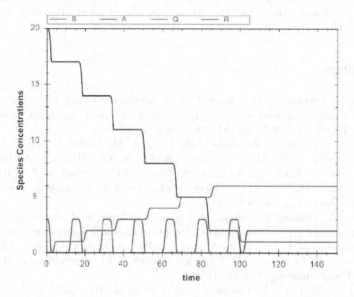

Fig. 6. Biochemical computation of the Euclidean division of A by B [25]

However, more work is needed on this schema to minimize the number of involved molecular species [26]. This is crucial to accomplish a complex computation within a confined biochemical environment. The challenge of implementing simple imperative programs with protein reaction systems in vesicles seems attainable in a near future with enormous applications for creating biosensors and personalized therapeutics at the microscopic scale.

6   Conclusion

This line of research in systems biology based on the vision of cell as computation, aims at mastering the complexity of cell processes, through the use of concepts and tools from theoretical computer science and the establishment of formal computation paradigms tightly coupled to experimental settings in cell biology. While for the biologist, as well as for the mathematician, the sizes of the biological networks and the number of elementary interactions constitute a complexity barrier, for the computer scientist the difficulty is not that much in the size of the networks than in the unconventional nature of biochemical computation. Unlike most programs, biochemical computation involve transitions that are stochastic rather than deterministic, continuous-time rather than discrete-time, poorly localized in compartments instead of well-structured in modules, and created by evolution instead of by rational design. It is our belief however that some form of modularity (functional if not structural) is required by an evolutionary system to survive, and that the elucidation of these modules in biochemical computation is now a key to master the analog aspects of biochemical computation, understand natural biochemical programs, and start controlling the cell machinery.

References

1. Angeli, D., Leenheer, P.D., Sontag, E.D.: A petri net approach to persistence analysis in chemical reaction networks. In: Biology and Control Theory: Current Challenges. LNCIS, vol. 357, pp. 181–216. Springer (2007)
2. Ashburner, M., Ball, C.A., Blake, J.A., Botstein, D., Butler, H., Michael Cherry, J., Davis, A.P., Dolinski, K., Dwight, S.S., Eppig, J.T., Harris, M.A., Hill, D.P., Issel-Tarver, L., Kasarskis, A., Lewis, S., Matese, J.C., Richardson, J.E., Ringwald, M., Rubin, G.M., Sherlock, G.: Gene ontology: tool for the unification of biology. Nature Genetics 25, 25–29 (2000)
3. Ballesta, A., Dulong, S., Abbara, C., Cohen, B., Okyar, A., Clairambault, J., Levi, F.: A combined experimental and mathematical approach for molecular-based optimization of irinotecan circadian delivery. PLOS Computational Biology 7(9) (2011)
4. Banâtre, J.-P., Le Métayer, D.: Chemical reaction as a computational model. Functional Programmming, 103–117 (1989)
5. Banâtre, J.-P., Priol, T.: Chemical programming of future service-oriented architectures. Jounral of Software 4, 738–746 (2009)
6. Bernot, G., Comet, J.-P., Richard, A., Guespin, J.: A fruitful application of formal methods to biological regulatory networks: Extending thomas' asynchronous logical approach with temporal logic. Journal of Theoretical Biology 229(3), 339–347 (2004)
7. Berry, G., Boudol, G.: The chemical abstract machine. Theoretical Computer Science 96 (1992)
8. Cardelli, L.: Brane calculi - interactions of biological membranes. In: Danos, V., Schachter, V. (eds.) CMSB 2004. LNCS (LNBI), vol. 3082, pp. 257–278. Springer, Heidelberg (2005)
9. Chabrier-Rivier, N., Chiaverini, M., Danos, V., Fages, F., Schächter, V.: Modeling and querying biochemical interaction networks. Theoretical Computer Science 325(1), 25–44 (2004)
10. Chaouiya, C.: Petri net modelling of biological networks. Briefings in Bioinformatics (2007)

11. Chelliah, V., Laibe, C., Novère, N.: Biomodels database: A repository of mathematical models of biological processes. In: Schneider, M.V. (ed.) Silico Systems Biology. Methods in Molecular Biology, vol. 1021, pp. 189–199. Humana Press (2013)

12. Cimatti, A., Clarke, E., Giunchiglia, E., Giunchiglia, F., Pistore, M., Roveri, M., Sebastiani, R., Tacchella, A.: NuSMV 2: An openSource tool for symbolic model checking. In: Brinksma, E., Larsen, K.G. (eds.) CAV 2002. LNCS, vol. 2404, p. 359. Springer, Heidelberg (2002)

13. Clarke, E.M., Grumberg, O., Peled, D.A.: Model Checking. MIT Press (1999)

14. Cousot, P., Cousot, R.: Abstract interpretation: A unified lattice model for static analysis of programs by construction or approximation of fixpoints. In: POPL 1977: Proceedings of the 6th ACM Symposium on Principles of Programming Languages, pp. 238–252. ACM Press, New York (1977)

15. Danos, V., Laneve, C.: Formal molecular biology. Theoretical Computer Science 325(1), 69–110 (2004)

16. De Maria, E., Fages, F., Rizk, A., Soliman, S.: Design, optimization, and predictions of a coupled model of the cell cycle, circadian clock, dna repair system, irinotecan metabolism and exposure control under temporal logic constraints. Theoretical Computer Science 412(21), 2108–2127 (2011)

17. Fages, F., Rizk, A.: On temporal logic constraint solving for the analysis of numerical data time series. Theoretical Computer Science 408(1), 55–65 (2008)

18. Fages, F., Soliman, S.: Abstract interpretation and types for systems biology. Theoretical Computer Science 403(1), 52–70 (2008)

19. Funahashi, A., Matsuoka, Y., Jouraku, A., Morohashi, M., Kikuchi, N., Kitano, H.: Celldesigner 3.5: A versatile modeling tool for biochemical networks. Proceedings of the IEEE 96(8), 1254–1265 (2008)

20. Gillespie, D.T.: General method for numerically simulating stochastic time evolution of coupled chemical-reactions. Journal of Computational Physics 22, 403–434 (1976)

21. Grafahrend-Belau, E., Schreiber, F., Heiner, M., Sackmann, A., Junker, B.H., Grunwald, S., Speer, A., Winder, K., Koch, I.: Modularization of biochemical networks based on a classification of petri net by T-invariants. BMC Bioinformatics 9(90) (February 2008)

22. Hansen, N., Ostermeier, A.: Completely derandomized self-adaptation in evolution strategies. Evolutionary Computation 9(2), 159–195 (2001)

23. Heitzler, D., Durand, G., Gallay, N., Rizk, A., Ahn, S., Kim, J., Violin, J.D., Dupuy, L., Gauthier, C., Piketty, V., Crépieux, P., Poupon, A., Clément, F., Fages, F., Lefkowitz, R.J., Reiter, E.: Competing g protein-coupled receptor kinases balance g protein and β-arrestin signaling. Molecular Systems Biology 8(590) (June 2012)

24. Hoops, S., Sahle, S., Gauges, R., Lee, C., Pahle, J., Simus, N., Singhal, M., Xu, L., Mendes, P., Kummer, U.: Copasi – a complex pathway simulator. Bioinformatics 22(24), 3067–3074 (2006)

25. Huang, D.-A., Jiang, J.-H., Huang, R.-Y., Cheng, C.-Y.: Compiling program control flows into biochemical reactions. In: ICCAD 2012: IEEE/ACM International Conference on Computer-Aided Design, San Jose, USA (November 2012)

26. Huang, R.-Y., Huang, D.-A., Chiang, H.-J.K., Jiang, J.-H., Fages, F.: Species minimization in computation with biochemical reactions. In: IWBDA 2013: Proceedings of the Fifth International Workshop on Bio-Design Automation. Imperial College, London (2013)

27. Hucka, M.: et al. The systems biology markup language (SBML): A medium for representation and exchange of biochemical network models. Bioinformatics 19(4), 524–531 (2003)

28. Hucka, M., Hoops, S., Keating, S.M., Nicolas, L.N., Sahle, S., Wilkinson, D.: Systems biology markup language (SBML) level 2: Structures and facilities for model definitions. In: Nature Precedings (December 2008)

29. Karr, J.R., Sanghvi, J.C., Macklin, D.N., Gutschow, M.V., Jacobs, J.M., Bolival Jr., B., Assad-Garcia, N., Glass, J.I., Covert, M.W.: A whole-cell computational model predicts phenotype from genotype. Cell 150(2), 389–401 (2012)

30. Kitano, H.: Towards a theory of biological robustness. Molecular Systems Biology 3, 137 (2007)

31. Kitano, H.: Systems biology: A brief overview. Science 295(5560), 1662–1664 (2002)

32. Kohn, K.W.: Molecular interaction map of the mammalian cell cycle control and DNA repair systems. Molecular Biology of the Cell 10(8), 2703–2734 (1999)

33. le Novere, N., Hucka, M., Mi, H., Moodie, S., Schreiber, F., Sorokin, A., Demir, E., Wegner, K., Aladjem, M.I., Wimalaratne, S.M., Bergman, F.T., Gauges, R., Ghazal, P., Kawaji, H., Li, L., Matsuoka, Y., Villeger, A., Boyd, S.E., Calzone, L., Courtot, M., Dogrusoz, U., Freeman, T.C., Funahashi, A., Ghosh, S., Jouraku, A., Kim, S., Kolpakov, F., Luna, A., Sahle, S., Schmidt, E., Watterson, S., Wu, G., Goryanin, I., Kell, D.B., Sander, C., Sauro, H., Snoep, J.L., Kohn, K., Kitano, H.: The systems biology graphical notation. Nature Biotechnology 27(8), 735–741 (2009)

34. Matsuno, H., Doi, A., Nagasaki, M., Miyano, S.: Hybrid petri net representation of gene regulatory network. In: Proceedings of the 5th Pacific Symposium on Biocomputing, pp. 338–349 (2000)

35. Matsuno, H., Tanaka, Y., Aoshima, H., Doi, A., Matsui, M., Miyano, S.: Biopathways representation and simulation on hybrid functional petri net. Silico Biology 3, 32 (2003)

36. Nabli, F., Fages, F., Martinez, T., Soliman, S.: A boolean model for enumerating minimal siphons and traps in petri nets. In: Milano, M. (ed.) CP 2012. LNCS, vol. 7514, pp. 798–814. Springer, Heidelberg (2012)

37. Nagasaki, M., Onami, S., Miyano, S., Kitano, H.: Bio-calculus: Its concept, and an application for molecular interaction. In: Currents in Computational Molecular Biology. Frontiers Science Series, vol. 30, Universal Academy Press, Inc. (2000) This book is a collection of poster papers presented at the RECOMB 2000 Poster Session.

38. Priami, C., Regev, A., Silverman, W., Shapiro, E.: Application of a stochastic name passing calculus to representation and simulation of molecular processes. Information Processing Letters 80, 25–31 (2001)

39. Reddy, V.N., Mavrovouniotis, M.L., Liebman, M.N.: Petri net representations in metabolic pathways. In: Hunter, L., Searls, D.B., Shavlik, J.W. (eds.) Proceedings of the 1st International Conference on Intelligent Systems for Molecular Biology (ISMB), pp. 328–336. AAAI Press (1993)

40. Regev, A., Panina, E.M., Silverman, W., Cardelli, L., Shapiro, E.: Bioambients: An abstraction for biological compartments. Theoretical Computer Science 325(1), 141–167 (2004)

41. Regev, A., Silverman, W., Shapiro, E.Y.: Representation and simulation of biochemical processes using the pi-calculus process algebra. In: Proceedings of the sixth Pacific Symposium of Biocomputing, pp. 459–470 (2001)

42. Rizk, A., Batt, G., Fages, F., Soliman, S.: A general computational method for robustness analysis with applications to synthetic gene networks. Bioinformatics 12(25), il69–il78 (2009)
43. Rizk, A., Batt, G., Fages, F., Soliman, S.: Continuous valuations of temporal logic specifications with applications to parameter optimization and robustness measures. Theoretical Computer Science 412(26), 2827–2839 (2011)
44. Rohr, C., Marwan, W., Heiner, M.: Snoopy - a unifying petri net framework to investigate biomolecular networks. Bioinformatics 26(7), 974–975 (2010)
45. Segel, L.A.: Modeling dynamic phenomena in molecular and cellular biology. Cambridge University Press, Cambridge (1984)
46. Senum, P., Riedel, M.: Rate-independent constructs for chemical computation. PLOS One 6(6) (2011)
47. Soliman, S.: Invariants and other structural properties of biochemical models as a constraint satisfaction problem. Algorithms for Molecular Biology 7(15) (May 2012)
48. Tyson, J.J.: Modeling the cell division cycle: cdc2 and cyclin interactions. Proceedings of the National Academy of Sciences 88(16), 7328–7332 (1991)
49. Uhlendorf, J., Miermont, A., Delaveau, T., Charvin, G., Fages, F., Bottani, S., Batt, G., Hersen, P.: Long-term model predictive control of gene expression at the population and single-cell levels. Proceedings of the National Academy of Sciences 109(35), 14271–14276 (2012)
50. Zevedei-Oancea, I., Schuster, S.: Topological analysis of metabolic networks based on petri net theory. Silico Biology, 3(29) (2003)

A Spatial Web Crawler for Discovering Geo-servers and Semantic Referencing with Spatial Features

Sonal Patil, Shrutilipi Bhattacharjee, and Soumya K. Ghosh

School of Information Technology,
Indian Institute of Technology Kharagpur, India
{sonalspatil,shrutilipi.2007}@gmail.com, skg@iitkgp.ac.in

Abstract. Improvement of technologies in the field of spatial data collection provide a lot of research opportunities in the field of *Geographic Information System*. The geospatial data are often dynamic in nature and available in heterogeneous format. The online spatial data sources are one of the key avenues for publishing and retrieving the geo-spatial data. Efficient discovery of these data sources through Internet, retrieval and analysis of useful information, is one of major challenges in this field. The paper proposes a framework for discovering the geo-spatial data sources using a spatial web crawler. This will facilitate processing of spatial queries involving distributed heterogeneous data repositories. This is being done with the help of the *Web Feature Service* (WFS) standard specification provided by *Open Geospatial Consortium* (OGC). Geo-spatial information is retrieved further for semantic annotations of the data sources using ontology. The semantic information is stored in the form of feature_type repositories as the area of interest lies around the geographic features provided by the geo-servers. The performance study analyzes the accuracy of discovery and semantic annotation of geo-servers for better understanding the framework.

Keywords: Geospatial Data, Data discovery, Spatial Web Crawler, Semantic Indexing, Ontology.

1 Introduction

The exponential growth of geo-spatial data offers enormous research scope to deliver accurate and efficient approaches for discovering and analyzing the spatial information through Internet. In 2005, article [1] reported that *NASA*'s *Earth Observing System Data and Information System* produced over 3 terabytes of data daily. This kind of gigantic amount of data limits the efficient retrieval of suitable geo-spatial data source and getting meaningful knowledge out of it. These limitations also affect the search related spatial attributes, stored as the thematic layers in *geographic information system* (*GIS*) [2].

A web crawler is an automated program or script to retrieve resources from Internet. It is provided with the input set of URLs. From the downloaded pages,

R. Natarajan (Ed.): ICDCIT 2014, LNCS 8337, pp. 68–78, 2014.

all the hyperlinks are extracted from the crawled pages and added to the queue. The process continues till the stopping criterion is met. It also indexes the pages which is used in search engines. Topical crawler is the web crawler which aims to search for a particular topic. The proposed work focusses on developing an efficient topical web crawler for discovering geo-spatial data sources in the Internet and extracting the meaningful information in the form of *feature_types* supported by those geo-servers. It is followed by the semantic indexing of data sources with respect to the stored *feature_types*. This work utilizes the *Web Feature Service (WFS)* [3] to get the metadata information related to geographic features provided by any geo-servers. *Open Geospatial Consortium (OGC)*[1] has established the *OpenGIS WFS* implementation specification so that the spatial data providers can use them to publish and retrieve their data on Internet. This work is further extended to distinguish spatial data sources as per their offered *feature_types* for efficient indexing and hence better search. *Ontology* [4] [5] is the tool to semantically describe the knowledge base, represent it formally and distinguish between its unique concepts. *Spatial feature ontology* is constructed for annotating geo-server with the proper *feature_types* reference. The *ontology*, used for the experiments, is being populated with the spatial features in the Indian context (refer to Fig. 3) but the coverage of the crawler is global. The results are found to be well balanced between *precision* and *recall* in terms of information retrieval. The overall objectives of this work are as follows,

- Building a spatial web crawler using *WFS* based on *OGC* standard.
- Building a domain *ontology* with spatial *feature_type*.
- Semantic matching using *ontology* and indexing of geo-servers with offered *feature_type* reference.
- Performing experiment with test seed URLs and analyzing the performance of the crawler in terms of accurate semantic annotations.

State of the art reports many research works regarding spatial web crawler. Developing topical web crawler is one of the utmost interesting areas to the researchers in the last few decade. Karkaletsis *et al.* [6] proposed a technique for identifying domain specific web sites and extracting interesting information from the associated web pages. Lopez *et al* [7] measured the performance of the public search APIs. For this, they have tested three main commercial search engines for discovering geographic web services, namely, Bing, Google and Yahoo!. Mukhopadhyay *et al.* [8] proposed a domain specific ontology based search engine for crawling and download the domain specific web pages in WWW. With reference to these works, some topical crawlers has been proposed for spatial web service discovery. Li *et al.* [9] have proposed an effective crawler to discover and update the services using *web map service* by *OGC* utilizing concurrent multi-threading technique. Jiang *et al.* [10] proposed a prototype system of WFS crawler based on the OpenGIS WFS Specification which can discover and update the service content of the WFS servers dynamically. A location-based search engine has been proposed by Ahlers *et al.* [11] which is capable to

---

[1] www.opengeospatial.org

derive spatial context from the unstructured web resources automatically. Their proposed indexer also assigns geo-context to the web-pages for further use.

The paper is organized into four sections. Section 1 gives the overall description of the problem and the proposed solution, followed by the present state of the art regarding the spatial web crawlers and discovery of geo-servers. In section 2, the proposed work is demonstrated with different modules. Performance evaluation is being carried out in the section 3 followed by analysis. Finally, the conclusion is drawn in the section 4.

2   Proposed Framework: WFS Crawler

The proposed spatial web crawler has been developed to focus on geo-spatial features available in the geo-servers. The overall architecture is discussed in this section followed by the implementation specifications and evaluation.

2.1   Crawler Architecture

The crawler developed for discovering data sources based on *WFS* includes *seed set, URLQueue, extraction module, WFS module, XML analyzer, ontology* and *WFS feature_type repository* to archive relevant WFS geo-servers and related *feature_types*. The proposed architecture of the crawler is illustrated in Fig. 1 with its components.

The initial seed set is the entry section for the crawler. First, all these URLs will be added to the *URLQueue* including the URLs extracted by the crawler. *URLQueue* acts as a buffer to store all the hyperlinks. Once the URL is evaluated to be WFS server, it is not neccessary that it will be linked to the other WFS server. Hence, the next URL from the *URLQueue* will be considered. This process is continuous. The proposed spatial crawler is divided into three main modules i.e. *extraction module, WFS module* followed by *analysis and indexing module*. These modules are discussed below.

Extraction Module: This module starts with the URL extracted from the *URLQueue* and reading its page source. Its job is to extract all the hyperlinks present in the page, convert them to absolute URLs, filter the duplicate URLs and then push them to the *URLQueue*. Duplicate URLs are filtered from the *URLQueue*. After completion of cycle of the URL through all the modules, the next URL will be extracted. This process will be continuous.

WFS Module: This module is responsible to check whether server is a WFS server. Extracted URL from *URLQueue* is checked to search for the keywords such as *GetCapability, request, WFS* etc. If the URL contains all these keywords, it is directly sent to *WFS module* otherwise the *GetCapabalities* request is generated for the extracted URL by appending URL with string
`"services?REQUEST=GetCapabilities&version=1.1.0&service=WFS"`

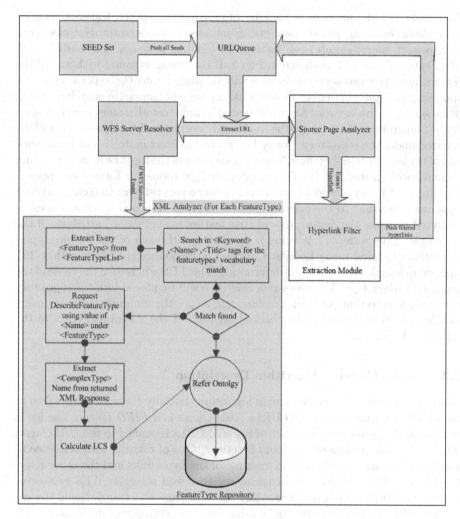

Fig. 1. Proposed Framework for Spatial Web Crawler

and the transformed URL will be sent to *WFS module*. The response of the *Get-Capabalities* request is searched to find tags <WFS_Capabilities>. If the tags are present in the XML response, then the URL represents the WFS server. The XML response is sent to the *analysis and indexing module*.

Analysis and Indexing Module: This module analyses the XML response sent by the *WFS module*. There are various tags present in the XML. The <FeatureTypeList> is extracted from the XML and for each of the <FeatureType> tag (under <FeatureTypeList> tag), the <keyword> tag (if present), the <title> and <name> tags are checked to see if any of them contains the words from any of the feature_type's vocabulary which is created for *ontology*. This *ontology* is built by organizing the spatial features, namely, *water-body, building, forest, road* etc. Some standard semantic relations (*such as hyponym, meronym* etc) can be used for building *ontology*. The basic format of <FeatureTypeList> is shown in Fig. 2. If the match is found with any of the *feature_type*, the geo-server reference will be placed into the repository corresponding to that particular *feature_type* as per the semantic matching using *ontology* e.g. if the keyword has word "canal", since "canal" comes under "water-body"(superclass of canal in the *ontology*), corresponding geo-server will be referred under the repository "water-body". If the direct match is not found with any of the keywords, using the <Name> node value of the tag <FeatureType> and "namespace" (if mentioned), *DescribeFeatureType* request is formed by appending string `"?service=WFS&version=1.1.0&request=DescribeFeatureType& typename="+name"` to the original URL. The XML returned by that request is analyzed to know the *feature_type* of that feature using "name" attribute of the <ComplexType> tag. That value is compared with each of the feature_type's vocabulary list and using Longest Common Subsequence (LCS) algorithm [12], maximum length subsequence is determined. This LCS will return the value of the matched *feature_type*. The geo-server reference will be placed into the repository corresponding to that particular *feature_type* as per the semantic matching using *ontology*. This is needed to be checked for each of the <FeatureType> of the <FeatureTypeList>.

2.2   Spatial Crawler Algorithm Description

Algorithm 1 gives the crawler's main algorithm. Initially the *seed set* is taken to be a file having number of seed URLs. *URLQueue* is a *FIFO Queue*. The file is read at start of procedure and each of the seed URLs is pushed to the *URLQueue*. This algorithm consists of two main functions. One of them is with reference to the *extraction module* which is extracting all the hyperlinks and the other refers to the next *WFS Module* to recognize whether web server is WFS geo-server or not. Function *CrawlURL* is crawling the web page and transforming the extracted URLs to the absolute URLs using function *TransformIntoAbsoluteURL*, followed by filtering of duplicate URLs which are already present in the repository, *URLQueue*. Before passing URL to *CheckWFSServer* function, the URL is checked whether it is in *GetCapabilities* Request form or not. If so, we are passing it with the TRUE indicator, otherwise FALSE indicator. In *CheckWFSServer* function, if the indicator is FALSE, the corresponding XML is retrieved by making *GetCapabilities* Request. The XML response is checked to verify whether the server is WFS geo-server by checking the presence of <WFS_Capability> tags. If the server is found to be a WFS geo-server, the XML response is sent to the next module for analysis. *Ontology* is used in the *analysis and indexing module*. It is implemented using *HashMap* which is mapping featuretypes to their parent featuretype. *HashSet* is used to store the vocabulary of all the featuretypes which are taken for this study. *HashSet* and *HashMap* are used to make the searching

```
<WFS_Capabilities>
...
   <FeatureTypeList>
   <Operations>
     <!--operations supported by all FeatureTypes-->
   </Operations>
   <FeatureType>
   <!--information about this FeatureType-->
              <Name>FeatureType Name</Name>
              <Title>FeatureType Title</Title>
              <Abstract>Short Description</Abstract>
              <Keywords>Keywords</Keywords>
              ...
              <Operations>
              <--operations supported for this FeatureType-->
              </Operations>
          </FeatureType>
          ...
          ...
          ...
          </FeatureTypeList>
...
</WFS_Capabilities>
```

Fig. 2. GetCapability Response

process faster. *Analyze* function uses the XML response to retrieve the list of *feature_types* provided by that geo-server. For each of the *feature_type*, the *ontology* is addressed to know the parent *feature_type*. The first phase is the direct matching of the values under tags <keyword>, <name> and <title> with each element in *HashSet FeatureTypeVocab* until it finds the match. If it does not find match, it will go to the next phase which makes *DescribeFeatureType* request to extract the *feature_type*. Longest Common Subsequence (LCS) algorithm is used further to find the LCS with each word from *HashSet FeatureTypeVocab* and the extracted *feature_type* name of the <FeatureType> being considered. One word from *FeatureTypeVocab* is selected which has length above LCS length threshold and has maximum length of LCS among all. This is being implemented by using function *ApplyLCS*. That match will be searched in *HashMap* to find the parent *feature_type*. After finding the parent *feature_type* in either of the phase, the geo-server URL is saved into the corresponding parent *feature_type* repository.

3 Performance Evaluation

The performance of the proposed framework is evaluated on the basis of three metrics namely precision, recall and F1-measure [13]. The efficiency of the crawler is measured by analyzing the relevant number of geo-servers found for particular *feature_type* and total number of expected or existing web servers supporting that corresponding *feature_type*.

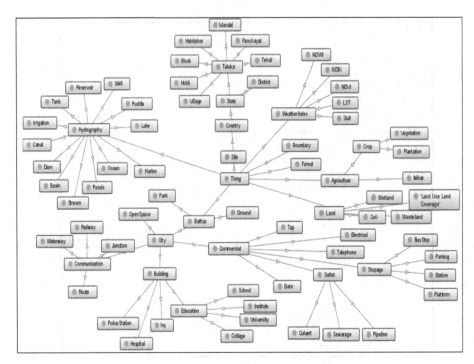

Fig. 3. FeatureType Ontology

For each *feature_type*, these three metrics are calculated, followed by average precision, average recall and average F1-measure for all the feature types. These are calculated based on the semantic annotations of geoservers using different LCS threshold, for the function ApplyLCS in Algorithm 1. *Ontology* displayed in Fig. 3 is used for our study.

The following seed URLs are taken for this case study. Some of the GIS websites are being used as seed to optimize the processing of web pages. Some of the results returned by the general search engines such as Google, for the keywords like "getcapabilities", "wfs", "request", "geoserver" are taken to be the other seeds.

- https://www.google.co.in/search?q=wfs+getcapabilities+
  request+geoserver
- http://www.bing.com/search?q=wfs+getcapabilities+
  request+geoserver
- http://www.gise.cse.iitb.ac.in
- http://bhuvan5.nrsc.gov.in
- http://203.110.240.68:8888/iitkgp-wms

Some of the geoservers discovered by the above seed URLs are referred for the performance evaluation. *GetCapabilities* request for these geoservers are listed below. First four geoservers are considered mainly for the experiments which are having mass data.

Algorithm 1. Spatial Crawler Algorithm

Input: SeedSet-Seed URLs, MaxURLs-Stopping Criterion
Result: List of WFS Servers and Indexed Documents
i = 0;
foreach *Seed in SeedSet* **do**
   | PushQueue(URLQueue,Seed);
   | i++;
end
while $i \neq MaxURLs$ **do**
   | WFSflag = false;
   | URL = PopQueue(URLQueue);
   | CrawlURL(URL);
   | **if** *URL contains "WFS" AND URL contains "request" AND URL contains "GetCapabilities"* **then**
      | WFSflag = true;
   | **end**
   | CheckWFSServer(URL,WFSflag);
   | i++;
end

CrawlURL(URL)
Input: URL
Result: Hyperlinks extracted after crawling Webpage
WebPage = ReadPageSource(URL);
URLList = ExtractHyperLinks(WebPage);
foreach *U in URLList* **do**
   | Trans_URL = TransformIntoAbsoluteURL(U);
   | **if** *Trans_URL NOT IN URLQueue* **then**
      | PushQueue(URLQueue,U);
   | **end**
end

CheckWFSServer(URL, WFSFlag)
Input: URL, WFSFlag
Result: Server is WFS geo-server or not AND XMLResponse of GetCapability
               Request
if $WFSFlag \equiv TRUE$ **then**
   | XMLResponse = ReadXML(URL);
else
   | XMLResponse = SendGetCapabilityRequest(URL);
end
if *XMLResponse CONTAINS WFS_Capabilities tag* **then**
   | Analyze(XMLResponse,URL);
end

Analyze(XMLResponse, URL, FeatureTypeVocab, FeatureOntology)
Input: XMLResponse, URL, FeatureTypeVocab, FeatureOntology
Result: Indexed Documents by FeatureTypes
initialization;
foreach *<FeatureType> in <FeatureTypeList>* **do**
   | Match = NULL; MatchFlag = FALSE;
   | **foreach** *F in FeatureTypeVocab* **do**
      | **if** *F MATCHES WITH Value of <Keyword> OR <Title> OR <Name>*
      then
         | Match = ExtractParentClass(F, FeatureOntology);
         | MatchFlag = TRUE;
         | Break;
      | **end**
   | **end**
   | **if** $MatchFlag \equiv FALSE$ **then**
      | NameVal = GetNameTagValue(FeatureType);
      | XML = GetDescribeFeatureTypeRequest(URL, NameVal);
      | TypeNameVal = ExtractTypeName(XML);
      | Match = ApplyLCS(TypeNameVal);
   | **end**
   | **if** $Match \neq NULL$ **then**
      | PutIntoRepository(URL, Match);
   | **end**
end

```
ApplyLCS(FeatureTypeName, FeatureTypeVocab, FeatureOntology)
Input: FeatureTypeName, FeatureTypeVocab, FeatureOntology
Result: Maximum Matching Subsequence from Vocabulary with the
         FeatureTypeName
Match = NULL; MaxLength = 0;
foreach F in FeatureTypeVocab do
    LCS = FindLCS(F, FeatureTypeName);
    if Length(LCS) > MaxLength AND Length(LCS) > LCS_Threshold then
        Match = F;
        MaxLength = Length(LCS);
    end
end
if Match ≠ NULL then
    ParentMatch = ExtractParentClass(Match, FeatureOntology);
    PutIntoRepository(URL, ParentMatch);
end
```

- `http://giswebservices.massgis.state.ma.us/geoserver/wms/services?REQUEST=GetCapabilities&version=1.1.0&service=WFS`
- `http://www.gise.cse.iitb.ac.in/geoserver/wfs/services?REQUEST=GetCapabilities&version=1.1.0&service=WFS`
- `http://bhuvan5.nrsc.gov.in/bhuvan/ows?service=wfs&version=1.1.0&request=GetCapabilities`
- `http://203.110.240.68:8888/iitkgp-wms/services?REQUEST=GetCapabilities&version=1.1.0&service=WFS`
- `http://www2.dmsolutions.ca/cgi-bin/mswfs_gmap?SERVICE=WFS&VERSION=1.0.0&REQUEST=getcapabilities`
- `http://mapserver.ngdc.noaa.gov/cgi-bin/Sample_Index?request=getcapabilities&service=wfs&version=1.1.0`
- `http://www.bsc-eoc.org/cgi-bin/bsc_ows.asp?version=1.1.1&service=WFS&request=GetCapabilities`

The *feature_types* present with these geo-servers are analyzed using the layer-preview facility present with those WFS services. The relevant *feature_types* that are actually supported by these geo-servers are collected manually for evaluation. Performance is measured based on various LCS threshold. If LCS is found to be above threshold length, it will be considered for further processing. Then the resultant *feature_type* is checked in the *ontology* shown in Fig. 3 and the corresponding geo-server is placed in that corresponding *feature_type's* superclass's repository. The precision model considered for each of the *feature_type* is as follows,

$$precision = \frac{(Number\_of\_relevant\_geoservers\_found)}{(Total\_Number\_of\_geoservers\_found)} * 100\% \qquad (1)$$

Average precision is calculated by taking average of precision of all the *feature_types*. It is observed that the precision has increased with increase in LCS length threshold. As the length of LCS is increasing, it tends to be a direct comparison between the two strings. Hence the occurrence of irrelevant results will get decreased. The recall is being calculated as follows,

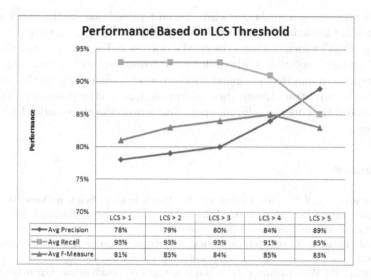

Fig. 4. Performance Evaluation of the Proposed Crawler based on LCS Threshold

$$recall = \frac{Number\_of\_relevant\_geoservers\_found\_in\_search}{Total\_Number\_of\_existing\_relevant\_geoservers} * 100\% \quad (2)$$

Average recall is calculated by taking average of all the *feature_types'* recall. It is observed that the recall is the maximum for the LCS threshold greater than 3. It is increasing from LCS length threshold greater than 1 up-to 3 and then it will start decrementing. With increment of LCS length, chances of finding word matches with vocabulary *FeatureTypeVocab* will get reduced resulting decrement in recall. Based on precision and recall, F1-measure i.e., balanced F-score of precision and recall, is calculated as follows,

$$F1 = 2 * \frac{(precision * recall)}{(precision + recall)} \quad (3)$$

Similarly, average F1-measure is calculated by taking average of F1-measure of all the *feature_types.* As shown in Fig. 4, it is observed that F1-measure is also increasing till LCS length threshold greater than 4 and then it starts decreasing. Since the result is following a trend of decremented recall beyond LCS length threshold greater than 4, the experiment is not carried out further. Again, for most of the featuretype words present in the vocabulary, average length is not more than length 5. Hence, it will increase precision beyond this threshold, but recall will definitely decrease.

4   Conclusion

Geospatial data are often voluminous, dynamic and heterogeneous in nature. The discovery of spatial data repositories over the Internet and information retrieval from these heterogeneous datasets are crucial for resolving spatial queries. This paper presents a spatial web crawler based on WFS (Web Feature Service) specification by OGC, which analyzes the spatial queries and searches for suitable geoservers for query resolution. It also indexes the geo-servers with respect to relevant feature types to annotate the semantic reference with them. This work can be extended further to extract the location information, geometric properties of spatial features and retrieving the relevant spatial data from the repositories for further processing.

References

1. Aeronautics, U.S.N., Administration, S.: Earth System Science Data Resources: Tapping Into a Wealth of Data, Information, and Services. National Aeronautics and Space Administration (2005)
2. Star, J., Estes, J.: Geographic information systems. Prentice-Hall, Englewood Cliffs (1990)
3. Vretanos, P.: Web feature service implementation specification. Open Geospatial Consortium Specification, 04–094 (2005)
4. Gruber, T.R.: Toward principles for the design of ontologies used for knowledge sharing. International Journal of Human-computer Studies 43(5), 907–928 (1995)
5. Bhattacharjee, S., Prasad, R.R., Dwivedi, A., Dasgupta, A., Ghosh, S.K.: Ontology based framework for semantic resolution of geospatial query. In: 2012 12th International Conference on Intelligent Systems Design and Applications (ISDA), pp. 437–442. IEEE (2012)
6. Stamatakis, K., Karkaletsis, V., Paliouras, G., Horlock, J., Grover, C., Curran, J.R., Dingare, S.: Domain-specific web site identification: the crossmarc focused web crawler. In: Proceedings of the 2nd International Workshop on Web Document Analysis (WDA 2003), Edinburgh, UK (2003)
7. Lopez-Pellicer, F.J., Florczyk, A.J., Béjar, R., Muro-Medrano, P.R., Zarazaga-Soria, F.J.: Discovering geographic web services in search engines. Online Information Review 35(6), 909–927 (2011)
8. Mukhopadhyay, D., Biswas, A., Sinha, S.: A new approach to design domain specific ontology based web crawler. In: 10th International Conference on Information Technology (ICIT 2007), pp. 289–291. IEEE (2007)
9. Li, W., Yang, C., Yang, C.: An active crawler for discovering geospatial web services and their distribution pattern–a case study of ogc web map service. International Journal of Geographical Information Science 24(8), 1127–1147 (2010)
10. Jiang, J., Yang, C.J., Ren, Y.C.: A spatial information crawler for opengis wfs. In: Sixth International Conference on Advanced Optical Materials and Devices, International Society for Optics and Photonics, pp. 71432C–71432C (2008)
11. Ahlers, D., Boll, S.: Location-based web search. The Geospatial Web: How Geo-browsers. Social Software and the Web 2.0 are Shaping the Network Society, 55–66 (2007)
12. Kondrak, G.: N-gram similarity and distance. In: Consens, M.P., Navarro, G. (eds.) SPIRE 2005. LNCS, vol. 3772, pp. 115–126. Springer, Heidelberg (2005)
13. Makhoul, J., Kubala, F., Schwartz, R., Weischedel, R., et al.: Performance measures for information extraction. In: Proceedings of DARPA Broadcast News Workshop, pp. 249–252 (1999)

Software Transactional Memory Friendly
Slot Schedulers

Pooja Aggarwal and Smruti R. Sarangi

Computer Science Department, IIT Delhi, New Delhi, India
{pooja.aggarwal,srsarangi}@cse.iitd.ac.in

Abstract. In this paper, we discuss the design space of highly concurrent linearizable data structures for slot scheduling. We observe that it is not possible to have high *fairness* across threads, and maximize *throughput* of the entire system simultaneously. Lock free algorithms are very fast, yet very *unfair*, and wait free algorithms follow the reverse trend. We thus propose a class of algorithms using software transactional memory (STM) that are in the middle of the spectrum. They equitably balance fairness and throughput, and are much simpler to design and verify.

Keywords: software transactional memory (STM), transactions, wait-free, lock-free, schedulers, slot scheduling.

1   Introduction

Multicore and manycore processors are increasingly replacing ASICs in large scale enterprise class systems. For example, multicore processors are beginning to be extensively used in high throughput networking systems [6], and high volume storage systems [7]. An integral component in all of these systems is the *scheduler*, whose role is to accept requests from multiple producers, and dispatch them to multiple consumers with respect to a given optimality criteria.

In this paper, we consider an important subset of schedulers namely *slot schedulers* [1] that discretize time into fixed-length timeslices called *slots*. We first discuss the design space of slot scheduling algorithms, and classify them on the basis of three attributes – *throughput*, *fairness*, and *complexity*. The number of requests scheduled per second is the throughput, and the ratio of the average number of requests scheduled per thread and the maximum number of requests scheduled per thread is referred to as *fairness*.

The main contribution of this paper is to propose parallel slot scheduling algorithms using software transactional memory(STM). In STM systems a block of code is treated as an atomic unit akin to a database transaction (obeys ACID properties). We use the DEUCE STM framework developed by Korland et. al. [3] for Java. DEUCE implements atomic blocks at the granularity of methods (annotated by the *@Atomic* keyword). Our algorithms are simpler than the corresponding lock-free and wait-free versions [4], provide strong consistency guarantees (linearizability), and equally balance fairness and throughput.

R. Natarajan (Ed.): ICDCIT 2014, LNCS 8337, pp. 79–85, 2014.
© Springer International Publishing Switzerland 2014

2   Basics of Slot Scheduling

Figure 4 shows an Ousterhout matrix [2] that is typically used for slot scheduling. Here, the columns represents time (in slots) and the rows represents resources (core, disk, network link), where we assume that resources are homogeneous. In this matrix (SCHEDULEMAP array), we maintain the status of all the slots. Each cell(slot) can either be *vacant* or *reserved*. We wish to schedule a request that occupies *numSlots* consecutive slots (one in each column) starting from a given slot number (*startSlot*). The *slotSchedule* operation returns the list of slots allotted to the thread. The state of a cell in the SCHEDULEMAP array can take three values: VACANT , MARKED or RESERVED . VACANT means that currently no request is scheduled for this slot. MARKED means that the cell is temporarily reserved, and RESERVED means that the slot is permanently reserved. The state of the slot changes as shown in Figure 2. An instance of the REQUEST class gets populated (see Figure 1) when a new request is placed. The *state* field maintains the state of the request and other fields as shown in Figure 2. The RECORD array stores the slots reserved by the thread.

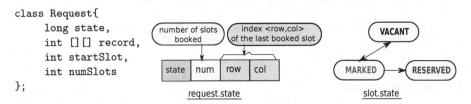

```
class Request{
    long state,
    int [][] record,
    int startSlot,
    int numSlots
};
```

Fig. 1. The REQUEST class

Fig. 2. Request.state and slot.state

3   Parallel Slot Scheduling Using STMs

3.1   The *SimpleScan* Algorithm

Assume that thread t_i places a request to book *numSlots* slots starting from time slot s. t_i first scans the SCHEDULEMAP array to find *numSlots* consecutive VACANT slots starting from slot s (Line 3). Next, t_i books these slots by changing the state of the slots from VACANT to RESERVED (Line 10). All the instructions in this method are enveloped in one transaction and are executed atomically (Line 1). The STM system monitors the transactions of the threads and if two or more threads concurrently access the SCHEDULEMAP array at the same index, it handles the conflict by allowing one thread to commit its transaction and abort/restart the other transaction(s) involved in the conflict.

3.2   The *SoftVisible* Algorithm

The main issue with the *SimpleScan* algorithm is that it creates one large transaction for processing the entire request. The probability of conflicts is high

with larger transactions, and thus we wish to design an algorithm that breaks
the schedule operation into several mini-transactions as shown in Figure 3. Each
transaction corresponds to the state of the request. It makes the changes done at
a cell level in the SCHEDULEMAP array immediately visible to concurrent threads
when the transaction commits.

Algorithm 1. *SlotSchedule- SimpleScan*

```
1: @Atomic
2: function slotSchedule (tid, s, numSlots)
3:    for i ∈ [s, SCHEDULEMAP .length] ∧ (slotCount < numSlots) do
4:       if ∃ j, SCHEDULEMAP [i][j] = VACANT then
5:          record[index++] ← j , slotCount++
6:       else
7:          reset slotCount and record, start searching again
8:       end if
9:    end for
10:   /* reserve the slot indicated by RECORD array by setting the threadId */
11: end function
end
```

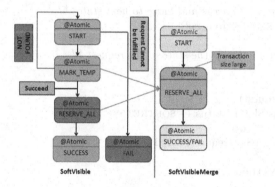

Fig. 3. Flowchart of the algorithms

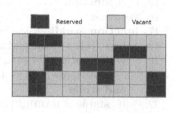

Fig. 4. The Ousterhout matrix for scheduling

Algorithm 2 shows the *SoftVisible* algorithm. A thread starts with the
findFirstSlot method, to find an earliest possible VACANT slot. The *markSlot*
method is then invoked (Line 5) that marks a VACANT slot, and changes its state
to MARKED. Concomitantly, the request moves to the (MARK_TEMP , *slotCount*)
state. Here, *slotCount* is equal to the number of slots that have already been
marked. After successfully finding the first slot, the *markRestSlots* method is
called to mark the rest of the required slots in adjacent columns. Once *numSlots*
slots are marked, the thread enters the RESERVE_ALL state and the state of the
slots changes from MARKED to RESERVED .

markSlot(): This method is invoked to change the state of a slot from VACANT
to MARKED in a given column of the SCHEDULEMAP array. This method accepts
two parameters- the request and the column id. It returns the booked slot (if
possible), and the *status*, which can be – SOFTRETRY , HARDRETRY , TRUE or

FALSE . SOFTRETRY means that all the slots in the column are in the MARKED state. In this case, we wait for the slots to turn into either VACANT or RESERVED (Line 4 and Line 19). HARDRETRY means that all the slots in a column are already in the RESERVED state. TRUE indicates that a slot is successfully marked, and FALSE indicates that the request cannot be scheduled because we reach the end of the SCHEDULEMAP array (thus transition to the FAIL state (Line 9)).

Algorithm 2. *SlotSchedule-SoftVisible*

```
 1: @Atomic
 2: function findFirstSlot(request)
 3:     startSlot ← request.getStartSlot() , status ← SOFTRETRY
 4:     while status ∈ (SOFTRETRY , HARDRETRY ) do
 5:         (status, row, col) ← markSlot(request,startSlot.col) /* index of the slot */

 6:         (status = HARDRETRY ) ? startSlot++ : startSlot)
 7:     end while
 8:     if status = FALSE then
 9:         newState ← FAIL /* unable to fulfill the request */
10:     else if status = TRUE then
11:         /* save the slot in the record array and move to next state */
12:         newState ← (MARK_TEMP , 1, row, col)
13:     end if
14:     request.state ← newState /* change the state of the request */
15: end function
16: @Atomic
17: function markRestSlots(request)
18:     (row, col) ← state.getLastSlot(), status ← SOFTRETRY
19:     while status = SOFTRETRY do
20:         (status, row, col) ← markSlot(request, col+1)
21:     end while
22:     if  status = HARDRETRY then
23:         newCol ← col +1
24:         newState ← (CANCEL , 0, 0, newCol) /* could not find VACANT slot */
25:     else if status = TRUE then
26:         /* save the slot allotted in the record array */
27:         if numSlots = slotNum then
28:             newState ← RESERVE_ALL /* all the slots are marked */
29:         else
30:             newState ← (MARK_TEMP , slotNum+1, row, col+1) /* some slots are
                left to be marked */
31:         end if
32:     end if
33:     request.state ← newState /* set the new request state */
34: end function
```

end

If the *markSlot* returns HARDRETRY , then it is clear that no slot in the specified column can be booked. If we are still looking to book our first slot, then we can start from the next column. However, if we have already booked some slots, then we need to cancel the request by moving to the CANCEL state (Line 24). We need to convert the state of all the MARKED slots to VACANT and clear the RECORD array.

SoftVisibleMerge Algorithm- Another way of implementing the *SoftVisible* algorithm is to merge the RESERVE_ALL and MARK_TEMP stages into one RESERVE_ALL stage. Thus, instead of having four to five transactions/stages per *slotSchedule* operation there can be three stages, as shown in Figure 3. This strategy performs slightly better (see Section 4) on our test system.

Proof: We can prove that irrespective of the STM model, all three of our algorithms obey sequential semantics, and are linearizable. The main idea of the proof is that we start searching for a new set of slots only when we encounter a column that has all of its entries in the RESERVED state. This ensures that we do not take decisions based on the temporary state of unfinished requests. Secondly, once a request has finished, its state in the SCHEDULEMAP array cannot be overwritten. We can use these two observations to prove linearizability.

Due to lack of space, we request the interested reader to kindly look at a companion technical report [5].

4   Evaluation

The performance of the proposed scheme was evaluated on a hyper-threaded four socket, 64 bit, Dell PowerEdge R820 server. We used the DEUCE STM framework. The performance of our slot scheduling algorithms is evaluated using a synthetic benchmark(similar to [4]). We use the Box-Muller transform (mean = 10, variance = $5*threadid$) to generate normal variates, and run the experiment till the fastest thread completes κ requests.

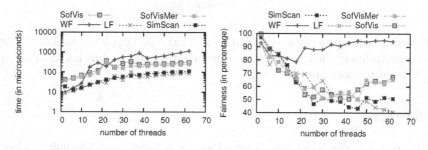

Fig. 5. Time   **Fig. 6.** *fairness*

We define two quantities – mean time per request (*time*) and fairness (*frn*). $frn = total\_requests\_completed/(\kappa \times NUMTHREADS)$. We set $\kappa = 10,000$, and vary the number of threads from 1 to 64. We repeat each experiment ten times and report the mean values. We compare all our algorithms with wait-free(WF) and lock-free(LF) algorithms as presented in [4].

Figures 5 and 6 show the results for *numslots* = 3. We observe that the *WF* implementation is 5-10 times slower than others. In terms of time taken per request, *SimScan* is as fast as *LF*. *SofVis* and *SofVisMer* lie in the middle of the spectrum with *SofVisMer* being faster by 20%. The reason for the overall trend is that *WF* and STM based algorithms have a fair amount of overhead. For similar reasons *SofVisMer* is faster than *SofVis* because it has lesser transactions. All our algorithms are roughly 1-2 orders of magnitude faster than algorithms with locks. Note that *SimScan* is also faster because an STM performs optimistic locking, whereas traditional locks are pessimistic.

The fairness results shown in Figures 6 and 8 show a reverse trend. *WF* is the most fair algorithm (*frn* > 90%). *LF* and *SimScan* are the most unfair algorithms because they follow a "winner take all" strategy. Their fairness values decrease from 92% for 2 threads to 50% for a system of 50 threads. Beyond 50 threads, *SimScan* is better than *LF* by 5-20%. In comparison, *SofVis* and *SofVisMer* start outperforming *SimScan* and *LF* in terms of fairness, and their *frn* values jump to 60-65% beyond 50 threads. As the granularity of transactions gets finer, the fairness across threads increases as they have a lesser number of aborts per commit (Figure 7).

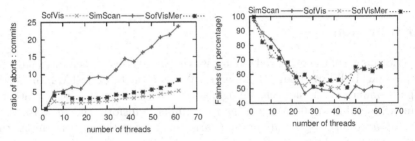

Fig. 7. Ratio of aborts to commits

Fig. 8. Fairness (STM based algorithms only)

We also tried adding the *helping* feature in STM based implementations. There was no performance benefit as the read-write set for the various helpers overlap and this led to more aborts.

References

[1] Brandon Hall: Slot Scheduling: General Purpose Multiprocessor Scheduling for Heterogeneous Workloads, Ph.D Thesis, University of Texas, Austin (2005)
[2] Ousterhout, J.K.: Scheduling Techniques for Concurrent Systems. In: International Conference on Distributed Computing Systems (1982)
[3] Korland, G., Shavit, N., Felber, P.: Non invasive concurrency with Java STM. In: MultiProg. 2010 (2010)

[4] Aggarwal, P., Sarangi, S.R.: Lock-free and Wait-free Slot Scheduling Algorithms. In: IPDPS 2013 (2013)

[5] Extended Discussion on STM Friendly Slot Scheduling Algorithms, posted at http://www.cse.iitd.ac.in/~srsarangi/files/papers/stmlong.pdf

[6] Liang, J.-M., Chen, J.-J., Wu, H.-C., Tseng, Y.-C.: Simple and Regular Mini-Slot Scheduling for IEEE 802.16d Grid-based Mesh Networks. In: Vehicular Technology Conference (2010)

[7] Zhu, Q., Chen, Z., Tan, L., Zhou, Y., Keeton, K., Wilkes, J.: Hibernator: Helping disk arrays sleep through the winter. In: SOSP 2005 (2005)

An Improved Approach of Decoupling in Mobile Cloud Computing

Sohini De[1], Alok Misra[2], and Suddhasil De[3]

[1] Siliguri Institute of Technology, West Bengal, India
sohini.de@acm.org
[2] S.R. Group of Professional Colleges Lucknow, UP, India
alokm@iitg.ernet.in
[3] Indian Institute of Technology Guwahati, Assam, India
suddhasil.de@acm.org

Abstract. Mobile Cloud Computing (MCC) augments resource capability of mobile/portable devices for efficient execution of their applications, which results in undesirable coupling of mobile applications and mobile cloud services. The existing approaches of decoupling between them can manage either logical mobility or physical mobility of different constituents of MCC, but not together at the same time. This paper proposes the notion of *hierarchical decoupling* in MCC, that manages both logical and physical mobility simultaneously. The proposed hierarchical decoupling follows a tiered approach, in which interactions of mobile applications with mobile cloud services are decoupled at two tiers using the tuple space model. At the top tier, decoupling manages logical mobility of mobile applications and mobile cloud services, whereas, decoupling at the bottom tier handles physical mobility of devices in dynamic and unreliable networks. This results in better decoupling between mobile applications and mobile cloud services, which, in turn, improves adaptability and robustness of MCC. A new mobile cloud architecture that realizes the proposed approach has also been presented in this paper.

Keywords: Cloud computing, mobile cloud computing, mobile application, mobile cloud service, decoupling, hierarchical decoupling, tuple space.

1 Introduction

The popularity of *cloud computing* paradigm [1] has stimulated the research of *Mobile Cloud Computing* (MCC) paradigm [2, 3]. The possibility of overcoming inherent limitations of mobile/portable devices, that have so far obstructed the daily activities of end-users, has come to light. MCC allows the end-users to lease different computing resources, operating platforms and/or application software as *mobile cloud services* on pay-per-use basis for augmenting the resource capability of their devices. This facilitates efficient execution of a wide variety of *mobile applications*, including mobile commerce, mobile learning, mobile healthcare, mobile gaming, (mobile) social networking etc. However, some recent reports [4, 5] hint that the soaring MCC market disregard personal usage of mobile cloud by individual subscribers (particularly, mobile end-users), due to

R. Natarajan (Ed.): ICDCIT 2014, LNCS 8337, pp. 86–91, 2014.
© Springer International Publishing Switzerland 2014

the challenges in *synergy* of mobile applications and mobile cloud services. Such challenges arise mainly because of the inherent limitations of wireless/mobile communications and shortcomings of mobile/portable devices. *Decoupling* (i.e. very loose coupling or practically no coupling) in interactions between mobile applications and mobile cloud services is necessary at this juncture, as it can mitigate obstructions in intercommunication between mobile computing and cloud computing, and improve adaptability as well as robustness of MCC.

Until recently, tight coupling exists in interactions between mobile applications and mobile cloud services. A recent proposal has suggested an approach of decoupling [6, 7], in which decoupling media are introduced at the junction of mobile computing and cloud computing, i.e. they are distributed in mobile/portable devices as well as base stations of wireless infrastructure networks. This approach separates the dynamic segment of MCC from its static counterpart, thereby counters the effects of physical mobility in MCC. However, handling of logical mobility of MCC has not been considered in this approach. Logical mobility can be initiated either through the possible migration of mobile application from one mobile/portable device to another [8], or through the possible migration of entities within a data center, like Virtual Machine Migration [9]. An additional notion of decoupling is required to counter the effects of logical mobility of different constituents of MCC. However, in the existing architectures of MCC [2, 3, 8, 10–16], multi-tier decoupling to handle both logical mobility and physical mobility at the same time is not present.

This paper proposes a notion of decoupling, termed as *hierarchical decoupling*, to counter the effects of both logical mobility of mobile applications and mobile cloud services (due to the virtual machine migration) as well as physical mobility of mobile/portable devices simultaneously. In hierarchical decoupling, bottom tier decouples the *mobile hosts* (i.e. runtime environments within the mobile/portable devices) from base stations to handle the effects of physical mobility, whereas mobile applications are decoupled from mobile cloud services at the top tier to handle the effects of logical mobility. The tuple space model [17] has been used as decoupling media in the proposed approach. At the bottom tier, mobile hosts as well as base stations hold individual tuple spaces for this purpose, while individual tuple spaces are also distributed to mobile applications and mobile cloud services at the top tier. The two tiers of decoupling act at different hierarchies in the interactions between mobile applications and mobile cloud services, advocating a better ability to counter the effects of both logical mobility and physical mobility. This improvement, in turn, improves adaptability and robustness of MCC. A new mobile cloud architecture incorporating hierarchical decoupling is also presented, which is also suitable in mobile, dynamic and unreliable environments. Rest of the paper is organized as follows. Section 2 discusses the proposed notion of hierarchical decoupling, and presents the new mobile cloud architecture that realizes hierarchical decoupling of mobile applications from mobile cloud services. Finally, Section 3 concludes the paper.

2　Proposed Notion of Hierarchical Decoupling in MCC

2.1　Hierarchical Decoupling

The hierarchical decoupling in MCC follows a tiered approach, where the decoupling media are arranged in two tiers between mobile applications and mobile cloud services. At the top tier, mobile applications are decoupled from mobile cloud services by placing the decoupling media at their respective interfaces, viz. mobile application interfaces and mobile cloud dispatchers respectively. The top tier of decoupling directly handles the effects of logical dynamics of mobile applications, so that their migrations have no effect while they are being serviced by mobile cloud services. It may be noted here that, mobile cloud dispatchers can also be separated from mobile cloud services (e.g. Information-Centric Data Center Network Architecture [18]); such approaches become orthogonal to the top-tier decoupling of proposed notion, and these two approaches can be combined together to support logical mobility of both mobile applications as well as mobile cloud services (via virtual machine migration). The combined effect can even improve the decoupling ability of mobile applications from mobile cloud services, thereby further improving the adaptability of MCC.

At the bottom tier, decoupling between mobile/portable devices and base stations of wireless infrastructure networks mitigates the unavailability factor of these devices due to mobility, dynamicity and unreliability in wireless networks. Thus, the bottom-tier of hierarchical decoupling directly counters physical dynamics of mobile applications in these devices. The bottom-tier decoupling also indirectly handles logical dynamics of mobile applications. Consequently, the integrated effect of these two tiers of hierarchical decoupling produces a better ability of separation of mobile applications from mobile cloud services.

2.2　Proposed Mobile Cloud Architecture

Figure 1 presents the proposed mobile cloud architecture, called *Hierarchically-Decoupled Mobile Cloud Architecture* (H-DMCA), that includes the ability of

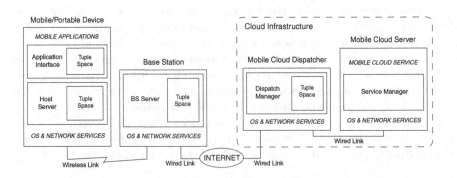

Fig. 1. Proposed Hierarchically-Decoupled Mobile Cloud Architecture (H-DMCA)

hierarchical decoupling between mobile applications and mobile cloud services using the tuple space model. In this architecture, mobile cloud services can be communicated and leased by mobile applications via mobile cloud dispatchers. The responsibility of a mobile cloud dispatcher is to forward the service requests to respective mobile cloud services, and direct the responses of such servicing back towards the requester mobile applications. As pointed out in [3], any architecture of MCC inherently incorporates dynamic environments at different levels, viz. wireless communication between mobile/portable devices and base stations, possibility of migration of mobile applications, and virtual machine migrations. In H-DMCA, these three segments of dynamics has been handled by hierarchical decoupling. As MCC is inherently decentralized in nature, multiple tuple spaces are distributed as decoupling media in these dynamic segments of H-DMCA. A tuple space is added to each of mobile application interface, mobile host, base station and mobile cloud dispatcher. The benefit of proposed H-DMCA is that not only physical mobility of mobile/portable devices can be handled, but also unreliability in communication between mobile/portable devices and base stations can be mitigated, as well as logical mobility of mobile applications and virtual machines (running mobile cloud services) can be managed. These benefits, in turn, reduces the effect of dynamics in MCC, when the mobile applications are being serviced by mobile cloud services. Irrespective of the nature of mobile applications, H-DMCA provides their adaptive servicing by mobile cloud services over unreliable wireless infrastructure networks.

The tuple spaces, included in H-DMCA, are tailored for efficient execution of decoupling functionalities. The structures of both tuples and antituples in these tuple spaces are unordered [19], which improves flexibility of mobile/portable devices in supporting multiple mobile applications and simplifies their design and development, as well as enables mobile cloud dispatchers to deal with virtual machine migrations comfortably. Moreover, these tuple spaces have indexed structures [19], which improves efficiency of mobile applications, mobile/portable devices, base stations and mobile cloud dispatchers. Also, the set of tuple space primitives for these tuple spaces are customized as per the requirement of decoupling. Instead of the conventional primitives in these tuple spaces, only a pair of primitives, viz. `inject` and `eject`, are defined for insertion and withdrawal operations. The `inject` primitive inserts one/more given tuple(s) into designated tuple space. Whereas, the `eject` primitive withdraws one/more available sought tuple(s) (i.e. tuples being looked up) from these designated tuple spaces.

The abilities of hierarchical decoupling in H-DMCA can be better clarified by an illustration. A mobile application (say, $\mathcal{A}$) is considered, which is requesting service (say, $\mathcal{S}$) from a mobile cloud service provider. In H-DMCA, $\mathcal{A}$ interacts with $\mathcal{S}$ via the tuple space at its interface $\mathcal{A}_I$ (denoted by $\mathbf{T}^{\mathcal{A}_I}$), tuple space at mobile host $\mathcal{H}$ of the device executing $\mathcal{A}$ (denoted by $\mathbf{T}^{\mathcal{H}}$), tuple space at base station $\mathcal{B}$ through which $\mathcal{H}$ accesses the mobile cloud (denoted by $\mathbf{T}^{\mathcal{B}}$), and tuple space at mobile cloud dispatcher $\mathcal{D}$ which interfaces with $\mathcal{S}$ (denoted by $\mathbf{T}^{\mathcal{D}}$). The interacting data containing service requests are transformed into tuples, and are stored in $\mathbf{T}^{\mathcal{A}_I}$, $\mathbf{T}^{\mathcal{H}}$, $\mathbf{T}^{\mathcal{B}}$ and $\mathbf{T}^{\mathcal{D}}$ successively on their way to be delivered from $\mathcal{A}$ to $\mathcal{S}$, and vice versa for return of service responses. The persistency of tuple space model supports such storage functionalities that are required for decoupling. For instance, the tuple $t_{\mathcal{A}}^1$, generated by $\mathcal{A}$ to intimate $\mathcal{S}$ about important service parameters, has to be delivered to $\mathcal{S}$. On its transit, $t_{\mathcal{A}}^1$ is stored first in $\mathsf{T}^{\mathcal{A}_l}$. At this moment, if $\mathcal{A}$ decides to migrate to another mobile host $\mathcal{H}'$ of a different mobile/portable device, $\mathcal{A}$ can easily do so without losing its interacting data. Apart from handling logical mobility of $\mathcal{A}$, interactions of $\mathcal{A}$ are also "time-decoupled", "name space-decoupled", "data space-decoupled" and "synchronization-decoupled", due to the presence of $\mathsf{T}^{\mathcal{A}_l}$. The tuple $t_{\mathcal{A}}^1$ is then stored in $\mathsf{T}^{\mathcal{H}}$ (considering that $\mathcal{A}$ is still executing at $\mathcal{H}$) prior to check the reachability of $\mathcal{B}$ from $\mathcal{H}$.

Once $\mathcal{B}$ is reachable from $\mathcal{H}$, $t_{\mathcal{A}}^1$ is withdrawn from $\mathsf{T}^{\mathcal{H}}$ to transfer to $\mathcal{B}$, from where it eventually reaches $\mathcal{D}$ and is stored in $\mathsf{T}^{\mathcal{D}}$. On availability of $\mathcal{S}$, $\mathcal{D}$ withdraws $t_{\mathcal{A}}^1$ from $\mathsf{T}^{\mathcal{D}}$ to deliver it to $\mathcal{S}$. The importance of $\mathsf{T}^{\mathcal{D}}$ lies in the fact that interacting data are preserved in it, if virtual machine running $\mathcal{S}$ migrates from one system to another in the middle of servicing. Thus, $\mathsf{T}^{\mathcal{D}}$ not only deals with logical mobility of $\mathcal{S}$, it also decouples interaction with $\mathcal{S}$ in several dimensions stated in the preceding paragraph. Similarly, response from $\mathcal{S}$ is converted to tuple $t_{\mathcal{A}}^2$, and is stored in $\mathsf{T}^{\mathcal{D}}$ on its way back to $\mathcal{A}$. When $t_{\mathcal{A}}^2$ reaches $\mathcal{B}$, it is stored in $\mathsf{T}^{\mathcal{B}}$ before reachability of $\mathcal{H}$ from $\mathcal{B}$ is found out. Eventually, $t_{\mathcal{A}}^2$ from $\mathsf{T}^{\mathcal{B}}$ reaches $\mathcal{H}$ and is stored in $\mathsf{T}^{\mathcal{H}}$. Finally, $t_{\mathcal{A}}^2$ reaches $\mathcal{A}$ via $\mathsf{T}^{\mathcal{A}_l}$. Thus, the effects of logical mobility and physical mobility, as well as dynamics and unreliability mitigates to a great extent in H-DMCA.

3   Conclusion

This paper has introduced the notion of hierarchical decoupling in MCC, which is not present in existing MCC architectures. The paper has also presented H-DMCA, a new mobile cloud architecture, where mobile applications are hierarchically decoupled from mobile cloud services by distributing multiple tuple spaces to constituents of H-DMCA. Moreover, the paper has illustrated the importance of H-DMCA as an adaptive MCC architecture.

References

1. Armbrust, M., Fox, A., Griffith, R., Joseph, A.D., Katz, R., Konwinski, A., Lee, G., Patterson, D., Rabkin, A., Stoica, I., Zaharia, M.: A View of Cloud Computing. Communications of the ACM 53(4), 50–58 (2010)
2. Dinh, H.T., Lee, C., Niyato, D., Wang, P.: A Survey of Mobile Cloud Computing: Architecture, Applications, and Approaches. Wireless Communications and Mobile Computing (2011), http://dx.doi.org/10.1002/wcm.1203
3. Fernando, N., Loke, S.W., Rahayu, W.: Mobile cloud computing: A survey. Future Generation Computer Systems 29(1), 84–106 (2013)
4. Hunter, R.: The why of cloud (December 2011), http://www.gartner.com/

5. Monaco, A.: A view inside the cloud (June 2012),
   http://theinstitute.ieee.org/technology-focus/technology-topic/
   a-view-inside-the-cloud
6. De, S., De, S.: Uncoupling in Services of Mobile Cloud Computing using Tuple Space model: Design and Formal Specifications. In: Proceedings of the 1st Workshop on Mobile Cloud Computing and Networking, MobileCloud 2013, pp. 27–31. ACM (July 2013)
7. Sabyasachi, A.S., De, S., De, S.: On the Notion of Decoupling in Mobile Cloud Computing. In: Proceedings of the 15th International Conference on High Performance Computing and Communication, HPCC 2013. IEEE Computer Society (November 2013)
8. Ma, R.K.K., Wang, C.L.: Lightweight Application-Level Task Migration for Mobile Cloud Computing. In: Proceedings of the 26th International Conference on Advanced Information Networking and Applications, AINA 2012, pp. 550–557. IEEE Computer Society (2012)
9. Shiraz, M., Abolfazli, S., Sanaei, Z., Gani, A.: A study on virtual machine deployment for application outsourcing in mobile cloud computing. The Journal of Supercomputing 63(3), 946–964 (2013)
10. Zhang, X., Kunjithapatham, A., Jeong, S., Gibbs, S.: Towards an Elastic Application Model for Augmenting the Computing Capabilities of Mobile Devices with Cloud Computing. Mobile Networks and Applications 16(3), 270–284 (2011)
11. Choi, M., Park, J., Jeong, Y.S.: Mobile cloud computing framework for a pervasive and ubiquitous environment. The Journal of Supercomputing 64(2), 331–356 (2013)
12. Shiraz, M., Gani, A., Khokhar, R.H., Buyya, R.: A Review on Distributed Application Processing Frameworks in Smart Mobile Devices for Mobile Cloud Computing. Communications Surveys & Tutorials 15(3), 1294–1313 (2013)
13. Kakadia, D., Saripalli, P., Varma, V.: MECCA: mobile, efficient cloud computing workload adoption framework using scheduler customization and workload migration decisions. In: Proceedings of the 1st Workshop on Mobile Cloud Computing and Networking, MobileCloud 2013, pp. 41–46. ACM (July 2013)
14. Ravi, A., Peddoju, S.K.: Energy Efficient Seamless Service Provisioning in Mobile Cloud Computing. In: Proceedings of the 7th International Symposium on Service Oriented System Engineering. SOSE 2013, pp. 463–471. IEEE (2013)
15. Lee, D., Lee, H., Park, D., Jeong, Y.S.: Proxy based seamless connection management method in mobile cloud computing. Cluster Computing (in press)
16. Sanaei, Z., Abolfazli, S., Gani, A., Buyya, R.: Heterogeneity in Mobile Cloud Computing: Taxonomy and Open Challenges. Communications Surveys & Tutorials (in press)
17. Gelernter, D.: Generative Communication in Linda. Transactions on Programming Languages and Systems 7(1), 80–112 (1985)
18. Ko, B.J., Pappas, V., Raghavendra, R., Song, Y., Dilmaghani, R.B., Lee, K.W., Verma, D.: An Information-Centric Architecture for Data Center Networks. In: Proceedings of the 2nd Workshop on Information-Centric Networking, ICN 2012, pp. 79–84. ACM (August 2012)
19. De, S., Nandi, S., Goswami, D.: Tuple space enhancements for mobile middleware. International Journal of Communication Networks and Distributed Systems (in press, 2013)

Value Added Services on Stationary Vehicular Cloud

Narayanan Vignesh, Rengaraj Shankar, Sundararajan Sathyamoorthy,
and V. Mary Anita Rajam

Department of Computer Science & Engineering
CEG, Anna University, Chennai
anitav@annauniv.edu

Abstract. Cloud computing is the use of computing resources that are delivered as a service over a network. Most of the mobile phones currently in use have less processing capability. A trivial solution to this resource poverty problem is compute offloading. Mobile clouds are not efficient with conventional internet cloud models and mobile computing approaches. The advancement in technology has made vehicles becoming more sophisticated through powerful on-board computing capabilities, tons of on-board storage, significant communication capabilities and virtually no power limitations. This paper proposes a communication mechanism for providing value added services on an opportunistically formed Stationary Vehicular Cloud by exploiting the idle vehicular resources that, now has become a thing of commonality in cities.

1 Introduction

Cloud computing maximizes the effectiveness of shared resources by the utilization of available remote infrastructures. The survey of more than 1,000 American adults conducted in August 2012 shows that, nearly one third see the cloud as a thing of the future, yet 97 percent are actually using cloud services today via online shopping, banking, social networking and file sharing [1].

Vehicular Cloud Computing is a distributed computing paradigm that comprises of heterogeneous domains of vehicular infrastructure, cloud computing, and wireless networks aiming to utilize the computational capabilities of vehicular resources. Rather than the cloud formed using vehicles in transit, this paper explores a Stationary Vehicular Cloud [SVC] formed using vehicles parked in a parking lot. The number of parked vehicles in a weekend in a railway station of a busy city is found to be around 1200 [2]. Many commercial organizations manufacture PCs for vehicles with high processing capacity at a very low cost [3]. The technology found in many mobiles these days are not capable enough to handle today's compute intensive applications. Our system tries to overcome the resource poverty problem by utilizing the processing capability available in the vehicles parked in parking lots.

The following scenario reflects potential benefits of this collaboration. If in a shopping mall, a suspect has to be identified from the frames sent by Closed Circuit Television [CCTV] cameras set up there, a lot of processing power is required. In this case, a viable solution would be to utilize the computational power of vehicular resources parked in the lot. Other potential applications of this system include distributed

R. Natarajan (Ed.): ICDCIT 2014, LNCS 8337, pp. 92–97, 2014.

information processing systems such as banking systems, railway reservation systems, massive multiplayer online games and virtual reality communities.

Our main contributions are: We describe a communication protocol that enables formation of a Stationary Vehicular Cloud (SVC) and communication between vehicles in the SVC. We provide mechanisms for assigning computational tasks to the vehicles participating in the SVC and for migrating tasks from vehicles whose departure is imminent. We report the results of the simulations done using ns2 simulator.

The paper is organized as follows: Section 2 briefs about the related work. Section 3 explains the proposed communication protocol's design. Section 4 discusses about the simulation results obtained. Section 5 concludes the paper.

2   Related Work

Lei Yang et al. [6] advised augmenting the execution of mobile data stream application on portable devices using cloud resources through computation partitioning, which aims at optimizing the partition of a data stream application between mobile and cloud such that the application has maximum speed/throughput in processing streaming data. Paramvir Bahl et al. [7] envisioned that new capabilities will enable mobile users to seamlessly utilize the cloud to obtain the resource benefits without incurring delays and jitter and without worrying about energy.

To overcome the issues of cloud availability and expensiveness, Vetriselvi et al. [9] created a cloud computing platform using mobile phones. The limitations of this approach are that the cloud itself may become overloaded. To overcome this, Don et al. [6] formed a grid with several virtual organizations in it. Whenever a single cloudlet gets overloaded, a Global Load Balancing Algorithm is employed.

Olariu et al. [4] [8] referred to a group of vehicles forming a vehicular cloud whose excess computing, communication, and storage resources can be coordinated dynamically and allocated to authorized users, as a vehicular cloud. They discussed potential vehicular cloud applications such as value-added and traffic-related applications.

Olariu et al. [4] envisioned a vehicular cloud involving cars in the parking lot of a typical international airport. They predict the parking occupancy given arrival and departure rates. They have not addressed the specific ways in which computational tasks are to be assigned to the participating vehicles and the ways in which tasks migrate from vehicles whose departure is imminent.

3   Communication in SVC

A dynamic group of vehicles in a parking lot is considered where the vehicles are typically on stay for several days and can form a stationary vehicular cloud (SVC). To be able to schedule resources and to assign computational tasks to the various cars in the vehicular cloud, it is necessary to have a picture of how the association, computational offloading and disassociation takes place which the following section deals about.

In the SVC, the node/vehicle that controls and coordinates the allocation of resources is called the SVC Master (SVC-M). The other nodes/vehicles in the SVC are
called SVC Participants (SVC-P). The SVC-M is responsible for synthesizing the
SVC, job scheduling and distribution and tariff tracking. The SVC-Ps get associated
with the SVC-M initially, get services and disassociate while leaving the cloud.

3.1   Association

Once a node wishes to associate itself into the SVC, it broadcasts an Association Request message. Here two cases are possible: In case the node does not receive any
ACK within a certain interval, it assumes that there is no SVC formed earlier and acts
as the SVC-M. In case there was an SVC-M earlier, the node would get an Association ACK from the SVC-M. Once the Association ACK is received, the SVC-P sends
the details of the resources it has viz. processing power, hard disk capacity, RAM size
and memory units through a Resource Definition message. The SVC-M on receiving
the Resource Definition populates a resource_table with the details about the
processing power, hard disk capacity and RAM size using SVC-P id as the primary
field.

3.2   Services

In this work, the following services have been considered to be provided in the SVC:
Computation as a Service, Storage as a Service, Local Browsing and Communication
as a Service. The sequences of interactions for the various services are detailed below.

Computation as a Service (CaaS)
In CaaS, the client sends a request for computation to the SVC-M through a CaaS
request packet from client to SVC-M. The appropriate node for compute offloading is
then found by the SVC-M using the information in the resource_table and svc_history
table maintained by it. The SVC-M selects the node with the maximum processing
power and the longest parking history. The SVC-M then contacts the selected node
through a CaaS request packet from SVC-M to SVC-P and thereby hands over the
computational data. The SVC-P does the necessary computation and returns the result
to the SVC-M through a CaaS Response from SVC-P to SVC-M. The SVC-M then
updates certain information in a CaaS_trace file like job id, the node that performed
the job, start and end time of the job. The SVC-M also updates the job success rate in
svc_history table. The SVC-M then sends back the result to the requesting client
through a CaaS response from SVC-M to Client.

Storage as a Service (SaaS)

SaaS Storage
In SaaS storage, the client initiates a storage request to the SVC-M through a SaaS
storage request packet from client to SVC-M along with the content to be stored. The
SVC-M finds the node with the maximum memory and availability using the information in the resource_table and the   svc_history table. The SVC-M then populates the

entries in an SaaS_trace table with the job id, client id, file name and the id of the SVC_P which stores the file. Then SVC-M contacts that respective node through SaaS request packet from SVC-M to SVC-P and sends the associated storage files to the SVC-P. The memory entry in the resource_table for the SVC-P is decreased. The SVC-P stores the intended data in its own storage location.

SaaS Retrieval
In SaaS retrieval, the client that stored data in the SVC initiates a storage retrieval request to the SVC-M through SaaS retrieval request packet from Client to SVC-M. The SVC-M now finds the SVC-P that currently holds the requested content using the client id, file name fields of the SaaS_trace table. The SVC-M contacts that SVC-P through SaaS retrieval request packet from SVC-M to SVC-P and sends the names of the files to be retrieved. The SVC-P returns the stored file contents to the SVC-M through SaaS retrieval response packet. The SVC-M updates the SaaS_trace table by removing the current storage history and also updates the memory units of SVC-P in the svc_history table. The SVC-M then sends the stored content to the requesting client through SaaS retrieval response packet from SVC-M to client.

Local Browsing
The client sends the local browsing (LB) request packet with the local browsing data such as music or data file names. The SVC-M populates the lb_trace table with entries lb id, client id that generated the LB request, process status and start time. The SVC-M then broadcasts the LB request packet from SVC-M to all SVC-Ps in the cloud. The SVC-Ps on receiving the LB request packet from SVC-M check whether the requested LB data is present in their file system and respond to the SVC-M through the LB Response packet with the contents of the file requested, if present. The SVC-M now updates the lb_trace table and sets the status and end time fields. The status field of lb_trace table serves as a contention resolving mechanism by which multiple responses from many SVC-Ps can be eliminated. The SVC-M then sends LB data to the client through LB Response packet from SVC-M to the Client.

Communication as a Service(COMaaS)
Here mailing is used as the communication service. The client sends a COMaaS request to the SVC-M which in turn broadcasts it to all SVC-Ps. The SVC-P which responds first acts as a mailing agent and forwards mails to intended recipients. The SVC-P also sends a response packet to the SVC-M as an acknowledgement to the sent mail by the COMaaS Response ACK packet, which is then forwarded to the client.

3.3   Disassociation

When an SVC-P intends to leave the SVC, it sends a Disassociation Request packet to the SVC-M. Here two cases arise: If the SVC-P currently does not have any SaaS Storage data then the SVC-M disassociates the SVC-P from the SVC by sending Disassociation ACK. Else, the SVC-M selects another SVC-P that is appropriate for handling the SaaS storage by considering the resource_table and svc_history tables and sends the newly selected SVC-P id to the SVC-P that needs to disassociate and asks the old SVC-P to handover the SaaS data that it currently has to the newly selected SVC-P. The old SVC-P sends the storage data to the new SVC-P and an ACK to the SVC-M indicating that it has done the assigned job. The SVC-M on receiving the ACK updates the SaaS_trace table and the resource_table to remove the disassociated SVC-P. The SVC-M then sends the Disassociation ACK to the old SVC-P.

4   Performance Analysis

The simulations were carried using the ns-2 simulator considering 25 nodes to be present in the cloud. The vehicle arrival rate was considered to be exponentially distributed. The performance was compared for the cases when requests arrive one after the other (that is after one request was serviced) and when requests arrive in parallel.

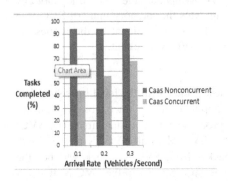

Fig. 1. Arrival Rate Vs CaaS Task Completed

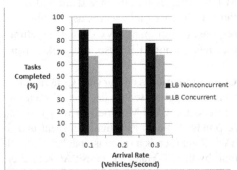

Fig. 2. Arrival Rate Vs SaaS Tasks Completed

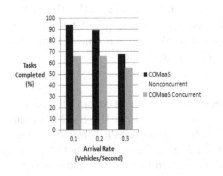

Fig. 3. Arrival Rate Vs COMaaS Tasks Completed

Fig. 4. Arrival Rate Vs LB Tasks Completed

For the simulations in the case of CaaS, an application where the client sends a set of target images and a source image to the SVC-M was considered. The SVC-M chooses an appropriate SVC-P and transfers all these images to the SVC-P. The SVC-P compares the target images with the source image and responds back to the SVC-M which in turn responds to the client. For simulations in the case of Local browsing, generation of a request for a file from the client was considered and the file was sent back to the client. For simulations in the case of COMaaS, a mail was sent from the client and the mail getting updated in the COMaaS trace was checked.

The graphs in Figures 1, 2, 3 and 4 show how performance of the SVC varies with respect to various arrival rates. It can easily be inferred from the above graphs that performance of the system is at the best when arrival rate is minimum or moderate and the system exhibits a very low performance at high arrival rates, the reason being that collision occurs between several control packets and results in loss of service.

5　　Conclusion

The main motive of this work is to overcome the resource poverty problem of certain lower end devices. The system designed is capable of handling any number of requests from the lower end devices, which would help, when the system is actually implemented real-time. This system is very flexible and can be implemented in any parking lot. The proposed protocol schedules jobs based on the time of arrival pattern the currently available vehicles. Results can be better if job scheduling is done by predicting the future availability of the vehicles based on their earlier arrivals and departures. The system can be modeled as a Continuous Time Markov Chain by which the availability of vehicles can be predicted thus achieving better performance.

References

1. Cloud Computing (2011), http://www.citrix.com/news/announcements/aug-2012/most-americans-confused-by-cloud-computing-according-to-national.html
2. Relief for car parking lot users at Central station (2011), http://www.thehindu.com/news/cities/chennai/relief-for-car-parking-lot-users-at-central-station/article1978901.ece
3. Commercial High End Cars (2012), http://www.incarpc.co.uk
4. Olariu, S., Eltoweissy, M., Younis, M.: Towards autonomous vehicular clouds. ICST Transactions on Mobile Communications and Applications 11(7-9), e2 (2011)
5. Abraham, D., Vetrian, V.: Decentralized Dynamic Load Balancing and Intersection Trust in Mobile Ad Hoc Grids. International Journal of Computer Science Issues 8(4), 236–244 (2011)
6. Yang, L., Cao, J., Tang, S., Li, T., Chan, A.T.S.: A Framework for Partitioning and Execution of Data Stream Applications in Mobile Cloud Computing. In: Proceedings of the Fifth International Conference on Cloud Computing, pp. 794–802 (2012)
7. Bahl, P., Han, R.Y., Li, L.E., Satyanarayanan, M.: Advancing the State of Mobile Cloud Computing. In: Proceedings of the Third ACM Workshop on Mobile Cloud Computing and Services, pp. 21–28 (2012)
8. Arif, S., Olariu, S., Wang, J., Yan, G., Yang, W., Khalil, I.: Datacenter at the Airport: Reasoning about Time-Dependent Parking Lot Occupancy. IEEE Transactions on Parallel and Distributed System 23(11), 2067–2080 (2012)
9. Vetriselvi, V., Parthasarathi, R.: Trace Based Mobility Model for Ad Hoc Networks. In: Third IEEE International Conference on Wireless and Mobile Computing, Networking and Communications, pp. 81–88 (2007)

FTM²: Fault Tolerant Batch Mode Heuristics in Computational Grid

Sanjaya Kumar Panda[1], Pabitra Mohan Khilar[2], and Durga Prasad Mohapatra[2]

[1] Department of Computer Science and Engineering, Indian School of Mines,
Dhanbad, India
[2] Department of Computer Science and Engineering, National Institute of Technology,
Rourkela, India
sanjayauce@gmail.com, {pmkhilar,durga}@nitrkl.ac.in

Abstract. Task scheduling is a complicated work in a grid computing environment because the resources are extremely unpredictable. In addition, there are many resources with varying functionalities. More importantly both resources and users are generally in different domains. They may join or leave at any period of time due to administrative reason, network failure or machine failure. It may degrade the performance of computational grid. So, we need a fault tolerant approach to work smoothly in the presence of failure. In this paper, we address the problem of machine failure in computational grid. The proposed system model uses the Round Trip Time (RTT) to detect the failure and the checkpointing strategy to recover from the failure. This model is applied to the traditional batch mode heuristics such as Min-Min and Max-Min. The proposed Fault Tolerant Min-Min (FTMin-Min) heuristic and Fault Tolerant Max-Min heuristic (FTMax-Min) (combinedly FTM²) are simulated using MATLAB. The experimental results are discussed and compared with the traditional heuristics. The results show that these approaches bypass the permanent machine failure and reduce the makespan.

Keywords: Batch mode, Min-Min, Max-Min, Scheduling, Fault tolerance, Grid.

1 Introduction

Grid resource allocation and task scheduling is very complicated work in grid computing because the resources are heterogeneous, distributed and dynamic in nature [1]. The resources are owned by different organizations or domains [2]. Moreover, each domain may have different security constraints and policies. If the security criteria do not met then the resource may leave at any period of time. Apart from this, the resource may leave due to network failure or machine failure [3]. It may degrade the performance of computational grid. Let us consider a real world problem to address the above problem. The real world grid projects are running in Berkeley Open Infrastructure for Network Computing (BOINC) middleware system [4]. For example, Search for Extra Terrestrial Intelligence (SETI@home) is a very famous grid project [5]. The projects are running on the user machine if the user is idle. But,

R. Natarajan (Ed.): ICDCIT 2014, LNCS 8337, pp. 98–104, 2014.

the user may leave the project due to some unavoidable circumstances like power failure, system failure, network failure and many more. So, the jobs are incomplete or unprocessed. In this paper, we address the above problem.

The Grid Referral Service (GRS) keeps track of all information about the grid resources. The delays between the GRS and the resource are divided into two types. They are communication and queuing delay. Communication delay measures the time taken to move from the GRS to the domain and/or the domain to the machine or vice-versa. Queuing delay measures the time taken to the domain and/or the machine to hold the message before it is processed. Finally, RTT is the essence of the above delay to send a message to the machine and acknowledge for the same. If a machine runs out due to some problems, the grid scheduler is responsible for mapping the tasks in such a manner that the overall performance remains intact. Checkpointing is one of the recovery mechanisms to recover from the failure.

The remainder of this paper is organized as follows. Section 2 briefly discusses related research in fault tolerance and grid scheduling. Section 3 gives the preliminaries. In Section 4, the proposed heuristics are discussed and presented. We conduct experiments in Section 5. Finally, we conclude in Section 6.

2   Related Work

Many works are going on the area of task scheduling and fault tolerance. The researchers and practitioners are attempting to minimize the makespan and increase resource (or machine) utilization. But, very few authors are addressing the problem of fault tolerance [6-12].

A task level fault tolerance is introduced by Priya et al. [8]. This approach considers retry, alternate machine, checkpointing and replication task level techniques. Khanli et al. [9] and Upadhya et al. [13] uses genetic algorithm to schedule the jobs. But, Guo et al. [14] uses ant colony optimization to solve multi-objective task scheduling. The machine may be failed due to hardware, software or application and operating system. Nazir et al. [7] addresses the machine failure problem. The Grid Information Service (GIS) keeps track of the information about the fault occurrence index. If the index value is low then the probability of failure is less. This strategy uses checkpointing technique to prone from failure. Abawajy [11] introduces distributed fault-tolerant scheduling policies based on job replication strategy. The replica of a job is scheduled in different machine to achieve fault tolerance. The primary aim is that at least one of the replicas gives correct result. Replication policy is of two types: static and dynamic. Anglano et al. [12] considers static replication policy where the number of replicas per task should not exceed the replication threshold.

In this paper, we have proposed two batch mode heuristic using RTT and checkpointing. To the best of our knowledge, this is the first fault tolerance work (in batch mode) using the benchmark data set by Braun et al. [15].

3   Preliminaries

3.1   Problem Definition

Let us consider a grid environment consists of m different types of jobs (or tasks) J_1, $J_2,...,J_m$ and n different types of resources (or machines) $R_1, R_2,..., R_n$. The problem is to map all jobs to the available resources such that the overall processing time is minimized. More importantly, if a resource runs out due to some problems then the proposed heuristic is able to handle it.

3.2   Scheduling Algorithms

There are many heuristics in batch mode heuristic. But, we have listed only two heuristics: Min-Min and Max-Min.

3.2.1   Min-Min
It is a two step heuristic. First, it finds the earliest completion time of each task. Second, it finds an earliest value from the first step. This heuristic takes $O(m^2n)$ time to map the tasks to the resources.

3.2.2   Max-Min
It is also a two step heuristic. This heuristic is a slight modification of Min-Min heuristic. In the second step, it finds a latest value rather than earliest value.

4   Proposed Heuristic

In this section, we present the two batch mode heuristics: FTMin-Min and FTMax-Min (combinedly FTM^2).

4.1   Description

The heuristics are divided into two phases: matching and scheduling. The matching phase is similar to the traditional Min-Min (or Max-Min) heuristic. The proposed fault tolerant technique is introduced in scheduling phase.

4.2   Heuristics

The primary mechanism of FTM^2 heuristic is defined in Algorithm 1. It is a two phase heuristic. First, this heuristic finds the completion time of all tasks on all machines (Lines 1-5). For each task, it finds an earliest completion time (Lines 6-8). Second, the task that has minimum (or maximum) earliest completion time is selected and assigned to the requesting machine (Line 9). Note that, minimum and maximum earliest completion time is applicable for FTMin-Min and FTMax-Min heuristic respectively. Thereafter, the Grid Machine Broker (GMB) finds the current status of the machine from GRS. Then, the GRS checks whether the machine is able to compute a task or not. It sends a message to the machine and waits for a reply. It also calculates the RTT as shown in Equation 1. If GRS will not get back the confirmation message in stipulated time (as shown in Equation 2), it concludes that the machine is failed or unable to respond to the request. The value of ζ is in between 1 to 2 (depends on the grid). If the machine fails then the GRS informs the GMB to reschedule another task. Then again, it obtains the current status of the machine from GRS. If the machine works normally then the task is assigned to the machine (Lines 10-15).

$$RTT_{T_i \rightarrow DN_j, M_k} = D_{GMB-DN_j} + D_{DN_j} + D_{DN_j-M_k} + D_{M_k} +$$

$$D_{M_k-DN_j} + D_{DN_j} + D_{DN_j-GMB} \qquad (1)$$

where $RTT_{T_i \rightarrow DN_j, M_k}$ = RTT of task T_i on machine M_k present in domain DN_j

$D_{GMB-DN_j} (D_{DN_j-GMB})$ = Communication delay between GMB (DN_j) and DN_j (GMB)

$D_{DN_j} (D_{M_k})$ = Delay on domain j (machine k) including queuing delay

$D_{DN_j-M_k} (D_{M_k-DN_j})$ = Communication delay between domain j (machine k) and machine k (domain j)

$$\text{Timeout} > \xi \times 2 \times (D_{GMB-DN_j} + D_{DN_j} + D_{DN_j-M_k}) + D_{M_k} \qquad (2)$$

Checkpointing strategy is used to recover the failure. If timeout occurs then the GRS requests the broker to roll back to the last consistent state. Furthermore, the GRS is not sending any task to that failed (or timeout) machine.

Algorithm 1. FTM² heuristic

1. **for** all tasks T_i in Task Queue (TQ)
2.   **for** all machine M_j
3. $C_{i,j} = E_{i,j} + R_j$ // Completion time = Execution time + Ready time
4.   **end for**
5. **end for**
6. **for** all tasks T_i in TQ
7.   Find minimum $C_{i,j}$ and machine M_j that holds it.
8. **end for**
9. Find the task T_h with minimum/maximum $C_{i,j}$ and machine M_j that holds it.
10. Find the status of machine M_j from GRS.
11. **if** (M_j == Faulty)
12.   Go to Step 9.
13. **else**   Assign task T_h to machine M_j that gives minimum $C_{i,j}$.
14. **end if**
15. Delete the task T_h from TQ and Update R_j.

Table 1. Numerical results of makespan value for 512 × 16, 1024 × 32 and 2048 × 64 instances respectively

Instance	Min-Min (512×16)	Min-Min (1024×32)	Min-Min (2048×64)	FTMin-Min (512×16)	FTMin-Min (1024×32)	FTMin-Min (2048×64)	Max-Min (512×16)	Max-Min (1024×32)	Max-Min (2048×64)	FTMax-Min (512×16)	FTMax-Min (1024×32)	FTMax-Min (2048×64)
u_c_hihi	8.1189E+06	2.0735E+07	1.8377E+07	2.1407E+07	9.2542E+07	6.7673E+07	1.2382E+07	3.2007E+07	2.7648E+07	1.9058E+07	7.7707E+07	6.8052E+07
u_c_hilo	1.6181E+05	2.1880E+06	1.8731E+06	3.2471E+06	9.2014E+06	6.6778E+06	2.0405E+05	3.2199E+06	2.7135E+06	2.8025E+05	7.5687E+06	6.5929E+06
u_c_lohi	2.6700E+05	2.0370E+03	1.8400E+03	6.7661E+05	9.2120E+03	6.7535E+03	3.9247E+05	3.1182E+03	2.7380E+03	6.2904E+05	7.4429E+03	6.8577E+03
u_c_lolo	5.4255E+03	2.2587E+02	1.8169E+02	1.0801E+04	9.4887E+02	6.6689E+02	6.9443E+03	3.2910E+02	2.6773E+02	9.1983E+03	7.7871E+02	6.6836E+02
u_i_hihi	3.5139E+06	5.9639E+06	3.2489E+06	8.7481E+06	1.3936E+07	4.7571E+06	8.0184E+06	1.3223E+07	6.5511E+06	1.2108E+07	2.0882E+07	1.1040E+07
u_i_hilo	8.0756E+04	5.5055E+05	3.2768E+05	1.5813E+05	1.2984E+06	4.8487E+05	2.5191E+05	1.2517E+06	1.1039E+06	2.1763E+05	2.0121E+06	1.2574E+06
u_i_lohi	1.0897E+05	6.2358E+02	3.2094E+02	2.9737E+02	1.3579E+03	4.8307E+02	2.5153E+02	1.3313E+03	6.9389E+02	3.9092E+02	2.2663E+03	9.429E+02
u_i_lolo	2.6401E+03	6.3720E+01	3.1040E+01	5.6108E+03	1.4079E+02	4.6520E+01	5.1766E+03	1.2753E+02	6.7940E+01	7.3042E+03	2.2828E+02	9.6640E+01
u_s_hihi	4.8348E+06	1.3558E+07	1.0826E+07	1.6121E+07	6.1872E+07	3.9099E+07	9.1951E+06	2.3282E+07	1.6694E+07	1.6855E+07	4.6608E+07	3.1368E+07
u_s_hilo	1.0327E+05	1.3175E+06	9.9935E+05	2.3919E+05	5.9335E+06	3.7126E+06	1.7262E+06	2.2329E+06	1.6607E+06	2.4758E+05	4.4402E+06	3.0262E+06
u_s_lohi	1.3738E+05	1.3546E+03	1.0135E+03	4.4101E+05	5.7314E+03	3.7054E+03	2.8205E+05	2.2049E+03	1.6190E+03	4.8025E+05	4.1854E+03	3.0513E+03
u_s_lolo	3.8068E+03	1.2871E+02	1.0283E+02	8.1789E+03	6.0615E+02	3.8993E+02	6.2318E+03	2.2347E+02	1.7043E+02	9.0163E+03	4.3121E+02	3.1886E+02

Table 2. Numerical results of machine utilization value for 512 × 16, 1024 × 32 and 2048 × 64 instances respectively

Instance	Min-Min (512×16)	Min-Min (1024×32)	Min-Min (2048×64)	FTMin-Min (512×16)	FTMin-Min (1024×32)	FTMin-Min (2048×64)	Max-Min (512×16)	Max-Min (1024×32)	Max-Min (2048×64)	FTMax-Min (512×16)	FTMax-Min (1024×32)	FTMax-Min (2048×64)
u_c_hihi	0.5234	0.4745	0.4435	0.5228	0.5032	0.5050	0.8769	0.8060	0.7590	0.7969	0.6889	0.6972
u_c_hilo	0.5909	0.4578	0.4290	0.5610	0.5046	0.5044	0.8519	0.8007	0.7624	0.7898	0.6879	0.6988
u_c_lohi	0.5347	0.4540	0.4371	0.5295	0.5013	0.5101	0.8547	0.8046	0.7585	0.7793	0.6886	0.6976
u_c_lolo	0.5895	0.4502	0.4448	0.5698	0.5003	0.5014	0.8536	0.8049	0.7592	0.7941	0.6861	0.7003
u_i_hihi	0.4745	0.4317	0.3892	0.4971	0.4630	0.4024	0.8842	0.8095	0.7698	0.7865	0.7399	0.6126
u_i_hilo	0.5728	0.4560	0.4219	0.5523	0.4639	0.4202	0.8522	0.8195	0.7797	0.8001	0.7451	0.6237
u_i_lohi	0.5262	0.4288	0.4209	0.4991	0.4731	0.4261	0.8760	0.8025	0.7731	0.8167	0.7368	0.7409
u_i_lolo	0.5939	0.4182	0.4347	0.5296	0.4445	0.4290	0.8539	0.8172	0.7696	0.7992	0.7504	0.7594
u_s_hihi	0.4726	0.3854	0.3031	0.4965	0.4695	0.4498	0.8740	0.8380	0.8297	0.7831	0.7552	0.7932
u_s_hilo	0.5653	0.3767	0.3270	0.5398	0.4797	0.4459	0.8602	0.8284	0.8206	0.7891	0.7195	0.7846
u_s_lohi	0.5030	0.3877	0.3562	0.5112	0.4796	0.4520	0.8844	0.8376	0.8257	0.7913	0.7393	0.7908
u_s_lolo	0.5753	0.3788	0.3470	0.5504	0.4776	0.4550	0.8576	0.8232	0.8312	0.7809	0.7542	0.7906

5   Experimental Study

In this section, we present the results of two batch mode heuristics defined in the previous section. The results are compared in terms of two performance measures: makespan and machine utilization. All the experiments are performed using MALAB R2010b version 7.11.0.584. We have considered Braun et al. [15] data sets (or instances) to evaluate the proposed heuristics. The general form of the instance is u_t_mmnn.o. Here, u indicates the uniform distribution; t indicates the nature of the matrix: consistent (c), inconsistent (i) and semi-consistent (s); mm indicates the task heterogeneity and nn indicates the machine heterogeneity. The value of mm or nn is either hi or lo. In this paper, we have taken three different sizes of the data sets: 512 × 16, 1024 × 32 and 2048 × 64. The first value denotes the number of tasks and the second value denotes the number of machines.

In 512 × 16 instances, eight numbers of machines are failed during simulation. The machine IDs are M_{10}, M_3, M_4, M_{15}, M_1, M_8, M_{16} and M_6. The machines are failed after the execution of the task ID T_{165}, T_{176}, T_{182}, T_{188}, T_{234}, T_{314}, T_{338} and T_{370} respectively. The numerical results of makespan value and machine utilization value are shown in Table 1 and 2 respectively. The RTT and checkpointing overhead are negligible for simplicity. Note that, Min-Min and Max-Min heuristics are very less makespan in Table 1 and 2. Because very few numbers of task are carried out. For instance, let us consider a 512 × 16 instance. In Min-Min, the total number of tasks executed in u_c_hihi instance is 512 − 172 (total number of failed task) = 340. The makespan is 8.1189E+06. But, the proposed FTMin-Min heuristic executes 512 tasks in the presence of failure. The makespan is 2.1407E+07. So, FTMin-Min heuristic gives better performance in the presence of failure.

6   Conclusion

In this paper, we have introduced FTM^2 heuristic. This heuristic is an extension of the existing Min-Min and Max-Min heuristic. The proposed heuristics address the problem of fault tolerance and its solution. The solution contains two important things: RTT and checkpointing. We have used Braun et al. [15] benchmark instances to simulate our heuristics. The results show that the proposed heuristics gives better task processing and minimize the makespan.

References

1. Buyya, R.: High Performance Cluster Computing. Pearson Education (2008)
2. Murshed, M., Buyya, R., Abramson, D.: GridSim: A Toolkit for the Modeling and Simulation of Global Grids, pp.1–15. Monash University
3. Duarte, E.P., Weber, A., Fonseca, K.V.O.: Distributed Diagnosis of Dynamic Events in Partitionable Arbitrary Topology Networks. IEEE Transactions on Parallel and Distributed Systems 23, 1415–1426 (2012)
4. BOINC, http://boinc.berkeley.edu/ (accessed on September 1, 2013)

5. SETI@home, http://setiathome.berkeley.edu/ (accessed on September 1, 2013)
6. Medeiros, R., Cirne, W., Brasileiro, F., Sauve, J.: Faults in Grids: Why are they so Bad and What can be done about it. In: Proceedings of the Fourth International Workshop on Grid Computing (2003)
7. Nazir, B., Khan, T.: Fault Tolerant Job Scheduling in Computational Grid. In: IEEE 2nd International Conference on Emerging Technologies, pp. 708–713 (2006)
8. Priya, S.B., Prakash, M., Dhawan, K.K.: Fault Tolerance-Genetic Algorithm for Grid Task Scheduling using Check Point. In: IEEE 6th International Conference on Grid and Cooperative Computing, pp. 676–680 (2007)
9. Khanli, L.M., Far, M.E., Rahmani, A.M.: RFOH: A New Fault Tolerant Job Scheduler in Grid Computing. In: IEEE 2nd International Conference on Computer Engineering and Applications, pp. 422–425 (2010)
10. Egwutuoha, I.P., Levy, D., Selic, B., Chen, S.: A Survey of Fault Tolerance Mechanisms and Checkpoint / Restart Implementations for High Performance Computing Systems. Journal of Supercomputering 65, 1302–1326 (2013)
11. Abawajy, J.H.: Fault-Tolerant Scheduling Policy for Grid Computing Systems. In: 18th International Parallel and Distributed Processing Symposium. IEEE (2004)
12. Anglano, C., Brevik, J., Canonico, M., Nurmi, D., Wolski, R.: Fault-aware Scheduling for Bag-of-Tasks Applications on Desktop Grids. In: Grid Computing Conference. IEEE (2006)
13. Upadhyay, N., Misra, M.: Incorporating Fault Tolerance in GA-based Scheduling in Grid Environment. In: IEEE World Congress Information and Communication Technologies, pp. 772–777 (2011)
14. Guo, S., Huang, H., Wang, Z., Xie, M.: Grid Service Reliability Modeling and Optimal Task Scheduling Considering Fault Recovery. IEEE Transactions on Reliability 60, 263–274 (2011)
15. Braun, T.D., Siegel, H.J., Beck, N., Boloni, L.L., Maheswaran, M., Reuther, A.I., Robertson, J.P., Theys, M.D., Yao, B.: A Comparison of Eleven Static Heuristics for Mapping a Class of Independent Tasks onto Heterogeneous Distributed Computing Systems. Journal of Parallel and Distributed Computing 61, 810–837 (2001)

SNAPWebD and SNAPSync: A Web Desktop and Transparent *sync* of NFS and Standalone System Logical Volumes

Anupama Potluri[1], Krishna Vutukuri[1], and Garvit Sharma[2]

[1] School of Computer and Information Sciences, University of Hyderabad
Hyderabad, India
[2] The LNM Institute of Information Technology, Jaipur, India
apcs@uohyd.ernet.in, {sskrishnavutukuri,garvits45}@gmail.com

Abstract. The web browser is the most ubiquitous software today on all kinds of devices including PCs, tablets and mobile phones. Access to high bandwidth network services has lead to the development of cloud computing where services such as applications or desktops can be accessed from remote servers through the Internet. In this paper, we present our work in developing a Web Desktop for the typical environments found in many corporates and educational institutions. These environments consist of Network File System (NFS) mounted home directories of users authenticated using Lightweight Directory Access Protocol (LDAP). *SNAPWebD*, our web desktop, which is a free and open source software, will allow users of such organizations to access their home directories and remote applications through the web browser. *SNAPSync* is the software that allows transparent syncing of the home directory from the cloud to local or NFS volumes of a user and vice versa. Together, these two applications allow a user to access their home directory from the cloud using any available device and also sync the changes transparently to local home systems. This keeps the information consistent across multiple systems without user intervention while allowing anytime, anywhere access through the web desktop.

1 Introduction

The Web Browser is an ubiquitous piece of software on almost all devices of communication today including PCs, Laptops, Tablets, Mobile phones etc.. This, combined with the availability of high bandwidth network access using 3G/4G mobile networks, has spurred the growth of *cloud computing*. Cloud computing is transparent access to various services in the network anywhere, anytime. One of the services that is gaining a lot of momentum is a desktop environment or an operating system through the browser called Web Desktop [1] and WebOS respectively [2–5]. This extends independence from hardware and specific operating systems for users and helps portability. There has also been development of software that keeps some of the files synchronized between the local and the

R. Natarajan (Ed.): ICDCIT 2014, LNCS 8337, pp. 105–110, 2014.
© Springer International Publishing Switzerland 2014

cloud versions such as *UbuntuOne* [6], *4sync* [7], *eyeSync* [4] and *GoogleDrive* [8].

In this paper, we present our work on providing a Web Desktop that is extremely lightweight and involves no installation of any software on the client system. It allows access to Lightweight Directory Access Protocol (LDAP) authenticated user accounts hosted on Network File System (NFS) logical volumes. We believe that this will be ideal for small offices and educational institutions. The IT challenge in implementing this software in an organization is minimal. While the web desktop allows access to users of their home accounts from any system at any time, typically, most users also have a laptop that they use for continuing the work at home rather than directly on the cloud. It is extremely useful to have all versions of the home directories synchronized with each other. Towards this end, we developed *SNAPSync*, that uses *rsync* as a library to synchronize the home directories. Many of the existing applications that allow synchronization only synchronize those files that exist in special directories/folders on the local system and not entire home directories.

The rest of the paper is organized as follows: the architecture and implementation of *SNAPWebD* is given in Section 2. The design of *SNAPSync* is given in Section 3. We conclude with Section 4 on enhancements planned in the future for these applications.

2   *SNAPWebD*

Virtualization of a desktop has long been used in Unix environments through software such as Virtual Network Computing (VNC) [9, 10]. Recently, software has been developed to access desktops through the web browser giving platform and OS independence. These are called Web Desktops. However, none of them have the capability to directly access already existing user accounts through the web browser. Many need installation of software on client side and use protocols such as Remote Desktop Protocol (RDP) [11] which is quite complex. *SNAP-WebD*[12] overcomes all of these limitations.

SNAPWebD architecture consists of the following minimum components: an LDAP server to authenticate the users, an NFS server to host the users' home directories, a web server that hosts *SNAPWebD* software and a client system that is used by the user to access the home directory via the web browser. In addition, if an organization hosts an application server from which the applications are transparently accessed, this is also supported by the web desktop. The basic architecture of *SNAPWebD* is given in Fig. 1. The web server is the only system where our software needs to be installed. All the other components of the IT infrastructure of an organization are untouched by our application. The web desktop software we have developed is also extremely lightweight in that it consists of a maximum of 2000 lines of JSP and JQuery code. Thus, the job of the IT administrator to enable the web desktop in an organization is highly simplified.

SNAPWebD works as follows: when the user types in the URL for *SNAPWebD*, the login page is displayed. The user's details are accepted and authenticated

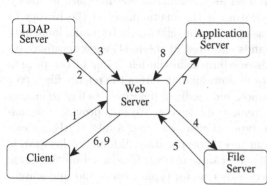

1. User logs in
2. User details sent to LDAP server
3. LDAP server sends validity of user
4. Web server sends request for mount to NFS server.
5. Web server mounts the user's home
6. Web server sends home directory details to the client.
7. Application request from client is forwarded to the application server.
8. Web server mounts the appln. server directory to launch the application.
9. Web server launches the application

Fig. 1. Proposed Web Desktop Architecture

using the LDAP server. The LDAP server returns the home directory information for the user who has logged in. Using the home information, *SNAPWebD*
software automatically and transparently mounts the corresponding NFS logical
volume, if needed. Then, the contents of the home directory are displayed on the
web browser. Similarly, whenever a user needs to launch an application, *SNAP-
WebD* software searches for the corresponding application in the local system,
the web server, the NFS file server and then the NFS application server in that
order. This is done so as to enhance the performance. As long as an application is
available on the local system, there is no need to connect to remote servers on the
network and run the application on the remote system. This helps performance
in three ways: firstly, there is no network load. Secondly, there is no load on the
remote server in terms of the number of running processes. Thirdly, working with
a local process is much faster than with a remote process. We use the application on a web server so as not to have further network traffic between the web
and file/application servers. On the other hand, if the file server volume is already
mounted, accessing the application from this volume is more efficient. Only if the
application is not found in any of the already mounted partitions does the software
load a new partition and use it. However, this order can be customized or the institution can load balance by having different types of applications in different application servers. To run an application on the remote system we use the following
Secure SHell (SSH) command: **sshpass -p "password" ssh user-name@NFS
Server-IP "application-command"**. The application display (xserver display)
should be exported to the client system before we run the application to open its
window in the local system. This is done by using the **DISPLAY** environment
variable and exporting it to the client IP address (**DISPLAY=Client-IP:0**).

We maintain a list of standard extension types for files and the applications associated with these file types in our software. We can also use a given application
to open a file. For example, to open a file called "ex.pdf", we invoke the application as follows: **sshpass -p "krishna.48" ssh -o StrictHostKeyCheck-
ing=no Krishna@10.5.0.95 "DISPLAY=10.5.1.0:0;okular ex.pdf"**.

We provide other interesting features in our web desktop. One feature is a lightweight terminal which can be used as a command line interface for many of the standard actions. Another feature is the maintenance of the history of actions taken since the login, such as opening the lightweight terminal, launching an application etc.. All the commands executed in the lightweight terminal are also stored and displayed when history button in the left frame of the page is clicked. A third feature is the ability to download files from the remote file server to the local system or other locally mounted media or devices as well as to upload the files from local system to the remote file server. We also provide a search feature for the web desktop. Three types of searches are possible: firstly, we can search for an application which launches the application, if found; otherwise, it displays an error message. Secondly, we can search for files based on the name of the files using wildcard characters as is true for typical command line search. The third search feature is a rudimentary search on the content of the files. The given string is searched for in the files of the home directory recursively and all the files that contain the given string are displayed in the left frame of the page.

Web Desktop to a Specified Remote Computer: The final feature of *SNAPWebD* is that it allows access to a local user account on a given system identified by its IP address or a logical name. We assume that this system runs the NFS server software. In this case, *SNAPWebD* software authenticates the user locally without using the LDAP server. Once the user is authenticated, the home directory of the user on that system is mounted on the web server and the user can access the files of that system. A user can access an NFS account and a local account on a different standalone system simultaneously using the web desktop. Files can be transferred from one system to the other by downloading from one system to the local system and then uploading it to the other.

A table comparing the features supported by various commercial and free software web desktop products and **SNAPWebD** is given in Table 1.

3   *SNAPSync*

SNAPSync[13] uses *rsync* as a library to perform the synchronization across various systems. It runs as a daemon on systems which need to be synchronized. We need to configure the remote system(s) and directory information to which the home directory on the local system needs to be synchronized. Once this configuration is complete, the synchronization is entirely transparent to the user. *SNAPSync* differs from other synchronization products as follows: it allows for home directory to be synchronized and not only those files and directories in a specially marked directory. Further, unlike *UbuntuOne* and many other synchronization tools, it maintains a journal. This helps in two ways. Firstly, if a user has made many changes while being offline, on connection to the Internet, the overhead associated with searching for modified files is removed. Secondly, a periodic update combines multiple edits to the same file into a single synchronization event. We use *inotify* just as *UbuntuOne* does but only to make a journal entry.

Table 1. Comparison of Features supported by SNAPWebD and Other Products

Features	Products			
	VNC	eyeOS	OVD	SNAPWebD
Display files and directories in a browser	NO	YES	YES	**YES**
Can a user get his personal desktop	YES	NO	NO	**YES**
Opening a file when the associated application does not exist in the remote system hosting the file	NO	NO	NO	**YES**
Ability to upload a file to the remote host from local system	NO	YES	YES	**YES**
Ability to download a file to the local host from the remote system	NO	YES	YES	**YES**
Lightweight terminal (execute all types of non-interactive commands)	NO	NO	NO	**YES**
Complete terminal (execute all types of commands)	YES	NO	NO	**YES**
Search for an application in user's remote system	YES	NO	NO	**YES**
Search for a file based on name	NO	NO	YES	**YES**
Search for a file based on content	NO	NO	NO	**YES**
Store the history of users' actions since login time	NO	NO	NO	**YES**
Accessing a specified standalone system (using its IP address)	NO	NO	NO	**YES**

The very first time that $SNAPSync$ runs, it simply dumps the entire contents to the remote system if this directory does not exist in the remote system. After that, every time a change is done to the local system, a journal is maintained of the changes made. Periodically, the $SNAPSync$ daemon checks the journal and synchronizes the modified files. The result of the operation is stored in a log file to indicate success or failure and the causes of failure. If the synchronization is a success, the corresponding entry in the journal file is deleted. If a $force\ sync$ command is issued, it attempts to flush all the changes currently in the journal to the remote system. This is useful before shutdown of a system to ensure that all changes are synchronized in the remote system. If the user shuts down the system without this option, the journal is still retained. Hence, the changes are synchronized in the future whenever both the local and remote systems are online.

The user may also use $SNAPWebD$ to modify the contents of the files in the cloud from a third party system or a mobile device. When the user returns to the home or office and goes online, we need to pull the changes from the cloud into the local system. This is the first step of the $SNAPSync$ daemon. Thus, by using both $SNAPWebD$ and $SNAPSync$, we can manipulate the home directory contents of users as well as synchronize them in a lightweight and transparent manner.

4 Conclusions and Future Work

We have developed a web desktop, *SNAPWebD*, that allows users to access their home directories hosted on NFS servers using the browser. While there are other web desktop applications – both free and commercial products – available, none of these work with existing infrastructure of most institutions/corporations where users' accounts are hosted on NFS servers. In *SNAPWebD*, we do not need any special software to be installed on the client system. One additional feature is the ability to access a user's account on any standalone remote system with *SNAPWebD* given its name or IP address. *SNAPSync* allows the user to pull changes to the home directory from the cloud to local systems and vice versa. This differs from other products in that there is no special directory whose contents are synchronized. A journal maintained of all changes made while the system is offline or online is used to flush the changes. A periodic synchronization leads to a more efficient utilization of bandwidth.

However, at this point of time, *SNAPWebD* and *SNAPSync* work only with Linux systems. In future, we plan to extend them to work with other operating systems as well as connect to VMs and allow access to VMs of users. We also need to explore the security considerations of *SNAPWebD*.

References

1. Web Desktop, http://en.wikipedia.org/wiki/Web_desktop
2. Silvestri, G.A.: Citrix XenDesktop 5.6 Cookbook. PACKT Publishing, Birmingham (2013)
3. Citrix: How Desktop Delivery Works, http://www.1st-computer-networks.co.uk/citrix-how-desktop-delivery-works.php
4. Norte, J.C.: Hybrid virtualization: optimal management of a companys IT resources (January 2012), http://resources.eyeos.com/ENG_virtualization_whitepaper.pdf
5. Open Virtual Desktop, http://www.ulteo.com/home/
6. Ubuntu One, https://wiki.ubuntu.com/UbuntuOne/TechnicalDetails
7. 4sync, http://en.wikipedia.org/wiki/4sync
8. Google Drive, https://support.google.com/drive/answer/2424384?hl=en&ref_topic=14942
9. VNC, http://en.wikipedia.org/wiki/Virtual_Network_Computing
10. Virtual Network Computing, http://virtuallab.tufreiberg.de/p2p/p2p/vnc/ug/howitworks.html
11. Remote desktop protocl, http://support.microsoft.com/kb/186607
12. Vutukuri, K.: SNAPWebD: a web desktop for Standalone desktop or Nfs server using APache (SNAP) web server, https://github.com/sskrishna/SNAPWebD
13. Sharma, G.: SNAPSync, https://github.com/garvitlnmiit/SNAPSync

Energy-Aware Multi-level Routing Algorithm
for Two-Tier Wireless Sensor Networks

Tarachand Amgoth[1], Nabin Ghosh[2], and Prasanta K. Jana[1]

[1] Department of Computer Science and Engineering, Indian School of Mines, Dhanbad
Jharkhand-826004, India
[2] School of Computer Engineering, KIIT University, Bhubaneswar
Odisha-751024, India
{tarachand.ism,nabin.ghosh11}@gmail.com,
prasantajana@yahoo.com

Abstract. Cluster-based multi-hop routing is one of the proficient techniques to prolong the network lifetime of wireless sensor networks (WSNs). In this technique, a cluster head (CH) sends its data packet via other CHs to the sink. However, in most of such routing techniques, a CH selects a single path to forward the data to the sink which results in imbalance energy consumption of some of the CHs along the path and hence limits the network lifetime. In this paper, we propose a new distributed energy-aware multi-level routing algorithm (EMRA) to maximize the network lifetime. In the proposed algorithm, CHs are assigned various levels based on the distance between the CHs and the sink. Furthermore, a backbone network (BN) is constructed over these CHs rooted at the sink. We devise a simple and efficient technique through which each CH in the BN selects a few CHs as forwarding nodes keeping the load balancing among the CHs. Simulation results show that the proposed algorithm outperforms the existing ones in terms of network lifetime.

Keywords: Clustering, wireless sensor networks, multi-level routing, network lifetime.

1   Introduction

A wireless sensor network (WSN) consists of tiny sensor devices capable of monitoring and recording the physical conditions such as temperature, humidity, vehicular movement, lighting conditions, pressure, noise levels, etc. Mission critical applications of WSNs include military applications, environmental monitoring, disaster systems and heath care [1]. The sensor nodes build the network autonomously after deployment and collect the data from the target area and send them to the sink wirelessly. In many applications, WSNs are deployed in harsh environments where replenishment of the sensor nodes is not feasible at all, but the sensor nodes are battery operated with limited power source. Therefore, the energy consumption of the sensor nodes is treated as the most serious issue for the long run operation of the WSN.

Clustering sensor nodes is an efficient technique which is known for energy saving of the sensor nodes [2]. In this approach, a two-tier WSN is formed by grouping sensor nodes into clusters in the lower tier. Each cluster has a leader referred as

R. Natarajan (Ed.): ICDCIT 2014, LNCS 8337, pp. 111–121, 2014.

cluster head (CH) and remaining nodes act as cluster members (CMs). CHs collect the data from their respective cluster members (CMs) and aggregate them. The CHs then send the aggregated data to the sink directly or via other CHs, thus forming the upper tier. There are two types of communication exist between CH and the sink, i.e., single-hop communication and multi-hop communication. In single-hop communication, CHs send their aggregated data to the sink directly. To avoid long haul communication between CHs and the sink multi-hop routing over sensor nodes is introduced. In multi-hop communication, CH sends its data packets via other CHs/intermediate sensor nodes to reach the sink. However, this technique introduces new overheads in the network, CHs near the sink burdened with heavy relaying load, load balance of the CHs and other issues. There are many multi-hop routing protocols have been proposed in the literature [3-12]. However, a major drawback in these techniques is that they select a single routing path between a CH and the sink. Such approaches excessively drain the residual energy of some of the CHs along the routing path and hence limit the network lifetime.

In this paper, we propose a new distributed energy-aware multi-level routing algorithm (EMRA) for WSNs to maximize the network lifetime. The proposed routing algorithm is divided into two phases; backbone network (BN) formation and routing. In BN, CHs are assigning with various levels based on the distance between CHs and the sink. Then, we develop a simple and elegant method by which each CH chooses a set of CHs as forwarding nodes to route the data. Next each CH distributes and transmits the data packet to these nodes according to the proposed cost function (CF) so that the load of the forwarding nodes is balanced and the energy consumed by the CHs is also minimized in the process of data routing. We perform experiments on the proposed algorithm and the results are compared with the existing ones such EADC [11] and EEPA [12].

Remaining sections of the paper are organized as follows. In Section 2, we present the related works followed by the system model for the proposed work in Section 3. In Section 4, we elaborate the algorithm. Simulation results are given in Section 5 and Section 6 concludes the paper.

2   Related Work

Many cluster-based routing protocols have been developed which can be found in [3-20]. These protocols are mainly divided two types, single-hop communication [13-20] and multi-hop communication [3-12]. In single hop communication, CHs collect the data from their CMs, aggregate them and then send it to the sink directly. An advantage of this technique is that the nodes near to the sink do not carry any incoming traffic and therefore no hot spot problem is raised in the network. However, these techniques suffer from excess drain of energy of the sensor nodes due to long haul communication with the sink and also energy consumption increases as number of CHs in the network increases, e.g., forced CHs [16]. On the other hand, in multi-hop communication, CHs forward their data via other CHs/intermediate sensor nodes. As a result, the transmission energy of the CHs is drastically reduced. In [11], author proposed a cluster based routing protocol for WSNs. In this approach, a node is selected as CH whose residual energy is greater than the average residual energy of its neighbor nodes. Further, each CH selects next hop CH as the forwarding node towards the sink which is based on the residual energy of the next hop CH and its number of CMs. An energy efficient and power aware (EEPA) multi-hop routing protocol has been proposed in [12]. In this protocol, each CH selects a set of intermediate CHs to build the path towards the sink. The selection of intermediate CH is based on its residual energy and distance with it. Finally, the path information receives by the sink which contains the residual energy of the CHs belong to the path. Similarly, the sink also receives the multiple path information from the same CHs. Then the sink calculates efficient path and acknowledges the same to the CH in the reverse direction of the same path. However, one common drawback in these techniques is that each CH selects only one forwarding CH to route all its incoming packets including its own data packet to the forwarding CHs. Such approach excessively drain the residual energy of some of the CHs due to imbalance of the relaying load.

In our work, we adopt the following strategies to overcome the above mentioned shortcoming:

1) Each CH finds a set of CHs towards the sink independently; among these CHs few nodes are selected as forwarding nodes whose residual energy are greater than equal to average residual energy of the CHs. This approach helps in selecting the CHs having relatively higher residual energy than others.

2) To balance the relaying load over these forwarding CHs, each CH distributes and transmits the data packets over these forwarding nodes. Distribute of data packets is according to the residual energy of the CHs and energy consumed to transmit data packet to these nodes.

3   System Model

Here, we present some assumptions made for the network model for the proposed algorithm followed by the energy model of the sensor nodes.

3.1   Network Model

We assume the following model of the WSN. A homogenous set of sensor nodes are deployed in the target area and the sensor nodes become static once they are deployed. The sink is also static and located outside the target area. Initially, the sensor nodes are charged with equal amount of energy. The sensor nodes are aware of their locations and the location of the sink.

In addition to this, we also assume that the WSN is a two tire network with the clusters of the sensor nodes. The sensor nodes are grouped into the clusters following some distributed clustering algorithm such as BDCP [20]. In this algorithm, selection of CHs is based on the residual energy of the sensor nodes and cluster formation is based on both the residual energy of the CHs and distance between CHs and the sensor nodes. Each sensor node belongs to only one cluster. Periodically, the role of CHs is rotated among the sensor node in order to balance their energy consumption of the CHs. CHs collect the data from their respective CMs and aggregate them. In contrast to the proposed algorithm, CHs send the aggregated data to the sink directly. A new set of CHs are selected for every new upcoming communication round in order to balance the energy consumption of the CHs. Here, we assume that the round in BDCP is quite similar to the communication round as adopted in LEACH [13] which is a well known protocol for WSNs.

3.2   Energy Model

The energy model of the sensor nodes is adopted from [13]. The energy consumed to transmit β-bit data packet over the distance $D_{(i,j)}$ where, $D_{(i,j)}$ is the distance between the node i and j is given as

$$E_{tx}(i, j) = \begin{cases} (\alpha_{tx} + \varepsilon_{fs}D_{(i,j)}^2)\beta & D_{(i,j)}) < d_0 \\ (\alpha_{tx} + \varepsilon_{mp}D_{(i,j)}^4)\beta & D_{(i,j)} \geq d_0 \end{cases} \tag{1}$$

where α_{tx} and α_{rx} are the energy dissipated in transmitting and receiving the data bit respectively. If the distance between the sender and receiver is less than d_0 then free space (ε_{fs}) channel model is used. Otherwise, multi-path fading (ε_{mp}) channel model is used. The energy consumed in receiving the β-bit data is given by

$$E_{rx}(j) = \alpha_{rx}\beta \tag{2}$$

4   Proposed Algorithm

The proposed protocol is divided into two phases, namely, backbone network formation and routing. They are subsequently discussed as follows.

4.1   Backbone Network (BN) Formation

Here, we devise a simple formula to find the level of a CH in the network. The whole region of the WSN is divided into various levels which is calculated as follows. Let $L(u)$ denote the level of the cluster head u which is calculated as follows

$$L[u] = \left\lceil \frac{D_{(u, sink)}}{r} \right\rceil \tag{3}$$

where r is the sensing range of the sensor nodes and $D_{(u, sink)}$ is the distance between the cluster head u and the sink. The distance between CHs and between CH and the sink is calculated based on the received signal strength by the CH or the sink [21]. This is a well known technique for distance measurement between two nodes in wireless sensor networks. By default, the level of the sink is assumed to be at zero level, i.e., $L[sink] = 0$. Each CH broadcast a control message within the range of kr (initially $k = 2$) to find its next hop neighbor CHs towards the sink. The message contains its identification number (ID), level (L). If there is no acknowledgement from any CHs within the timeout period of the range kr $(k = 2)$ then the node increments the k value, i.e., $k = 3$, and again broadcast the same control message, where k is the constant coefficient. This process continues until the CH receives the acknowledgement from any of its next hop CHs. Note that, the value of k never crosses the 2 until the first node dying in the network. If a CH receives the control messages especially from higher level CHs then the node replies with the message consisting of its ID, residual energy (E). Thus the backbone network is formed with the CHs by their message receipt and acknowledgement. The pseudo code of the proposed BN formation is presented in the following Fig. 1.

Algorithm: BN Formation

(01) **for** i = 1 **to** N_{CH} **do** /*N_{CH} is the number of CHs*/
(02) $L[u_i] = D_{(ui,sink)})/r$;
(03) **end for**
(04) $k = 1$;
(05) **for** i = 1 **to** N_{CH} **do**
(06) CH u_i broadcast control message in the range kr
(07) **If** no ack. received **then**
(08) k++;
(09) **goto to** step 6;
(10) **else**
(11) continue;
(12) **end for**

Fig. 1. Pseudo code for BN formation

4.2   Routing

In this phase, each CH selects a few lower level CHs from which it receives the acknowledgment. Let us assume that cluster head u belongs to the level $L[u]$ and it receives acknowledgment from the set of CHs, $v_1, v_2, \ldots, v_p$ such that that $L[v_i] < L[u]$, $\forall i, 1 \leq i \leq p$. Then, let μ be the average residual energy of the CHs which is calculated as follows

$$\mu = \frac{\sum_{i=1}^{p} E_r[v_i]}{p} \tag{4}$$

In the routing process, the cluster head u can forward data through any cluster head v_i which has residual energy greater than or equal to μ. By using μ, the CHs having relatively higher residual energy than the others can be selected for data forwarding. After forwarding the data packets, the residual energy of these CHs will be closer to that of the remaining CHs, whose residual energy is less than μ, thereby balancing the energy consumption of the CHs. Let w_1, w_2, w_3, w_4, ..., w_m are such CHs whore residual energy is greater than or equal to μ, where $m \leq p$. Then, cluster u distributes the data packets into following ratios

$$[\text{CF}(u, w_1)] : [\text{CF}(u, w_2)] : [\text{CF}(u, w_3)] : [\text{CF}(u, w_4)] : \cdots \cdots \cdots : [\text{CF}(u, w_m)] \tag{5}$$

and send the data packets to the CHs, where cost function (CF) is given by the following formula

$$\text{CF}(u, w) = \frac{E_r[w]}{E_{tx}(u, w)} \tag{6}$$

Here, $E[w]$ is the residual energy of the cluster head w and $E_{tx}(u, w)$ is the energy consumed by the cluster head u while transmitting a data packet (β-bit size) to the cluster head w (refer equation 1). For example, cluster head u has 6 packets to transmit to the sink. Let x, y, and z are selected as forwarding CHs and their given ratios of the CF are 3: 2: 1. Then, node u transmits 3, 2 and 1 data packets to CHs x, y and z respectively. Therefore, relaying load of the CHs is equalized with respect to their energy and the transmission energy of the node u is also considered.

Lemma 1. The message complexity for a CH to join the BN in worst case is $O(L)$ where L is a level of a CH in the network.

Proof. CH broadcast the control message within the range kr (initially, $k = 2$) to find its forwarding CHs. In case of unsuccessful attempt to find forwarding CHs it increments k and broadcast the same control message within the range kr ($k = 3$) and this process continues until $k = L$. The reason is that in the range of kr ($k = L$) a CH finds the sink finally. Therefore, the message complexity of a CH to join the BN is $O(L)$ in worst case.

Lemma 2. The time complexity of the proposed algorithm is $O(N)$ for N sensor nodes in the network.

Proof. Each CH calculates L and μ independently by using equations 3 and 4. This is done in constant time. According to equation 5, a CH needs to process N-1 CHs' residual energy in order to distribute the data packets to these CHs. Therefore, this operation can be done in $O(N)$ time.

5   Simulation Results

In this section, we test the performance of proposed algorithm EMRA and the results are compared with EADC [11] and EEPA [12]. We evaluated the proposed algorithm by considering two metrics namely, network lifetime and energy consumption. In our work, we quantify the network lifetime into two categories; (i) network lifetime when first node dies and (ii) network lifetime when fifty percent of nodes die. We also calculated the average energy consumed by the alive sensor nodes in the network and average remaining residual energy of the CHs to justify the network lifetime. Simulation program was written in Dev C++ and Matlab. The parameters used in the simulation program are shown in Table.1. Note that sink is assumed to be located at (0, 0) position, i.e., left corner of the target region.

Table 1. Parameters used in simulation and their values

Parameter Name	Notation	Value
Target area	A	100 ×100 m sq.
Sink location	S	(0,0)
No. of sensor nodes	N	200 to 500
Residual energy	E_r	0.5 J
Tx range	r	25 m
Control packet size	C_p	100 bits
Data packet size	D_p	500 bits
Tx or Rx electronics	α_{tx} or α_{rx}	50nJ/m^2/bit

In our experiments, we choose two types of network topology; (i) random and (ii) grid. In random topology, sensor nodes are randomly deployed in the target area whereas in grid deployment, sensor nodes are placed on the intersection of grid lines. These two scenarios are shown in Fig. 2(a) and 2(b) respectively. We study the performance of EMRA, EADC and EEPA by varying sensor nodes from 200 to 500 in both the scenarios.

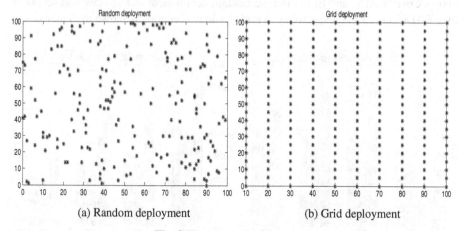

(a) Random deployment   (b) Grid deployment

Fig. 2. Topology of the network

5.1   Network Lifetime

In this section, we compared the network lifetime of EMRA (proposed algorithm) with EADC and EEPA in both the network deployment scenarios. From Fig. 3(a) and 3(b), we find that the proposed algorithm outperforms others in terms of network lifetime ($N = 200$).

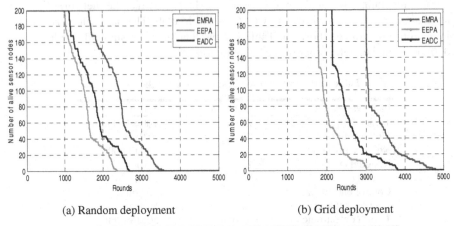

(a) Random deployment   (b) Grid deployment

Fig. 3. Network lifetime of various algorithms

We also tested the performance of the EMRA with those of EADC and EEPA by deploying 200, 300, 400 and 500 sensor nodes to find the lifetime of the network in two different cases, i) when first node dies and ii) when fifty percent of node die. From Fig. 4(a) and 4(b), we observe that EMRA attains minimum 45% and 60% lifetime enhancement over EADC and EEPA when first node died in both the scenarios. Similarly, Fig. 5(a) shows that EMRA achieves minimum 40% and 60% network over EADC and EEPA in case random deployment and 25-45% and 454-60% over EADC and EEPA respectively in grid topology scenario, as shown in Fig. 5(b).

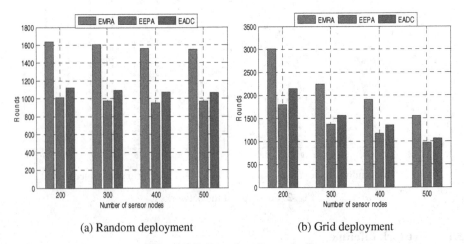

(a) Random deployment   (b) Grid deployment

Fig. 4. Lifetime when first node dies

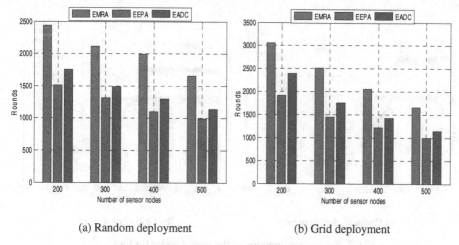

(a) Random deployment   (b) Grid deployment

Fig. 5. Lifetime when fifty percent of the node dies

5.2   Energy Consumption

To justify the network lifetime, we also measured energy consumption aspects of the sensor nodes. Here, we consider two metrics in our experiments, namely, average remaining residual energy of CHs and energy consumption of the sensor nodes. Fig. 6(a) and 6(b) show that the energy consumption of the CHs for EMRA is minimal as compared to EADC and EEPA. Fig. 7(a) and 7(b) demonstrates that the amount of energy spent by the sensor nodes in EMRA is very less as compared to EADC and EEPA.

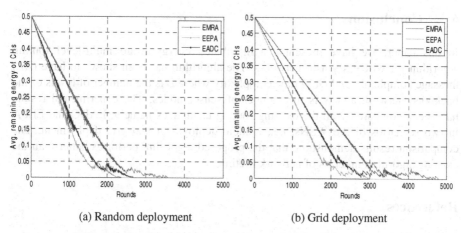

(a) Random deployment   (b) Grid deployment

Fig. 6. Average remaining residual energy of the CHs (in Joules)

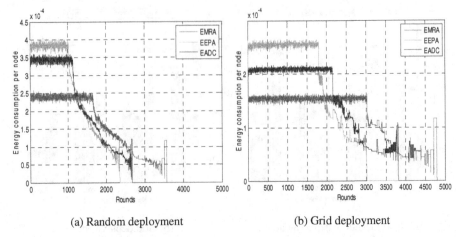

(a) Random deployment   (b) Grid deployment

Fig. 7. Energy consumption of the sensor nodes (in Joules)

The main reasons for better performance of the proposed algorithm can be summarized and justified as follows

1) The BN constructed in EMRA is a multi-level structure and sink is at the top of the BN. In this structure, each CH has multiple routes towards the sink and each CH divides data packets and transmits to the forwarding CH in such way that the energy consumption of the CHs is balanced. Hence the network lifetime is enhanced.
2) Furthermore, the selection criterion for forwarding CHs also contributed to the enhancement of the network lifetime.

6   Conclusion

In this paper, we have presented a distributed energy-aware multi-level routing algorithm for wireless sensor networks. The algorithm has been shown to have $O(L)$ message complexity and $O(N)$ time complexity where L is the number of levels of the backbone network and N is the number of sensor nodes. The experimental results have been compared with the existing routing techniques namely, EADC and EEPA in two scenarios of the WSNs, i.e., random deployment and grid deployment. The comparison results demonstrate that the proposed algorithm performs better than the existing algorithm in terms of network lifetime.

References

1. Akilidz, I.F., Su, W., Sankarasubramaniam, Y., Cayirci, E.: Wireless sensor networks: survey. Computer Networks 38, 393–422 (2002)
2. Abbasi, A.A., Younis, M.: A survey on clustering algorithms for wireless sensor networks. Computer Communication 30, 2826–2841 (2007)

3. Akkaya, K., Younis, M.: A survey on routing protocols for wireless sensor networks. Ad-Hoc Networks 3, 325–349 (2005)
4. Youssef, M., Younis, M., Arisha, K.A.: A constrained shortest-path energy-aware routing algorithm for wireless sensor networks 2, 794–799 (2002)
5. Ahmed, E.A.A., Abdulla, H.N., Nei, K.: Extending the lifetime of wireless sensor networks: A hybrid routing algorithm. Computer Communications 35, 1056–1063 (2012)
6. Boukerche, A., Pazzi, R.W.N., Araujo, R.B.: Fault-tolerant wireless sensor network routing protocols for the supervision of context-aware physical environments. Journal of Parallel and Distributed Computing 66, 586–599 (2006)
7. Perillo, M., Cheng, Z., Heinzelman, W.: On the problem of unbalanced load distribution in wireless sensor networks. In: Global Telecommunication Conference Workshops, pp. 74–79 (2004)
8. Muruganathan, S.D., Ma, D.C.F., Bhasin, R.I., Fapojuwo, A.: A centralized energy-efficient routing protocol for wireless sensor networks. IEEE Radio Communications 43, 8–13 (2005)
9. Liu, Y., Wang, Z.: Maximizing energy utilization routing scheme in wireless sensor networks based on minimum hops algorithm. Computers and Electrical Engineering 38, 703–721 (2012)
10. Fariborzi, H., Moghavvemi, M.: EAMTR: energy aware multi-tree routing for wireless sensor networks. IET Communication 3, 733–739 (2009)
11. Jiguo, Y., Yingying, Q., Guangui, W., Xin, G.: A cluster-based routing protocol for wireless sensor with non-uniform node distribution. International Journal of Electronics and Communications 66, 54–61 (2012)
12. Yu, M., Kin, K.L., Ankit, M.: A dynamic clustering and energy efficient routing techniques for sensor networks. IEEE Transaction on Wireless Communications 6, 3069–3079 (2007)
13. Heinzelman, W.B., Chandrakasan, A., Balakrishnan, H.: Energy-efficient communication protocols for wireless microsensor networks. In: Proceedings of Hawaii International Conference on System Sciences (2000)
14. Younis, O., Fahmy, S.: HEED: a hybrid, energy-efficient, distributed clustering approach for ad hoc sensor networks. IEEE Transaction on Mobile Computing 3, 366–379 (2004)
15. Ye, M., Li, C.F., Chen, G.H., Wu, J.: EECS: an energy efficient clustering scheme in wireless sensor networks. In: IEEE International Performance Computing and Communication Conference, pp. 535–540 (2005)
16. Cao, Y., He, C.: A distributed clustering algorithm with an adaptive backoff strategy for wireless sensor networks. IEICE Transactions on Communications 89-B(2), 609–613 (2006)
17. Navid, A., Alireza, V., Xu, W., Maria, G., Majid, S.: Cluster size optimization in sensor networks with decentralized cluster-based protocols. Computer Communication 35, 207–220 (2012)
18. Dimokas, N., Katsaros, D., Manolopoulos, Y.: Energy-efficient distributed clustering in wireless sensor networks. J. of Parallel Distributed Computing 70, 371–383 (2010)
19. Nauman, A., William, P., William, R., Shyamala, S.: A multi-criterion optimization technique for energy efficient cluster formation in wireless sensor networks. Information Fusion 12, 202–212 (2011)
20. Amgoth, T., Jana, P.K.: BDCP: A backoff-based distributed clustering protocol for wireless sensor networks. In: Proceedings of the International Conference on Advances in Computing, Communication and Informatics, pp. 1012–1016 (2013)
21. Patwari, N., O'Dea, R.J., Wang, Y.: Relative location in wireless networks. In: Proceedings of the IEEE Vehicular Technology Conference, vol. 2, pp. 1149–1153 (2001)

Minimum Range Assignment Problem for Two Connectivity in Wireless Sensor Networks

Bhawani Sankar Panda and D. Pushparaj Shetty

Computer Science and Application Group,
Department of Mathematics,
Indian Institute of Technology Delhi, Hauz Khas,
New Delhi 110016, India
{bspanda, prajshetty}@maths.iitd.ac.in

Abstract. A wireless sensor network (WSN) is modeled as weighted directed graph, with each sensor in the plane representing a vertex. The edges represent the link between two sensors. A cost function $c : E \to \mathbb{R}^+$ is associated with each edge E. The power of a node v is the maximum cost of its incident edges. The sum of powers of all nodes $v \in V$ is the total power of the graph. A graph $G = (V, E)$ is 2-connected and remains connected even if any one node is deleted from the graph. Fault tolerance is an important property of a network, which demands two or higher connectivity. In this paper we consider the problem of assigning transmit power to the nodes of a WSN, such that the resulting topology is two node-connected and the the total power of the network is minimized. The minimum power two-connected subgraph (MP2CS) problem is known to be NP-hard. We give a polynomial reduction from strong minimum energy topology problem to MP2CS problem. This leads to an alternate NP-hard proof for MP2CS problem. We propose a heuristic for MP2CS, which is based on MST augmentation. Through simulation we show that the proposed heuristics performs better than the existing heuristic for MP2CS problem. We then consider a special case of MP2CS problem, called the minimum power k backbone 2-connected subgraph(MPkB2CS) problem. We prove that MPkB2CS problem can be solved optimally in $O(n^3)$ time for $k = 2$, and propose a 2-approximation algorithm for $k = 3$. We show that MPkB2CS problem admits an approximation algorithm with approximation ratio $\frac{3(k+1)}{2}$ for $k > 3$.

Keywords: Wireless Sensor Networks, Topology Control Problem, Transmission Power Assignment, Heuristics, Graph Theory, Minimum Spanning Tree.

1 Introduction

Wireless Sensor Networks (WSNs) find wide applications in several fields [1]. A WSN is modelled using a weighted directed graph $G = (V, E, c)$, where vertex set V corresponds to the set of sensor nodes and edge E represents the link between two sensors and $c : E \to \mathbb{R}^+$ is the cost function. The cost function

R. Natarajan (Ed.): ICDCIT 2014, LNCS 8337, pp. 122–133, 2014.

here determines the assignment of transmission powers to the nodes. Let H be a spanning subgraph of G. For a vertex $u \in V$, the power of u is the maximum cost of an edge in H, incident on u, i.e $P_H(u) = \max_{uv \in E} c(uv)$. The total power of H is given by $P(H) = \sum_{u \in V} P_H(u)$. The power assignment problem is also called range assignment problem.

In the wireless communication the power needed to to support a link uv is $|uv|^\alpha$, where $|uv|$ is the Euclidean distance between u and v, α is *distance-power gradient* [2], which may vary between 2 and 5 depending on the various environmental factors. In our formulation we choose $\alpha = 2$. Given a set of sensor nodes S, a range assignment for S is a function $r : S \to \mathbb{R}^+$. The cost of a range assignment r is the sum of overall power consumption, that is

$$cost(r) = \sum_{v \in S} r(v).$$

Given a range assignment r for a set of sensors S, the following two kinds of communication graphs are defined in [5].

- $\overrightarrow{G_r} = (S, A_r)$ is a directed graph, for range assignment r where the radio stations present in S represents the vertices and A_r represents the edge set, where $A_r = \{(s_i, s_j)| \ d(s_i, s_j)^2 \leq r(s_i)\}$. In other words, a directed edge (x, y) indicates that y is within the range of x.
- $G_r = (S, E_r)$ is an undirected graph, for range assignment r where the radio stations present in S represents the vertices and E_r represents the edge set, where an edge $uv \in E_r$ if and only if node u can send data to node v and v can send data to u, that is, $uv \in E_r$ if and only if $\min(r_u, r_v) \geq d(u, v)^2$. In other words, G_r contains only bidirectional edges. When there are only bidirectional edges the range assignment is called *symmetric*.

Topology control problem in WSNs is to find a communication subgraph that satisfies some prescribed properties such as connectivity, bi-connectivity, minimum degree etc. The topology control by adjusting the transmit powers of nodes in a multihop wireless network is studied in [12]. The different connectivity requirements like simple connectivity, strong connectivity and broadcast are discussed in [7]. For more details about topology control in WSN, we refer to [9,13].

Fault-tolerance is an important network property, which demands 2 or high connectivity between any two nodes. Fault tolerance is often measured by node-connectivity. A graph is said to be k-node/edge-connected if and only if there are k-node/edge-disjoint paths between every pair of vertices [14]. It may be noted that if a graph is k-node connected, then it is also k-edge connected, but the converse is not true. For this reason, and because node connectivity is important for resilience to node failures and hotspots, we shall consider only vertex connectivity. We will denote k-node connectivity as k-connectivity. Thus when $k = 1$ the graph is *connected* and if $k = 2$, it is *biconnected*.

In general minimum power(range) assignment problem is to find a subgraph H of G such that H satisfies some connectivity constraint and $P(H)$ is minimum. A biconnected network, unlike a merely connected one, has the desirable property that the loss of any single node or link will not partition the network. Furthermore, it affords multiple-path redundancy between every pair of nodes enabling fault tolerance, load balancing or both [12].

In this paper we consider a Minimum Power 2 Connected Subgraph (MP2CS) problem. Given a graph G, representing a WSN, MP2CS problem is defined as the problem of finding a subgraph H of G such that H is 2-connected and the total power $P(H)$ is minimum. MP2CS problem is known to be NP-hard [3]. We establish an alternate proof for NP-hardness of MP2CS problem. We propose a heuristic for MP2CS based on MST-augmentation technique. We compare the performance of our heuristic with existing heuristics. We then consider a special case of MP2CS problem called the minimum power k-backbone 2-connected subgraph (MPkB2CS) problem and propose algorithms for this MPkB2CS problem.

2   Related Work

Minimum power bi-connectivity problem is studied by Lloyd et al. [10]. They studied the the general topology control problem as a triple of the form $\langle \mathbb{M}, \mathbb{P}, \mathbb{O} \rangle$, where $\mathbb{M} \in \{\text{Dir,Undir}\}$ represents the graph model, $\mathbb{P}$ represents desired graph property and $\mathbb{O} \in \{\text{MaxP, TotalP}\}$ (abbreviation for maximum power and total power) represents minimization objective. The minimum power biconnectivity problem is proved to be NP-hard in the journal version of the same paper by Calinescu and Wan [3]. They proposed a MST-augmentation based approximation algorithm for minimum power bi-connectivity problem. They proved that performance ratio of MST-augmentation based algorithm is at most 8. They provided a constant approximation algorithm with ratio 4 for min-power 2-connectivity. The approximation results for minimum power k-connectivity problem is given by Jia et al. [8]. More recently, Zeev Nutov [11] gave an improved approximation ratio of 3 and 4 for MPkCS problem for $k = 2$ and $k = 3$ respectively.

3   NP-Hardness of MP2CS

Given an undirected graph G, representing a WSN, the Strong Minimum Energy Topology (SMET) problem seeks to find a spanning tree T of G such that $P(T)$ is minimum. SMET problem is studied by Cheng et al. [4] and they proved that SMET problem is NP-hard. A feasible solution for SMET is a spanning tree. We propose an alternate NP-hardness proof for MP2CS by establishing a reduction from SMET to MP2CS problem. The alternate proof helps us to understand the solution to MP2CS problem in terms of SMET problem.

Problem: Strong Minimum Energy Topology (SMET) Decision Problem
Instance: (K_n, w, M), where K_n is a complete graph with n nodes, $w : E(K_n) \to \mathbb{R}^+$ is a weight function and M is a positive real value.
Question: Does there exist a spanning tree T of K_n such that $P(T) \leq M$? The following theorem recalls that SMET problem is NP-complete

Theorem 1. [4] *SMET problem is NP-complete.*

Problem: Minimum Power two Connected Subgraph (MP2CS) Decision Problem.

Instance: (K_n, w, M), where K_n is a complete graph with n nodes, $w : E(K_n) \to \mathbb{R}^+$ is a weight function, and M is a positive real value.

Question: Does there exist a 2-node-connected subgraph H of K_n such that $P(T) \leq M$?

We prove that MP2CS problem is NP-complete.

Theorem 2. *MP2CS problem is NP-complete.*

Proof. Given a subgraph H, we can test if H has 2-connected property in $O(n^2)$ time for a graph with n nodes. It can be tested if $P(H) \leq M$ in polynomial time. So MP2CS$\in$NP. The NP-hardness of MP2CS is established using a reduction from SMET problem. Let (K_n, w, M) be an instance of SMET problem. We construct an instance (K_{n+1}, w', M') of MP2CS problem as follows:

Let $V(K_n) = \{v_1, v_2, \ldots, v_n\}$. Set $V(K_{n+1}) = V(K_n) \cup \{u\}$. The weight function w' is defined as follows. $w'(v_i v_j) = w(v_i v_j)$ for all $1 \leq i, j \leq n$, $w'(v_i u) = 1, 1 \leq i \leq n$. The construction for $n = 4$ is illustrated in Figure 1. Note that the instance (K_{n+1}, w', M') of MP2CS problem can be constructed in polynomial time from an instance (K_n, w, M) of SMET problem.

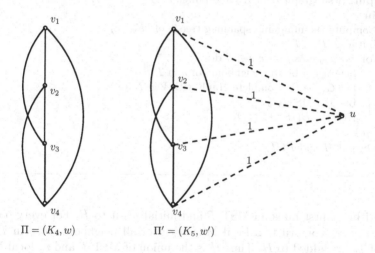

$\Pi = (K_4, w)$ $\Pi' = (K_5, w')$

Fig. 1. Reduction from SMET to MP2CS

Claim. K_n has a spanning tree T such that $P(T) \leq M$ if and only if K_{n+1} has a 2 connected subgraph H such that $P(H) \leq M + 1$.

Without loss of generality it is assumed that the cost of each edge in K_n is greater than or equal to 1.

First assume that T is a spanning tree of K_n such that $P(T) \leq M$. Consider a subgraph H, where $V(H) = V(T) \cup \{u\}$ and $E(H) = E(T) \cup_{i=1}^{n} (uv_i)$. By this we can see that H is 2 connected. The power assigned $P(H) \leq P(T) + 1 \leq M + 1$

Next assume that H is a 2-connected subgraph of K_{n+1} such that $P(H) \leq M+1$. Since $P(H) \leq M+1$, vertex u connected to all $v_i \in V(K_n)$. Now consider the subgraph T with $E(T) = E(H) \setminus \cup_{i=1}^{n}(v_i u)$ and $V(T) = V(H) \setminus \{u\}$. We can see that T is a spanning tree of K_n such that $P(T) \leq (M+1) - 1 = M$.

So (K_n, w, M) is an yes instance of SMET problem if and only if $(K_{n'}, w', M+1)$ is an yes instance of MP2CS problem.

So we conclude that MP2CS problem is NP-complete.   □

4   MST-Augmentation Algorithm for MP2CS

Calinescu and Wan [3] presented an algorithm for minimum power biconnected spanning subgraph H by augmenting an MST. Their algorithm is presented in Algorithm 1 for completeness. The vertices of G that are adjacent to a vertex $u \in V(G)$ are called the *neighbours* of u in G. $N_G(u) = \{x | xu \in E(G)\}$ is the *neighbourhood* of u in G.

Algorithm 1. MST-Augmentation for MP2CS problem

Input: (K_n, w), where K_n is a complete graph having cost function w
Output: A subgraph H of K_n and power $P(H)$
1 **begin**
2 | Compute the minimum spanning tree T of (K_n, w) ;
3 | Initialize $H = T$;
4 | **for** *each non-leaf node $v \in T$* **do**
5 | | Let $N_T(v)$ be the neighbours of v in T;
6 | | Let G_v be the complete graph with $V \in N_v(T)$;
7 | | Let $T_v = MST(G_v)$;
8 | | $E(H) = E(H) \cup E(T_v)$;
9 | **end**
10 | Output H and $P(H)$;
11 **end**

Algorithm 1 first finds an MST T and initializes it to H. For every non-leaf node $v \in T$, it constructs a local MST T_v over all neighbours of v in T. The edges of T_v are added to H. Thus H is the union of MST T and n_i local MSTs, where n_i is the number of non-leaf nodes. The following lemma shows that the subgraph H is 2-connected.

Lemma 1. [3] *Subgraph H generated by MST-augmentation algorithm is 2-Connected.*

5   Proposed Heuristic for MP2CS Problem

In this section, we propose a new heuristic for MP2CS problem which is also based on MST-augmentation. The existing Algorithm 1 constructs a local MST of the neighbours of every non leaf node. Then augments the MST with these local MSTs. We can see that for each non leaf node v, the size of local MST is $|N(v)| - 1$. The total size is the sum of all local MSTs over non-leaf nodes. But if we consider augmentation at the leaf nodes, the size of Local MST is $n_l - 1$, where n_l is the number of leaf nodes. With this motivation we propose our algorithm below. We first obtain the solution for SMET and then augment it to get solution to MP2CS.

Algorithm 2. MST-Aug-leaf for MP2CS problem

   Input: (K_n, w), where K_n is a complete graph having cost function w
   Output: A subgraph H of K_n and power $P(H)$
1 **begin**
2   Compute the minimum spanning tree T of (K_n, w) ;
3   Let $L(T)$ be the set of leaf nodes in T;
4   Let G_v be the complete graph with $V(G_v) = L(T)$;
5   Let $T_v = \text{MST}(G_v)$;
6     $E(H) = E(T) \cup E(T_v)$;
7   Output H and $P(H)$;
8 **end**

Algorithm 2 first computes a minimum spanning tree T of K_n. It constructs another minimum spanning tree T_v over all the graph induced by the the leaf nodes of T. The subgraph H is the union of T and T_v.

Lemma 2. *Subgraph H generated by Algorithm 2 is 2-connected.*

Proof. Let T be a MST generated in Step 2 of the Algorithm 2. Let $L = \{u_1 \ldots u_l\}$ be the set of leaf nodes in T. A spanning tree T_v over the nodes in L connects all leaf nodes. Since H contains the union of T and T_v, there are two vertex disjoint paths between any every pair of vertices in H. Hence H is 2-node connected. □

The following lemma explains the time complexity of Algorithm 2.

Lemma 3. *The running time of Algorithm 2 is $O(n^2 \log n)$*

Proof. The popular Kruskal's algorithm and Prim's algorithm for MST takes $O(n^2 \log n)$ time. Algorithm MST-Aug-leaf computes MST twice: one for K_n and other over graph G_v, induced by leaf nodes T. Merging the two MSTs take $O(n)$ time. The time taken to compute $P(H)$, the transmission power assignment is at most $O(n^2)$. Hence the total running time is $O(n^2 \log n)$. □

6   Experimental Results

We implement the heuristics based on the general approach outlined in [10]. Step 2 of this outline asks for a edge subgraph with specific property $\mathbb{P}$. The property $\mathbb{P}$ in our case is 2-node connected subgraph. We implement the existing heuristic MST-Aug proposed by Calinescu and Wan [3] and our proposed heuristic MST-Aug-leaf. It may be noted that when the specific property $\mathbb{P}$ is simple connectivity, then problem is called SMET [4]. So we include these three heuristics, namely MST, MST-aug and MST-aug-leaf in our comparison.

In our experiments we consider n nodes randomly distributed in a square grid of size 1000×1000. The transmission power needed for a sensor s_i to send packet to a sensor s_j is given by the power function $f(s_i, s_j) = t.d^{\alpha}$, where t is a function of signal-to-noise ratio at s_i, d is the Euclidean distance between i and j and α is a constant related to path loss. In typical experiments α is between 2 to 5. In our computational experiments we set $t = 1$ and $\alpha = 2$.

Our algorithm is run for increasing value of n in steps of 5 starting from $n = 25$. For each value of n, the algorithm is run 100 times and average of these values for total power is reported in Table 1 for selected values of n. The last column in the table indicates the percentage of times when proposed heuristics is better than MST-aug.

Table 1. Comparison of Total power consumption

No.of.Nodes	SMET-power	MST-aug	MST-aug-leaf	% better
25	883992	2167023	2234865	36
30	873933	2084514	2054713	46
40	845180	2083801	1918005	67
50	828196	2008568	1930113	70
60	811428	1973361	1834057	75
70	826902	1989699	1831497	85
80	817447	1999197	1801398	91
90	801242	1979941	1753221	98
100	801433	1982573	1743454	93
110	798960	1962206	1721757	96
120	797089	1953228	1709284	98
130	782698	1928711	1684042	98
140	778764	1890343	1665384	99
150	778874	1885629	1642799	100
160	769100	1879536	1641684	100
170	778324	1882527	1619894	100
180	762178	1859630	1625437	100
190	768196	1886227	1611462	100
200	768295	1902505	1601238	100

The total power consumption is plotted in Figure 2. This shows that for $n > 25$ proposed heuristic consumes less power on an average. For $n > 100$, the percentage of times the proposed heuristic gives better result is almost 100. The plot corresponding to our proposed algorithm is shown by legend MST-Aug-leaf in Figure 2.

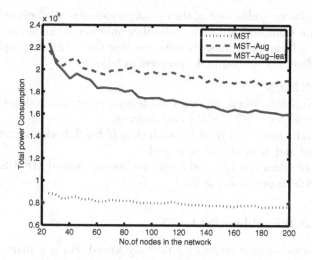

Fig. 2. Total power for the heuristics

Some applications demand computation of maximum power. So we plot the maximum power computed by our algorithm in Figure 3. As our algorithm is run several times for each value of n with different seed for random number in every run, it important to establish the stability of our algorithm. The variance of the total power is plotted in Figure 4. The almost overlapping plot for MST-aug and MST-aug-leaf is an indication that our algorithms are stable.

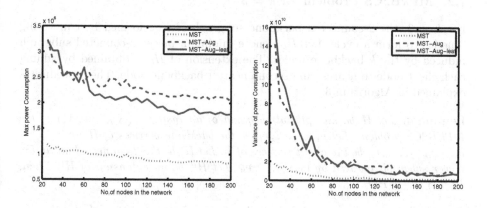

Fig. 3. Maximum power consumption   **Fig. 4.** Variance of total power

7   Minimum Power k Backbone 2 Connected Subgraph

As most WSN are hierarchical in nature [6]. Therefore it is useful to consider minimum power k backbone 2 connected subgraph (MPkB2CS). In this arrangement there are k-backbone nodes, rest of the $(n - k)$ nodes are called *client nodes*. The client nodes can communicate with each other only via backbone nodes. The k-backbone nodes form a 2-connected structure and the entire subgraph H is also 2-connected. Formally, we define the problem as follows.

Problem: MPkB2CS

Instance : (K_n, k, w), where K_n is a complete graph with n nodes, k is positive integer and $w : E(K_n) \to \mathbb{R}^+$ is the cost function.

Question: Find a subgraph H of K_n such that H has k backbone nodes, which are 2-connected and H is also 2-connected.

MPkB2CS problem can be considered as a special case of MP2CS. Below we consider MPkB2CS problem $k \geq 2$.

7.1   MPkB2CS Problem for $k = 2$

For $k = 2$, we can see that problem is trivially solved. For any pair of backbone nodes (x, y), connect the remaining $n - 2$ nodes, that is $V \setminus \{x, y\}$ to both x and y. The resulting subgraph is 2-connected as every client node form a cycle with backbone nodes (x, y). Since there are $\binom{n}{2}$ (x, y) pairs, and connecting $n-2$ nodes to (x, y) takes $O(n)$ time, MP2B2CS problem can be solved optimally in $O(n^3)$ time. Hence we have the following theorem.

Theorem 3. *MPkB2CS problem can be solved optimally in $O(n^3)$ time for $k = 2$.*

7.2   MPkB2CS Problem for $k = 3$

For $k = 3$, the 2-connected backbone subgraph can be formed by connecting 3 nodes to form a cycle. Let H_k denote minimum power 2-conncted subgraph induced by the k backbone nodes. The extension of H_k is obtained by adding each client node to nearest and second nearest backbone node. The procedure is explained in Algorithm 3.

Lemma 4. *Let H be an optimal subgraph of an instance (K_n, w, k, M) of the MPkB2CS problem. Let $v_1, v_2, \ldots, v_k$ be the backbone vertices of H and $v_{k+1}, v_{k+2}, \ldots, v_n$ be the client vertices of T. Let H' be the 2-connected minimum power subgraph induced by $v_1, v_2, \ldots, v_k$. Let H'' be an extension of H'. Then, $P(H'') \leq \frac{k+1}{2} P(H)$.*

Proof. T'' is a 2-connected subgraph of K_n. Let $m = \max\{w(xy)|xy \in E(H) \setminus E(H')$. So $P_H(v_i) \geq m$ for some $i \in \{1, 2, \ldots, k\}$. Hence, $P(H) \geq 2m$. Note that $P_{H''}(v) \leq P_H(v)$ for all $v \in V \setminus \{v_1, v_2, \ldots, v_k\}$. Since $P_{H''}(v_j) = \max\{P_H(v_j), m\}, 1 \leq j \leq k$, $P(H'') \leq (k - 1)m + P(H)$. Since $P(H) \geq 2m$, $P(H'') \leq \frac{k-1}{2} P(H) + P(H) \leq \frac{k+1}{2} P(H)$.   □

The following algorithm explains the construction of a minimum power k backbone 2-connected subgraph.

Algorithm 3. Extension of H_k

Input: H_k and complete graph K_n
Output: Extension of H_k
1 **begin**
2 | Let $V(H_k) = \{v_1 \ldots v_k\}$;
3 | **for** $i = 1$ *to* k **do**
4 | | $X_{i_k} = \emptyset$;
5 | **end**
6 | **for** *each* $a \in V - \{v_1 \ldots v_k\}$ **do**
7 | | $i_1 =$index: $\min_{j=1 \ldots k}(av_j)$;
8 | | $X_{i_1} = X_{i_1} \cup a$;
9 | | $i_2 =$index: secondMin $_{j=1 \ldots k}(av_j)$;
10 | | $X_{i_2} = X_{i_2} \cup a$;
11 | **end**
12 | $E_H = E_H \cup E_i$, where $E_i = v_i x | x \in X_i 1 \le i \le k$;
13 **end**

Algorithm 4. Algorithm MPkB2CS

Input: (K_n, w, k), where K_n is a complete graph having cost function w and k is a fixed integer constant.
Output: A subgraph H with k backbone nodes
1 **begin**
2 | Let H be any arbitrary 2 connected subgraph of K_n having exactly k backbone vertices.
3 | **for** *each subset* V_k *of* $V(K_n)$ *of* k *elements* **do**
4 | | Compute H', the 2-connected minimum power subgraph induced by $v_1, v_2, \ldots, v_k$.
5 | | **if** $P(Extension(H')) \le P(H)$ **then**
6 | | | $H = Extension(H')$;
7 | | **end**
8 | **end**
9 | output(H);
10 **end**

Theorem 4. *MPkB2CS problem has a 2-approximation algorithm time for* $k = 3$.

Proof. Step 4 of Algorithm MPkB2CS can be computed optimally for $k = 3$, as cycle involving 3 vertices forms the minimum power 2-connected subgraph. There are $\binom{n}{k}$ subsets of $V(K_n)$ of size k, where k is a fixed constant, the number of iterations in Step 3 of the algorithm is $O(n^k)$. The Extension(H') and $P(H')$ can be computed in $O(n)$ time. Hence Algorithm MPkB2CS takes $O(n^{k+1})$ time. Since k is a fixed constant, it is a polynomial time algorithm.

Let H^* be an optimal power 2-connected subgraph with k backbone nodes. Let H' be the 2-connected subgraph induced by these k backbone nodes. Let

H'' be an extension of H'. From Lemma 4, $P(H'') \leq \frac{k+1}{2}P(H^*)$. Let H be the output of Algorithm 4. Clearly $P(H) \leq P(H'')$. So $P(H) \leq \frac{k+1}{2}P(H^*)$. For $k = 3$, $P(H) \leq 2P(H^*)$. □

7.3 MPkB2CS Problem for $k > 3$

For $k > 3$, forming a 2-connected backbone subgraph becomes non trivial. As we know that MP2CS problem is NP-complete, the following corollary follows.

Corollary 1. *MPkB2CS problem is NP-hard for $k > 3$.*

There are many approximation results for MPkCS. The following lemma shows the most recent result.

Lemma 5. *[11] MPkCS has approximation ratio of 3 for $k = 2$.*

Theorem 5. *MPkB2CS problem has $\frac{3(k+1)}{2}$-approximation algorithm time for $k > 3$.*

Proof. The Step 4 of the Algorithm 4 is to compute MP2CS of the k backbone nodes. From Lemma 5, this computation has a performance ratio of 3. From Theorem 4, computing the extension of H_k and finding minimum power subgraph among these has performance ratio of $\frac{k+1}{2}$. Hence MPkB2CS problem has approximation ratio of $\frac{3(k+1)}{2}$ for $k > 3$. □

8   Conclusion

In this paper we studied the minimum power 2-connected subgraph (MP2CS) problem. We established a simple alternate proof for NP-harness of MP2CS. We proposed a MST-augmentation based heuristic for MP2CS problem. By simulation study, we showed that the proposed heuristics performs better as the number of nodes n increases. We studied a special case of the MP2CS problem called Minimum power k backbone 2-connected subgraph (MPkB2CS) problem, and proposed a 2-approximation algorithm for MPkB2CS for $k = 3$ and $\frac{3(k+1)}{2}$-approximation algorithm for $k > 3$.

References

1. Akyildiz, I.F., Su, W., Sankarasubramaniam, Y., Cayirci, E.: Wireless sensor networks: a survey. Computer Networks 38(4), 393–422 (2002)
2. Boukerche, A.: Handbook of algorithms for wireless networking and mobile computing. CRC Press (2005)
3. Calinescu, G., Wan, P.-J.: Range assignment for high connectivity in wireless ad hoc networks. In: Pierre, S., Barbeau, M., An, H.-C. (eds.) ADHOC-NOW 2003. LNCS, vol. 2865, pp. 235–246. Springer, Heidelberg (2003)

4. Cheng, X., Narahari, B., Simha, R., Cheng, M.X., Liu, D.: Strong minimum energy topology in wireless sensor networks: Np-completeness and heuristics. IEEE Transactions on Mobile Computing 2(3), 248–256 (2003)
5. Clementi, A.E.F., Huiban, G., Penna, P., Rossi, G., Verhoeven, Y.C.: Some recent theoretical advances and open questions on energy consumption in ad-hoc wireless networks. In: Proceedings of the 3rd Workshop on Approximation and Randomization Algorithms in Communication Networks (ARACNE), pp. 23–38 (2002)
6. Estrin, D., Govindan, R., Heidemann, J., Kumar, S.: Next century challenges: Scalable coordination in sensor networks. In: Proceedings of the 5th Annual ACM/IEEE International Conference on Mobile Computing and Networking, pp. 263–270. ACM (1999)
7. Fuchs, B.: On the hardness of range assignment problems. Networks 52(4), 183–195 (2008)
8. Jia, X., Kim, D., Makki, S., Wan, P.J., Yi, C.W.: Power assignment for k-connectivity in wireless ad hoc networks. Journal of Combinatorial Optimization 9(2), 213–222 (2005)
9. Labrador, M.A., Wightman, P.M.: Topology Control in Wireless Sensor Networks: with a companion simulation tool for teaching and research. Springer (2009)
10. Lloyd, E.L., Liu, R., Marathe, M.V., Ramanathan, R., Ravi, S.S.: Algorithmic aspects of topology control problems for ad hoc networks. Mobile Networks and Applications 10(1-2), 19–34 (2005)
11. Nutov, Z.: Approximating minimum-power k-connectivity. In: Coudert, D., Simplot-Ryl, D., Stojmenovic, I. (eds.) ADHOC-NOW 2008. LNCS, vol. 5198, pp. 86–93. Springer, Heidelberg (2008)
12. Ramanathan, R., Rosales-Hain, R.: Topology control of multihop wireless networks using transmit power adjustment. In: Proceedings of the Nineteenth Annual Joint Conference of the IEEE Computer and Communications Societies, INFOCOM 2000, vol. 2, pp. 404–413. IEEE (2000)
13. Santi, P.: Topology Control in Wireless Ad Hoc and Sensor Networks. John Wiley & Sons Ltd. (2005)
14. West, D.B.: Introduction to Graph Theory. Prentice Hall (2001)

A Digital-Geometric Approach for Computing Area Coverage in Wireless Sensor Networks

Dibakar Saha[1], Nabanita Das[2], and Shyamosree Pal[3]

[1,2] Advanced Computing and Microelectronics Unit,
Indian Statistical Institute, Kolkata, India
dibakar.saha10@gmail.com
ndas@isical.ac.in
[3] National Institute of Technology, Jamshedpur, India
shyamosree.pal@gmail.com

Abstract. Given a set of n sensor nodes distributed randomly over a 2-D plane, this paper addresses the problem of computing the area covered by the sensors assuming that each sensor covers a circular area of radius r. To make the computation simple, instead of considering real circles, a digital geometry based approach is followed here. A detailed study on intersection of digital circles reveals many interesting properties that lead to the development of a novel $O(n \log n)$ centralized algorithm using simple arithmetic operations for computing the area covered by n uniform digital circles. Next, a distributed version of the same is proposed to select a subset of nodes to cover a given area. Comparison with earlier works by simulation shows that the proposed distributed algorithm improves the estimated area coverage significantly.

Keywords: Digital Circle, Number-Theoretic Representation of Digital Circle, Intersection of Digital Circles, Area Coverage, Point Containment.

1 Introduction

In the present age of pervasive computing and communication, embedded systems, sensor networks, vehicular networks etc. are applied for various purposes like precision agriculture, homeland security, weather forecasting, surveillance, environment monitoring, smart health care technologies etc. In such environments, nodes with limited computation and communication capabilities are deployed in large number with the objective of providing services to the entire region under consideration. Hence recently, the classical problem of covering a plane with certain shapes has revived with great interest. In most of the works in this area, authors concentrated on the coverage problem [6], [9] and also focused on the optimal deployment of nodes to cover the area [7], [16]. For wireless sensor networks, efficient methods have been proposed by which a node can decide to go to the sleep mode to conserve energy if it finds that its sensing region is already covered by the awake nodes [5]. However, these techniques enable us either to

R. Natarajan (Ed.): ICDCIT 2014, LNCS 8337, pp. 134–145, 2014.

deploy the nodes in a predetermined way, or after deployment to dynamically schedule the nodes to guarantee full coverage. But in case, the region is not fully covered, it does not provide any direct information about the extent of coverage. In many applications, it may be the case that $80-90\%$ coverage is sufficient. Also, for large networks, or networks in inaccessible areas, it may not be always possible to deploy the nodes in predetermined positions. For these situations, in this paper, we assume that n nodes are distributed randomly on a 2-D plane. Each node covers a circular region of uniform radius. How to compute the area covered by all the nodes? With real circles in continuous paradigm, the straightforward way to calculate the area is obviously computation intensive, and therefore not feasible for nodes with limited computing power and small memory. The algorithms proposed in [11], [15] divide the region into square grids and then cover each grid with a sensor node. The coverage area of a sensor node is computed by taking the maximum square inscribed within the circle for simpler computation of covered area. Authors in [12], [13] proposed algorithms for the *Connected Set Cover Partitioning problem* in sensor networks. To make the computation simple as well as to have better approximation of covered area, in this paper, a digital geometry-based approach is followed where each real circle is represented as a digital circle [2],[3],[8]. In continuous paradigm, an $O(n\log^2 n)$ algorithm is developed in [14] to construct a generalized Voronoi diagram for a set of n circular discs that helps to compute the area in terms of circular sectors and quadrangles. A more efficient $O(n \log n)$ algorithm for circle intersection/union using a particular generalization of Voronoi diagram called power diagrams is presented in [1]. But to the best of our knowledge, so far no study has been reported on estimating the area covered by a set of digital circles. In this paper, based on the interesting properties of digital circles, a novel $O(n \log n)$ centralized algorithm has been developed to compute the area covered by n uniform digital circles distributed randomly. The computation involves simple arithmetic operations only. Next, a distributed version of the same is proposed based on the local neighborhood information at each node to select a subset of nodes to cover a bounded area. Simulation studies show that the proposed distributed algorithm improves the estimated area coverage significantly compared to the earlier approaches.

The paper is organized in the following way: Section 2 describes the preliminaries of digital circles. Section 3 presents properties of intersecting digital circles. Section 4 describes the features of the area covered by a given set of digital circles and the algorithms for area computation. Section 5 shows the simulation results and finally Section 6 concludes the paper.

2   Preliminaries

With the advent of the new digital geometry paradigm in computation, the digital circle being a simple and prevalent geometric primitive has been studied extensively. Here follows a brief outline of the representation of digital circles following the number-theoretic approach presented in [2].

Let $\mathcal{C}^{\mathcal{Z}}(p,r)$ be the digital circle corresponding to a given real circle $\mathcal{C}^{\mathcal{R}}(p,r)$ with center at $p \in \mathcal{Z}^2$ and radius $r \in \mathcal{Z}^+$. Fig. 1 shows a digital circle with center at $O(0,0)$ and radius $r = 11$. Here, $\mathcal{C}^{\mathcal{Z}}(p,r)$ essentially represents the set of grid points in $\mathcal{Z}^2$ lying on the circumference of the digital circle. From the *8-axes symmetry* of digital circles [4], [3], it is obvious that just the set of points of one octant of the circle (as shown in Fig. 1) is sufficient to generate the complete circle. Also, given the set of points on the circle $\mathcal{C}^{\mathcal{Z}}(O,r)$, where O is the origin of the co-ordinate system in $\mathcal{Z}^2$, the circle $\mathcal{C}^{\mathcal{Z}}(p,r)$ can be generated easily. In

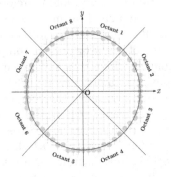

Fig. 1. Digital Circle $\mathcal{C}^{\mathcal{Z}}(O,11)$ **Fig. 2.** Runs of $\mathcal{C}^{\mathcal{Z}}(O,11)$ in octant 1

[2], authors proposed a simple and very useful number-theoretic representation of digital circles that is followed in this paper. By this method, for a digital circle $\mathcal{C}^{\mathcal{Z}}(O,r)$, $O(0,0)$ the origin, the points of the first octant, as shown in Fig. 2, can be generated from a sequence of integer intervals $(I_0, I_1, ..., I_{k_{max}})$, where
$I_k = [0,\ r-1]\ for\ k = 0,$
$\quad = [(2k-1)r - k(k-1),\ (2k+1)r - k(k+1) - 1]\ ,\ for\ 1 \le k \le k_{max}.$
If l_k be the number of integer squares lying within the interval I_k, $\mathcal{C}^{\mathcal{Z}}(O,r)$ will have a sequence of l_k consecutive points in octant-1, whose ordinates are $(r - k)$.

It is said that I_k represents a *run* of points on the digital circle, and l_k is termed as the corresponding *run length*, $0 \le k \le k_{max}$.

Remark 1. k_{max} essentially stands for the distinct integer values of the ordinates of the points lying in octant 1. From Fig. 2, it is evident that $k_{max} = (r - NI(\frac{r}{\sqrt{2}}))$, where $NI(x)$ denotes the integer nearest to x.

Example 1. For a digital circle $\mathcal{C}^{\mathcal{Z}}(O,11)$ with center $O = (0,0)$ and radius $r = 11$, $k_{max} = (r - \frac{r}{\sqrt{2}}) = 3$. The intervals I_k, $0 \le k \le k_{max}$, and the corresponding *run lengths* l_k are:
$I_0 = [0,10]$, the integer squares within this interval are: $1,4,9$, hence $l_0 = 3$. Similarly, $I_1 = [11,30]$, $l_1 = 2$, $I_2 = [31,48]$, $l_2 = 1$, $I_3 = [49,64]$, $l_3 = 1$.

The first octant of the digital circle $\mathcal{C}^{\mathcal{Z}}(O,11)$ is represented as a sequence of l_k's, as $(3,2,1,1)$ and can be generated as shown in Fig. 2.

3 Intersection of Two Digital Circles

So far, extensive studies on digital circles have been made to generate digital circles, to characterize and recognize digital circles and circular arcs from a given set of digital curves and curve segments in an image etc. This paper explores a new application area of digital circles that is for computing the area covered by a set of circles. The number-theoretic approach of digital circle representation [2] is applied here to make the computation simple and elegant. Following that approach, in this section, we study some additional properties of digital circles that help to compute the covered area.

3.1 Point Containment

Let $C^Z(p, r)$ be a digital circle with center at p and radius r corresponding to a real circle $C^R(p, r)$.

Lemma 1. *The Euclidean distance, r' of any point on $C^Z(p, r)$ from p lies within the range $r - \frac{1}{2} < r' < r + \frac{1}{2}$.*

Proof. Follows directly from the property that the deviation of the grid points on the digital circle either along the x axis or y axis from the real circle is always less than $\frac{1}{2}$ [2].

Theorem 1. *A digital query point q is a point on the circumference of the digital circle $C^Z(p, r)$, if and only if the Euclidean distance r' of q from the center p lies in the range $(r - \frac{1}{2} < r' < r + \frac{1}{2})$.*

Proof. Follows directly from Lemma 1.

3.2 Run Position of a Circumference Point

Given a point $Q(x', y')$ on the circumference of a digital circle $C^Z(p, r)$, we can easily find the octant in which Q lies depending on the position of Q relative to $p(x, y)$. On that octant, the run k that contains Q is given by $k = r - |y' - y|$, if Q lies in octant 1, 4, 5 or 8, else $k = r - |x' - x|$.

3.3 Intersection Points

Two digital circles are said to intersect each other if they share some common area, including the degenerate case, where the two just touch each other at the boundary with zero overlapped area. Unlike the real circles, where at any intersection, the circles have just a single common point, it is interesting to see that two digital circles can intersect in three different ways according to the number of points lying on the circumference of both digital circles at any intersection, as shown in Fig.s 3-5:

- A single common point on the circumference (Fig. 3)
- No common point (Fig. 4).
- More than one contiguous common points (Fig. 5)

In each of the three cases, the digital circles are said to be intersecting.

Lemma 2. *Existence of at least one common point on the circumference is a sufficient condition for intersection of two digital circles, but it is not a necessary condition.*

Proof. Evident from Fig.s 3-5.

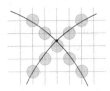 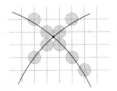 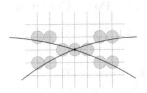

Fig. 3. Intersection with a single common point

Fig. 4. Intersection with no common point

Fig. 5. Intersection with multiple common points

Remark 2. From the *8-axes symmetry* of digital circles, it is evident that if we have the knowledge of one intersection point of two digital circles, the other one can be obtained by appropriate reflection.

3.4   Algorithm for Finding Intersection Points

Now, given two digital circles with their centers $c_1(x_1, y_1)$ and $c_2(x_2, y_2)$ and radius r, let us find the intersection points if it exist. For multiple common points at any intersection, only one end point is sufficient. From Lemma 1, it is obvious that the two may intersect if and only if the distance between c_1 and c_2 is less than $(2r + 1)$.

Algorithm 1 presents the steps. It finds the intersection points in $O(1)$ time assuming the circles to be real circles with $(x_1 \leq x_2)$. Next by local search around the point (just by two comparisons), the exact intersection point on the digital circle is identified.

4   Area Coverage by a Set of Digital Circles

To compute the area covered by a set of n digital circles with radius r distributed randomly over a 2-D plane, here we propose an iterative procedure. In each iteration, the covered area is represented in terms of a sequence of intersection points defining the boundary of that area. The intersection points are detected following the technique given in [14] that considered a set of monotone objects.

Algorithm 1. Intersection points

Input: circle centers : $c_1(x_1, y_1)$, $c_2(x_2, y_2)$, radius : r
Output: list of intersection points: p_1, p_2
Step 1: Compute distance d between c_1 and c_2;
Step 2: if $d \geq (2r + 1)$ then
  | Exit (Circles are disjoint);
else
$$h \leftarrow \sqrt{(r^2 - (\tfrac{d}{2})^2)} \; ;$$
$p_1(x) = [\frac{x_1+x_2}{2} + (h * \frac{y_2-y_1}{d})]$, $p_1(y) = [\frac{y_1+y_2}{2} - (h * \frac{x_2-x_1}{d})]$;
Check if $p_1(x, y)$ or any of its two immediate neighbor points lies on the circumferences of both c_1 and c_2 then
    | Find the symmetric point p_2:
$$p_2(x) = x_2 + x_1 - p_1(x), \; p_2(y) = y_2 + y_1 - p_1(y);$$
  end
end

4.1 Intersection of a Set of Monotone Objects

In [14], given a set S of n monotone objects B_i, $1 \leq i \leq n$, authors presented an $O(n \log n)$ algorithm to detect if there is an intersection between any two objects of S. Here we apply a modification of the algorithm to find all the intersection points for a given set of digital circles with same radius r. For completeness, a brief outline of the algorithm is included here.

Definition 1. *An object B is monotone in the direction of x-axis if the boundary of B consists of an upper portion and a lower portion and both portions extend monotonously along the x-axis.*

It is evident that a digital circle is a monotone object, and if we draw a vertical line at $x = x_i$, it will cut some circles in vertical segments. Given a set S of n digital circles $S = \{C_1, C_2, ...C_n\}$, let us make a linearly ordered list $\mathcal{L}$ of $2n$ x-ordinates of the leftmost and rightmost points (a_i and b_i respectively) of the circles C_i in S, $1 \leq i \leq n$. Sweeping from left, at each point $x = x_i$, $x_i = a_i$ or b_i, a linearly ordered list $L(x_i)$ is generated with the set of circles intersected by the vertical line where the circle C_i precedes C_j if the lower point of the segment of $x = a_i(b_i)$ cut by C_i is lower than that of C_j. It is evident that at each step the list $L(x_i)$ changes by exactly one element, one insertion when $x_i = a_j$, or one deletion when $x_i = b_j$, $1 \leq j \leq n$. Hence, to detect if there is any intersection, only the newly adjacent pairs of circles in $L(x_i)$ are to be tested. We apply our algorithm *Intersection Points* for this purpose. Maintaining the list L as a $2-3$ tree, the processing of each $L(x_i)$ can be done in $O(\log n)$ time. Hence, the algorithm completes in $O(n \log n)$ time provided the following operations can be done in constant time, as has been mentioned in [14]:

- To check whether a pair of objects B_i, $B_j \in S$ intersect each other
- To find the points with maximum and minimum abscissa in each $B \in S$.
- For a given abscissa x, to find the point (x, y) in each $B \in S$.

In case of a digital circle, we have shown in section 3.4 that the first operation can be done in constant time. Also, it is obvious that the next two operations are straightforward and can be computed in constant time. So, we can identify all the intersection points in $O(n \log n)$ time. However, it is to be noted that the algorithm proposed in [14] only checks if there is any intersection among the given monotone objects, and it terminates if one intersection is obtained. Here we use the same algorithm to identify all the intersection points existing among the digital circles in S. It is evident that the time complexity remains the same. From the algorithm proposed in [14], here we prove an interesting result on the maximum number of intersection points possible among a set of monotone objects.

Theorem 2. *Given a set of n monotone objects distributed randomly over a 2-D plane, the total number of intersection points is always upper bounded by $6n$.*

Proof. From the algorithm of [14], it is evident that at each step of sweeping at $x = x_i$, $x_i \in \mathcal{L}$ (the list of the leftmost and the rightmost points of the objects), the list $L(x_i)$ experiences a single change, either an insertion, when $x_i = a_j$, a leftmost point, or a deletion when $x_i = b_j$, a rightmost point of a monotone object. In case of an insertion, at most two newly adjacent pairs of objects may appear (if the insertion is anywhere except at the two ends of the list, when just one newly adjacent pair appears). In case of a deletion, it is evident that at most one pair becomes newly adjacent. For each newly adjacent pairs there may be at most two intersection points. Since $\mathcal{L}$ contains exactly n leftmost points a_i and n rightmost points b_i, it proves the upper bound.

Given a set S of n digital circles, applying the above algorithm [14], for each circle $C_i \in S$, a list of intersection points of $I(C_i)$ is maintained, ordered in clockwise direction which are on the boundary of the covered area. After an intersection point $I_{i,j}$ between circles C_i and C_j, is obtained, it is checked if the point is included in any circle C_k, $k \neq i, j$, adjacent with both the circles C_i and C_j in $\mathcal{L}$. If not, the point is a boundary point of the area covered by S, and is included in a list of boundary points $\mathcal{I}$, and also in $I(C_i)$ and $I(C_j)$. Next, an appropriate traversal along $\mathcal{I}$ can compute the covered area. The following section describes the details of this procedure.

4.2   Area Computation

The area of a digital circle C can be computed by treating it as an isothetic cover, and traversing its boundary in cyclic order [10], as shown in Fig. 6 . Here each run corresponds to a vertical strip of area.

It is to be noted that for octants in the upper half of C, i.e., octants 1, 2, 7 and 8, the area of the columns associated with each run are taken to be positive, and for the other octants, the corresponding column areas are considered to be negative. The total sum gives the area covered by C.

Given the list of boundary points $\mathcal{I}$, starting from any arbitrary intersection point $I_{i,j}$, for area computation, the exact arc of either along C_i or along C_j is to be identified that is to be traversed for area computation.

Definition 2. *At any intersection point $I_{i,j}$ on the boundary, for each intersecting circle C_i and C_j, the valid path for boundary traversal is the clockwise or anticlockwise path along C_i or C_j that lies outside the other circle.*

Given two circles C_1 and C_2 intersecting at I_1 and I_2, Fig. 7 shows the valid path along C_1 and C_2 respectively. Given an intersection point P between C_1 and C_2, here follows an $O(1)$ algorithm to find the valid path.

Algorithm 2. Valid path detection

Input: circle C, intersection point P,*octant*, *run*
Output: direction
Depending upon the *octant* and *run* information find the next neighbor point P' on C in clockwise direction;
if P' *lies inside the other circle associated with P* **then**
  | *direction* ← 1 // anti clockwise direction
else
  | *direction* ← 0 // clockwise direction
end
Return *direction* and terminate;

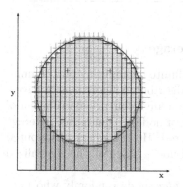

Fig. 6. Area computation

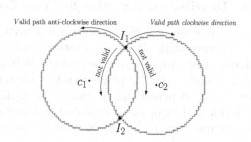

Fig. 7. Valid path between intersection points

4.3 Centralized Algorithm for Area Coverage

The centralized algorithm 3 presents a brief outline of the steps for computing the area covered by a set of digital circles.

Complexity Analysis: In step 1, to sort all a_i, b_i, it requires $O(n \log n)$ time. In step 2, insertion or deletion requires $O(\log n)$ time, since the individual intersection point lists are sorted in clockwise direction. Therefore, step 2 requires $O(n \log n)$ time. In step 3, we need to traverse along the circumference of the circle. If there are n circles, in the worst case, it will take $O(n.r)$ time, r is the radius of the circle. Therefore, the time complexity of the centralized algorithm is $O(n \log n + n.r)$, i.e., $O(n \log n)$, for a constant r.

Algorithm 3. Centralized algorithm

Input: Circles $C := \{c_1, c_2, \ldots, c_n\}$
Output: Area : A_{tot}
Step 1: for *each circle $c_i \in C$* **do**
| Compute a_i and b_i and include in $\mathcal{L}$ in sorted order;
end
Step 2: for $i = 1$ *to* $2n$ **do**
| **if** $\mathcal{L}(i) = a_j$ **then** include c_j in L in sorted order ;
| **if** $\mathcal{L}(i) = a_j$ *or* b_j *and* $c_j = L(k)$ *and if both* $L(k-1)$ *and* $L(k+1)$ *exist in* L **then**
| | check if intersection point between circles of any pair $(L(k-1), L(k), L(k-1))$ is
| | included within the third one;
| | update the intersection lists;
| | **if** $\mathcal{L}(i) = b_j$ **then** delete $L(k)$ from L;
| **end**
end
Step 3: while $\mathcal{I} \neq \phi$ **do**
| Select first intersection point $i \in \mathcal{I}$ & $j \leftarrow null$;
| **while** $i \neq j$ **do**
| | Select circle c_i of i which is not recently traversed and find *valid path direction*;
| | $j \leftarrow$ next point in $I(c_i)$ & find octant and run position of i and j;
| | Traverse along the valid path from i to j, and compute the area A_{tot};
| | $i \leftarrow j$ & $c_i \leftarrow$ not recently traversed circle;
| | $j \leftarrow$ next point of $I(c_i)$;
| **end**
| Remove all traversed intersection points from $\mathcal{I}$;
end
Step 4: Exit

4.4   Distributed Algorithm for Area Coverage

For wireless sensor networks with nodes having limited computing and communication capabilities it is always better to adopt distributed algorithms to have a solution. Here, we consider the problem that given any arbitrary distribution of n sensor nodes on a $2D$ plane, to select a subset of nodes to guarantee coverage over a certain percentage of area to be monitored. Here a simple distributed algorithm is developed to compute the subset of nodes based on the centralized area computation technique described above.

It is assumed that the *sink* node selects a *leader* node randomly who joins the subset CL and initiates the subset selection procedure by broadcasting a *candidate* message with the current CL. On receiving that message, a node $i \notin CL$ computes the area $A_{add}(i)$ that it can contribute if it joins CL following the centralized algorithm 3. Each node $\in CL$ selects the neighbor with highest $A_{add}(i)$ and sends *select* message with its id and A_{add} to its parent. At each round, each node $i \in CL$, selects one of its free neighbors $N(i)$ such that the area covered by $(CL \cup N(i))$ is maximum. Based on this information from all nodes in CL, the *leader* includes the node with maximum A_{add} in CL and broadcasts *include* message to start the next round until either the area covered A_{tot} exceeds the required area limit A_{th}, or $\cup_{\forall i \in CL} N(i) = \phi$. It is assumed that each node knows the locations of itself and its neighbors.

Complexity Analysis: In the distributed algorithm, in response to the *candidate* message, when a new neighbor joins CL, a free node computes the area covered by its neighbors in CL and itself following the *Centralized Algorithm 3.* Therefore, per node the computation complexity is $O(d^2 \log d)$ where d is the

---

Algorithm 4. Distributed Algorithm

Input: CL, threshold area:A_{th}
Output: A_{tot}
if *node* $j \notin CL$, $\{C\} \leftarrow j$ **then**
    if *receives candidate message* **then**
        if *exists neighbors* $k \notin C$ *and* $k \in CL$ **then**
        | include $\forall k$ in C and call algorithm 3;
        end
        sends *add area* message to its sender with A_{add};
    end
    If receives *include(j)* message, update CL and broadcasts *candidate* message;
else
    if *receives add area message* **then**
        if *i is leader* **then**
        | selects the node-k with maximum A_{add} and broadcasts *include(k)* message;
        | If $A_{add} \geq A_{th}$ broadcasts *terminate* message;
        else
        | Select the node-k with maximum A_{add} and sends *select(k)* message to parent;
        end
    end
end

---

maximum degree of a node. The message complexity is $O(|CL|)$, where $|CL| \leq n$, is the total number of nodes selected in the output subset.

5   Simulation Results

Extensive simulation studies have been made to evaluate the performance of the centralized and distributed algorithms. For simulation study, N nodes, $10 \leq N \leq 25$, are distributed randomly over a 500×500 grid area. The radius r is varied between 10 to 45 units. The area computed by the centralized algorithm in each step, as nodes are included one by one is shown in Fig. 10. It shows the comparison of covered areas computed by our proposed algorithm and by approximating the area of each sensor as the maximum square inscribed within the circle of radius r [11] as has been shown in Fig.s 8 and 9 respectively. From Fig. 10, it is evident that the proposed algorithm reports more area than that in [11], as is expected. Moreover, as the number of nodes grows, the difference between the computed areas increases significantly.

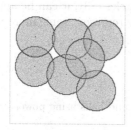
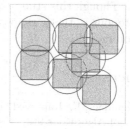

Fig. 8. Area coverage by digital circles   **Fig. 9.** Area coverage by square grids

Fig. 11 shows the variation of covered area with radius r. Here, also with increase in r, the difference of areas grows. For, the distributed algorithm, Fig.12 shows how the computed area grows with rounds. The comparison shows that in

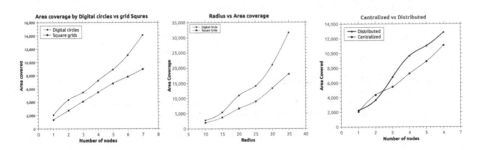

Fig. 10. Variation of area coverage with number of nodes

Fig. 11. Variation of area coverage with radius

Fig. 12. Growth of covered area with rounds/ number of nodes

the centralized case, area grows slower than that in distributed one. It is expected as in the centralized case, we include the nearest nodes along the x-axis, one after another irrespective of its additional area, whereas in the distributed algorithm in each round the node with maximum additional area is selected.

6   Conclusion

In this paper, we have addressed the problem of computing the area covered by a set of sensors distributed randomly, assuming that each sensor covers a circular area of radius r. To make the computation simple, instead of considering real circles, a digital geometry based approach is followed here. We propose an $O(n \log n)$ centralized algorithm for computing the area covered by sensors using simple arithmetic operations only. Also, a distributed version is developed to select a subset of nodes to cover an area. Simulation studies show that the proposed distributed algorithm improves the estimated area coverage compared to the earlier works. It would be interesting to find the comparison of the real area and the estimated area and its dependence on the radius which is yet to be completed. Though this study considers digital circles only, it can be applied to any monotonous isothetic shapes as well that may represent some more realistic propagation models.

References

1. Aurenhammer, F.: Improved algorithms for discs and balls using power diagrams. Journal of Algorithms 9(2), 151–161 (1988)
2. Bhowmick, P., Bhattacharya, B.B.: Number-theoretic interpretation and construction of a digital circle. Discrete Applied Mathematics 156(12), 2381–2399 (2008)

3. Bresenham, J.: A linear algorithm for incremental digital display of circular arcs. Commun. ACM 20(2), 100–106 (1977)
4. Foley, J.D., Dam, A.V., Feiner, S.K., Hughes, J.F.: Computer graphics: principles and practice. 2 edn.
5. Gallais, A., Carle, J., Simplot-Ryl, D., Stojmenovi, I.: Localized sensor area coverage with low communication overhead. IEEE Transactions on Mobile Computing 7(5), 661–672 (2008)
6. Huang, C.F., Tseng, Y.C.: The coverage problem in a wireless sensor network. In: Proceedings of the 2nd ACM International Conference on Wireless Sensor Networks and Applications, WSNA, pp. 115–121. ACM, New York (2003)
7. Kershner, R.: The number of circles covering a set. American Journal of Mathematics 61(3), 665–671 (1939)
8. McIlroy, M.D.: Best approximate circles on integer grids. ACM Trans. Graph. 2(4), 237–263 (1983)
9. Meguerdichian, S., Koushanfar, F., Potkonjak, M., Srivastava, M.B.: Coverage problems in wireless ad-hoc sensor networks. In: Twentieth Annual Joint Conference of the IEEE Computer and Communications Societies, IEEE INFOCOM, vol. 3, pp. 1380–1387 (2001)
10. Pal, S., Bhowmick, P., Biswas, A.: Facet: A fast approximate circularity estimation technique. In: Second International Conference on Emerging Applications of Information Technology (EAIT), pp. 106–109 (2011)
11. Pervin, N., Layek, D., Das, N.: Localized algorithm for connected set cover partitioning in wireless sensor networks. In: 1st International Conference on Parallel Distributed and Grid Computing (PDGC), pp. 229–234 (2010)
12. Saha, D., Das, N.: Distributed area coverage by connected set cover partitioning in wireless sensor networks. In: First International Workshop on Sustainable Monitoring through Cyber-Physical Systems (SuMo-CPS), In Conjunction with ICDCN, Mumbai, India (2013)
13. Saha, D., Das, N.: A fast fault tolerant partitioning algorithm for wireless sensor networks. In: Third International Conference on Advances in Computing and Information Technology (ACITY), pp. 227–237. CSIT-AIRCC Digital Library, Chennai (2013)
14. Sharir, M.: Intersection and closest-pair problems for a set of planar discs. SIAM Journal on Computing 14(2), 448–468 (1985)
15. Yan, T., He, T., Stankovic, J.A.: Differentiated surveillance for sensor networks. In: Proceedings of the 1st International Conference on Embedded Networked Sensor Systems, SenSys 2003, pp. 51–62. ACM (2003)
16. Yu, Z., Teng, J., Li, X., Xuan, D.: On wireless network coverage in bounded areas. In: Proceedings IEEE INFOCOM, pp. 1195–1203 (2013)

Effect of Choice of Discretization Methods on Context Extraction from Sensor Data – An Empirical Evaluation

Sangeeta Mittal[1], Krishna Gopal[1], and Shankar Lall Maskara[3]

[1] Jaypee Institute of Information Technology Noida, UP, India
smittal.150210@gmail.com, krishna.gopal@jiit.ac.in
[2] G-2W, Soura Niloy Housing Complex, 1 - Kailash Ghosh Road,
Kolkata – 700008, India
maskara.shankar@gmail.com

Abstract. Data from sensor logs in raw form is generally continuous valued. This data from multiple sensors in continuous stream becomes voluminous. For knowledge discovery like extraction of context, from these datasets, standard machine learning algorithms or their variations are used as classifier. Most classification schemes require the input data to be discretized. The focus of this paper is to study merits of some popular discretization methods when applied on noisy sensor logs. Representative methods from supervised and unsupervised discretization, like binning, clustering and entropy minimization are evaluated with context extraction. Interestingly, unlike common perception, for discretization of sensor data, supervised algorithms do not have a clear edge over unsupervised.

Keywords: Sensor Streams, Sensor Classifiers, Discretization, Context Extraction.

1 Introduction

Small sensing devices capable of sensing multiple modalities in users' surroundings are rapidly finding importance [1]. Sensors like RFIds for Identification of movable and non-movable objects, location tags, accelerometers, weather sensors are available for fine grained sensing. The salient features of sensor data are different data rates, many features, lots of noise and redundancy. When sensors sense different physical phenomenon extractions of meaningful abstractions like current context, from raw data becomes necessary. This may require different computation methods for different sensors. The sensor data also has to be pre sanitized and processed to meet the requirements of context extraction algorithms [2]. One of these is discretization of continuous valued sensor data to make it finite valued. Most algorithms to deduce useful and actionable high-level information like context and situation cannot perform on real valued data [3]. In this work, we apply various discretization techniques for sensor data processing. The effect of ten popular methods on context extraction accuracy at the controller is studied. For the purpose of comparison, a publicly available, benchmark, multi sensor data from human monitoring domain is used [4].

R. Natarajan (Ed.): ICDCIT 2014, LNCS 8337, pp. 146–151, 2014.

The Opportunity dataset is manually annotated with daily life activities of a user living in a sensor rich environment. These annotations are considered as contexts in which the user is currently in. Here we take "mode of locomotion" as the context to be extracted. There are many context modeling and extraction approaches [5]. Based on the study in [6] and [7], Bayesian belief network with K2 algorithm for structure creation is used as context extraction model. This paper investigates the impact of different discretization techniques used at sensors in context classifier performance at controller. Accuracy and Model Computation Time are main evaluating parameters. The paper is organized as follows. In Section 2, discretization methods used and the context extraction mechanisms based on Bayesian Belief Networks are described. The dataset used and analysis of performance are discussed in section 3. The paper is concluded in last section.

2   Wireless Sensor Data - Discretization and Context Extraction

Sensors perpetually generate and transmit raw data to a sink or intermediate sensors. To increase usability and decrease communication costs, raw data is often discretized. Lots of discretization methods are available in machine learning literature [8]. It would be interesting to study their performance with noisy sensor data. The dataset used here has 13% of missing values. First step is to impute these missing values by replacing with previous available value [9]. The rate at which sensors sense data is much higher than the rate at which humans comprehend data. Moving Average based smoothing is thus applied as next step to reduce its rate and lower the effect of outliers [10]. These are followed by discretization to have a compact representation of data and making it suitable for use by machine learning methods deployed at sink. The final preprocessed data is presented to a classifier that attempts to extract the desired context. Discretization though compromises data quality as granularity is reduced. Therefore, there's a need to study its impact before using. Many discretization approaches have been defined in machine learning .The methods that do discretization independent of the classes of data are called unsupervised discretization methods [8]. Methods of this type studied here are equal frequency, equal width binning, Proportional K Interval Discretization, Self Organizing Maps and K Means Clustering for each attribute. On the other hand, some methods take into account the target class for discretization of data attributes. These are called supervised discretization methods. Examples studied here are Fuzzy Discretization, Recursive Minimal Entropy Partitioning, Kononeko's MDL method, Naïve and Semi Naïve Discretization and Boolean reasoning. Various models have been designed that make the context extraction transparent to the sources of context, that is, sensors [11]. Methods like Object based, entity- relation, ontology based modeling have been proposed. Given the uncertain nature of sensor data, probabilistic modeling based on Bayesian Belief Network (BBN) has been developed in [6]. The BBN represents joint probability, P (A, C) where A = $\{a_1.....a_n\}$ is set of data variables and C the class variable. The classifier Z: A $\rightarrow$ C is a function that maps an instance of A to a value of C. Exact Inference Junction tree algorithm performing inference by enumeration and variable elimination is used.

3   Experiments and Evaluation

The Opportunity dataset [4] consists of simulated Activities of Daily Living (ADLs) related to a breakfast scenario. The data contains daily human activities recorded on various subjects inside a simulated studio apartment. A wide variety of body-worn, object based, and ambient sensors – in total, 72 sensors from 10 modalities mostly accelerometers and inertial measurement units with 15 wireless and wired sensor networks in the home environment are used. Each subject performed one drill session, which has about 20 repetitions of some predefined actions in one sequence of sensory data, and five ADLs. Annotation for modes of gestures, modes of locomotion, and high-level activities is also provided. For our analysis, we consider the sensors placed on knee, hip and shoes as one cluster. Data from these sensors of the subject S1 are used for context extraction. We intend to extract from our Bayesian belief network based classifier the context of four modes of locomotion that is, stand, walk, sit and lie. As stated earlier, the manually labelled ground truth of these modes is available. It can be seen from figure 1 that the dataset does not exhibit a uniform distribution across the parameters.

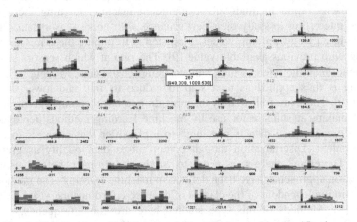

Fig. 1. Visualization of 24 of the total 34 attributes used in classification

3.1   Evaluation Metrics and Methods

Bayesian Belief Network based classifier is used for predicting class labels of test instances. For a given dataset $D = \{d_1, d_2 .... d_n\}$, there is a set $T = \{t_1, t_2, ... t_n\}$, of ground truth labels already known. For evaluation, 10 fold cross validation is used. In this evaluation, in ten iterations, random $n*9/10$ values are used for training classifier and remaining, $k = n/10$ values are used for testing. The classifier produces a set $P = \{p_1, p_2, ... p_k\}$ of predicted labels. These numbers are used to evaluate various parameters described as follows. The Kappa Coefficient measures the agreement of prediction with actual class labels. Possible values for it range from -1 to +1, which are total disagreement and agreement respectively. The used dataset is unbalanced in terms of class distribution in training sets. Therefore multiple evaluation measures are used. Accuracy is the measure of fraction of correctly classified test instances. True Positive Rate or Recall is the ratio of correctly classified instances of a class with total instances of that class. False Positive Rate tells how frequently a class is confused with other classes. For example, an unlabeled locomotion class may be classified as any other class. Precision of a particular class gives the percentage of instances where its labeling is correct against the total labeling done for that class. Computation Time to build the classifier from discretized data is also taken as a metric.

3.2   Results

We report the recognition performance using the classifier discussed in Section 2. A subset of opportunity dataset, that is, data of subject 1 classifying modes of locomotion are used. Raw sensor data had 13% missing values. These values were imputed simply by previous available values in the current setup. The original data is available at 30 Hz. It is down-sampled to 2Hz as none of the actions to be recognized last lesser than half a second. As human activities don't finish and start at sharp times, during resampling an overlapping window of 250 milliseconds is taken. This processed data is then used for discretization by various methods enumerated in section 2. For clustering based methods like K-means and SOM, discretization is achieved by clustering one sensor attribute at a time. The discretized data is used by a BBN classifier to predict the mode of current locomotion of the user. Results are then evaluated by different parameters as defined earlier in this section. Evaluation results of all discretization algorithms are shown in figure 2. The PKID algorithm performs best in accuracy, precision and recall. Considering the kappa coefficient, the self-organizing map gives best value. PKID in this parameter is close second. All supervised algorithms have accuracy very close to each other. The supervised algorithms produced better output than unsupervised as none of the data got rejected by the classifier, and as a result accuracy is same as recall. This is not so in unsupervised methods.

In figure 3, the average performance of supervised and unsupervised algorithms is compared. As is evident from the graph, the supervised algorithms do not provide significant gain in performance, given their training cost. On the other hand, the unsupervised algorithms do not require and class information and can learn discretization only from the sensor data. Even then, their performance is at par with the supervised ones. Both the methods although require batch processing and hence memory requirements are inadvertent in the sensor. The supervised algorithms have clear edge in many other data mining applications. Interestingly, from figure 3, it is evident that here the unsupervised counterparts are also giving comparable results. This may be due to imputations done in large number of missing values. The resultant data thus obfuscates the relationship between instances and class label. No such information is made use of in unsupervised methods. Thus, simple unsupervised discretization is also a good choice for sensors data.

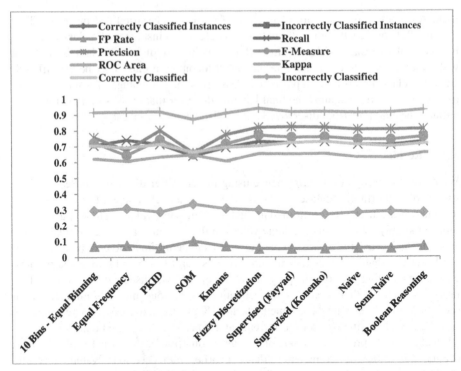

Fig. 2. Comparison of various performance metrics on different discretization methods

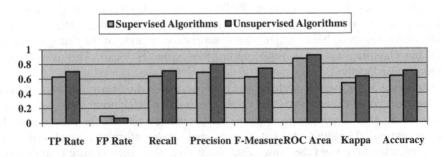

Fig. 3. Mean of Performance Evaluation of Supervised and Unsupervised Discretization

Discretization itself is a one-time process; hence computation time of classifier model was taken as an evaluation measure. Once the discretized data is made available, most of the algorithms give output that is suitable for real time generation of classifier in very short time of 0.05 sec approx. Output data from K means and Naïve algorithms was found to take longer time to build the classifier model, as these two algorithms generate a very large number of cut points or intervals for each attribute.

4   Conclusions

Discretization is an important step in processing of sensors data streams. Impact of popular supervised and unsupervised discretization algorithms have been evaluated for classification of noisy sensor data in this paper. It is observed that unlike other data mining domains there is no clear edge between two types of discretization approaches possibly due to obfuscation of instance-class relationship in presence of imputed values. Overall, the PKID algorithm works marginally better than all others. It is concluded that for multivariate sensors data unsupervised methods are preferable due to their computational simplicity and comparable performances.

References

1. McGrath, M., Dishongh, T.: Wireless Sensor Networks for Healthcare Applications. Artech House, London (2010)
2. Figo, D., Diniz, P.C., Ferreira, D.R., Cardoso, J.M.: Preprocessing techniques for context recognition from accelerometer data. Personal and Ubiquitous Computing 14(7), 645–662 (2010)
3. Randell, C., Muller, H.: Context awareness by analysing accelerometer data. In: Proceedings of The Fourth International Symposium on Wearable Computers, pp. 175–176. IEEE (2000)
4. Roggen, D., et al.: Collecting complex activity data sets in highly rich networked sensor environments. In: Seventh International Conference on Networked Sensing Systems, Kassel, Germany (June 2010)
5. Kulkarni, R.V., Anna, F., Kumar, G.V.: Computational intelligence in wireless sensor networks: A survey. IEEE Communications Surveys & Tutorials 13(1), 68–96 (2011)
6. Mittal, S., Aggarwal, A., Maskara, S.L.: Application of Bayesian Belief Networks for context extraction from wireless sensors data. In: Proceedings of 14th International Conference on Advanced Communication Technology (ICACT), South Korea,, pp. 410–415 (2012)
7. Mittal, S., Gopal, K., Maskara, S.L.: A Versatile Lattice Based Model for Situation Recognition from Dynamic Ambient Sensors. International Journal on Smart Sensing and Intelligent Systems 6(1), 403–432 (2013)
8. Chmielewski, M.R., Grzymala-Busse, J.W.: Global discretization of continuous attributes as preprocessing for machine learning. International Journal of Approximate Reasoning 15(4), 319–331 (1996)
9. Gemmeke, J.F., Van Hamme, H., Cranen, B., Boves, L.: Compressive sensing for missing data imputation in noise robust speech recognition. IEEE Journal of Selected Topics in Signal Processing 4(2), 272–287 (2010)
10. Mittal, S., Aggarwal, A., Maskara, S.L.: Online Cleaning of Wireless Sensor Data Resulting in Improved Context Extraction. International Journal of Computer Applications 60(15), 24–32 (2012)
11. Claudio, B., et al.: A survey of context modelling and reasoning techniques. Pervasive Mobile Computing 6(2), 161–180 (2010)
12. Fatourechi, M., et al.: Comparison of evaluation metrics in classification applications with imbalanced datasets. In: Seventh IEEE International Conference on Machine Learning and Applications, pp. 777–782 (2008)

Discrete Krill Herd Algorithm – A Bio-Inspired Meta-Heuristics for Graph Based Network Route Optimization

Chiranjib Sur and Anupam Shukla

Soft Computing and Expert System Laboratory
ABV- Indian Institute of Information Technology & Management, Gwalior
{chiranjibsur,dranupamshukla}@gmail.com

Abstract. Krill Herd Algorithm (KHA) is creature inspired meta-heuristic search algorithm, inspired by the tiny sea creature krill and its style of living, which can be utilized in optimization solution foundation of NP – Hard problems. In this paper we have adopted the various activities of the creature and described a discrete version of the Krill Herd Algorithm for the first time which is favorable for graph network based search and optimization problems. KHA is operated on a multi-parametric road graph for search of optimized path with respect to some parameters and evaluation function and the convergence rate is compared with Ant Colony Optimization (ACO) and Intelligent Water Drop (IWD) algorithms. The proposed KHA works well when it comes to decision making and path planning for graph based networks and other discrete event based optimization problems and works on the principle of various random exploration schemes following some parameters which decides whether to include a node/edge or not. Due to the dynamicity of the road network with several dynamic parameters, the optimized path tends to change with intervals, the optimized path changes and will bring about a near fair distribution of vehicles in the road network and withdraw the excessive pressure on the busy roads and pave the way for proper exploitation of the underutilized.

Keywords: Discrete Krill Herd Algorithm, vehicle route optimization, path planning in graphs, combinatorial optimization.

1 Introduction

Road management has become an issue with the increase in the number of vehicles and due to the existing inefficient traffic management system. An effort has been very common on for path planning problem, but if the number of agents increases the least path criteria can become a bottleneck. Unlike the computer data network where this kind of congestion is handled with hard hand like packet drop and differential services, in road network there is no scope of such treatment and the only way of optimization is through efficient route discovery and enhance waiting delay. An effort has been made in the description of Discrete Krill Herd Algorithm (DKHA) and its application for road network optimization and management. Krill Herd Algorithm is

R. Natarajan (Ed.): ICDCIT 2014, LNCS 8337, pp. 152–163, 2014.

first described by Gandomi and Alavi [5] in 2012, and is characterized by the time varying cummulation of movement affected by other krill individuals, foraging action, random diffusion. The mathematical expressions [5] which describes the traditional KHA mainly supports the continuous search domain (CSD) like numerical equation but fails to suit the discrete search domain (DSD) like graph based problems and discrete event based problems. [8] describes the application of an improved KHA for global numerical optimization and [9] describes the introduction of levy search equation in the KHA giving rise to Lévy-Flight Krill Herd Algorithm. Apart from ACO [10] and IWD [11] there is hardly any bio-inspired meta-heuristics which can be applied for the graph based problems. The rest of the paper is organized as Section 2 describes the modified krill herd algorithm, Section 3 illustrates the discrete version in details, Section 4 provides the method obtained, Section 5 is for results and Section 6 concludes with future work.

2   Krill Herd Algorithm and Mathematics

Krill are small crustaceans creatures having the characteristics of prawn but comparatively are very small in size and their volume constitutes considerable part of the living organisms under the sea. Originally word krill is of Norwegian origin meaning "tiny fry of fishes", but later the word meant a different kind of organism on which many aquatic animals feed on. The biologists consider krill as having vital tropic connection as they reside at the bottom of the food chain. Krill mostly feed on phytoplankton (algae) but there are species that are both carnivorous and omnivorous fed on fish larvae and zooplankton. Krill themselves constitutes as diet of many large sea animals like whale, fishes, seals etc. and even penguins.

Krill have various kinds of species which are present at oceans all over the world and each of them have diverse features of living, movement, reproduction, food habit, moulting, predation, lifespan, swarming, migration etc. Species may be adapted to certain conditions of its habitat but in general Krill remains in deep water during the day time to avoid predation and at night goes to the upper layer of the sea bed for phytoplankton. The proposed Krill Herd Algorithm constitute of the following steps which are being discussed with respect to both the continuous and discrete search space problem implementation.

2.1   Concentration Enhancement Movement

Krill possess highly developed sense organs which sense the phytoplankton level of the adjacent environment and move towards the high concentration as consumption is mainly through filter feeding, and the chance of getting maximum phytoplankton in their comb-like appendages is only in high concentration region. The Krill actually detects a chemical secretion of the phytoplankton and can estimate the density of its presence. It must be mentioned that the applicability of the algorithm for both CSD and DSD is discussed, though only for DSD we have simulated.

In (CSD) this movement direction will actually be favored if the fitness value of the new position is enhanced with respect to local best solution or sometimes for the global best solution at that moment. The number of options or direction of path scrutinized by a krill will depend on the variation step $x_{t+1} = x_t + \delta$. For DSD the path offered can be many but not unlimited like in CSD and hence the decision making phenomenon will constitute of the path chosen depending on probability function.

Concentration investigation depends on the dimension vector of parameters $\{p_1, p_2, \ldots, p_n\}$ and weight $\{w_1, w_2, \ldots, w_n\}$ and is represented as :

$$f_j(p_1, p_2, \ldots, p_n) = \begin{cases} MIN\forall[\psi(p_1), \psi(p_2), \ldots, \psi(p_n)] \\ MIN[\omega_1\psi(p_1) + \omega_2\psi(p_2) + \ldots + \omega_n\psi(p_n)] \end{cases} \tag{1}$$

where $f_j(\ )$ is the estimation factor. However a probability factor can be generated as

$$P_{ij} = \frac{f_j()}{\sum f_k()} \tag{2}$$

For DSD there can be g available paths, but only h < g paths are considered for movement and the selection is dependent on the less weighted edges for better enhancement of path. Now for the DSD we can argue that the step imitates ACO or greedy algorithm like attitude. But experiment has shown that, when an algorithm works out stochastically, the combination of a balanced serialization of deterministic and probabilistic approach yield better outcome than only the individuals, hence the justification of this step. For CSD the selection of path is random where $x_{t+1} = x_t + k_1(\Delta x)$ where x_t is the position at iteration t and x belong to N dimension where N is an integer value and N > 0. Also -1 < k_1 < 1 is an adaptive variable which adapts with the difference in fitness between the positions x_t and x_{t+1} and k_1 is proportional to $|J_t - J_{t+1}|$. If difference is more then take bigger steps and if less then take smaller steps.

2.2   Phototatic Swarming Movement

Photophores organ in krill is capable of emitting light through an "enzyme-catalyzed chemiluminescence reaction" [4] where the chemical is interestingly not produced by the organism itself but is acquired as part of their diet. Hence it clearly indicated that the krill which is more glowing possesses more quality food than any other else and this attracts all the krill (capable of visualization) to accumulate in that swarm in search of quality food. In CSD the concentration of the light emitted by an individual within a certain radius range will attract more krill towards itself. Glowing light will indicate good solution opportunity in that region. In Firefly Algorithm [13] the agents are attracted only towards the global best or iteration best while in Glowworm Swarm Optimization [12] the agents are attracted towards other agents with varying range less than equal to sensor range. But in Discrete Krill Herd Algorithm the range of the agents is fixed. This means that the agents, who are isolated or in other words who don't have agents in range, will induce exploration and thus a control criterion to balance between exploration and exploitation. The fixed range factor depends on the environment, and the requirement for search based problem. $x_{t+1} = x_t + rand()$ or $x_{t+1} = x_t + \epsilon$ where ϵ is the directional parameter towards another agent. However in the

DSD the presence of better krill (wrt to fitness) only in the adjacent nodes will actually attract the krill no matter how weighted the two nodes are connected with. Proper swarming movement will create opportunity of successful reproduction (see Reproduction & Genetic Crossover) of the best ones. It is to be mention that the swarming movement accumulate the krill towards the expected best solution search space, but the solution won't stuck to the local best as there are several randomize mutation phenomenon (see Moulding) for scattering of the organisms to unexplored part of the search space. The mathematical expressions representing the attraction movement are:

$$L_1^k = MAX(l_1, l_2, \ldots, l_n) \tag{3}$$

$$L_2^k = [\sum \frac{(l_1 + l_2 + \ldots + l_n)}{n}] \tag{4}$$

where n number of krill are present at a certain node and there are k number of paths available and l_d is the fitness value for the dth Krill and MAX is used to represent better solution which is maximum for maximization problems and minimum for minimization problems. L_1^k and L_2^k are the two types of illumination factor through which decision makings that can be achieved, where the former depicts the maximum of all and the latter concentrates on any of the   better than averages of all.

2.3   Random Movement

Krill move cautiously to prevent invasion of the predators. But random movement is a carefree movement for both CSD and DSD. This occurs when krill is confused because available paths are either equally important or equally unpredictable when it comes to investigation with the local heuristic information and other calculated network parameters. Greedy exploration occurs in this operation.

2.4   Reproduction and Genetic Crossover

Reproduction occurs when there are suitable krill that are having chromosome having common point of intersection(s). The fitness of produced offspring may or may not be enhanced and is related to uncertainty. The example in Fig.1 will clearly illustrate the process of reproduction along with genetic crossover.

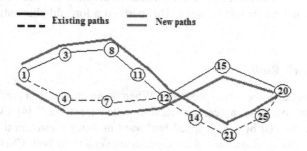

Fig. 1. Reproduction & Crossover in DKHA

Let us consider that the participating krill in reproduction have the gene or chromosomes which represent the path traversed while making its movement for food throughout the network. Now the crossover cum reproduction will create offspring having knowledge of the combined effect of their parents. Say if the first parent have traversed through 1, 3, 8, 11, 12, 15, 20 and the other parent have traversed 1, 4, 7, 12, 14, 21, 25,20 then the one point crossover can occur through 12 and the new offspring will have combination of path as 1, 3, 8, 11, 12, 14, 21, 25, 20 and 1, 4, 7, 12, 15, 20 and they are totally new combinations which might have not traversed by an individual krill. The genetic crossover is opportunistic depending on the common point(s). More than one point crossover is also possible. However if reproduction of two individual of no common points occurs then the generated combination of offspring will have no fitness as far as solution of the problem is concerned.

After reproduction, there are two kind of hatching process of the eggs. In one case the female lets the eggs deposited at the ocean bed and the eggs hatch there. This is called "non-sac-spawners". In that case at node 20 the reproduction will occur. Whereas in another the female are "sac spawners" [4] and carries the eggs until it hatches. In that case the reproduction will occur at some other subsequent node where the agent has moved on. In the former case the new krill starts exploration at that node itself, whereas in the latter the krill starts exploration at some other node as they are carried by the female. In the latter case it is considered that the unhatched krill can actually keep track of the path traversed by the female. The chance of reproduction is more when there is an accumulation of best krill (highly illuminated, energized, and fed). This example is suitable for DSD, in CSD the reproduction phenomenon will not possess any genetic crossover like this but may constitute of that described in traditional Genetic Algorithm for the best ones.

2.5   Predator's Prey

This step reflects the process of death or elimination of krill from the swarm, which are less fit, having less food, energy and incapable of "escape reaction called lobstering" [4]. Through this phenomenon the elimination of the weak krill occurs to pave the way for new generation of krill which will more concentrate in the better part of the search space. Also this phenomenon occurs randomly and the weak krill are eaten up. Reproduction must follow this step to avoid lessening of the krill counts. In DSD the weak krill are attacked at the nodes, whereas in the CSD the weak krill gets struck at coordinates and are unable to move. This perhaps a forceful elimination of the not fitted krill.

2.6   Predator's Rush

The krill camouflage to confuse predators. When being chased by a predator, the krill camouflage and performs a "escape reaction called lobstering" [4] like movement which is characterized by a high speed backward movement through the water. This kind of movement is characterized by random movement in both CSD and DSD to promote the chances of exploration. Difference between "random movement" and "predator's rush" is that the former takes decision for forward movement and not towards the direction from where it has come from, while in the latter it can move backward to some previous node. This kind of movement is helpful when somehow there occurred looping in graph based network and hence the agent want to regenerate itself through this movement.

2.7 Moulting

Moulting is the mode of shedding off a certain part of the body which is capable of enhanced regeneration. This occurs in krill in the form of a shell on the backside of the organism. Mainly it is hormonal, but species have shown that it is also a way of decoy and can create confusion for the predators. This phenomenon is reflected in both CSD and DSD by the sudden change of position of the krill to a new position, less explored, which is an equivalent to the process of the mutation in genetic algorithm. This uncertain exile to unexplored area is automatically handled in CSD but in case of DSD the best intermediate path between the initial and final node is included in the chromosome of the moulted krill.

3   Discrete Krill Herd Algorithm

The discrete KHA will constitute of decision making as selection of an event or not, like a state space transition and no intermediate halts or investigation. But the most important aspect of this discrete KHA, suitable for graph based problems, is that there is no requirement of any discrete equations. On the same platform it can be generalized to all kind of continuous space search problems. The presence of mutation category steps like Random Movement, Predator's Rush and Moulting there is possibility that in spite of swarming there will high probability of coming out of local optimization to global optimization. Random movement is a slow carefree movement, while Predator's Rush is randomized escape movement of considerable levels and is more than one. However the Moulting is a sudden deportation to a random node. The flow diagram of the algorithm is provided in Fig. 3.

4   Methods and Algorithms

Discrete Krill Herd Algorithm is used for the road management problem of maneuvering the excessive flow of vehicles through the other optimized path of the network. A herd of krill will scatter through the network in search of optimum path and will be evaluated on the basis of a weighted parameter fitness function. The following algorithm is used in the simulation for optimized path planning. The road network considered in Fig. 2 is of 25 nodes and 45 edges and each of the edges are having fixed parameters like distance and a dynamic parameters average waiting time. The presence of constantly changing parameters concerns how fast the algorithm works and how efficient the optimized path is, when already the dynamic parameters tends to change with time and the validity of the optimized path gradually diminishes. In this work we have shown that the efficient route foundation between node A and node Y is being made with DKHA, ACO and IWD and the best convergence rate is with DKHA.

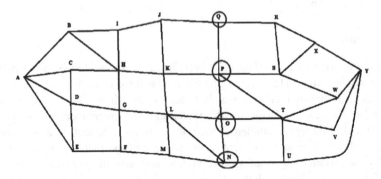

Fig. 2. Road Graph Network

There are a few considerations and approximations that are opted to ensure implementation simplicity of the road network and the application of the nature inspired heuristic possible. The vehicles considered here are of same size irrespective of its type and the velocity is considered constant. The road network parameters are modeled and changed randomly considering that the other vehicles from other regions are also making their normal transportation. The individual contribution for waiting time for each segment of the road is not considered, instead an average of all for a particular crossing is considered. The overall fitness is calculated by the summation of all the parameters of the edges of the derived path. The fitness function is kept simple and non-linear non-weighted sum of traveling time and waiting time. The main purpose of the algorithm is finding the multi-variable based optimized best path for the vehicles and analyzes the variation in total time and thus compare with the Ant Colony Optimization and Intelligent Water Drop algorithms for optimized path.

$$f_1 = \sum_{k=1}^{k=n} D_k \quad \& \quad f_2 = \sum_{k=1}^{k=n} AWT_k \tag{5}$$

where f_1 and f_2 are the two equations and D_k is the distance and AWT_k is the average waiting time for the path $k \in \{i,j\}$ where i and j are the two nodes and there exist a link between them. Fitness function is defined as $f = (f_1/V + f_2)$ where V is the velocity normalization factor to make both f_1 and f_2 of the same time unit and f_1/V becomes travelling time.

4.1   Discrete KHA for Optimized Route Search

In this portion some implementation details of the Discrete Krill Herd Algorithm are being discussed according to the graph based scenario problem and the criteria for decision of occurrence of any operation of the algorithm.

Step 1: Initialize Road Graph G = (V, E) and Road Parameters Matrix {p_1, p_2 ,...., p_k } for k parameters. Here k = 2.

Step 2: Initialize krill matrix consisting of ID, chromosome for path traversed, number of nodes, sum of parameter vector, illumination factor or fitness.

Step 3: Initialize normalized illumination factor (L^k) of each node depending on the krill present there and $0 \leq L^k \leq 1$.

Step 4: IF L^k of adjacent nodes ≥ Threshold

     Calculate P_{ij} for n_2 number of paths according to Equation (3,4) where $n_2 \leq$ number of available paths

     Perform Phototatic Swarming Movement

    IF L of adjacent nodes < Threshold

     Calculate P_{ij} for n number of paths according to Equation (1,2) where $n \leq$ number of available paths

     Perform Concentration Enhancement Movement

    IF P_{ij} is same for more than one path

     Perform Random Movement

where $0 \leq$ Threshold ≤ 1 can be margin for decision making which can be constant or can be adaptive which is generated randomly and then treated.

Step 5: IF fitness of krill very poor

    Perform Predator's Prey operation

Step 6: IF number of krill are dead

    Choose the best swarms at node

    Randomly choose krill with common gene point(s)

    Perform Reproduction

    Perform Crossover of Gene

    IF Swarm Size < Threshold

     Perform non-sac-spawners hatching

    IF Swarm Size > Threshold

     Perform sac-spawners hatching

where Threshold can be random for adaptive situation or can be a function of the Swarm size and the paths available. If the Swarm size is too big for the available paths, then better is sac-spawners hatching, else the other one.

Step 7: IF fitness of krill very low or looping occurred

    Perform Predator's Rush

    IF fitness of krill very low

     Perform Predator's Prey operation or looping occurred (looping is one of the main reasons for deterioration of the fitness)

    Else

     Perform lobstering

Step 8: IF illumination factor of krill very low

    Perform Moulting

Step 9: IF the krill reached destination

    Calculate the fitness value

Step 10: Update the best path matrix with global best

Step 11: Provide the best path matrix to the vehicles

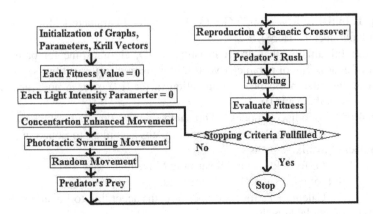

Fig. 3. Flow Diagram for Discrete Krill Herd Algorithm

5 Computational Results and Graphs

The following graphs are the results of the simulation performed to estimate the success and appropriateness of the algorithm with respect to complexity and events and the result is compared with Ant Colony Optimization (ACO) and Intelligent Water Drops (IWD) algorithms and the KRILL (DKHA) in Fig. 4-8 represents the performance of Discrete Krill Herd Algorithm (DKHA). The results show that the convergence rate of the DKHA is quicker than the others. This is because in DKHA the exploration is more and elaborated than in ACO and IWD. However the complexity of the DKHA is also more both with respect to space and time and gain is achieved in quick convergence. Another salient feature of the DKHA is that if the graph is "partly region biased" then it can achieve good result. The term "partly region biased" means that the graph has similar kind of nodes/edges or similar kind of events in clusters and hence when events like reproduction occurs it achieves good results. Like in the road graph in Fig. 2, we have considered that the outer roads are like bypass and are high way like roads and have low waiting time and high in distance whereas the middle one are with low distance and high waiting time. So when events like reproduction occurs at the outer regions then it may happen that the offspring may explore better paths with optimized waiting time and considerably better distance. The performance in other models is opportunistic and subjected to randomness (balance between exploration and exploitation) and experimentation.

Fig. 4-8 show how the convergence rate of the three algorithms (ACO, IWD, DKHA) with respect to Travelling time (distance), Waiting time and Total time (Travelling time + Waiting time). Total time is the multi-objective fitness considered here. In all the cases the DKHA outperforms the other two, where the search movement is considered here is only for Total time and the performance for the Travelling time & Waiting time is being extracted from the evaluation for 40 krill agents for each out of 30 iterations. Another important point that needs to be mentioned here is that though the search is for Total time based optimization, the search is well scattered and also covers many other parts of the graph to contribute for the search. Also the reproduction and elimination of agents in the graph must not eliminate all the agents at one part of the graph and care must be taken care through controlling the numbers of regeneration and elimination.

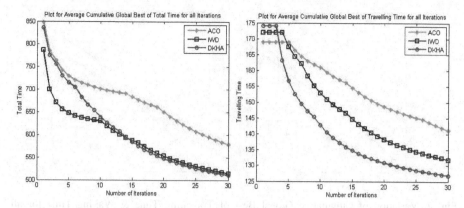

Fig. 4. Variation of Average Cumulative Global Best of Total & Travelling Time for all Iterations

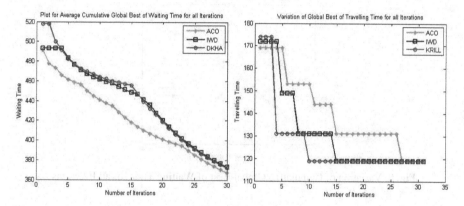

Fig. 5. Variation of Average Cumulative Global Best of Waiting Time & Global Best of Travelling Time for all Iterations

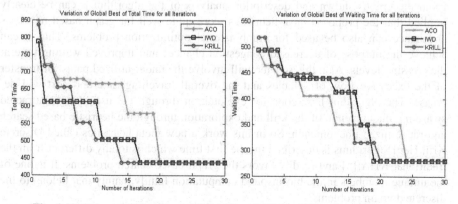

Fig. 6. Variation of Global Best of Total Time & Waiting Time for all Iterations

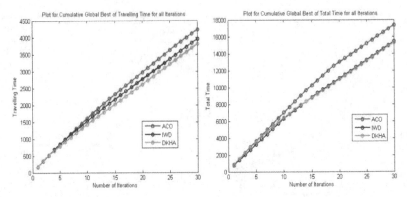

Fig. 7. Variation of Cumulative Global Best of Travelling Time & Waiting Time for all Iterations

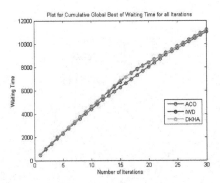

Fig. 8. Variation of Cumulative Global Best of Waiting Time for all Iterations

6   Conclusion and Future Works

From the graphs shown and description analysis of the algorithm it can be clearly implied that the proposed meat-heuristics work quite well for graph based networks and hence can also be used for combinatorial optimization problems. Thus it can achieve the purpose of decreased congestion chances and improved waiting time at the crossing levels. Also this scheme will involve the under-utilized paths for transfer of the excessive flow of vehicles and the overall travelling time and cost will decrease. The algorithm has scope for exploitation through the use of light attracted swarming phenomenon of the krill and exploration through the heuristic based search and randomized phenomenon. So in this work a new meta-heuristics called Discrete Krill Herd algorithms is described for the first time which is totally different from the traditional KHA [5] and readily favors the graph based search problems. It is one of the unique members in the bio-inspired computation family mainly that belong to the discrete domain problems.

There are a lot of work remains when it comes to comparing how efficient is the algorithm when compared to other meta-heuristics and also depending on the cost function how it performs for all other NP-Hard problems. The system is likely to change its behavior when it comes to other road network system and different arrival rate of vehicles. The work also involves how to develop its parameters making the system more adaptive while selecting its choice of step variations in movements. The occurrences of the steps are mostly random which makes the algorithm suitable for hard problems. An investigation of the importance of each step in the whole meta-heuristics can also be done.

References

1. Everson, I. (ed.): Krill - Biology, Ecology and Fisheries. Blackwell Science Ltd. (2000)
2. Tarling, G., Lesser, M. (eds.): Advances in Marine Biology, vol. 57. Academic Press, Elsevier (2010)
3. Yang, Z., Lu, S., Liu, X.: Combined Traffic Signal Control and Route Guidance: Multiple User Class Traffic Assignment Model versus Discrete Choice Model. In: IMACS Multiconference on Computational Engineering in Systems Applications, October 4-6, vol. 2, pp. 1957–1964 (2006)
4. Krill (2012), http://en.wikipedia.org/wiki/Krill
5. Gandomi, A.H., Alavi, A.H.: Krill Herd: a new bio-inspired optimization algorithm. Communications in Nonlinear Science and Numerical Simulation 17(12), 4831–4845 (2012)
6. Alves, D., van Ast, J., Cong, Z., De Schutter, B., Babusandka, R.: Ant colony optimization for traffic dispersion routing. In: 2010 13th International IEEE Conference on Intelligent Transportation Systems(ITSC), pp. 683–688 (2010)
7. Zong, X., Xiong, S., Fang, Z., Li, Q.: Multi-ant colony system for evacuation routing problem with mixed traffic flow. In: 2010 IEEE Congress on Evolutionary Computation (CEC), pp. 1–6 (2010)
8. Wang, G., Guo, L., Duan, H., Wang, H., Liu, L., Li, J.: Incorporating mutation scheme into krill herd algorithm for global numerical optimization. Neural Computing and Applications.
9. Wang, G., Guo, L., HosseinGandomi, A., et al.: Lévy-Flight Krill Herd Algorithm. Mathematical Problems in Engineering 2013, Article ID 682073, 14 pages (2013)
10. Dorigo, M., Gambardella, L.M.: Ant Colony System: A Cooperative Learning Approach to the Traveling Salesman Problem. IEEE Transactions on Evolutionary Computation 1(1), 53–66 (1997)
11. Shah-Hosseini, H.: The intelligent water drops algorithm: a nature-inspired swarm-based optimization algorithm. International Journal of Bio-Inspired Computation 1(1/2), 71–79 (2009)
12. Krishnanand, K., Ghose, D.: Glowworm swarm optimization for simultaneous capture of multiple local optima of multimodal functions. Swarm Intelligence 3(2), 87–124 (2009)
13. Yang, X.-S.: Firefly algorithms for multimodal optimization. In: Watanabe, O., Zeugmann, T. (eds.) SAGA 2009. LNCS, vol. 5792, pp. 169–178. Springer, Heidelberg (2009)
14. Kennedy, J., Eberhart, R.: Particle swarm optimization. In: Proc. IEEE Int. Conf. Neural Networks, vol. 4, pp. 1942–1948 (1995)

A New Number System Using Alternate Fibonacci Numbers as the Positional Weights with Some Engineering Applications

Koushik Sinha[1], Rabindranath Ghosh[2], and Bhabani Prasad Sinha[3]

[1] HP Labs, Bangalore, India
sinha_kou@yahoo.com
[2] St. Thomas' College of Engineering and Technology, Kolkata, India
rnghosh@gmail.com
[3] A.C.M. Unit, Indian Statistical Institute, Kolkata, India
bhabani@isical.ac.in

Abstract. Fibonaccian number system (FNS) that uses $\{0, 1\}$ as the digit set with Fibonacci numbers as the positional weights, has many interesting properties which can be exploited for various applications. We propose here a new number system, termed as the Tri-digit Fibonaccian Number System (TFNS), with alternate Fibonacci numbers as the positional weights for the various digits in the representation. We show that TFNS provides asymmetric distribution of the three digits (0, 1 and 2) in representing numbers with a pair of consecutive 2's never appearing in a valid codeword. These properties can conveniently be utilized for typical engineering applications, e.g., message encoding for low-energy communication systems and variable length encoding with self-delimiting code.

Keywords: Fibonacci Number, Fibonacci Number System, Tridigit Fibonacci Number System, Silent Communication, Energy-efficient Communication.

1 Introduction

In many engineering applications, the Fibonacci number system (FNS) [13] has been used with remarkable success. Such applications include VLSI chip design (in minimizing crosstalk among the data buses inside a processor chip [10]), synchronization control [8], compression of large sparse bit-strings [5], robust transmission of binary strings [2], and so on. Another possible application is in the area of low-power wireless communication systems [6, 11, 12] where asymmetry in the numbers of symbols to be transmitted through the wireless channel is exploited in minimizing the transmitter and/or receiver energy. If Fibonaccian number system is used to give positional weights to binary digits for representation of decimal numbers, a marked asymmetry may be observed so far as the numbers of 0's and 1's in the resulting codewords are concerned. These asymmetric characteristics can be exploited for saving energy in communication, particularly in low-power wireless sensor networks. However, if conventional FNS is used, the number of bits representing a given decimal number increases compared to the binary number system. As a result, the savings of energy for low-power wireless communication systems may not be substantial. This motivates us to propose a new

R. Natarajan (Ed.): ICDCIT 2014, LNCS 8337, pp. 164–175, 2014.

number system called the *Tri-digit Fibonaccian Number System* (TFNS), which provides asymmetric distribution in the number of 0's, 1's and 2's used in representing the all possible numbers, along with a substantial reduction in the number of digits, so as to bring about significant energy savings in wireless communication systems. Also in the proposed TFNS, a pair of 2's will never appear in a valid codeword. Thus, TFNS can be used for variable length encoding of integers in data using a pair of 2's as separators between consecutive integers in the data stream.

2 Preliminaries

We denote the nth ($n \geq 0$) number in the Fibonacci sequence $< 0, 1, 1, 2, 3, 5, 8, \ldots >$ as F_n, where $F_0 = 0, F_1 = F_2 = 1, F_3 = 2, F_4 = 3, F_5 = 5$ and so on. In FNS, the ith bit position ($i \geq 0$, $i = 0$ being the least significant bit) has the positional weight of F_{i+2}. In the literature, there exist different versions of FNS which have different representations of the same decimal number [10]. However, the normal form of FNS [8] always provides a unique representation of a given decimal number N in FNS as shown in table 1. Also, an interesting result regarding the Fibonacci numbers is that a positive integer can be expressed uniquely in terms of a sum of non-consecutive Fibonacci numbers as in Zeckendorf representation of numbers [13]. However, it may be noted that the positional weights in all such representations [8, 13] consist of all the Fibonacci numbers in order, leading to a representation of a number in terms of a string of 0's and 1's only.

One interesting property of the normal form of FNS is that if the $i^{th}(i > 0)$ bit is 1, then the $(i - 1)^{th}$ bit must be a 0. It is easy to prove by induction on n that out of all possible n-bit valid strings of 0's and 1's in FNS there are exactly F_n strings which have a 1 and F_{n+1} strings which have a 0 at the msb. This hypothesis is true for $n = 3$. Assuming that the hypothesis is true for $n = n$ we note that there can not be two consecutive 1's in FNS representation. Hence, to form $(n + 1)$-bit numbers in FNS from all possible n-bit numbers in FNS, we can append either a 0 or a 1 on the msb side of F_{n+1} such n-bit numbers having a 0 at the $(n - 1)^{th}$ bit position. But we can append only a 0 on the msb side of F_n n-bit numbers which have a 1 at the $(n - 1)^{th}$ bit position. Thus, the total number of valid $(n + 1)$-bit numbers in FNS having a 1 at its msb = F_{n+1}, while those with a 0 at the msb = $F_{n+1} + F_n = F_{n+2}$. Thus, the hypothesis is also true for $n = n + 1$. The total numbers of 0's and 1's appearing at any bit position (starting from the most significant bit (msb)) of an n-bit FNS representation of all decimal numbers in the range $0 \leq N \leq F_{n+2} - 1$, can be visualized by means of an edge-weighted binary tree as shown in Fig. 1.

In Fig. 1, the root node labeled as '*' has the left child labeled as '0' with the corresponding edge weight of F_{n+1}, and a right child labeled as '1' with the corresponding edge weight of F_n, meaning thereby that considering the representation of all possible numbers, there are F_{n+1} 0's and F_n 1's at the msb (i.e., $(n - 1)^{th}$ bit position). This left child '0' of '*', in turn, has a left child labeled as '0' with the corresponding edge weight of F_n and a right child labeled as '1' with the corresponding edge weight of F_{n-1}, meaning that the codes which have a 0 at the msb, have a total of F_n 0's and F_{n-1} 1's at the $(n - 2)^{th}$ bit position. On the other hand, the right child '1' of '*' has

Table 1. Numbers Represented in FNS, TFNS and Decimal System

FNS					Corresponding decimal number	TFNS			
Weights $\Longrightarrow$	$F_6 = 8$	$F_5 = 5$	$F_4 = 3$	$F_3 = 2$	$F_2 = 1$		$F_8 = 21$	$F_6 = 8$	$F_4 = 3$	$F_2 = 1$
	0	0	0	0	0	0	0	0	0	0
	0	0	0	0	1	1	0	0	0	1
	0	0	0	1	0	2	0	0	0	2
	0	0	1	0	0	3	0	0	1	0
	0	0	1	0	1	4	0	0	1	1
	0	1	0	0	0	5	0	0	1	2
	0	1	0	0	1	6	0	0	2	0
	0	1	0	1	0	7	0	0	2	1
	1	0	0	0	0	8	0	1	0	0
	1	0	0	0	1	9	0	1	0	1
	1	0	0	1	0	10	0	1	0	2
	1	0	1	0	0	11	0	1	1	0
	1	0	1	0	1	12	0	1	1	1

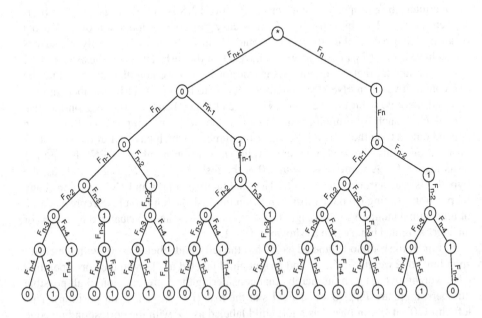

Fig. 1. Tree for FNS

only one (left) child labeled as '0' (as two consecutive bits can not be 1) with the corresponding edge weight of F_n, meaning that the codes which have a 1 at the msb, have a total of only F_n 0's at the $(n-2)^{th}$ bit position.

Asymptotic proportions of 0's and 1's in the numbers in FNS have been derived by P. H. St. John [7]. However, we derive these values here in a slightly different way as follows. From the above construction of the binary tree in Fig. 1, the total number of 0's in n-bit representation of all decimal numbers in the range 0 to $F_{n+2} - 1$ (both inclusive) is given by:

$$
\begin{aligned}
\nu_0 &= F_{n+1} + (F_n + F_n) + (F_{n-1} + F_{n-1} + F_{n-1}) + \ldots \\
&= F_{n+1} + 2F_n + 3F_{n-1} + 5F_{n-2} + 8F_{n-3} + \ldots \\
&= F_2 F_{n+1} + F_3 F_n + F_4 F_{n-1} + F_5 F_{n-2} + F_6 F_{n-3} + \ldots + F_{n+1} F_2
\end{aligned}
\tag{1}
$$

Similarly, the number of 1's denoted by ν_1 is given by:

$$
\begin{aligned}
\nu_1 &= F_n + F_{n-1} + (F_{n-2} + F_{n-2}) + (F_{n-3} + F_{n-3} + F_{n-3}) + \ldots \\
&= F_n + F_{n-1} + 2F_{n-2} + 3F_{n-3} + 5F_{n-4} + 8F_{n-5} + \ldots \\
&= F_1 F_n + F_2 F_{n-1} + F_3 F_{n-2} + F_4 F_{n-3} + F_5 F_{n-4} + \ldots + F_n F_1
\end{aligned}
\tag{2}
$$

Let $G(z) = F_0 + F_1 z + F_2 z^2 + F_3 z^3 + F_4 z^4 + \ldots$.
Thus, $G^2(z) = (F_0 + F_1 z + F_2 z^2 + F_3 z^3 + F_4 z^4 + \ldots)^2$ and the coefficient of z^{n+3} in $G^2(z)$ is given by:
$$(F_{n+3}F_0 + F_{n+2}F_1 + F_{n+1}F_2 + \ldots + F_2 F_{n+1} + F_1 F_{n+2} + F_0 F_{n+3})$$
$$= \nu_0 + 2F_{n+2}F_1.$$
Now, $G(z) = \frac{1}{\sqrt{5}}[(1 - \phi z)^{-1} - (1 - \bar{\phi} z)^{-1}]$ as in [9], where $\phi = \frac{\sqrt{5}+1}{2}$ and $\bar{\phi} = \frac{\sqrt{5}-1}{2}$.
So,

$$
G^2(z) = \frac{1}{5}[(1 - \phi z)^{-2} + (1 - \bar{\phi} z)^{-2} - 2(1 - \phi z)^{-1}(1 - \bar{\phi} z)^{-1}]
$$

Hence, the coefficient of z^{n+3} in $G^2(z)$ is:

$$
\frac{1}{5}[(n+4).\phi^{n+3} + (n+4).\bar{\phi}^{n+3} - 2(\phi^{n+3}.\bar{\phi}^0 + \phi^{n+2}.\bar{\phi} + \ldots + \phi^1.\bar{\phi}^{n+2} + \phi^0.\bar{\phi}^{n+3}]
$$

Let $S = \phi^{n+3} + \phi^{n+2}.\bar{\phi} + \ldots + \phi.\bar{\phi}^{n+2} + \bar{\phi}^{n+3}$.
So, $S[1 - \frac{\bar{\phi}}{\phi}] = \phi^{n+3} - \frac{\bar{\phi}^{n+4}}{\phi} = \frac{\phi^{n+4} - \bar{\phi}^{n+4}}{\phi}$
Hence, $S = \phi^{n+4} - \bar{\phi}^{n+4}$, as $\phi - \bar{\phi} = 1$.
Therefore,

$$
\nu_0 = \frac{1}{5}[(n+4)(\phi^{n+3} + \bar{\phi}^{n+3}) - 2(\phi^{n+4} - \bar{\phi}^{n+4})]
\tag{3}
$$

Putting the values of ϕ and $\bar{\phi}$ in the above expression of ν_0, we get the number of 0's in all n-bit valid codewords. Hence, we get the number of 1's in all n-bit valid codewords as,

$$\nu_1 = nF_{n+2} - \nu_0 \tag{4}$$

For large n, $\nu_0 \approx \frac{(n+4-2\phi)\phi^{n+3}}{5} = \frac{(n+0.764)\phi^{n+3}}{5}$. The ratio of ν_0 to the total number of bits nF_{n+2} asymptotically tends to $\frac{\phi}{\sqrt{5}} = 72.36\%$. Such a large asymmetry in the number of 0's and 1's would have been nicely exploited in certain applications involving low energy wireless communication (such as, in wireless sensor networks) as used by Sinha et al. in [11, 12], by keeping the transmitter silent or OFF during the dominant symbols (0's in this case) and thereby reducing the average power of signal transmission.

On the other hand, corresponding to m-bit binary representation of numbers, we need n bits in FNS where n is the least integer satisfying the inequality $F_{n+2} - 1 > 2^m - 1$. Noting that $F_{n+2} \approx \frac{\phi^{n+2}}{\sqrt{5}}$ for large n, $\frac{\phi^{n+2}}{\sqrt{5}} > 2^m$, i.e., $n \approx \lceil \frac{m \log 2 + \log \sqrt{5}}{\log \phi} \rceil - 2$. For $m = 8, 16, 32, 64, 128, 256, 512$ and 1024, the corresponding values of n are 12, 23, 46, 92, 185, 369, 738 and 1475, respectively. The ratio $\frac{n}{m}$ asymptotically tends to 1.44. This shows that the number of bits in FNS representation is 1.44 times higher than that of the original binary representation. Such an increase in the length of the code may not be desirable in many engineering applications.

3   Proposed Tri-digit Fibonaccian Number System

To overcome the above problem of increase in the length of a codeword in FNS, we propose here a number system in which i) the digits at each digit-position will be taken from the set $\{0, 1, 2\}$, and ii) the positional weight at the ith ($i \geq 0$), digit-position ($i = 0$ corresponds to the least significant digit-position) is equal to F_{2i+2}. That is, the positional weights at different digit-positions are $F_2, F_4, F_6, \ldots$, with F_2 as the weight of the least significant digit. We term this number system as the *Tri-digit Fibonaccian Number System* (TFNS). In TFNS the weights at different digit-positions are alternate numbers in the Fibonacci sequence. Given a decimal number $N < F_{2k+2}$ for some k, we can represent N in its equivalent TFNS form using k digits $d_0, d_1, d_2, \ldots, d_{k-1}$ by the decimal-to-TFNS conversion algorithm $DTFNS$ as given below :

Following the above conversion algorithm $DTFNS$, the representations of all decimal numbers in the range 0 to 12 (both inclusive) using 4 digits in TFNS are shown in Table 1. Note that the decimal number 8 is *uniquely* represented as 0100 in TFNS using the above conversion algorithm. Although another possible representation of the decimal number 8 in TFNS with the above positional weights could be 0022, this representation cannot be obtained by the algorithm $DTFNS$. This is because of the *if* statement in line 2 which, in effect, forces the number to be represented by using non-zero digits at the highest possible digit positions, whenever possible.

Lemma 1. *Let N be a decimal number whose representation in TFNS is $2111\ldots1$ having $(k - 1)$ 1's following a '2'. Then the decimal number $N + 1$ will be represented by $1000\ldots0$, with k 0's after the '1'.*

Algorithm 1. $DTFNS$

Input: Decimal number N, integer k such that $N < F_{2k+2}$
Output: Equivalent TFNS form for N

```
1  forall i = k - 1 downto 0 do
2      if N ≥ 2F_{2i+2} then
3          d_i ← 2;
4          N ← N - 2F_{2i+2};
5      else if N ≥ F_{2i+2} then
6          d_i ← 1;
7          N ← N - F_{2i+2};
8      else
9          d_i ← 0;
```

Proof: We first note that $F_{2n+2} = F_{2n+1} + F_{2n} = F_{2n} + F_{2n-1} + F_{2n} = 3F_{2n} - F_{2n-2}$. Thus, if we subtract three from a digit and add one to the two digits on either side and apply this process repeatedly then we can form patterns like $(+1,-3,+1)$, $(+1,-2,-2,+1)$, $(+1,-2,-1,-2,+1)$, $(+1,-2,-1,-1,-2,+1)$ and so on with any number of minus 1's between the two minus 2's, all having the value zero. Hence, any substring of the form $x, 2, 1 * n, 2, y$ with $x, y \in \{0, 1, 2\}$ and n as an integer greater than or equal to zero, can be replaced by $(x + 1), 0 * (n + 2), (y + 1)$ by adding the sequence $(+1, -2, (-1) * n, -2, +1)$ (representing zero) to that substring, without changing the value of the string. This sort of arithmetic is similar to that used in FNS [1, 3]. Specifically, by above logic, if a decimal number N is represented in TFNS as $2111\ldots1$ having $(k - 1)$ 1's following a '2', then $N + 1$ will be represented by $1000\ldots0$, with k 0's after the '1'. That is, $N + 1 = F_{2n+2}$. By virtue of the conversion algorithm $DTFNS$, $N + 1$ will indeed be represented as $1000\ldots0$ in TFNS, with k 0's after the '1'. $\qquad \square$

Because of lemma 1 it follows that if we consider n-digit representation of numbers in TFNS, then all possible 3^n code values will not be generated by the algorithm $DTFNS$. Our proposed number system primarily differs from the Zeckendorf number system in having the alternate Fibonacci numbers as positional weights. Such a choice of alternate Fibonacci numbers in the positional weights leads to a number representation using three digits 0, 1 and 2 for any digit position. Moreover, Zeckendorf representation does not have two consecutive 1's but there will be no two consecutive 2's in TFNS representation as stated in the following lemma.

Lemma 2. *TFNS representation of any given number may have consecutive 1's, but no consecutive 2's.*

Proof: Follows from the same logic given in the proof of lemma 1. $\qquad \square$

The property given in lemma 2 leads to an immediate application of TFNS in variable length encoding for minimizing the code length, with a pair of consecutive 2's as a delimiter. The properties given in lemmas 1 and 2 lead to unequal distribution in the total number of 0's, 1's and 2's in the TFNS coding of numbers for any given n-digit representation. A careful look at the digit generation process in the algorithm $DTFNS$ would help us in finding the exact distribution of the numbers of 0's, 1's and 2's in the TFNS code values. We follow this digit generation process (starting from the most

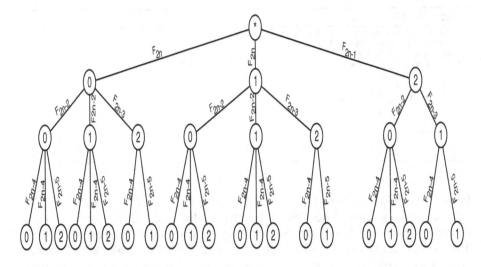

Fig. 2. Tree for TFNS

significant digit position) for all possible codes with n digits (to represent numbers in the range 0 to $F_{2n+2} - 1$) by constructing a weighted ternary tree T shown in Fig. 2 as follows.

First, we start at the root of T and insert its 3 children nodes labeled as 0, 1 and 2 (with three edges connected from the root to these three nodes), meaning thereby that the leftmost digit position of the code values can be filled by a 0, 1 or 2. Since a '0' at the leftmost digit position will appear for all the numbers having the decimal values ranging from 0 to F_{2n}, the weight of the edge connecting the root to its child node labeled as 0, will be set as F_{2n}. So is also the case with the weight of the edge connecting the root to its child labeled as '1'. But the weight of the edge connecting the root to the child labeled as '2' will be $F_{2n+2} - 2F_{2n} = F_{2n-1}$. We now derive expressions for the distribution of 0's, 1's and 2's in TFNS.

4   Deriving TFNS Digit Distributions

From Figure 2 we see that the total number of 0's in all the n-digit valid codewords representing all numbers in the range 0 to $F_{2n+2} - 1$ (both inclusive) is given by:

$$\nu_0' = F_{2n} + 3F_{2n-2} + 8F_{2n-4} + \ldots = F_2 F_{2n} + F_4 F_{2n-2} + F_6 F_{2n-4} + \ldots + F_{2n} F_2$$

Similarly, the total number of 1's in all valid codewords is:

$$\nu_1' = F_{2n} + (2F_{2n-2} + F_{2n-3}) + \ldots$$
$$= F_1 F_{2n} + (F_3 F_{2n-2} + F_2 F_{2n-3}) + \ldots + (F_{2n-1} F_2 + F_{2n-2} F_1)$$

And, the total number of 2's in all the valid codewords is:

$$v_2' = F_1 F_{2n-1} + 2 F_{2n-3} + 5 F_{2n-5} + \ldots$$
$$= F_1 F_{2n-1} + F_3 F_{2n-3} + F_5 F_{2n-5} + \ldots + F_{2n-1} F_1$$

To express v_0', v_1' and v_2' in closed form we proceed as follows.
Let $G(z) = F_0 + F_1 z + F_2 z^2 + F_3 z^3 + F_4 z^4 + \ldots$.
Thus, $G(z)$ is given by $G(z) = \frac{z}{1-z-z^2}$ as in [9].
Now, $G(-z) = F_0 - F_1 z + F_2 z^2 - F_3 z^3 + F_4 z^4 + \ldots$.
Hence, we have:

$$\frac{G(z) + G(-z)}{2} = F_0 + F_2 z^2 + F_4 z^4 + F_6 z^6 + \ldots = H(z), \quad \text{(say)}.$$

That is,

$$H(z) = \frac{z^2}{(1-z^2)^2 - z^2} = \frac{z^2}{1 - 3z^2 + z^4}$$
$$= \frac{z^2}{(1 - \alpha z^2)(1 - \beta z^2)}, \quad \text{(say)},$$

where α and β are given by:

$$\left. \begin{array}{r} \alpha + \beta = 3 \\ \alpha \beta = 1 \end{array} \right\} \tag{5}$$

Hence, $\alpha = \frac{3+\sqrt{5}}{2} = 1 + \phi$ and $\beta = \frac{3-\sqrt{5}}{2} = 1 - \bar{\phi}$.
Also, $H^2(z) = (F_0 + F_2 z^2 + F_4 z^4 + \ldots)^2$, in which the coefficient of z^{2n+2} is $F_0 F_{2n+2} + F_2 F_{2n} + F_4 F_{2n-2} + \ldots + F_{2n+2} F_0 = v_0'$.
Hence,

$$H(z) = \frac{z^2}{[1 - (1+\phi)z^2][1 - (1+\bar{\phi})z^2]}$$
$$\Rightarrow H^2(z) = \frac{z^4}{[1 - (1+\phi)z^2]^2 [1 - (1+\bar{\phi})z^2]^2}$$

Let $(1+\phi)z^2 = x$ and $(1-\bar{\phi})z^2 = y$. Then, $H^2(z) = \frac{z^4}{(1-x)^2(1-y)^2}$.
Hence, the coefficient of z^{2n+2} in $H^2(z)$

= the coefficient of z^{2n-2} in $(1-x)^{-2}(1-y)^{-2}$
= the sum of the coefficients of $x^i y^j$ in $(1-x)^{-2}(1-y)^{-2}$ with $i + j = n - 1$
$= (1+\phi)^0 \cdot 1 \cdot n(1-\bar{\phi})^{n-1} + 2(1+\phi)(n-1)(1-\bar{\phi})^{n-2}$
$\quad + 3(1+\phi)^2(n-2)(1-\bar{\phi})^{n-3} + \ldots + n(1+\phi)^{n-1} \cdot 1 \cdot (1-\bar{\phi})$.

4.1   Computation of ν_0'

Collecting the terms from the right hand side of the above expression and noting that $(1 + \phi)(1 - \bar{\phi}) = 1$, we get $\nu_0' = n(1 + \phi)^{n-1} + 2(n - 1)(1 + \phi)^{n-3} + 3(n - 2)(1 + \phi)^{n-5} + \ldots + n(1 + \phi)^{1-n}$.

Replacing $(1 + \phi)$ by α, we get,

$$\nu_0' = n\alpha^{n-1} + 2(n - 1)\alpha^{n-3} + 3(n - 2)\alpha^{n-5} + \ldots + n\alpha^{1-n} \tag{6}$$

And, $$\frac{\nu_0'}{\alpha^2} = n\alpha^{n-3} + 2(n - 1)\alpha^{n-5} + \ldots + (n - 1).2.\alpha^{1-n} + n\alpha^{-n-1} \tag{7}$$

Subtracting eqn (7) from eqn (6) we get

$\nu_0'(1 - \frac{1}{\alpha^2}) = n\alpha^{n-1} + (n - 2)\alpha^{n-3} + (n - 4)\alpha^{n-5} \quad + (n - 6)\alpha^{n-7} + \ldots + [n - 2(n - 1)]\alpha^{1-n} - n\alpha^{-n-1}$

$= n(\alpha^{n-1} + \alpha^{n-3} + \alpha^{n-5} + \ldots) - 2(\alpha^{n-3} + 2\alpha^{n-5} + 3\alpha^{n-7} + \ldots)$

$= \frac{n\alpha^{n-1}(1-\gamma^n)}{1-\gamma} - 2\alpha^{n-3}\left[\frac{1-\gamma^{n-1}}{(1-\gamma)^2} - \frac{(n-1)\gamma^{n-1}}{1-\gamma}\right] - n\alpha^{-1-n}$, where $\gamma = \frac{1}{\alpha^2}$.

Thus,

$$\nu_0' = \frac{1}{1 - \gamma}\left(\frac{n\alpha^{n-1}(1 - \gamma^n)}{1 - \gamma} - 2\alpha^{n-3}\left[\frac{1 - \gamma^{n-1}}{(1 - \gamma)^2} - \frac{(n - 1)\gamma^{n-1}}{1 - \gamma}\right] - n\alpha^{-1-n}\right) \tag{8}$$

That is,

$$\nu_0' = \frac{n\alpha^{n-1}(1 - \gamma^n)}{(1 - \gamma)^2} - 2\alpha^{n-3}\left[\frac{1 - \gamma^{n-1}}{(1 - \gamma)^3} - \frac{(n - 1)\gamma^{n-1}}{(1 - \gamma)^2}\right] - \frac{n\alpha^{-1-n}}{1 - \gamma} \tag{9}$$

4.2   Computation of ν_1' and ν_2'

We have, $\nu_2' = F_1 F_{2n-1} + F_3 F_{2n-3} + \ldots + F_{2n-1}F_1$.
Let $H'(z) = \frac{1}{2}[G(z) - G(-z)] = F_1 z + F_3 z^3 + F_5 z^5 + \ldots$
Hence, ν_2' is the coefficient of z^{2n} in $H'^2(z)$.
Now, $H'(z)$ can be written as:

$$\frac{1}{2}\left[\frac{z}{1 - z - z^2} - \frac{-z}{1 + z - z^2}\right] = z\left[\frac{1 - z^2}{1 + z^4 - 3z^2}\right]$$

Denoting z^2 by δ, we get,

$$\frac{1 - z^2}{1 + z^4 - 3z^2} = \frac{1 - \delta}{1 - 3\delta + \delta^2} = \frac{1 - \delta}{(1 - \alpha\delta)(1 - \beta\delta)}$$

where α and β are given by eqn (5).

Now,

$$\frac{1}{1-\alpha\delta} + \frac{1}{1-\beta\delta} = \frac{2-(\alpha+\beta)\delta}{1-3\delta+\delta^2}$$

$$= \frac{2-3\delta}{1-3\delta+\delta^2}$$

and,

$$\frac{1}{1-\alpha\delta} - \frac{1}{1-\beta\delta} = \frac{(\alpha-\beta)\delta}{1-3\delta+\delta^2}$$

$$= \frac{\sqrt{5}\delta}{1-3\delta+\delta^2}$$

$$\Rightarrow \frac{2(1-\delta)}{1-3\delta+\delta^2} = \frac{2-3\delta+\delta}{1-3\delta+\delta^2}$$

$$= \frac{1}{1-\alpha\delta} + \frac{1}{1-\beta\delta} + \frac{1}{\sqrt{5}}\left[\frac{1}{1-\alpha\delta} - \frac{1}{1-\beta\delta}\right]$$

We can therefore express $H'(z)$ as $\frac{z}{2}\left[\frac{C_1}{1-\alpha z^2} + \frac{C_2}{1-\beta z^2}\right]$, where $C_1 = 1 + \frac{1}{\sqrt{5}}$ and $C_2 = 1 - \frac{1}{\sqrt{5}}$.

Hence, $H'^2(z) = \frac{z^2}{4}\left[\frac{C_1}{1-\alpha z^2} + \frac{C_2}{1-\beta z^2}\right]^2$

$= \frac{z^2}{4}\left[C_1(1-\alpha z^2)^{-1} + C_2(1-\beta z^2)^{-1}\right]^2$

$= \frac{z^2}{4}[C_1^2(1+2\alpha z^2+3\alpha^2 z^4+4\alpha^3 z^6+\ldots) + C_2^2((1+2\beta z^2+3\beta^2 z^4+4\beta^3 z^6+\ldots)$
$+ 2C_1C_2(1+\alpha z^2+\alpha^2 z^4+\alpha^3 z^6+\ldots)(1+\beta z^2+\beta^2 z^4+\beta^3 z^6+\ldots)]$

Thus, $\nu_2' =$ coefficient of z^{2n} in $H'^2(z)$ and is given by the expression,

$$\frac{1}{4}[C_1^2 n\alpha^{n-1} + C_2^2 n\beta^{n-1} + 2C_1C_2(\beta^{n-1} + \beta^{n-2}\alpha + \beta^{n-3}\alpha^2 + \alpha^{n-1})]$$

Let $S' = \beta^{n-1} + \beta^{n-2}\alpha + \beta^{n-3}\alpha^2 + \ldots + \beta\alpha^{n-2} + \alpha^{n-1}$.
Thus we get:

$$S'(1 - \frac{\beta}{\alpha}) = \alpha^{n-1} - \frac{\beta^n}{\alpha}$$

$$\Rightarrow S' = \frac{\alpha^n - \beta^n}{\sqrt{5}}, \qquad \text{since} \quad \alpha - \beta = \sqrt{5}$$

Hence,

$$\nu_2' = \frac{1}{4}\left[C_1^2 n\alpha^{n-1} + C_2^2 n\beta^{n-1} + 2C_1C_2\frac{(\alpha^n - \beta^n)}{\sqrt{5}}\right] \qquad (10)$$

Using the values of ν_0' and ν_2' from eqns (9) and (10) respectively, the total number of 1's in all n-digit valid codewords is thus given by:

$$\nu_1' = nF_{2n+2} - \nu_0' - \nu_2' \qquad (11)$$

Table 2. Comparison of values of ν'_0, ν'_1 and ν'_2 for different values of n

m	n	ν'_0	ν'_1	ν'_2
8	6	954	864	444
16	12	632916	556416	267384
32	23	4.87153×10^{10}	4.22352×10^{10}	1.96227×10^{10}
64	46	4.03077×10^{20}	3.46847×10^{20}	1.5813×10^{20}
128	93	3.6107×10^{40}	3.09529×10^{40}	1.39756×10^{40}
256	185	2.04551×10^{79}	1.75032×10^{79}	7.86544×10^{78}
512	369	3.29995×10^{156}	2.82114×10^{156}	1.2647×10^{156}
1024	738	1.1288×10^{311}	9.64587×10^{310}	4.31886×10^{310}

The number of bits required for representing all m-bit binary numbers is given by the smallest integer n satisfying the inequality $F_{2n+2} - 1 > 2^m - 1$. Noting that $F_{2n+2} \approx \frac{\phi^{2n+2}}{\sqrt{5}}$ for large n, $\frac{\phi^{2n+2}}{\sqrt{5}} > 2^m$. That is,

$$n \approx \left\lceil \frac{m \log 2 + \log \sqrt{5}}{2 \log \phi} \right\rceil - 1 \tag{12}$$

For $m = 8, 16, 32, 64, 128, 256, 512$ and 1024, the corresponding values of n are 6, 12, 23, 46, 93, 185, 369 and 738, respectively. The ratio $\frac{n}{m}$ asymptotically tends to 0.72. Compared to base three, the ratio is equal to $\frac{\log(3)}{2 \log \phi} = 1.14$. In Table 2, we have shown the values of ν'_0, ν'_1 and ν'_2 for some values of n with $m = 8, 16, 32, 64, 128, 256, 512$ and 1024. It appears that for large n, the frequencies of occurrences of 0, 1 and 2 in all the valid codewords of TFNS asymptotically tend to 42.2%, 38.2% and 19.6%, respectively. This fact, together with the reduction in length of codewords compared to binary numbers, may be suitably exploited in many engineering applications, e.g., in reducing substantial amount of energy consumed by both the transmitter and receiver in wireless communication systems - similar to the energy-efficient communication techniques described in [11, 12].

5   Conclusion

In this paper, we have proposed the Tri-digit Fibonaccian number system in which the numbers of 0's, 1's and 2's in the representation of decimal numbers using this new number system are very much asymmetric in nature. We have derived expressions for the numbers of 0's, 1's and 2's in a bit-stream of any arbitrary length n. When n is high, the percentage of 0's, 1's and 2's in long bit-streams will asymptotically become 42.2%, 38.2% and 19.6%, respectively. In conventional ternary number system the number of 0's, 1's and 2s appearing in all the codewords are 33.3% each. The unequal distribution of the three digits is a characteristic feature of the the proposed TFNS system. Also, the code length in this new number system is reduced by a factor of 0.72 compared to the binary code of a given decimal number. For large bit-streams these characteristics may be appropriately utilized in typical engineering applications, e.g., for substantial savings of energy in communication systems. Other applications include variable length coding with a pair of consecutive 2's as delimiter for minimizing the code length. Future research may include use of TFNS in VLSI chip design for minimizing crosstalks among data buses inside the processor, arithmetics with TFNS (similar to those in FNS [1,3]), and exploring other number systems using odd numbered Fibonacci numbers or every third Fibonacci number as the positional weights.

References

1. Ahlbach, C., Usatine, J., Frougny, C., Pippenger, N.: Efficient Algorithms for Zeckendorf Arithmetic. The Fibonacci Quarterly 51(3), 249–255 (2013)
2. Apostolico, A., Fraenkel, A.: Robust transmission of unbounded strings using fibonacci representations. IEEE Transactions on Information Theory 33, 238–245 (1987)
3. Fenwick, P.: Zeckendorf Integer Arithmetic. The Fibonacci Quarterly 41, 405–413 (2003)
4. Fraenkel, A.S.: Systems of Numeration. Amer. Math. Monthly 92(2), 105–114 (1985)
5. Fraenkel, A., Klein, S.: Combinatorial Algorithms on Words, vol. F12, pp. 169–183 (1985)
6. Ghosh, R.N., Sinha, K., Sinha, B.P., Datta, D.: TSS: an energy efficient communication scheme for low power wireless networks. In: Proc. 27th IEEE Intl. Performance Computing and Communications Conf (IPCCC), USA, pp. 85–92 (December 2008)
7. St. John, P.H.: On the Asymtotic Proportions of zeros and Ones in Fibonacci Sequences. The Fibonacci Quarterly 22(2), 144–145 (1984)
8. Kautz, W.: Fibonacci codes for synchronization control. IEEE Transactions on Information Theory 11, 284–292 (1965)
9. Knuth, D.E.: The Art of Computer Programming, 3rd edn., vol. 1. Pearson Education (1997)
10. Mutyam, M.: Preventing crosstalk delay using fibonacci representation. In: IEEE Intl. Conf. on VLSI Design, pp. 685–688 (2004)
11. Sinha, K., Sinha, B.P., Datta, D.: CNS: a new energy efficient transmission scheme for wireless sensor networks. Wireless Networks 16(8), 2087–2104 (2010)
12. Sinha, K., Sinha, B.P., Datta, D.: An energy-efficient communication scheme for wireless networks: a redundant radix-based approach. IEEE Transactions on Wireless Communications 10(2), 550–559 (2011)
13. Zeckendorf, E.: Reprsentation des nombres naturels par une somme des nombres de Fibonacci ou de nombres de Lucas. Bull. Soc. Roy. Sci. Liege 41, 179–182 (1972)

User Profiling Based on Keyword Clusters
for Improved Recommendations

Deepa Anand[1] and Bonson Sebastian Mampilli[2]

[1] CMR Institute of Technology, AECS Layout, Bangalore, Karnataka 560037, India
deepanand@gmail.com
[2] Christ University, Bangalore, Karnataka 560029, India
bonson.sebastian@res.christuniversity.in

Abstract. Recommender Systems (RS) have risen in popularity over
the years, and their ability to ease decision-making for the user in various domains has made them ubiquitous. However, the sparsity of data
continues to be one of the biggest shortcomings of the suggestions offered. Recommendation algorithms typically model user preferences in
the form of a profile, which is then used to match user preferences to
items of their interest. Consequently, the quality of recommendations is
directly related to the level of detail contained in these profiles. Several
attempts at enriching the user profiles leveraging both user preference
data and item content details have been explored in the past. We propose
a method of constructing a user profile, specifically for the movie domain,
based on user preference for keyword clusters, which indirectly captures
preferences for various narrative styles. These profiles are then utilized
to perform both content-based (CB) filtering as well as collaborative
filtering (CF). The proposed approach scores over the direct keyword-
matching, genre-based user profiling and the traditional CF methods
under sparse data scenarios as established by various experiments. It
has the advantage of a compact user model representation, while at the
same time capturing the essence of the styles or genres preferred by the
user. The identification of implicit genres is captured effectively through
clustering without requiring labeled data for training.

1 Introduction

The role of Recommender Systems (RS) in combating the information overload
problem and their ability to trim information spaces and ensure manageability
of the information that users need to process to make decisions have made them
an indispensable part of several web-based systems. As newer applications of RS
keep cropping up, they give rise to several new challenges. The types of RSs vary
depending on the type of input on which the recommendations are based.

We propose an approach to cluster keywords such that the clusters so formed
correspond to the narrative details and styles implicit in the set of keywords.
These clusters are treated as representing a unique narrative style. The extent
to which a movie belongs to the group formed by the keyword clusters as well
as the users interest in each cluster are computed to construct the item and user

R. Natarajan (Ed.): ICDCIT 2014, LNCS 8337, pp. 176–187, 2014.
© Springer International Publishing Switzerland 2014

profile, respectively. The proposed approach has the advantage of a condensed item/user profile representation while encoding the rich content and narrative style information derived from the available folksonomy within the compressed profiles. The proposed approach is evaluated by comparing it against some state-of-the-art methods combining a hybrid of CF and CB methods. The experimental results establish the effectiveness of the proposed approaches under sparse data situations.

2   Literature Review

2.1   Collaborative Filtering and Content-Based Filtering

CF systems are more popular than CB systems. CB techniques offer suggestions based on the content descriptions of items that the user has preferred in the past. On the other hand, as items are often difficult to describe, CF techniques base their recommendations only on the ratings expressed by the users about the items in the domain, emulating our everyday advice-seeking behavior from family and friends.

2.2   Content-Based User Profiles

In an attempt to compress the size of the user profile, several approaches construct content-based user profiles that reflect the interest a user has in a particular content feature [2]. In the film domain, movies are classified on the basis of a number of characteristics, which include actors, directors, writers, music directors, and genres. Genre is an information-rich classification, as it provides a lot of information about the movies narrative style and is proven to be the driving factor behind a user liking or disliking a movie.[3][2] suggest a method of representing the interest of a user for movies through Genre Interestingness Measures (GIM), which combines the user preference for movies and the genres of the movies liked. Once compact user profiles are constructed, CF based on similarities between compact user profiles is done. Genres of movies are typically coined by experts who do not assign the degree to which the movie belongs to the genre. Such genre assignments also typically lack information about sub-genre or minor genres, as witnessed in the genres assigned to movies in IMDb. A similar approach based on keywords and tags is proposed in [4]. The authors propose two measures, namely Weighted Tag Rating Recommender and Weighted Keyword Rating Recommender, where the ratings as well as the tag information is used to construct a user profile consisting of the interest of each user in a keyword/tag. Such a constructed profile is then used to estimate the user similarity to perform CF. The disadvantage of the proposed method is that even though the recommendation fuses both the CF and CB systems, the user profile remains large, especially in the presence of a large keyword/tag set. Another similar work, which only attempts content-based filtering, combines keywords associated with movies with the ratings [5] through tag clouds. Tag clouds for each user are constructed for each distinct value of rating. This is performed by considering each movie rated by the user with a specific rating and then collecting the keywords associated with these movies to form the keyword/tag cloud for the user for the corresponding ratings. Once tag clouds for each user are constructed for each rating value, the keywords associated with each movie are compared to the tag clouds and the rating corresponding to the tag cloud containing most keywords for the movie is assigned to the movie. In the end, the movies are ordered in descending order to be presented to the user. A similar content-based approach constructs item profiles as a set of keywords, where the similarity between items is computed based not only on the set of keywords shared but also on whether they have been tagged by keywords that are similar [5] . The drawbacks of these approaches [5] are that it follows only the CB approach, and like the previous work, has a user profile that consists of keywords, and hence is voluminous. Another approach has been suggested in [6] where the information is taken from tags or folksnomies and used to compute fuzzy Genre belongingness for movies. This information is then used to improve recommendations.

An approach to suggest items without any user input [7] utilizes the movie synopsis and analyzes it based on Natural Language Processing (NLP) techniques that take advantage of information in natural language descriptions. Information about the movie genres associated with each movie is used along with the movie synopsis to extract the keywords corresponding to each genre. Clustering is then performed on the set of genres, where two genres are deemed similar if they share a large common set of keywords. Genres thus identified to lie in the same cluster are then merged to form new genres and the topic signature for each keyword, which is a vector of keywords associated with each genre, is generated. The resultant topic signatures thus generated are used to generate topic vectors for each movie. An estimate of movie similarities are then derived based on a comparison of these topic vectors. This approach using topic signatures has not been directly used for recommendation but for the task of listing movies similar to a particular movie. Moreover, it relies on the information about the movie genres and is not applicable when this information is unavailable. Since the keyword identification is genre-driven, other sub-genres that may be implicit in the data would not be detected. [8] focus on clustering genres based on the set keywords shared by them. A hierarchical clustering is done for the genres to get the distance and complete linkage dendogram for genres. Next, the genre groups are retrieved using Principal Component Factor Analysis (PCFA). The authors conclude that the results of hierarchical clustering and PCFA are quite similar.

3   Proposed User/Item Profiles Using Keyword Clusters

The motivation behind the proposed approach is to construct profiles of users and items that accurately depict user interest while being compact enough to allow for the efficient computation of recommendations. The proposed approach utilizes the keywords with which various movies are tagged. Let the set of users be U={u1,u2,, un}, the set of movies be I = { i1,i2,,im}, and the set of keywords assigned to the items in the item set be K={k1,k2,,kl} be. Let R_{n*m} be the set of ratings assigned by users to various items. Let A_{m*k} be the set of keywords assigned to a movie such that:

$$A(i,j) = \begin{cases} 1, \textit{if keyword } j \textit{ has been assigned to movie } i \\ 0, \textit{otherwise} \end{cases} \tag{1}$$

We extract information about movies from the movie website IMDb. IMDb assigns every movie with a set of genres, keywords, plot summary etc., comprising the narrative content in addition to other content details such as actors, directors, etc. In the proposed work, we investigate the use of keywords to automatically inform about the movie content. The rationale behind not utilizing genres is that the IMDb-coined genres are broad, overlapping and not detailed, because the major and minor genres are not distinguished. Moreover, IMDb-coined genres do not contain enough information about sub-genres for instance, the crime genre may have sub-genres such as gang, heist, serial killer movies, etc. We aim to investigate the relative effectiveness of keywords alone in measuring and distinguishing between various movie content types. Unlike other keyword-based methods[5] that build movie profiles based on keywords contained within them, we follow a dual step process grouping keywords into clusters thus allowing the inherent genre/sub-genre to emerge and building the profile for each item based on its membership in different clusters. For example, we took the movie, The Sound Of Music, and saw that the genres of the movie are: Biography, Drama, Family, Musical, and Romance. However, we have a total of 100 keywords and if we analyze the keywords, we can classify them further, and in the process, find other hidden classifications or sub-genres. The keywords for the movie have been divided on the basis of clustering of the sub-genres in the movie, based on which we can classify the movie into 8 sub-classifications. Some of the sample keywords and their classifications are shown in Table 1. If we analyze the table above, we see that the classifications Religion, Awards, Thriller, Location and War are present in the genre classification but not in the base genre classification in IMDb. Thus, RS algorithms can use these cluster classifications to give better recommendation results. This is shown in Figure 1.

Table 1. Clusters for the movie "The Sound of Music"

Cluster Classification	Keyword Examples
Family (26)	children, single father, ...
Location (13)	austria, salzburg folk festival, salzburg austria, ...
Romance (9)	love, marriage proposal, ...
Religion (17)	nun, convent, postulant, abbey, ...
War (5)	nazi, anschluss, nazi officer, messenger, ...
Musical (14)	party, ballroom dancing, singing family, ...
Thriller (9)	pursuit, chase, escape, hiding place, sabotage, ...
Awards / Classification (7)	based on novel, based on stage musical, ...

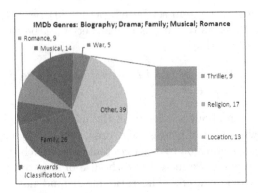

Fig. 1. Sound of Music: Tags not mentioned in Genres

For comparison, we have taken two movies, The Chronicles of Narnia and Oz the Great and Powerful (2013) as they both belong to the same genres classification which are Adventure, Family and Fantasy. The Chronicles of Narnia has 166 keywords out of which 65 keywords do not belong to the classified genres of the movie. Similarly, the movie Oz the Great and Powerful (2013) has 83 keywords out of which 26 keywords do not belong to the classified genres of the movie. On analysis, it was found that approximately 95 percent of the unclassified tags in both the movies were related to the Action genre.

If we analyze both the movies by genres or by keyword-to-keyword matching, these movies would not match based on keywords related to action. However, by clustering keywords, we can see that the movies have a large amount of Action genre keywords, which make them quite similar to other movies of the Action genre. This is the information that can be extracted and then used for better recommendations by clustering keywords.

To perform clustering of keywords, the movie keyword matrix is considered. We used the spectral clustering methods proposed in [9] as they are much more efficient than traditional methods. The clustering algorithm requires specification of the distance between keyword pairs. We compute the distances as a function of the cosine similarity. The formula is as follows:

$$Dist(k_1, k_2) = 1 - \frac{\sum_{x=1}^{m} C(i_x, k_1) \cdot C(i_x, k_2)}{\sqrt{\sum_{x=1}^{m} C(i_x, k_1)^2} \sqrt{\sum_{x=1}^{m} C(i_x, k_2)^2}} \qquad (2)$$

The number of clusters is a parameter that is important but at the same time difficult to fix in advance. To overcome this shortcoming, we create clusters with different starting values for the number of clusters and then follow a series of splits and merges of the various clusters till convergence. To do this, we first perform spectral clustering with a small number of clusters from 5 to 10. The steps that follow are a variant of the divisive clustering method. The distance, i.e. average distance between the ith and jth keyword of a cluster C denoted as k_c^i and k_c^j with n_c keywords in the cluster, is computed as follows:

$$Scatter(C) = \frac{2\sum_{i=1}^{nC}\sum_{j=i+1}^{nC} dist(k_c^i, k_c^j)}{n_c(n_c - 1)} \qquad (3)$$

At every step in the splitting process, each existing cluster C is split into clusters using a cluster size of 2, 3, 4 and 5 denoted by $C2 = \{C_2^1, C_2^2\}$, $C3 = \{C_3^1, C_3^2, C_3^3\}$ and similarly C4, C5. The average intra-cluster distances of these clusters are then compared with the intra-cluster distance of the original cluster. We choose the number of sub-clusters according to the number that minimizes this distance. At any time during the splitting, if any of the alternatives splits the original cluster into a size less than a minimum threshold T, the alternative is discarded. After all the clusters have been split, we compute the intra- and inter-cluster distances between each pair of clusters as:

$$Dist(C_1, C_2) = \frac{\sum_{i=1}^{nC1}\sum_{j=1}^{nC2} dist(k_c^i, k_c^j)}{n_{c1}n_{c2}} \qquad (4)$$

Clusters whose intra-cluster distance is more than the distance of the cluster from other clusters are considered for merging, provided the intra-cluster distance of the merged cluster is also less than the intra-cluster distances of both clusters. Clusters i and j may be merged if $Dist(C_{ij}, C_{ij}) < Dist(C_i, C_j) < Dist(C_i, C_i)$ and $Dist(C_{ij}, C_{ij}) < Dist(C_i, C_j) < Dist(C_j, C_j)$ where C_{ij} is the merged cluster. The splitting and merging phases iterate until there are no more splits of merges or a maximum of N iterations are performed. Let C=$\{C1, C2, ..., C_p\}$ be the set of clusters found after the splitting and merging phases and let the keyword cluster associations be represented by the matrix KC where KC(i,j)= 1 if keyword i is assigned to cluster j. We next estimate the movie profiles in terms of their membership in each genre/sub-genre represented by each of the clusters. We follow the simple strategy of counting the number of keywords describing the movie that are also present in the cluster. The cluster profile for a movie Ij for the Cluster Ck is thus defined as:

$$CP(I_j, C_k) = \sum_{k \in K} A(i_j, k) \cdot KC(k, C_k) \qquad (5)$$

Some clusters may have keywords that are more generic or may represent a genre that is more frequent across movies than other genres and, consequently, movies may have a higher count for this cluster. To overcome this bias, we divide the counts for each movie for a cluster by the maximum that any movie has for that cluster, i.e.:

$$CPN(I_j, C_k) = \frac{CP(I_j, C_k)}{max_{X \in I} CP(X, C_k)} \qquad (6)$$

Further, we normalize all the rows so that the sum of membership of a movie to various clusters adds up to one.

The user profile (UP) for each user in terms of their interest in various types of narrative content can be constructed by combining the ratings of the movies with the cluster profile for each movie, and is computed as $UP = R \cdot CPN$. The user interest that was initially expressed using the ratings matrix R is now represented by UP. The advantage offered by this approach is the compactness of the user profile due to the reduction in the number of components in the user profile because the number of items is much larger than the number of clusters. Moreover, the profiles so obtained are also denser because a user watching even one movie that may have some degree of representation in a cluster would ensure that some degree of interest of the user for the cluster can be computed. Once the user profiles are constructed, we use the user/item profile in order to perform both CB and CF. The interest of a user in a particular item is the function of the overlap between the sets of clusters, which is highly appreciated by the user and the clusters to which the movie belongs. Thus the interest of a user u_x for a movie i_y is computed as:

$$Interest(u_x, i_y) = \sum_{k=1}^{p} UP(u_j, k) \cdot CPN^T(k, i_y) \qquad (7)$$

Where CPN^T is the transpose of the item profile matrix. To perform CB filtering for user u_x, the interest is computed for each movie not experienced by the user, and the movies are presented in decreasing order of interest according to the number of items to be recommended. In this paper, we refer to this method as the Keyword Cluster-enabled Content-Based recommender (KC-CB).

On the other hand, the constructed user and item profiles can be harnessed to perform user- and item- based CF by computing the similarities between users or items using the constructed user profiles. Because the user profile will be denser, the similarities computed should be more accurate, and consequently, the user neighborhood would be richer, thus ensuring a better quality of recommendations. In this paper, we refer to this method as Keyword Cluster-enabled Collaborative Filtering recommender (KC-CF). Our claims are verified in the next section where we present the results of the experimental evaluation.

4   Experimental Evaluation

To affirm our claim that keyword cluster-based user and item profiling provides an edge over the previously proposed approaches, we compare it against competing recommendation approaches. The first one is the recommendations based on pure keyword-based user profiles as proposed in [5] where a users interest in various keywords/tags is evaluated and this in turn is used for the recommendations. This approach and its collaborative filtering variant are referred to in this paper as Keyword Content Based recommenders (K-CB) and Keyword Collaborative Filtering recommenders (K-CF), respectively. We also compare the proposed approach against genre-based profiling, where user interest in explicitly specified movie genres is computed and is used as a basis for recommendations, referred to as Genre Content-Based recommenders (G-CB) and Genre Collaborative Filtering recommenders (G-CF). We also contrast the performance of our approach against the traditional user and item-based CF (UCF and ICF).

We perform the experiments on the MovieLens dataset consisting of 943 users and 1682 movies. For each of the movies, we extract the set of keywords from the IMDb database. In addition, we utilize the set of 31468 keywords assigned to a set of 371417 movies/TV shows available at IMDb for training and for cluster formation. From this set of keywords, we retained the top 5000 most frequently occurring keywords for clustering. Movies that did not have any keywords from the selected list were removed. The minimum size of the clusters for the splitting and merging phases is set to 30. We experiment with different initial cluster sizes. To compare the performance of the proposed recommender, the ratings data is divided into training and test sets. We experiment with four sparsity configurations wherein 5%, 10%, 50% and 90% of the ratings data is retained in the training and the rest are in the test set. These give rise to configurations R5, R10, R50 and R90, respectively. The training data is used in constructing the user profiles, i.e., in deriving the users interest in the genres represented by the clusters. In case of CF, the training data is also used for aggregating the preferences of user/item neighborhoods. We arrive at the top N recommendations with varying recommendation list sizes. We vary these in the range of 10 to 60 with intervals of 10. The results of the various experiments are compared using the Precision, Recall and Ranked Accuracy metrics. While the Precision metric measures the fraction of recommendations provided that are useful to the user, and the Recall metric measures the fractions of useful items offered to the user, the Ranked Accuracy metric measures the degree of alignment of ranking of items in the recommendation list to the actual ranks [10]. The following subsections present the result of various experiments.

4.1 Effect of Initial Cluster Size

This series of experiments is performed to investigate the extent to which the number of clusters and the clustering style affect the quality of recommendations. The aim is also to investigate the relative merit of the splitting and merging phases after clustering as compared to a single level of clustering. To perform this comparison, we perform recommendations using cluster sizes of 20 and 60, where the numbers of clusters are directly specified, i.e., clustering was performed using a pre-specified number of clusters. We denote the methods by C20 and C60, respectively. We also perform Clustering using Splitting and Merging (CSM) using different initial cluster sizes of 5, 10, 15 and 30, which we refer to as CSM-5, CSM-10, CSM-15 and CSM-30, respectively. Figure 2 presents the results of performing recommendations using each of these schemes. As seen in the figure, the splitting of clusters into sub-clusters aids in improving the precision, recall and the ranked accuracy of recommendations. In the simple clustering strategy, choosing a larger number of clusters does result in a slight improvement in the recommendation quality. Using the approach followed in the paper of splitting and merging clusters, we notice that even with an initial cluster size of 5, we are able to get results where the quality is as good as C-20 in the simple clustering. Simply increasing the number of clusters need not improve the recommendation with respect to all metrics. This is clear from the fact that CSM-15 does not perform as well as CSM-5 or 10 with respect to precision and recall, but performs well when measured by the ranked accuracy metric. We notice that when the initial cluster size is 30, the approach followed gives the best results in terms of all the three metrics. Hence, for the following experiments, we follow CSM-30.

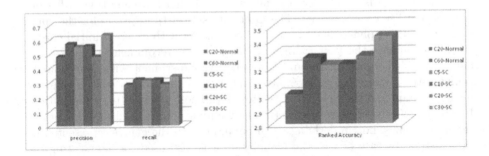

Fig. 2. Precision Vs Recall Vs Ranked Accuracy

4.2   Effect of Sparsity

In this section, we present the result of experiments that evaluate the merit of the various approaches under varying sparsity environments. To do this, we utilize the R5, R10 and R50 configurations, and for each configuration, vary the recommendation list size in the range 10-50. Figures 3, 4 and 5 presents the results of comparison of content-based techniques in terms of precision, recall and ranked accuracy.

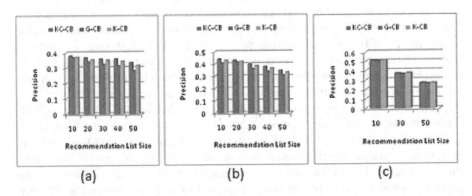

Fig. 3. Comparison of precision of content-based methods KC-CB, G-CB and K-CB for various sparsity levels (a) Sparsity level 95% (b) Sparsity level 90% (c) Sparsity level 50%.

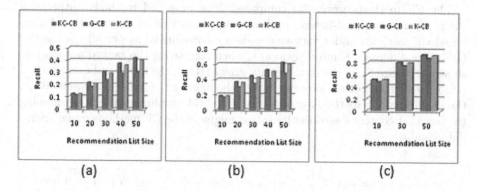

Fig. 4. Comparison of recall of content-based methods KC-CB, G-CB and K-CB for various sparsity levels (a) Sparsity level 95% (b) Sparsity level 90% (c) Sparsity level 50%.

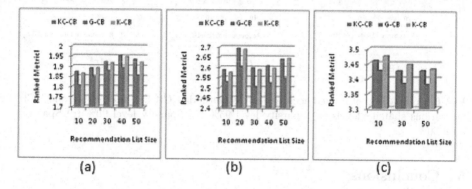

Fig. 5. Comparison of ranked accuracy of content-based methods KC-CB, G-CB and K-CB for various sparsity levels (a) Sparsity level 95% (b) Sparsity level 90% (c) Sparsity level 50%

As is clearly seen for very sparse conditions (i.e. R5 and R10), the proposed approach works better than the genre-based and keyword-based profiling methods in terms of all the three metrics, but for lower sparsity levels, the approaches do not differ much from each other. Moreover, as the recommendation list size increases, the precision drops whereas the recall sees an increase. It can also be noticed that both the proposed and the keyword-based methods substantially outperform the genre-based profiling method. The difference between the proposed method and the keyword-based method is less, but the proposed approach is able to achieve better results with profiles that are much shorter than keyword-based methods. Under dense data situations, the keyword-based methods slightly outperform the proposed method.

The CF methods were also compared. The proposed methods outperform the genre and keyword-based profiling methods as well as the traditional user-based CF methods under very sparse data environments as per all the metrics (R5). The difference is more noticeable when comparing the ranked accuracy as shown in Figure 6. As the data density grows (R10), the keyword-based method performs slightly better. However, when the density is further increased (R50), the traditional CF method outperforms all hybrid profiling methods, reinforcing the fact that content-based methods best augment the CF methods under sparse data conditions.

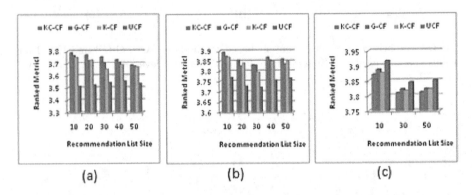

Fig. 6. Comparison of ranked accuracy of CF methods KC-CF, G-CF, K-CF and UCF for various sparsity levels (a) Sparsity level 95% (b) Sparsity level 90% (c) Sparsity level 50%

5   Conclusions

In this work, we proposed and evaluated an approach for the automatic construction of user profiles based on implicit genre-driven keyword clusters. Data extracted from the IMDb website consisting of movies and their associated keywords were employed to cluster the keywords according to their usage in various movies. The clusters so derived were deemed to represent movie categories based on their narrative content. User profiles based on their interest in the various keyword groups were constructed and utilized both for both content-based and collaborative filtering. As compared to other hybrids between content and CF systems, based on keyword comparisons or genre content, the proposed approach offers the advantage of a compact profile representation while at the same time being able to capture rich content-based information in these profiles. Moreover, the proposed approach does not require any labeled training set to learn the implicit categories because it employs clustering, an unsupervised learning technique. The merit of the proposed approach both in the CB and the CF versions were proven through various experiments where the proposed approaches outperformed competing approaches on sparse datasets. As the data density grew, however, the traditional CF approaches performed better than the hybrids.

The proposed approach only investigates the use of keywords in analyzing the movie content. However, descriptions of movies are available through synopsis, plot storyline and the crowd-sourced movie reviews, tags, tweets, etc. The various sources of information about the same entity may be exploited to determine the single source or a combination of sources that delivers the most accurate descriptions of the con-tents from an RS perspective. In future, we plan to compare and contrast these various sources in terms of their ability to improve the recommendation quality. Additionally, it would be interesting to explore the expansion of tags/keywords based on online thesauri, such as Wordnet[11], etc.

References

1. Pazzani, M.J., Billsus, D.: Content-based recommendation systems. In: Brusilovsky, P., Kobsa, A., Nejdl, W. (eds.) Adaptive Web 2007. LNCS, vol. 4321, pp. 325–341. Springer, Heidelberg (2007)
2. Anand, D.: Group movie recommendations via content based feature preferences. International Journal of Scientific & Engineering Research 4, 1–5 (2013)
3. Al-Shamri, M.Y.H., Bharadwaj, K.K.: Fuzzy-genetic approach to recommender systems based on a novel hybrid user model. Expert Systems with Applications 35, 1386–1399 (2008)
4. Liang, H., Xu, Y., Li, Y., Nayak, R., Shaw, G.: A hybrid recommender systems based on weighted tags. In: 10th SIAM International Conference on Data Mining, SDM 2010 (2010)
5. Nagar, S.: A hybrid recommender: user profiling from tags/keywords and ratings. PhD thesis, Kansas State University (2012)
6. Anand, D., Mampilli, B.S.: Folksonomy-based fuzzy user profiling for improved recommendations. Expert Systems with Applications (2013)
7. Ho, K.W.: Movies genres classification by synopsis (2008)
8. Bulut, H., Korukoglu, S.: Analysis and clustering of movie genres. Journal of Computing 3 (2011)
9. Yangqiu, S., Hongjie, B., Chih-Jen, L., Chang, E.: Parallel spectral clustering in distributed systems. Pattern Analysis and Machine Intelligence 33, 568–586 (2011)
10. Herlocker, J.L., Konstan, J.A., Terveen, L.G., Riedl, J.T.: Evaluating collaborative filtering recommender systems. ACM Trans. Inf. Syst. 22, 5–53 (2004)
11. Degemmis, M., Lops, P., Semeraro, G.: A content-collaborative recommender that exploits wordnet-based user profiles for neighborhood formation. User Modeling and User-Adapted Interaction 17, 217–255 (2007)

Equilibrium Balking Strategy
in an Unobservable $GI/M/c$ Queue
with Customers' Impatience

Dibyajyoti Guha[1], Abhijit Datta Banik[1], Veena Goswami[2], and Souvik Ghosh[1]

[1] School of Basic Sciences, Indian Institute of Technology
Samantapuri, Nandan Kanan Road, Bhubaneswar-751 013, India
[2] School of Computer Application, KIIT University
Bhubaneswar-751024, India
{dg11,adattabanik}@iitbbs.ac.in, veena@kiit.ac.in,
souvikghosh1989@yahoo.com

Abstract. We consider an equilibrium threshold balking strategy in an unobservable $GI/M/c$ queue with customers' impatience. Upon arriving a customer decides whether to join or balk the queue based on random probability known as joining probability (f). Once a customer decides to join the system it initiates an impatient timer with random duration T, such that, if customers' service is not completed before the timer expires, the customer abandons the system. The waiting time of a customer in system has been associated with a linear cost-reward structure for estimating the net benefit if a customer chooses to participate in the system. The study has been limited to unobservable queue where the information regarding system-length is unknown to the arriving customer. The proposed analysis is based on a root of the characteristic equation formed using the probability generating function of embedded pre-arrival epoch probabilities. Therefore, we obtain the stationary system-length distribution at pre-arrival and arbitrary epochs and thereby we obtain mean system sojourn time. Finally, we present numerical results in the form of graphs for observing net benefit against different model parameters. The proposed model has applications in the modeling of balking and impatient behavior of incoming calls in a call center, multi-core computing, multi-path routing in delay sensitive communications networks.

Keywords: Renewal arrival, multi-server, balking strategy, reneging, roots, infinite-buffer, Padé-Laplace method.

1   Introduction

Many practical queueing systems are often encountered with the situation where customers are allowed to depart before joining (known as balking) the queueing system. In a reneging queueing system, the customers become impatient after joining the queue, i.e. the customers may depart the system after the expiration of the patience timer before completing service. Teletraffic analysis in a

R. Natarajan (Ed.): ICDCIT 2014, LNCS 8337, pp. 188–199, 2014.

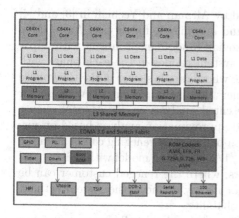

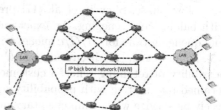

Fig. 1. $GI/M/c$ model for multi-core computing

Fig. 2. $GI/M/c$ model for multi-path routing

call center or data center is an ideal example where the customers exhibits the balking and reneging behavior in a multi-server queueing system. The difference between balking and reneging is that the customers decide probabilistically to participate in the queueing system at the time of arrival where as in case of reneging the customer may abandon the system at the expiration of a timer after joining the system. There are two kinds of balking strategy: (1) Observable cases: The arriving customer has the information of the system-length before joining the system; (2) Unobservable cases: The arriving customers has no information about the system-length at the arrival epoch. The proposed model is also applicable in multi-core computing, multi-path routing in delay sensitive communications networks, as shown in Fig. 1 and Fig. 2. Balking strategy with various model parameters and their results are summarized in [11] with extensive bibliographical references. An $M/M/1$ queue with unreliable server have been analyzed by Economou et al. in [8]. In recent times, Economou and Kanta [7] have also considered an $M/M/1$ constant retrial queueing system. Balking strategy with setup/ closedown times for an $M/M/1$ queue have been considered by Sun et al. [18]. A balking strategy from reliability perspective for $M/M/1$ queue have been studied by Wang and Zhang [19] with unreliable server and delayed repair. Guo and Hassin [9] considered Markovian vacation queueing models with N-policy with and without the information about mean delay. Recently Liu et al. [14] have considered equilibrium threshold strategies for observable queueing system with single vacation policy. The assumption of vacation is implicit in the references mentioned [8,7,18,19,9,14].

An $M/M/1/N$ queue with balking and reneging have been investigated by Ancker and Gafarian [1]. Abou-EI-Ata et al. [2] considered the multiple servers queueing system $M/M/c/N$ by combining balking and reneging. Wang et al. [20] extended works of [2] to study an $M/M/c/N$ queue with balking, reneging and server breakdowns. Queueing models with single and multiple servers with customers impatience have been analyzed by Altman and Yechiali in [3] and [4] when the server(s) is (are) on vacation and unavailable for service. An $M/M/c$ queues in a 2-phase (fast and slow) Markovian random environment with impatient customers is reported in [15]. The system resides in the each phase with an exponentially distributed random time whose rate is slower in the slow phase and higher in the fast phase. The customers become impatient when the server is in slow phase. Shawky et al. [17] presented analysis on $H_k/M/c/N$ queues with balking and reneging. An exact and approximation analysis based on virtual queueing time for $M/G/c$ queues with balking and reneging can be found in [13]. Kumar et al. [16] discussed an $M/M/1/N$ queueing model with balking and possibility of retaining reneged customers, where the reneged customer can be retained into system with probability p or it may abandon the system without receiving service with complementary probability.

In this paper, we investigate an equilibrium threshold balking strategy in an unobservable $GI/M/c$ queue with customers' impatience. A reward-cost structure is assumed in the system which attracts the customer to join the queueing system. Each customer incurs a cost which is proportionate to the mean waiting time of the customer.

2   Description and Analysis of the Model

We consider an equilibrium threshold balking strategy in an unobservable $GI/M/c$ queue with customers impatience wherein the inter-arrival times of successive arrivals are independent and identically distributed (i.i.d.) random variables with general distribution function $A(u)$ $(u \geq 0)$, a probability density function (p.d.f.) $a(u)$ $(u \geq 0)$, Laplace-Stieltjes (LST) transform $a^*(s)$ and mean $1/\lambda$. The service discipline is first-come, first-served (FCFS). The service time follows exponential distribution with parameter μ'.

Consider the system just before an arrival which are taken as embedded points. Let $t_0, t_1, t_2, \dots$ be the time epochs at which successive arrivals occur and t_n^- denote the time epochs just before the arrival instant t_n. The inter-arrival times $T_{n+1} = t_{n+1} - t_n$, $n = 0, 1, 2, \dots$ are i.i.d.r.vs. with common distribution function $A(x)$. The state of the system at t_i^- is defined as $\{N_s(t_i^-)\}$, where $N_s(t_i^-)$ is the number of customers in the system. The process $\{N_s(t_i^-)\}$ is an embedded Markov chain with the state space $\Theta = \{(k), k \geq 0\}$. In limiting case let us assume $\pi_n^- = \lim_{i \to \infty} P(N_s(t_i^-) = n)$, $n \geq 0$, where π_n^- represents the probability that there are n customers in the system just prior to an arrival epoch of a customer.

We assume that the arriving customers have the options to decide whether to join or balk upon their arrival. We model this decision by assuming that each customer receives a reward of R units for completing service and is charged a cost of G units per time unit that he remains in the system (sojourn time). We also assume that customers are risk neutral and wish to maximize their net benefit. At the arrival instant the customer decides whether to join or balk the queue based on random probability known as joining probability (f). Once a customer decides to join the system it initiates an impatient timer with random duration T, which follows an exponential distribution with parameter η, such that, if customers' service is not completed before the timer expires, the customer abandons the system. The patience timer T is exponentially distributed whose density function is given by $r(t) = \eta e^{-\eta t}$. The assumption regarding reneging is that the service times for those customers who eventually will renege without being served are not included in the calculation of the sojourn time. Thus, the effective departure rate of customers from the system due to reneging or completion of service is $\mu = \mu' + \eta$.

2.1 System-Length Distribution at Pre-arrival Epoch

In this subsection, we analyze system-length distribution at the pre-arrival epoch. Let d_k $(k \geq 0)$ represents the probability that k customers have been departed during an inter-arrival time given that all the c servers are busy during the inter-arrival time duration. Let $a_{k+1,j}$ be the probability that an arriving customer finds k $(k \leq c-1)$ customers in the system while the next arriving customer finds j $(0 \leq j \leq k)$ customers in the system. As a result, exactly $k+1-j$ customers have been departed during an inter-arrival time of a customer. Similarly, $b_{k+1,j}$ be the probability that an arriving customer finds k $(k \geq c)$ customers in the system while the next arriving customer finds j $(0 \leq j \leq c-1)$ customers in the system. Therefore, for all $k \geq 0$, we have

$$a_{k,j} = P(N_s(t_i^-) = j | N_s(t_{i-1}^-) = k-1) \text{ where } (0 \leq k-1 \leq c-1), \ (1 \leq j \leq k),$$
$$= \int_0^\infty \binom{k}{j} e^{-\mu j t}(1 - e^{-\mu t})^{k-j} dA(t),$$

$$b_{k,j} = P(N_s(t_i^-) = j | N_s(t_{i-1}^-) = k-1) \text{ where } (k-1 \geq c), \ (1 \leq j \leq c-1),$$
$$= \int_0^\infty \int_0^t \frac{(\mu c)^{k-c} u^{k-c-1} e^{-c\mu u}}{(k-c-1)!} \binom{c}{j} e^{-\mu j(t-u)} (1 - e^{-\mu(t-u)})^{c-j} \, du \, dA(t),$$

$$d_k = \int_0^\infty \frac{(c\mu t)^k}{k!} e^{-c\mu t} dA(t), \quad a_{k,0} = 1 - \sum_{j=1}^k a_{k,j}, \quad b_{k,0} = 1 - \sum_{j=1}^{c-1} b_{k,j} - \sum_{j=0}^{k-c} d_j.$$

We can simplify $a_{k,j}$ as

$$a_{k,j} = \int_0^\infty \binom{k}{j} e^{-\mu j t}(1 - e^{-\mu t})^{k-j} dA(t)$$

$$= \int_0^\infty \binom{k}{j} e^{-\mu j t}(-1)^{k-j}(e^{-\mu t} - 1)^{k-j} dA(t)$$

$$= \int_0^\infty \binom{k}{j} e^{-\mu j t}(-1)^{k-j} \sum_{l=0}^{k-j} \binom{k-j}{l} e^{-\mu t(k-j-l)}(-1)^l dA(t)$$

$$= \int_0^\infty \binom{k}{j} \sum_{l=0}^{k-j} (-1)^{k-j+l} \binom{k-j}{l} e^{-\mu t(k-j-l+j)} dA(t)$$

$$= \binom{k}{j} \sum_{l=0}^{k-j} (-1)^{k-j+l} \binom{k-j}{l} \int_0^\infty e^{-\mu t(k-l)} dA(t)$$

$$= \binom{k}{j} \sum_{l=0}^{k-j} (-1)^{k-j+l} \binom{k-j}{l} a^*(\mu(k-l)).$$

Similarly $b_{k,j}$ can be simplified as

$$
\begin{aligned}
b_{k,j} &= \int_0^\infty \int_0^t \frac{(\mu c)^{k-c} u^{k-c-1} e^{-c\mu u}}{(k-c-1)!} \binom{c}{j} e^{-\mu j(t-u)} (1 - e^{-\mu(t-u)})^{c-j} du \, dA(t) \\
&= \frac{(\mu c)^{k-c}}{(k-c-1)!} \binom{c}{j} \int_0^\infty \int_0^t e^{-c\mu u} u^{k-c-1} e^{-\mu j(t-u)} (1 - e^{-\mu(t-u)})^{c-j} du \, dA(t) \\
&= \frac{(\mu c)^{k-c}}{(k-c-1)!} \binom{c}{j} \int_0^\infty \int_0^t g(u) h(t-u) du \, dA(t),
\end{aligned}
\tag{1}
$$

where $g(u) = e^{-c\mu u} u^{k-c-1}$ and $h(t-u) = e^{-\mu j(t-u)} (1 - e^{-\mu(t-u)})^{c-j}$. Thus, the second integral is the convolution of $g(u)$ and $h(t-u)$, so the whole integral is the LST of the convolution of these two functions. The LST of $g(t)$ can be computed as

$$\int_0^\infty e^{-st} e^{-c\mu t} t^{k-c-1} dt = \frac{(k-c-1)!}{(s+c\mu)^{k-c}}.
\tag{2}$$

Similarly the LST of $h(t)$ can be obtained as

$$
\begin{aligned}
\int_0^\infty e^{-st} h(t) dt &= \int_0^\infty e^{-st} e^{-\mu j t} (1 - e^{-\mu t})^{c-j} dt \\
&= \int_0^\infty e^{-\mu t(s/\mu + j)} (1 - e^{-\mu t})^{c-j} dt \quad [\text{if } z = 1 - e^{-\mu t}, \therefore \frac{dz}{dt} = \mu e^{-\mu t}] \\
&= \frac{\int_0^1 e^{-\mu t(s/\mu + j - 1)} z^{c-j} dz}{\mu} = \frac{\int_0^1 (1-z)^{-\mu t(s/\mu + j - 1)} z^{c-j} dz}{\mu} \\
&= \frac{\Gamma(j + s/\mu) \Gamma(c - j + 1)}{\mu \Gamma(c + s/\mu + 1)}.
\end{aligned}
\tag{3}
$$

The literature on queueing theory shows that distributions having Laplace-Stieltjes transform as a rational function cover a wide range of distributions that arise in applications, see Botta et al. [5]. In view of this, we consider those distributions that have rational Laplace-Stieltjes transform of the form $v(s) = P(s)/Q(s)$, where degree of the polynomial $Q(s)$ is n and that of the polynomial $P(s)$ is at most n. Thus, the convolution of (2) and (3) can be expressed as

$$\frac{(k-c-1)!}{(s+c\mu)^{k-c}} \frac{\Gamma(j+s/\mu)\Gamma(c-j+1)}{\mu \Gamma(c+s/\mu+1)} \simeq \frac{(k-c-1)!(c-j)!}{\mu} \frac{P(s)}{Q(s)},$$

where $\frac{P(s)}{Q(s)} \simeq \frac{\Gamma(j+s/\mu)}{(s+c\mu)^{k-c}\Gamma(c+s/\mu+1)}$. We consider that inter-arrival time is following a PH-type distribution having parameters $(\boldsymbol{\alpha}, \boldsymbol{B})$ with density $a(t) = $

$\alpha e^{Bt}B^0$. By replacing $a(t) = \alpha e^{Bt}B^0$ in (1), $b_{k,j}$ can be written as

$$b_{k,j} = \frac{(\mu c)^{k-c}}{(k-c-1)!}\binom{c}{j}\int_0^\infty\int_0^t e^{-c\mu u}u^{k-c-1}e^{-\mu j(t-u)}(1-e^{-\mu(t-u)})^{c-j}du\,dA(t)$$

$$=\frac{(\mu c)^{k-c}}{(k-c-1)!}\binom{c}{j}\int_0^\infty \alpha e^{Bt}\int_0^t e^{-c\mu u}u^{k-c-1}e^{-\mu j(t-u)}(1-e^{-\mu(t-u)})^{c-j}du\,dt\,B^0$$

$$=\frac{(\mu c)^{k-c}}{(k-c-1)!}\binom{c}{j}\int_0^\infty \alpha e^{Bt}\int_0^t g(u)h(t-u)du\,dt\,B^0$$

$$\simeq \frac{(\mu c)^{k-c}c!}{j!\mu}\alpha.[\frac{P(s)}{Q(s)}|_{s=-B}].B^0. \tag{4}$$

We use Padé-Laplace method in (4) (see Harris and Marchal [10]) to approximate $b_{k,j}$ by a rational function of order (m,n). Hence $b_{k,j}$ can be expressed as

$$b_{k,j}\simeq\frac{(\mu c)^{k-c}c!}{j!\mu}\alpha.[\frac{P(s)}{Q(s)}|_{s=-B}].B^0. \tag{5}$$

Let us define f be the joining probability when the arriving customer chooses to join the system. The probability generating function (p.g.f.) of d_k is given by

$$\overline{D}(z) = \sum_{k=0}^\infty d_k z^k = a^*(c\mu - c\mu z). \tag{6}$$

Observing the state of the system at two consecutive pre-arrival epochs, we get the following difference equations:

$$\pi_0^- = f(\sum_{k=0}^{c-1}\pi_k^- a_{k+1,0} + \sum_{k=c}^\infty \pi_k^- b_{k+1,0})$$

$$+(1-f)(\pi_0^- + \sum_{k=1}^{c-1}\pi_k^- a_{k,0} + \sum_{k=c}^\infty \pi_k^- b_{k,0}), \tag{7}$$

$$\pi_i^- = f(\sum_{k=i-1}^{c-1}\pi_k^- a_{k+1,i} + \sum_{k=c}^\infty \pi_k^- b_{k+1,i})$$

$$+(1-f)(\sum_{k=i}^{c-1}\pi_k^- a_{k,i} + \sum_{k=c}^\infty \pi_k^- b_{k,i}),\quad 1\le i\le c-1, \tag{8}$$

$$\pi_i^- = f\sum_{k=i-1}^\infty \pi_k^- d_{k+1-i} + (1-f)\sum_{k=i}^\infty \pi_k^- d_{k-i},\quad i\ge c. \tag{9}$$

We define probability generating function (p.g.f.) of π_i^- $(i\ge c)$ as $\pi_c^{-*}(z) = \sum_{i=c}^\infty \pi_i^- z^{i-c}$. Multiplying (9) by z^{i-c}, summing them and using the definition of p.g.f. of π_i^- $(i\ge c)$, $\pi_c^{-*}(z)$ can be expressed as

$$\pi_c^{-*}(z) = \frac{\pi_c^- - f\sum_{i=1}^\infty \frac{d_i}{z^{i-1}}\sum_{j=0}^{i-1}\pi_{c+j}^- z^j - (1-f)\sum_{i=0}^\infty \pi_{c+i}^- z^i \sum_{k=i}^\infty \frac{d_k}{z^k}}{1-(1-f+fz)\overline{D}(\frac{1}{z})}. \tag{10}$$

The expression in (10) is analytic and convergent in $|z| \leq 1$. We need to calculate zeros in the denominator of (10). We know that the equation $1 - (1 - f + fz)\overline{D}(\frac{1}{z}) = 0$ has exactly one root in the region $|z| > 1$. Since the equation $1 - (1 - f + fz)\overline{D}(\frac{1}{z}) = 0$ has one root outside the unit circle, the function $1 - (1 - f + \frac{f}{z})\overline{D}(z) = 0$ has one zero ω inside the unit circle $|z| < 1$. As $\pi_c^{-*}(z)$ is an analytic function of z for $|z| \leq 1$, applying the partial-fraction method, we obtain

$$\pi_c^{-*}(z) = \frac{K_1}{1 - \omega z}, \tag{11}$$

where K_1 is the constant to be determined. Now, equating the coefficient of z^{i-c} from both sides of (11), the pre-arrival epoch probabilities can be obtained as

$$\pi_i^- = K_1 \omega^{i-c}, \ i \geq c. \tag{12}$$

Let us compute the pre-arrival epoch probabilities of π_i^- for $i \geq c$. The constant K_1 can be determined by considering $\sum_{i=c}^{\infty} \pi_i^- = 1$. Hence, $K_1 = 1 - \omega$ and $\pi_i^- = (1 - \omega)\omega^{i-c}$. At this point, we have c unknown probabilities π_i^- for $i = 0 \cdots c - 1$. One can obtain c equations for solving c unknown probabilities π_i^- ($\forall i = 0 \cdots c - 1$) by considering the Equations (7) and (8) where we have c unknown probabilities π_i^- ($\forall i = 0 \cdots c - 1$) and π_i^- ($\forall i \geq c$) known probabilities. The desired probabilities of system-length at pre-arrival epoch can be obtained by normalization condition $\sum_{i=0}^{\infty} \pi_i^- = 1$.

2.2   System-Length Distribution at Arbitrary Epoch

In this subsection, we derive the expression for steady-state system-length distribution at arbitrary epochs. We have applied the classical argument based on renewal theory (see Chaudhury, Templeton [6]) which relates the steady-state system-length distribution at an arbitrary epoch to that at the corresponding pre-arrival epoch. Let $\widehat{d}_k$ ($k \geq 1$) represents the probability that k customers have been departed during residual inter-arrival time given that all the c servers are busy during the residual inter-arrival time duration. Let $\widehat{a}_{k,j}$ and $\widehat{b}_{k,j}$ be the corresponding probability of $a_{k,j}$ and $b_{k,j}$, respectively while considering residual inter-arrival time instead of inter-arrival time. Hence for all $k \geq 0$, we have

$$\widehat{d}_k = \int_0^{\infty} \frac{(c\mu t)^k}{k!} e^{-c\mu t} \lambda(1 - A(t))dt, \ (k \geq 0),$$

$$\widehat{a}_{k,j} = \int_0^{\infty} \binom{k}{j} e^{-\mu j t}(1 - e^{-\mu t})^{k-j} \lambda(1 - A(t))dt,$$

$$= \text{where } (0 \leq k - 1 \leq c - 1), \ (1 \leq j \leq k),$$

$$\widehat{b}_{k,j} = \int_0^{\infty} \int_0^t \frac{(\mu c)^{k-c} u^{k-c-1} e^{-c\mu u}}{(k-c-1)!} \binom{c}{j} e^{-\mu j(t-u)} (1 - e^{-\mu(t-u)})^{c-j} du \lambda(1 - A(t))dt,$$

$$= \text{where } (k - 1 \geq c), \ (1 \leq j \leq c - 1),$$

$$\widehat{a}_{k,0} = 1 - \sum_{j=1}^{k} \widehat{a}_{k,j}, \text{ and } \widehat{b}_{k,0} = 1 - \sum_{j=1}^{c-1} \widehat{b}_{k,j} - \sum_{j=0}^{k-c} \widehat{d}_j.$$

Let us derive the p.g.f. of $\widehat{d_k}$ which is denoted by $\widehat{D}(z)$. We use the LST of probability density function (pdf) of residual inter-arrival time as given in Kleinrock [12], $\int_0^\infty e^{-st}\lambda(1-A(t))dt = \lambda\frac{1-a^*(s)}{s}$,

$$\widehat{D}(z) = \sum_{k=0}^\infty z^k \int_0^\infty \frac{(c\mu t)^k}{k!} e^{-c\mu t}\lambda(1-A(t))dt$$

$$= \int_0^\infty e^{-(c\mu - c\mu z)t}\lambda(1-A(t))dt = \lambda\frac{1-a^*(c\mu - c\mu z)}{c\mu - c\mu z}.$$

Similarly, $\widehat{a}_{k,j}$ can be expressed as

$$\widehat{a}_{k,j} = \int_0^\infty \binom{k}{j} e^{-\mu jt}(1-e^{-\mu t})^{k-j}\lambda(1-A(t))dt$$

$$= \binom{k}{j}\sum_{l=0}^{k-j}(-1)^{k-j+l}\binom{k-j}{l}\int_0^\infty e^{-\mu t(k-l)}\lambda(1-A(t))dt$$

$$= \binom{k}{j}\sum_{l=0}^{k-j}(-1)^{k-j+l}\binom{k-j}{l}\lambda\frac{1-a^*(\mu(k-l))}{\mu(k-l)}.$$

As the inter-arrival time is following a PH-type distribution with parameters (α, B) then the residual inter-arrival time follows a PH-type distribution with parameters (β, B) where the stationary probability vector β satisfies $\beta(B + B^0\alpha)=0$. System length at an arbitrary epoch π_i can be obtained from pre-arrival epoch probability π_i^- ($\forall i \geq 0$) by employing $\widehat{d}_k, \widehat{a}_{k,j}$ and $\widehat{b}_{k,j}$ which is given below

$$\pi_0 = f(\sum_{k=0}^{c-1}\pi_k^-\widehat{a}_{k+1,0} + \sum_{k=c}^\infty \pi_k^-\widehat{b}_{k+1,0})$$

$$+(1-f)(\pi_0 + \sum_{k=1}^{c-1}\pi_k^-\widehat{a}_{k,0} + \sum_{k=c}^\infty \pi_k^-\widehat{b}_{k,0}), \tag{13}$$

$$\pi_i = f(\sum_{k=i-1}^{c-1}\pi_k^-\widehat{a}_{k+1,i} + \sum_{k=c}^\infty \pi_k^-\widehat{b}_{k+1,i})$$

$$+(1-f)(\sum_{k=i}^{c-1}\pi_k^-\widehat{a}_{k,i} + \sum_{k=c}^\infty \pi_k^-\widehat{b}_{k,i}), \quad 1 \leq i \leq c-1, \tag{14}$$

$$\pi_i = f\sum_{k=i-1}^\infty \pi_k^-\widehat{d}_{k+1-i} + (1-f)\sum_{k=i}^\infty \pi_k^-\widehat{d}_{k-i}, \quad i \geq c. \tag{15}$$

3   Performance Measures

3.1   Mean System-Length and Sojourn Time Analysis

Computation of mean system-length and mean sojourn time are the key aspects of performance measures for queueing system. Steady-state system-length distribution at arbitrary epochs obtained in (13) - (15) is used to compute the mean system-length. Thus, the mean system-length is given as $L = \sum_{k=0}^{\infty} k\pi_k$. Waiting time in the system can be obtained from the pre-arrival epoch probabilities π_i^- that we have derived in Section 2.1. Let $W_a^*(s)$ denotes the Laplace-Stieltjes transform of the distribution function of the sojourn time of an arriving customer. Hence, $W_a^*(s)$ can be given by

$$W_a^*(s) = 1 - f + f \sum_{j=0}^{c-1} \pi_j^- \left(\frac{\mu}{s+\mu}\right) + f \sum_{j=c}^{\infty} \pi_j^- \left(\frac{c\mu}{s+c\mu}\right)^{j+1-c}. \qquad (16)$$

Let W be the r.v. denoting the sojourn time of an arriving customer. Thus, the mean of the sojourn time of an arriving customer is given by

$$E[W] = f \sum_{j=0}^{c-1} \frac{\pi_j^-}{\mu} + f \sum_{j=c}^{\infty} \pi_j^- \frac{j+1-c}{c\mu}. \qquad (17)$$

By the help of Little's law, mean system sojourn time $E[W]$ can be obtained from mean system-length $E[W] = \frac{L}{\lambda}$. The compliance of Little's law has been verified numerically for moderate values of ρ and c.

3.2   An Equilibrium Balking Strategy for Unobservable Queue

There is a finite service charge G that has to be paid by every customer who passes through the system after completing service. We denote it as $\Delta = R - G.E[W]$, the net benefit of a customer who has been served. The basic assumption about reward-cost structure is that system attracts a customer to participate even when the system is empty at the arrival instant of the customer. Using similar derivations as in Equation (17), the mean sojourn time of an arriving customer in an empty system (denoted by S_{wait}) is given by $S_{wait} = \sum_{j=1}^{c-1} \frac{\pi_j^-}{\mu}$. In other words, the reward for service is bigger than the cost of an arriving customer who finds the system empty, which is given as follows

$$R > G.S_{wait} = G \sum_{j=1}^{c-1} \frac{\pi_j^-}{\mu}.$$

The particular value of f which produces Δ closest to zero is the desired equilibrium joining probability. Let us denote the equilibrium joining probability as f_Δ. It is observable that the reward R is proportionate to the mean waiting time in system. Hence, the net benefit $\Delta = R - G.E[W]$ is also depending on mean waiting time in the system.

4   Numerical Results

This section presents numerical results to demonstrate how the joining probability influences net benefit with considering two aspects: Case 1: Different traffic

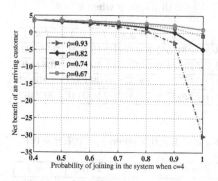

Fig. 3. f vs Δ for different values of μ when $c=4$

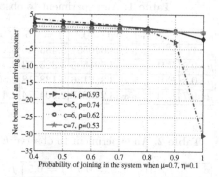

Fig. 4. f vs Δ for different values of c when $\mu = 0.7, \eta = 0.1$

intensity by changing the service rate (μ) for fixed value of c; Case 2: Different traffic intensity for different values of c but μ remains constant. Let us consider $PH/M/c$ model where inter-arrival time is a PH-type distribution having the representation $(\boldsymbol{\alpha}, \boldsymbol{B})$ where $\boldsymbol{B} = \begin{pmatrix} -5 & 0 & 3 \\ 1 & -5 & 2 \\ 1 & 3 & -10 \end{pmatrix}$ and $\boldsymbol{\alpha} = (0.35\ 0.45\ 0.20)$, with $\lambda = 2.978723$. The reneging parameter remained constant $\eta = 0.1$. By following the cost-reward constraint, we have kept $R = 8, C = 6$ to be constant throughout the experiment.

The net benefit for various joining probabilities for different values of traffic intensity while c remains constant (case 1) and c kept on increasing (case 2), is represented in Fig. 3 and Fig. 4, respectively. From Fig. 3, it can be seen that the net benefit is decreasing when the joining probabilities are increasing for each of the traffic intensity taking the value of $\rho = 0.67, 0.74, 0.82, 0.93$, while $c = 4$ through out the experiment. The equilibrium joining probability corresponding to case 1 is $f_\Delta = 1, 0.9, 0.9$ for $\rho = 0.74, 0.82, 0.93$, respectively. The net benefit never becomes zero when $\rho = 0.67$. Fig. 4 shows similar kind of decreasing net benefit when the joining probabilities are increasing for each of values of $c = 4, 5, 6, 7$, when $\mu = 0.7, \eta = 0.1$ The equilibrium joining probability corresponding to case 2 is $f_\Delta = 1, 1, 0.9$ for $\rho = 0.62\ (c = 6), 0.74\ (c = 5), 0.93\ (c = 4)$, respectively. The net benefit is always non-negative when $\rho = 0.53\ (c = 7)$.

A tabular representation of Fig. 3 and Fig. 4 is shown in Table 1 and Table 2, respectively. We have presented a scenario where $\rho = 0.74$ remains same for different combinations of c, μ, e.g. $\mu = 0.8$ and $c = 4$ (see row 2, Table 1) and $\mu = 0.7$ and $c = 5$ (see row 3, Table 2). It is visible that $\mu = 0.8$ and $c = 4$ produces less sojourn time compared to $\mu = 0.7$ and $c = 5$. It is an indication that an increase of service rate by $(0.8 - 0.7)/0.7$ proportion has more impact on reducing mean sojourn time in comparison with an increase of the number of servers by $(5 - 4)/4$ proportion.

Table 1. An experiment to observe $E[W]$ for different ρ when $c = 4$

μ	$E[W]$	$f = 0.4$	$f = 0.5$	$f = 0.6$	$f = 0.7$	$f = 0.8$	$f = 0.9$	$f = 1$
$\mu=1$	$E[W]_{\rho=0.67}$	3.640551	3.483346	3.289418	3.042016	2.702272	2.160621	0.959224
$\mu=0.9$	$E[W]_{\rho=0.74}$	3.521595	3.325253	3.075633	2.742324	2.252745	1.391438	-0.844460
$\mu=0.8$	$E[W]_{\rho=0.82}$	3.387136	3.138518	2.809666	2.343724	1.596378	0.093999	-4.866042
$\mu=0.7$	$E[W]_{\rho=0.93}$	3.228818	2.904274	2.449008	1.742697	0.433512	-2.990116	-30.24920

Table 2. An experiment to observe $E[W]$ for $c = 4, 5, 6, 7$ when $\mu = 0.7, \eta = 0.1$

c	$E[W]$	$f = 0.4$	$f = 0.5$	$f = 0.6$	$f = 0.7$	$f = 0.8$	$f = 0.9$	$f = 1$
c=7	$E[W]_{\rho=0.53}$	0.532693	0.458900	0.361475	0.242898	0.119455	0.050295	0.029993
c=6	$E[W]_{\rho=0.62}$	1.471397	1.336969	1.164467	0.947626	0.678269	0.336339	-0.178311
c=5	$E[W]_{\rho=0.74}$	2.385867	2.179768	1.913846	1.561243	1.058076	0.204006	-2.071733
c=4	$E[W]_{\rho=0.93}$	3.228818	2.904274	2.449008	1.742697	0.433512	-2.990116	-30.24920

5   Conclusion

In this paper, we have investigated an equilibrium threshold balking strategy in an unobservable $GI/M/c$ queue with customers' impatience based on a root of the characteristic equation formed using the probability generating function of embedded pre-arrival epoch probabilities. We have obtained the steady-state distributions of the number of customers in the system at pre-arrival and arbitrary epochs. On the similar direction, the analysis of renewal input batch arrival queue with multi-server with balking and reneging is an interesting problem for future work.

Acknowledgements. The second and fourth author acknowledges partial financial support from the Department of Science and Technology, New Delhi, India research grant SR/FTP/MS-003/2012.

References

1. Ancker Jr., C.J., Gafarian, A.: V. Some queueing problems with balking and reneging: I. Operations Research 11, 88–100 (1963)
2. Abou-El-Ata, M.O., Hariri, A.M.A.: The $M/M/C/N$ queue with balking and reneging. Computers and Operations Research 19, 713–716 (1992)
3. Altman, E., Yechiali, U.: Analysis of Customers Impatience in Queues with Server Vacations. Queueing Systems 52, 261–279 (2006)
4. Altman, E., Yechiali, U.: Infinite-Server Queues with System's Additional Tasks and Impatience Customers. Technical Report, Tel Aviv University (April 2005)
5. Botta, R.F., Harris, C.M., Marchal, W.G.: Characterisation of generalised hyperexponential distribution functions. Stochastic Models 3(1), 115–148 (1987)
6. Chaudhury, M.L., Templeton, J.G.C.: A first course in bulk queues. Wiley, New York (1983)

7. Economou, A., Kanta, S.: Equilibrium customer strategies and social-profit maximization in the single-server constant retrial queue. Naval Research Logistics 58, 107–122 (2011)

8. Economou, A., Kanta, S.: Equilibrium balking strategies in the observable single-server queue with breakdowns and repairs. Operations Research Letters 36, 696–699 (2008)

9. Guo, P., Hassin, R.: Strategic behavior and social optimization in Markovian vacation queues. Operations Research 59, 986–997 (2011)

10. Harris, C.M., Marchal, W.G.: Distribution Estimation using Laplace Transforms. INFORMS Journal on Computing 10(4), 448–458 (1998)

11. Hassin, R., Haviv, M.: To Queue or Not to Queue: Equilibrium Behavior in Queueing Systems. Kluwer Academic, Boston (2003)

12. Kleinrock, L.: Queuing Systems, Volume 1: Theory. John Willey & Sons, New York

13. Liqiang, L., Kulkarni, V.G.: Balking and Reneging in $M/G/s$ Systems: Exact Analysis and Approximations. Probability in the Engineering and Informational Sciences 22(3), 355–371 (2008)

14. Liu, W., Ma, Y., Li, J.: Equilibrium threshold strategies in observable queueing systems under single vacation policy. Applied Mathematical Modelling 36, 6186–6202 (2012)

15. Perel, N., Yechiali, U.: Queues with slow servers and impatient customers. European Journal of Operational Research 201(1), 247–258 (2010)

16. Rakesh, K., Sumeet, K.S.: An $M/M/1/N$ Queueing Model with Retention of Reneged Customers and Balking. American Journal of Operational Research 2(1), 1–5 (2012)

17. Shawky, A.I., El-Paoumy, M.S.: The interarrival hyperexponential queues: $H_k/M/c/N$ with balking and reneging. Stochastics and Stochastic Reports 69(1), 67–76 (2000)

18. Sun, W., Guo, P., Tian, N.: Equilibrium threshold strategies in observable queueing systems with setup/closedown times. Central European Journal of Operational Research 18, 241–268 (2010)

19. Wang, J., Zhang, F.: Equilibrium analysis of the observable queues with balking and delayed repairs. Applied Mathematics and Computation 218(6), 2716–2729 (2011)

20. Wang, K.-H., Chang, Y.-C.: Cost analysis of a finite $M/M/R$ queueing system with balking, reneging and server breakdowns. Mathematical Methods of Operations Research 56(2), 169–180 (2002)

Energy-Aware H.264 Decoding

Arani Bhattacharya, Ansuman Banerjee, and Susmita Sur-Kolay

Indian Statistical Institute
arani89@gmail.com, {ansuman,ssk}@isical.ac.in

Abstract. The increasing use of more resource-intensive multimedia applications in communication has made it essential to ensure better utilization of available computing resources. At the same time, energy consumption has turned out to be one of the most important resource constraints in modern systems. Digital videos are an important part of multimedia, and a large number of video standards are currently available. In this paper, we work on the most commonly used video standard named H.264. We propose a method to reduce the energy consumption involved in video decoding by selective degradation of video quality. Experiments on the LIVE video database show that our proposed method is quite effective in practice.

1 Introduction

The rise of both environmental concerns as well as limits placed on performance by energy dissipation has given rise to energy-aware computing. Moreover, embedded systems having limited sources of energy are increasingly being used for more and more complex tasks. Designers are, therefore, increasingly looking at ways of reducing the energy footprint of their applications [1].

In order to make them more user-friendly, computing systems are gradually turning towards communication through multimedia such as graphics, audio and videos. While this increasing use of multimedia has made computer systems more accessible to people, it has also made it essential to ensure that such systems have enough resources to deal with these demands. Since energy is one of the more important resources, building energy-efficient systems has turned out to be an important goal of designers.

With improvements in processor speeds according to Moore's Law [2], energy consumption by processors have gradually increased. In embedded systems, the amount of energy consumption is limited by the capacity of the power source. In desktop and server systems, energy consumption is limited by the amount of heat dissipation possible within the die area [3]. Thus, the constraint on energy consumption has placed a limit on the performance of embedded, desktop as well as server systems. An increasingly popular theme of research today is to limit the amount of energy consumption at the software level. This has been done at compiler-level, operating system level as well as at the application level. At the application level, energy-aware design of various commonly used software such as virtual machines, wireless sensors and video decoders are currently topics of active research [1].

R. Natarajan (Ed.): ICDCIT 2014, LNCS 8337, pp. 200–211, 2014.
© Springer International Publishing Switzerland 2014

A video decoder is an essential component in the playback of video files. Video decoders are, thus, commonly used on mobile devices having limited sources of energy. Thus, reducing energy consumption of video decoders is likely to enable users of mobile devices to decode more high resolution videos.

Among the many available video standards currently available, H.264 is the most commonly used standard. This is because H.264 offers very good video compression with little loss of quality[4]. For this reason, H.264 is widely used in both desktop and mobile platforms. It is also very commonly used for video streaming.

In this paper, we present a method to perform energy-aware decoding of H.264 videos. For simplicity, we have concentrated here only on intra-coded frames, i.e. frames in which information is derived solely from decoded pixels present in the same frame. We show that significant gains in energy consumption can be made by lowering quality of the video during the process of decoding. We perform experiments to show the trade-off between energy gain and video quality.

The rest of this paper is organized as follows. Section 2 briefly discusses the H.264 standard, existing methods of measuring energy consumption of a modern computing system and ways of measuring quality of videos. Section 3 describes our technique of reducing the energy footprint during the process of video decoding. The experiments performed and observations recorded are then discussed in Section 4. Section 5 lists some other work related to energy-aware video decoding, and the ways in which they differ from our contribution. Section 6 concludes this paper.

2   Background

2.1   H.264 Standard

A H.264 video [5,6] consists of a sequence of frames. A frame is an array of luma samples (related to luminance) and two corresponding arrays of chroma samples (related to red and blue chrominance). Each frame is further divided into spatial units called slices. A slice consists of blocks of 16 x 16 pixels, known as macro-blocks (MB). A macro-block contains type information describing the choice of methods used to code the macro-block, prediction information such as intra prediction mode, and coded residual data. Within a macro-block, luma samples may be coded as one of the three types of block sizes, namely 4x4, 8x8 or 16x16 pixels. Chroma samples are commonly coded as blocks of 8x8 pixels.

Reconstruction is an important step in the decoding of an H.264 video frame. Reconstruction of a decoded macro-block involves obtaining the data from neighbouring macro-blocks based on which motion prediction had been made by the encoder. This cannot be done independently, but only after fetching data of neighbouring macro-blocks. In an intra-coded video frame, all dependencies are in the same frame of video. The H.264 standard specifies four neighbours for a macro-block in an intra-frame, namely, left, top-left, top and top-right. For example, in Figure 2.1, the macroblock labelled 5 has the macroblocks labelled 4, 1, 2 and 3 as its left, top-left, top and top-right neighbours respectively. In addition, a macroblock includes a variable amount of residual information that cannot be inferred from previous macroblocks. This residual information is converted into frequency domain using a modified form of Discrete Cosine Transform (DCT), and then stored within the encoded bitstream.

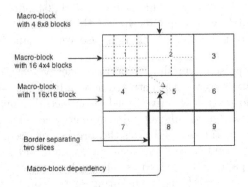

Fig. 1. A 3x3 H.264 frame

2.2   Measurement of Energy Consumption

In order to enable energy-aware computation, it is essential to monitor the amount of energy or power consumed while running a program. This can be done by reading the Model-Specific Registers (MSRs) which are available on almost all modern processors. Intel, in particular, allows the application user to read the amount of energy or power consumed by a code fragment by reading its MSR registers through its RAPL (Running Average Power Limit) driver.

Using RAPL to obtain energy consumption has two major disadvantages. First, it cannot measure energy consumption at very low granularity, i.e. the energy consumed is given in multiples of 125 mJ. Second, it does not quantify the energy consumption involved in different stages of instruction execution. Third, it is not possible to easily eliminate the energy consumption involved in the execution of background processes. Thus, it is not possible to suggest improvements in software design by simply using RAPL output without first studying the reasons which lead to high energy consumption [7].

In order to understand better the relation between program instructions and energy consumption, power models have been developed that can estimate the energy consumption involved depending on the number of instructions fetches, number of memory accesses at different levels of cache accesses and other factors. It has been shown that energy consumption by an architectural component is proportional to its activity ratio. The activity of an architectural component here refers to the number of operations performed by it per unit time. These power models allow us to recognize the components that consume more power, and thus point us towards techniques to reduce energy consumption by suggesting methods to reduce the number of operations performed by some component. In this paper, we have used one such power model to develop ways to reduce energy consumption of video decoders [8].

2.3 Measures of Video Quality

Measuring quality of video decoding is an active area of research. Our work focuses on measuring the quality of video obtained after the entire process of decoding is completed. This essentially implies that the decoded video obtained after degradation can be compared with another reference video decoded without degradation. This process of measuring video performance is known as Full-Reference video quality measurement. Wang et al. [9] provides an excellent survey of traditional methods of video quality along with their drawbacks.

The most commonly used method to rate the quality of videos is qualitative measurement, where the videos are shown to many different users. The users then rate the quality of videos, and a mean of these ratings is taken as a measure of video quality. However, quantitative measures of video decoding are more convenient to calculate and widely used as baseline for further studies. In this paper, we have used quantitative measures to measure the compare the quality of the degraded videos.

The traditionally most common Full-Reference video quality measure is Peak Signal-to-Noise Ratio (PSNR). Peak Signal-to-Noise Ratio is obtained by:

$$PSNR = 10log_{10}\frac{MAX_I^2}{MSE}$$

where MSE or Mean Square Error is the square of the sum of differences in intensity of each color element, and MAX_I is the maximum possible intensity, which is obtained using the number of bits used to represent a particular color component. There are two different types of PSNR that can be used:

1. Average PSNR: In this case, the PSNR of each image is obtained individually, and their arithmetic mean is then calculated.
2. Global PSNR: In this case, the MSE of the entire video is first obtained, and then its ratio with the maximum possible intensity is obtained. The logarithmic operation is applied on this ratio. This method basically concatenates all the frames of the video to form a single image of very large dimension, and then calculates its PSNR [10].

PSNR, though still widely used as a metric to measure video qualities, merely compares the differences between the reference video and the output video. This metric does not always agree with the human perception of video quality. Thus, researchers continued to look for better metrics of video quality.

A metric that is widely used to measure quality of images is the Structural Similarity Index Metric (SSIM). It uses the formula

$$SSIM = \frac{(2\mu_x\mu_y + c_1)(2\sigma_{xy} + c_2)}{(\mu_x^2 + \mu_y^2 + c_1)(\sigma_x^2 + \sigma_y^2 + c_2)}$$

where μ_x is the average value of pixels along the width of a frame, μ_y is the average value of pixels along the height of a frame, σ_x^2 is the variance of pixels along its width, σ_y^2 is the variance of pixels along its height, σ_{xy} is the covariance of x and y, c_1 and c_2 are constants that are typically used to stabilize the division with a weak denominator. SSIM is a linear metric that gives a number between 1 and -1, with 1 being returned when the reference and the test frame are identical to each other.

PSNR and SSIM, taken together, are the most common measures of video quality used nowadays by far. However, it has been observed that these two metrics do not take into account the interaction between different frames, or any information present in a video about the motion of objects [11].

One metric that takes into account the motion information and has been shown to provide a much better measure of video quality is the MOtion-based Video Integrity Evaluation (MOVIE) index, developed at the Laboratory for Image and Video Engineering at University of Texas, Austin. The MOVIE index consists of two distinct components — spatial and temporal MOVIE. The spatial index uses comparison techniques similar to other video quality assessment algorithms such as PSNR, but with much more detailed information. The temporal index captures any temporal distortions introduced into the video. Experiments have shown that the MOVIE index has a much higher correlation with human perception of video quality [12].

3   Methodology

In order to demonstrate the efficacy of our method, we need to first determine the amount of power or energy consumed by the decoder process. This requires calibrating the power model that we have selected with our processor. The next step involves profiling of the video decoder to determine the steps in the decode process that take up significant chunks of the total power consumption. Finally, we modify the video decoder in order to reduce the amount of energy consumed. These three steps are discussed in detail in the following subsections.

3.1   Calibration of Power Model

We have used a power model where the total power consumption can be decomposed into that of individual architectural components [8]. The motivation behind using such a power model is two-fold:

1. It allows us to determine the architectural components that consume most power, which in turn helps us identify the steps where reducing power consumption would be most beneficial,

2. it allows us to study the relation between macroblock properties and the power consumption involved in decoding them. In general, RAPL does not give the required level of precision required to obtain the power consumption involved in decoding each macroblock, and

3. it eliminates the effect of background processes.

In this power model, the power consumption of a component is assumed to be directly proportional to the activity ratio of each component. This power model considers a system to be made up of the following components:

1. Processor Frontend (FE),
2. Integer unit (INT),
3. Floating-point unit (FPU)
4. Single Instruction Multiple Data unit (SIMD)
5. Branch Prediction Unit (BPU),
6. L1 cache
7. L2 cache,
8. Memory and bus.

To obtain the weights associated with each architectural component, we have profiled the modified microbenchmark suite used in [8][1]. The microbenchmarks have been designed in such a way that it is easily possible to separate the power consumption of each individual component. This has helped us minimize the chances of regression error. The weights thus obtained (Figure 2) have been validated by profiling the SPEC2006 benchmarks on an Intel Core 2 Duo T9600 processor, containing 64 KB of split L1 cache, and 6 MB of unified L2 cache. The decoder that we worked with, does not use any floating-point and SIMD instructions, hence, we neglected the power consumption of these units in the above computation.

Profiling of the individual components has been done using Performance Application Programming Interface (PAPI) [7], which uses hardware counters to obtain various performance metrics. The total power consumed by the system has been measured using Intel Running Average Power Limit (RAPL) drivers. To ensure that power from other programs do not interfere with the total power, all other applications have been turned off as far as possible. Each microbenchmark has been run for 30 seconds each. This time limit has been imposed through asynchronous signals to ensure minimum interference in processor performance.

3.2   Profiling of Video Decoder

We have used the video decoder of Joint Model reference software [13], which has been developed by the video standardization team for better understandability of the standard. We have profiled separately the process of CABAC (entropy decoding), motion compensation and application of loop filter to conclude that the process of motion compensation consumes the largest amount of power.

---

[1] Freely available at http://rbertran.site.ac.upc.edu/tools/micro.tar.bz2

Component	Power (mW)
Front-end, P_{FE}	789
Integer unit, P_{INT}	261
Floating-point unit, P_{FPU}	502
Branch Processing unit, P_{BPU}	1908
L1 cache, P_{L1}	856
L2 cache, P_{L2}	24437
Front-side Bus, P_{FSB}	8852
Static power (constant), P_{STATIC}	8701

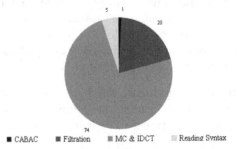

■ CABAC   ■ Filtration   ■ MC & IDCT   ▦ Reading Syntax

Fig. 2. Power weightages of different microarchitectural components

Fig. 3. Energy Consumption at Different Stages of Decoder

We have, therefore, concentrated on minimizing the power consumption during motion compensation.

The process of motion compensation essentially involves obtaining the pixel values of the predecessor macroblocks and summing them up with the residual data present in the encoded data. This fetching of residual data incurs significant power expense, since data has to be fetched from main memory, and then calculated for each pixel. By selectively ignoring some of the residual data, it is possible to significantly lower the amount of power consumption involved while minimizing the loss of video quality. This neglecting of residual data is done at the macroblock-level, where macroblocks satisfying some properties are selected as victims and their residual data is left unused.

3.3   Modification of Video Decoder

Using power analysis, we observed that a major amount of power consumption occurs due to the fetching of residual data. In order to reduce the amount of power consumption involved, we degrade the quality of some macroblocks by ignoring a portion of the residual data. The pixel data of such macroblocks is obtained solely through motion compensation. However, arbitrarily selecting macroblocks for such degradation would adversely affect the quality of video and render it unfit for use. We therefore, propose a heuristic that intelligently degrades video quality in order to minimize its effect on video quality.

Our strategy considers two major factors involved in selecting which macroblocks to ignore –the amount of power that decoding a macroblock requires, and the effect of degrading the macroblock on other neighbouring macroblocks. The quality of pixels in neighbouring macroblocks could degrade if we arbitrarily choose macroblocks for degradation, due to the presence of drifts. Since macroblock dependencies can exist in the form of long chains, an error introduced at some point in the macroblock could be transmitted to macroblocks much farther from the origin. To avoid such errors, we preferably choose macroblocks having fewer dependencies.

Algorithm 1. SelectVictimBlock

1: $S[MB] \leftarrow ReadMBSyntax$
2: $D[MB] \leftarrow GetDependencies(S[MB])$
3: $A[MB] \leftarrow meanQuantization(S[MB])$
4: **if** $mode = 1$ **then**
5:     $R[MB] \leftarrow ResidualData$
6:     $DecodeMB(S, D, R)$
7: **else if** $mode = 2$ **then**
8:     **if** $Quantization(S[MB]) < A[MB]$ **then**
9:         $O[MB] \leftarrow DependencyCount(S[MB])$
10:        **if** $O[MB] \neq 0$ **or** $NeighboursDegraded(S[MB]) = FALSE$ **then**
11:            $R[MB] \leftarrow ResidualData$
12:        **end if**
13:    **end if**
14: **else if** $mode = 3$ **then**
15:    **if** $Quantization(S[MB]) < A[MB]$ **then**
16:        **if** $O[MB] > 1$ **or** $NeighboursDegraded(S[MB]) = FALSE$ **then**
17:            $R[MB] \leftarrow ResidualData$
18:        **end if**
19:    **end if**
20: **end if**
21: $DecodeMB(S, D, R)$

We have investigated degradation strategies for different classes of videos and come up with three different options (or modes, as used in the algorithm above) in which our algorithm works. These options are as below:

- Mode 1: No degradation,
- Mode 2: Degradation less than α, and
- Mode 3: Degradation more than α,

where α is a context-dependent parameter to be provided by the user. The actual value of α may vary for different classes of videos. In our experiments, we have chosen α as 12%.

Algorithm 1 shows our overall strategy. The algorithm selects macroblocks whose residual data will be ignored. The macroblocks are selected based on the mode in which the user wants the decoder to run, the number of dependencies of the macroblock, and also depending on whether any adjacent macroblocks have been degraded. In the algorithm, variable S refers to the syntax elements of a macroblock, D refers to the list of dependencies, A is a temporary variable that stores the mean quantization value of macroblocks and R stores the list of blocks within a macroblock in which residual data is present. The variable O refers to the list of outgoing edges from a block. The function $ReadMBSyntax$ parses the syntax elements of the bitstream and populates the data structure of the macroblock. The function $GetDependencies$ then uses the data dependency information stored in the data structure to obtain the data dependency information required for motion compensation. The function *meanQuantization* returns the mean of the quantization step sizes among all macroblocks within the frame.

As shown in Algorithm 1, while running in no degradation mode, the video is decoded without any modifications. For all other modes where degradation is necessary, macroblocks with lower quantization step than average are first selected. Within these macroblocks, those blocks on which no other blocks outside depend, are selected for degradation in mode 2. The residual data of these blocks are ignored, and the pixel data for these are obtained solely using motion compensation. For mode 3, blocks which have one or fewer dependencies are selected for degradation. However, if its neighbouring block has already been degraded, then it is left untouched in order to ensure that the changes are not reflected over too large an area of the frame.

4   Experiment and Results

One major problem faced by researchers while working on video quality is the lack of standard benchmark videos present that is widely accepted in academia or industry. In order to mitigate this problem, the LIVE database for videos was developed [14,15,16]. The LIVE Video Quality Database contains ten uncompressed high-quality videos. These videos are – bs (blue sky), mc (mobile and calendar), pa (pedestrian area), rb (river bed), rh (rush hour), sf (sunflower), sh (shield), st (station), tr (tractor) and pr (park run). The videos are given in the form of planar 4:2:0 yuv files at a resolution of 768 × 432. They have been extensively used for subjective and objective video quality assessment. Seven of the videos have a frame rate of 25 frames per second, while the rest have a frame rate of 50 frames per second. The videos that are used by the Video Quality Experts Group (VQEG) for standardization of measures of video quality which have been made available are also a part of this database. We have used these videos for this work.

We have used the Joint Model reference software [13] version 18.3 to perform our experiments. The decoder is executed to decode the encoded video, and the energy consumption as well as PSNR of the decoded video is then recorded. Now, the decoder is modified as discussed in Section 3, and then this modified decoder is used to decode the same reference video. The measures of quality of the two versions of the decoded video so obtained are then calculated.

As discussed in Section 2, there is no single widely accepted measure of video quality. We have, therefore, provided results on four different metrics to better understand the amount of video degradation resulting from our strategy. The metrics used are a) average PSNR b) global PSNR c) average SSIM and d) average of the MOVIE indices. Both average and global PSNR as well as SSIM of the videos have been calculated using the open-source software *libyuv*[10]. MOVIE index has been calculated using the software provided by the original proposers of the method. The activation ratio of each unit has been calculated using the open-source Performance Application Programming Interface (PAPI) version 5.2.0 [17]. This has been multiplied by the weights given in Figure 2

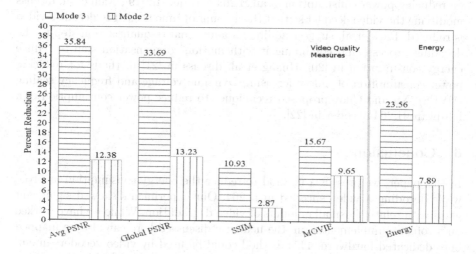

Fig. 4. Degradation of video quality for Modes 2 (bars with vertical grid lines) and 3 (bars with horizontal grid lines) VS. Reduction in energy consumption with respect to Mode 1 (no degradation)

and then the static power is added. The value obtained is multiplied by the time required to perform the decoding in order to determine the total energy consumed.

Fig. 4 shows the arithmetic mean of video quality degradation, measured in average and global PSNR, SSIM and MOVIE, and the corresponding energy gain, taken over each of the ten videos. We note that, as expected, more energy gains are made in Mode 3 than in Mode 2. Similarly, greater loss of video quality is seen in Mode 3 as compared to Mode 2. This can be explained by observing that the quality of video decreases with an increase in the number of victim macroblocks. We select more macroblocks in Mode 3 than in Mode 2, and, therefore, the quality of videos in Mode 3 reduces further. We also note that, in each case, the loss in quality as measured using PSNR was greater than the other video metrics. This can be explained by observing that PSNR does not take into account human perception, unlike SSIM and MOVIE index, and so the value of PSNR reduces even if introducing an error does not reduce video quality according to human perception.

5 Related Work

Minimization of energy for software and hardware systems has become an important area of active research. In [1], Ahmad and Ranka provide a good survey of methods, both at hardware and software level, of reducing energy computation.

Since H.264 is widely used in resource-constrained systems, improving its performance has long been a source of active research. In [18], Chang et al. work on reducing power consumption of an H.264 encoder. In [19], Nam et al. discuss modifying the video decoder so that the amount of time needed to decode a video is reduced. Park et al. suggest adding an additional re-quantization step to the decoding process, and combining it with motion compensation step to reduce energy consumption in [20]. Huang et al. discuss in [21] methods for reducing power consumption of a decoder using Dynamic voltage and frequency scaling (DVFS). Xu and Choy proposed techniques to reduce power consumption of a hardware H.264 decoder in [22].

6   Conclusion

In this paper, we present a method to reduce the energy consumption involved while decoding a video encoded in H.264. Our experiments showed significant gains with relatively small amounts of video degradation. While we have worked on a software implementation, the heuristic discussed here can also be mapped onto dedicated hardware. This method could be used by video decoders in embedded and streaming systems to prolong the lives of their power sources, and lead to lower energy consumption in desktop systems. As future work, we plan to integrate this method along with parallelization [23] for use in modern multi-core systems.

References

1. Ahmad, I., Ranka, S.: Handbook of Energy-Aware and Green Computing-Two Volume Set (2012)
2. Moore, G.E., et al.: Cramming more components onto integrated circuits (1965)
3. Hennessy, J.L., Patterson, D.A.: Computer architecture: a quantitative approach. Elsevier (2012)
4. Schwarz, H., Wiegand, T.: The emerging JVT/H.264 video coding standard. In: Proc. of IBC (2002)
5. Richardson, I.E.: The H. 264 advanced video compression standard. Wiley (2011)
6. Wiegand, T., Sullivan, G.J., Bjontegaard, G., Luthra, A.: Overview of the H. 264/AVC video coding standard. IEEE Transactions on Circuits and Systems for Video Technology 13(7), 560–576 (2003)
7. Weaver, V.M., Johnson, M., Kasichayanula, K., Ralph, J., Luszczek, P., Terpstra, D., Moore, S.: Measuring energy and power with PAPI. In: 2012 41st International Conference on Parallel Processing Workshops (ICPPW), pp. 262–268. IEEE (2012)
8. Bertran, R., Gonzalez, M., Martorell, X., Navarro, N., Ayguade, E.: Decomposable and responsive power models for multicore processors using performance counters. In: Proceedings of the 24th ACM International Conference on Supercomputing, pp. 147–158. ACM (2010)
9. Wang, Z., Bovik, A.C.: Mean squared error: love it or leave it? a new look at signal fidelity measures. IEEE Signal Processing Magazine 26(1), 98–117 (2009)
10. libyuv - yuv scaling and conversion functionality (2013), http://code.google.com/p/libyuv/ (accessed: August 18, 2013)
11. Wang, Z., Bovik, A.C., Sheikh, H.R., Simoncelli, E.P.: Image quality assessment: From error visibility to structural similarity. IEEE Transactions on Image Processing 13(4), 600–612 (2004)

12. Seshadrinathan, K., Bovik, A.C.: Motion tuned spatio-temporal quality assessment of natural videos. IEEE Transactions on Image Processing 19(2), 335–350 (2010)

13. Shring, K.: H.264-avc joint model software (2013), http://iphome.hhi.de/suehring/tml/ (accessed: July 8, 2013)

14. Seshadrinathan, K., Soundararajan, R., Bovik, A.C., Cormack, L.K.: Study of subjective and objective quality assessment of video. IEEE Transactions on Image Processing 19(6), 1427–1441 (2010)

15. Seshadrinathan, K., Soundararajan, R., Bovik, A.C., Cormack, L.K.: A subjective study to evaluate video quality assessment algorithms. In: IS&T/SPIE Electronic Imaging, pp. 75270H–75270H. International Society for Optics and Photonics (2010)

16. Live video database (2013), http://live.ece.utexas.edu/research/quality/live_video.html (accessed: August 18, 2013)

17. Papi (2013), http://icl.cs.utk.edu/papi/software/index.html (accessed: September 4, 2013)

18. Chang, H.-C., Chen, J.-W., Wu, B.-T., Su, C.-L., Wang, J.-S., Guo, J.-I.: A dynamic quality-adjustable H. 264 video encoder for power-aware video applications. IEEE Transactions on Circuits and Systems for Video Technology 19(12), 1739–1754 (2009)

19. Nam, H.-M., Jeong, J.-Y., Byun, K.-Y., Kim, J.-O., Ko, S.-J.: A complexity scalable h. 264 decoder with downsizing capability for mobile devices. IEEE Transactions on Consumer Electronics 56(2), 1025–1033 (2010)

20. Park, S., Lee, Y., Lee, J., Shin, H.: Quality-adaptive requantization for low-energy MPEG-4 video decoding in mobile devices. IEEE Transactions on Consumer Electronics 51(3), 999–1005 (2005)

21. Huang, Y., Chakraborty, S., Wang, Y.: Using offline bitstream analysis for power-aware video decoding in portable devices. In: Proceedings of the 13th Annual ACM International Conference on Multimedia, pp. 299–302. ACM (2005)

22. Xu, K., Choy, C.-S.: Low-power bitstream-residual decoder for H. 264/AVC baseline profile decoding. EURASIP Journal on Embedded Systems 2009, 9 (2009)

23. Bhattacharya, A., Banerjee, A., Sur-Kolay, S., Basu, P., Karmakar, B.: A cache-aware strategy for h.264 decoding on multi-processor architectures. In: VLSI Design and Test XVII (2013)

A Cost Effective Approach for Analyzing
Software Product Lines

Ganesh Khandu Narwane[1], Shankara Narayanan Krishna[2],
and Anup Kumar Bhattacharjee[3]

[1] HBNI, Mumbai
[2] IIT Bombay, Mumbai
[3] BARC, Mumbai
{ganeshk,krishnas}@cse.iitb.ac.in, anup@barc.gov.in

Abstract. In the area of Software Product Lines(SPL), most of the
research work focuses on automated analysis of SPLs and the traceability relation between the problem domain and solution domain. An SPL
with few features can generate billions of products; to analyze such a
large product space, we need efficient analysis operations. For a given
specification, we can get many possible implementations; choosing one
implementation from this is a non-trivial task. In this paper, we extend
the work on analyzing software product lines to propose a cost effective approach that fetches products from a given SPL based on various
factors. When there are multiple implementations for a given specification, then it is the cost factors which determine the product selection.
To this end, we propose a revised formal framework for SPLs with cost
factors. This approach has been implemented in a tool SPLANE-CF
(SPL Analysis Engine with Cost Factors). We illustrate the efficiency of
SPLANE-CF on a fairly large size case study.

1   Introduction

Software Product Line (SPL) is a software development paradigm to jointly
design a family of closely related software *products* in an efficient and cost-
effective manner. The starting point of an SPL is the *scope*, which is a collection
of all features of the products in the SPL.

The scope defines the problem space of the SPL, in the sense that it describes
the expectations and objectives of the family. The description is typically organized as a feature diagram [1] that expresses the variability of the SPL in
terms of relations or constraints (exclusion, dependency) between the features
and defines all the possible products in the family.

The next important step in SPL is the development of *core assets*, a collection
of reusable artifacts. The core assets, in some sense, defines the solution space
of the SPL and are developed to meet the expectations set forth in the problem
space [2]. They are developed for a systematic reuse across the different products
in the SPL [3,4]. The core assets, like the features, may also have exclusion and
dependency constraints. Given the problem and solution spaces for an SPL, as
defined by the scope and the core assets, the notion of *traceability*, that involves

R. Natarajan (Ed.): ICDCIT 2014, LNCS 8337, pp. 212–223, 2014.
© Springer International Publishing Switzerland 2014

relating the artifacts at the two levels [2] comes in. There are many relationships possible, the most useful and natural one is the *implementability* relation which associates each feature in the scope with a set of core assets that are required for implementing the feature(s) [5]. In this work, we introduce *cost relationships* that relate each component in the core assets with cost factors like price, performance rating, etc. Industrial size SPLs has huge number of features and components, which make the analysis a non-trivial task. So, our focus in this work is the formal modeling and analysis of traceability and cost relation in an SPL.

In the literature, formal modeling and analysis of variability at the feature level, has been studied extensively and several efficient tools have been built to carry out the analyses [6,7]. The main idea behind all these works is that the variability analysis can be reduced to SAT solving of appropriate Boolean formula over variables modeling the feature level variability [8,9,10,11,2,12,13,14,15]. Many of the recent works on traceability are confined to an informal treatment [16,17,18,19]. Some works have chosen a formal approach based either on SAT solving [20] or on configuration knowledge [6]. We have chosen Quantified Boolean Formula (QBF) to improve the scalability. QBF is a powerful generalization of satisfiability problem were the variables are universally and existentially quantified. QBFs also have the ability to nest the quantified variables, which make it more expressive then SAT formulas. SAT can be used to encode any NP problem, but QBF allow us to encode PSPACE problems. However, cost related analysis operations cannot be handled by QBF solvers alone. For such operations, we seperate the QBF part and the cost related part: the QBF part is handled by the state of the art QSAT solver CirQit [21] and the cost part is solved by a cost processing module in our proposed tool.

The following summarizes the contributions and focuses on the improvements.

- A simple and abstract set-theoretic semantics of SPL with variability constraints, traceability and cost factors are proposed. This extends earlier work [22], where cost factors were not considered.
- We add several new analysis problems, useful for relating the features, core assets and cost in an SPL.
- We continue using Quantified Boolean Formulae (QBF) for modelling these problems. The QBF approach was first proposed in [22].
- A tool SPLANE-CF, has been developed, which models feature diagrams, core assets, traceability relations and cost relations. Apart from the new analysis operations proposed here, SPLANE-CF also enables SPL developers to perform existing operations in the literature [6] over feature diagrams.

SPLANE-CF is a feasible solution for automated analysis of feature models together with assets and cost. We believe that this article opens the opportunity to new forms of analysis involving variability models, assets, cost and traceability relations.

The paper is organized as follows: In section 2, we give the basic definition of an SPL model, traceability as well as cost relations. Section 3 describes the operations used for analyzing SPLs. Finally, in section 4, we describe our tool SPLANE-CF and also illustrate its working on a fairly large size case study.

2   Model of SPL : Traceability and Cost Relation

Consider an SPL with three features, namely, Anti-Brake Skidding (ABS), Electronic Stability Control (ESC) and Lane Centering (LC). The set $\{ABS, ESC, LC\}$ forms the *scope* of the SPL. Variants of vehicles may be derived from different combination of these features. These different subsets, called *specifications* of a vehicle, are often decided by business reasons and form the *PL Specification* of the SPL. For example, the PL specification may contain $\{ABS, LC\}$, $\{ABS, ESC\}$ or $\{ABS, ESC, LC\}$. These features need several components for their implementation, e.g., feature specific sensors, control softwares, ECUs (Electronic Control Unit) and actuators. All these components together form the *core assets* of the SPL. A specific *implementation* consists of a set of components. For example, a skid sensor, a brake sensor, ABS control software and ABS ECU, brake actuator, lane sensor, lane centering control software and steering actuator together constitute an implementation. All the possible implementations (or, variants) in the SPL constitute the *PL implementation*. Each component is associated with the cost factors. Cost factors may have various attributes like price, performance, etc. Let say the specification $\{LC\}$ is implemented by the implementation $\{sensors\}$, but there may be various *sensors* with different quality and price. For such specification we may get n number of *implementation* and to select better *implementation* as per the specification, *cost factors* play's very important role. It allow the analyst to select the most optimized product from the given set, based on cost factors. In this section, we define some key terms associated with software product lines.

Specification and Implementation: The set of all features found in any of the products in a productline defines the *scope* of the productline. We denote the scope of a productline by $\mathcal{F}$. A scope $\mathcal{F}$ consists of a set of features, denoted by small letters $f, g \ldots$. Specifications are subsets of features in the scope and is denoted by $F, G, \ldots$ and so on, with possible subscripts. On the other hand, the collection of components in the productline defines the *core assets* and is denoted as $\mathcal{C}$. Small letters c, d etc. represent components while implementations (subsets of components) are denoted by capital letters C, D etc. with possible subscripts.

Traceability: A feature is implemented using a non-empty subset of components in the core asset $\mathcal{C}$. For example, the feature ABS is implemented by a skid sensor, brake sensor, brake controller ECU and a brake actuator. This relationship is modeled by the partial function $\mathcal{T} : \mathcal{F} \rightarrow \wp(\wp(\mathcal{C}) \setminus \{\emptyset\})$, where $\wp$ is used to represent a powerset. When $\mathcal{T}(f) = \{C_1, C_2, C_3\}$, we interpret it as the fact that the set of components C_1 (also, C_2 and C_3) can implement the feature f. When $\mathcal{T}(f)$ is not defined, it denotes that the feature f does not have any components to implement it.

Cost Relation: A component has various cost factors associated with it like price, performance rating, etc. Cost relation is defined as a function $\mathcal{E}(c) = \langle Price, Rating \rangle$, where c is a component and $\{Price, Rating\}$ are the cost factors. Cost function will return a tuple with cost attribute for particular component. Let's say $\mathcal{E}(c_1) = \langle 100, 7 \rangle$, means a component c_1 has $price = 100$ and performance $rating = 7$ out of 10.

Definition 1 (SPL). *An SPL Ψ is defined as a quadruple $\langle \overline{\mathcal{F}}, \overline{\mathcal{C}}, \mathcal{T}, \mathcal{E} \rangle$, where $\overline{\mathcal{F}} \in \mathcal{P}(\mathcal{P}(\mathcal{F}) \setminus \{\emptyset\})$ is the PL specification, $\overline{\mathcal{C}} \in \mathcal{P}(\mathcal{P}(\mathcal{C}) \setminus \{\emptyset\})$ is the PL implementation, $\mathcal{T}$ is the traceability relation and $\mathcal{E}$ is the cost relation. ($\mathcal{P}$ represent the power set symbol).*

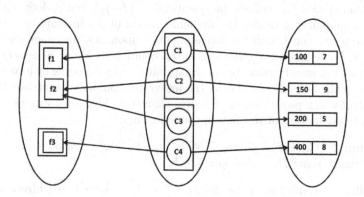

Fig. 1. The Example SPL

Example 1. *Consider the SPL $\Psi = (\overline{\mathcal{F}}, \overline{\mathcal{C}}, \mathcal{T}, \mathcal{E})$ with 3 features f_1, f_2, f_3 and 4 components c_1, c_2, c_3 and c_4, shown pictorially in Figure 1. The solid rectangles denote specifications and implementations. The hyper-edges from sets of components to features denote the traceability relation and the edges from components to cost factors denotes the cost relations.*

- $\overline{\mathcal{F}} = \{F_1 : \{f_1\}, F_2 : \{f_2\}, F_3 : \{f_1, f_2\}, F_4 : \{f_3\}\}$,
- $\overline{\mathcal{C}} = \{C_1 = \{c_1, c_2\}, C_2 = \{c_3, c_4\}\}$,
- $\mathcal{T}: f_1 \rightarrow \{\{c_1\}\}, f_2 \rightarrow \{\{c_2\}, \{c_3\}\}, f_3 \rightarrow \{\{c_4\}\}$.
- $\mathcal{E}: c_1 \rightarrow \langle 100, 7 \rangle, c_2 \rightarrow \langle 150, 9 \rangle, c_3 \rightarrow \langle 200, 5 \rangle, c_4 \rightarrow \langle 400, 8 \rangle$.

From $\mathcal{T}$, it is clear that f_1 requires c_1 for its implementation, f_3 requires c_4 for its implementation, while c_2 or c_3 can implement f_2. The $\mathcal{E}$ relation denotes that the component c_1 has price 100 and performance rating 7 out of 10.

The Implements relation A feature is *implemented* by a set of components C, denoted $implements(C, f)$, if C includes a non-empty subset of components C' such that $C' \in \mathcal{T}(f)$. It is obvious from the definition that if $\mathcal{T}(f) = \emptyset$, then f is not implemented by any set of components. In Example 1, f_1 is implemented by implementations C_1, f_2 is implemented by C_1 and C_2, and f_3 is implemented by C_2 but not by C_1.

In order to extend the definition to specifications and implementations, we define a function $Provided\_by(C)$ which computes all the features that are implemented by $C : Provided\_by(C) = \{f \in \mathcal{F} | implements(C, f)\}$. In Example 1,

$Provided\_by(C_1) = \{f_1, f_2\}$ and $Provided\_by(C_2) = \{f_2, f_3\}$. With the basic definitions above, we can now define when an implementation exactly implements a specification.

Definition 2 (Realizes). *Given $C \in \overline{C}$ and $F \in \overline{\mathcal{F}}$, $Realizes(C, F)$ if $F = Provided\_by(C)$.*

The *realizes* definition given above is rather strict. Thus, in the above example, the implementation C_1 realizes the specification $\{f_1, f_2\}$, but it does not realize $\{f_1\}$ even though it provides the implementation of f_1. In many real-life use-cases, due to the constraints on packaging of components, the exactness may be restrictive. For example, a *roll-over control* component is not necessary for an ABS feature but may be packaged in the stability control module by a component provider. In the absence of a choice, the integrator company has to buy the roll-over control which provides more features than is decided for a variant[1]. Hence, we relax the definition of *Realizes* in the following.

Definition 3 (Covers). *Given $C \in \overline{C}$ and $F \in \overline{\mathcal{F}}$, $Covers(C, F)$ if $F \subseteq Provided\_by(C)$ and $Provided\_by(C) \in \overline{\mathcal{F}}$.*

The additional condition ($Provided\_by(C) \in \mathcal{F}$) is added to address a tricky issue introduced by the *Covers* definition. Suppose that the scope $\mathcal{F}$ in Example 1 consisted of only two specifications $\{f_1\}$ and $\{f_2\}$. This models two variants with mutually exclusive features. The implementation C_1 implements $\{f_1\}$. Without the proviso, we would have $Covers(C_1, \{f_1\})$. However, since $Provided\_by(C_1) = \{f_1, f_2\}$, it actually implements both the features together, thus violating the requirement of mutual exclusion.

The set of products of the SPL are now defined as the specifications, and the implementation covering them through the traceability relation.

Definition 4 (SPL Products). *Given an SPL $\Psi = \langle \overline{\mathcal{F}}, \overline{C}, \mathcal{T}, \mathcal{E} \rangle$, the products of the SPL denoted $Prod(\Psi)$, is the set of all specification-implementation-Cost $\langle F, C, E \rangle$ where $Covers(C, F)$ and E is the tuple with costing attributes.*

Thus, in Example 1, we see that among the potential 8 products (4 specifications × 2 implementations) the valid products are $\langle C_1, F_1, \langle 250, 7 \rangle \rangle$, $\langle C_1, F_2, \langle 250, 9 \rangle \rangle$, $\langle C_1, F_3, \langle 250, 8 \rangle \rangle$, $\langle C_2, F_2, \langle 600, 5 \rangle \rangle$ and $\langle C_2, F_4, \langle 600, 8 \rangle \rangle$.

3   Analysis Operations

Industrial product lines are generally large in size, which make it difficult to analyze. To automate the analysis on such a large SPLs, formal analysis operations are presented in our previous work [22]. The proposed analysis operations in [22] doesn't provide the optimized results. In our current work, we redefined most of the analysis operations with cost factors. Cost factors, allow to choose

---

[1] This example is hypothetical. Usually, such extra components can be disabled by calibration parameters either by the provider or by the integrator.

the optimized entry from the millions or billions of available options. The QBFs formulation for the below analysis operations can be found in [22] and the cost factor analysis is done by SPLANE-CF. Given an SPL $\langle \overline{\mathcal{F}}, \overline{\mathcal{C}}, \mathcal{T}, \mathcal{E} \rangle$, we define the following analysis problems. The problems center around the new definition of SPL product.

1. A given SPL model $\langle \overline{\mathcal{F}}, \overline{\mathcal{C}}, \mathcal{T}, \mathcal{E} \rangle$ is *valid*, if there exists at least one specification ($\overline{\mathcal{F}} \neq \emptyset$) and one implementation ($\overline{\mathcal{C}} \neq \emptyset$). Let's assume a feature model with three features f_1, f_2 and f_3. The feature f_1 is a root and the features f_2 and f_3 are the mandatory children of f_1. An *excludes* relation exists between f_2 and f_3. The feature model cannot have any specification because of *excludes* relation and such an SPL is not a *valid model*.

2. In a given SPL model $\langle \overline{\mathcal{F}}, \overline{\mathcal{C}}, \mathcal{T}, \mathcal{E} \rangle$, if all the features have a traceability relation with the components which implement it, such a traceability relation is called as *complete traceability relation*. Similarly, if all the components has a cost relation with the cost factors, then such relation is called as *complete cost relation*. The preliminary properties- *valid model*, *complete traceability relation* and *complete cost relation* should hold before analyzing any other properties.

3. Let us assume an SPL model $\langle \overline{\mathcal{F}}, \overline{\mathcal{C}}, \mathcal{T}, \mathcal{E} \rangle$ which is a *valid model* but none of the implementation C covers any of the specification F. Such a model is called as *void product model* i.e. the model is not able to return a single product.

4. In a given SPL model $\langle \overline{\mathcal{F}}, \overline{\mathcal{C}}, \mathcal{T}, \mathcal{E} \rangle$, the *Cost function for a feature* is defined as $\mathcal{E}(f) = set\ of\ \langle C, \langle Price, Rating \rangle \rangle$ where f is a feature, C is the set of components which implements the feature f i.e., $\mathcal{T}(f) = \{C\}$ and $\{Price, Rating\}$ are the cost factors. Internally, this function calls the traceability relation to get the set of components implementing the feature f and then applies the cost relation on each of the component sets. Let's say $\mathcal{T}(f) = \{C_1, C_2\}$, $C_1 = \{c_1, c_2\}$ and $C_2 = \{c_2, c_3\}$. Assume $\mathcal{E}(c_1) = \langle 100, 4 \rangle$, $\mathcal{E}(c_2) = \langle 50, 7 \rangle$ and $\mathcal{E}(c_3) = \langle 200, 9 \rangle$ then, $\mathcal{E}(f) = \{\langle C_1, 150, 5.5 \rangle, \langle C_2, 250, 8 \rangle\}$. One should note that, *price* cost factor uses the *addition* function and *rating* cost factor uses *average* function. The relation between cost factors and operation functions like *addition*, *average*, etc can be set in the SPL model.

5. In a given SPL model $\langle \overline{\mathcal{F}}, \overline{\mathcal{C}}, \mathcal{T}, \mathcal{E} \rangle$, *Costing function for specification* is defined as $\mathcal{E}(F) = set\ of\ \langle C, \langle Price, Rating \rangle \rangle$ where F is a specification, C is the implementation which *Covers* the specification F and $\{Price, Rating\}$ are the cost factors. Lets say $F = \{f_1, f_2\}$, $C_1 = \{c_1, c_2\}$, $C_2 = \{c_1, c_2, c_3\}$ and $C_3 = \{c_1, c_2, c_3, c_4\}$. Assume $\mathcal{E}(c_1) = \langle 100, 4 \rangle$, $\mathcal{E}(c_2) = \langle 50, 7 \rangle$, $\mathcal{E}(c_3) = \langle 200, 9 \rangle$ and $\mathcal{E}(c_4) = \langle 500, 8 \rangle$, also $\mathcal{T}(f_1) = \{c_1\}$ and $\mathcal{T}(f_2) = \{c_2\}$. Then, $\mathcal{E}(F) = \{\langle C_1, 150, 5.5 \rangle, \langle C_2, 350, 5.5 \rangle, \langle C_3, 850, 5.5 \rangle\}$. Without the cost factor we may randomly choose any of the implementation from $\{C_1, C_2, C_3\}$ as all of them covers specification F. From traceability of f_1 and f_2 it is clear that, to implement F, the required components are c_1 and c_2. The presence of c_3 and c_4 are redundant so it is not going to affect the overall performance

rating of the product, but it results in bearing unnecessary cost of component c_3 and c_4 in the product.

6. In a given SPL model $\langle \overline{\mathcal{F}}, \overline{\mathcal{C}}, \mathcal{T}, \mathcal{E} \rangle$, *Costing function for implementation* is defined as, $\mathcal{E}(C) = \langle Price, Rating \rangle$ where C is a implementation and $\{Price, Rating\}$ are the cost factors. Lets say $C_1 = \{c_1, c_2\}$ and $C_2 = \{c_2, c_3, c_4\}$. Assume $\mathcal{E}(c_1) = \langle 100, 4 \rangle$, $\mathcal{E}(c_2) = \langle 50, 7 \rangle$, $\mathcal{E}(c_3) = \langle 200, 9 \rangle$ and $\mathcal{E}(c_4) = \langle 500, 8 \rangle$. Then, $\mathcal{E}(C_1) = \langle 150, 5.5 \rangle$ and $\mathcal{E}(C_2) = \langle 750, 8 \rangle$.

7. In a given SPL model $\langle \overline{\mathcal{F}}, \overline{\mathcal{C}}, \mathcal{T}, \mathcal{E} \rangle$ the cheapest tuple with respect to cost factors is found by the function $minCost(X)$, where X can be a given *PL specification, PL implementation* or *SPL*. When $minCost(X)$ is applied on specification, implementation or SPL, the function returns the cheapest feature, component or product respectively. Similarly, the costliest tuple is found by the function $maxCost(X)$, where X can be a PL specification, PL implementation or *SPL*.

8. The homogeneity of an SPL model is defined by a function $homo(X)$, where X can be a given *feature model, component model* or *SPL model*. The function returns the degree to which a given X is homogeneous. The homogeneity of X is calculated as follows[23]: $Homo(X) = 1 - \dfrac{\#uq}{\#tp}$, where, $\#uq$ are the number of unique variations in X and $\#tp$ are the total number of variations in X. Similarly, we define function $Hete(X)$ to measure heterogeneity of X. The heterogeneity of X is calculated as follows: $Hete(X) = \dfrac{\#uq}{\#tp}$.

9. The commonality of an SPL model is defined by a function $Common(X)$ with respect to Y, where X can be a given *specification, implementation* or *product* and Y can be a given *feature model, component model* or *SPL model* respectively. The function returns the commonality Pranoti J Tapase percentage of X calculated as follows[23]: $Common(X) = \dfrac{\#cx}{\#tx} * 100$, where, $\#cx$ are the number of variations in Y which contain X and $\#tc$ are the total number of variations in Y.

10. The variability of an SPL model is defined by a function $Vari(X)$ where X can be a given *feature model, component model* or *SPL model*. The function returns the variability factor of X calculated as follows[23]:
$Vari(X) = \dfrac{\#p}{2^n}$, where, $\#p$ are the number of variation in X and n is the number of leaf nodes in a model.

4   Validation

In order to validate the approach presented throughout this paper, a tool called SPLANE-CF for the automated analysis with cost factors have been developed and a tablet product line(TPL) based example presented and analyzed.

4.1   SPLANE-CF

SPLANE-CF (Software Product Line Analysis Engine with Cost Factors) is designed and developed to analyze the traceability between the features and implementation assets with cost factors. Nowadays, there are a large set of tools that enable the reasoning over feature models. The state of the art tool in the SPL domain *FaMa*, is restricted to analyze only feature models. *SPLANE* [22] is the first prototype tool capable of reasoning over feature models and a set of implementations. Here, we extend SPLANE to *SPLANE-CF* by providing new and refined analysis operations based on cost factors.

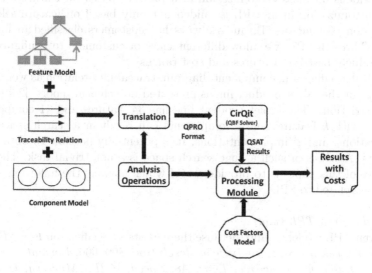

Fig. 2. SPLANE-CF reasoning process

The reasoning process performed by SPLANE-CF is shown in the Figure 2. First, SPLANE-CF takes as inputs a feature model, a traceability relationship, a component model and a cost factors model. Second, depending on the selected analysis operation, SPLANE-CF constructs the QBF and encodes it in QPRO format by using *boole2qpro* converter [24]. But the tool will not encode the cost factors in QBF, as no SAT or QSAT solver is able to handle it. QPRO format is a standard input file format in non-prenex, non-CNF form. SPLANE-CF invokes the QSAT solver CirQit [21] in the back-end to check the satisfiability of the generated QBFs in QPRO format. In case, the operation is satisfiable, cost processing module is invoked to calculate the cost for that operation and the results are provided to the user. In case of unsatisfiability, cost processing module will not be invoked, but the user will be intimated for the unsatisfiability. The choice of the QSAT solver CirQiT that SPLANE-CF invokes is based upon performance: CirQit has solved the most number of problems in the non-prenex, non-CNF track of QBFEval'10 [25].

Tablet product line(TPL) will be used to illustrate the SPL analyses and experimental results obtained through the tool SPLANE-CF.

Tablet Product Line (TPL) - Casestudy A tablet is a mobile computer. It is differentiated from smart phone by its large size and high processing capability, but are not as good as laptops. Tablets are getting popular because of it features like portability, touch screen, web access, operations through gestures, etc. Now a days, we see lot of tablets with many such features in the market. The price of a tablet is directly proportional to the number of features and the quality of components used (in general, irrespective of the brands). Product lines pave the way for the mass customization of the products. All of the existing work in SPL, focus on mass customization of a product based on feature selection. Mass customization in an SPL is guided not only based on feature selection, but also on cost factors. Business always has customers classified in financial ranges. Through SPL, we allow different class of customers to configure their own products based on features and cost ranges.

The feature diagram, component diagram, traceability relation as well as cost relations for the tablet product line is presented in technical report [26] (due to page restriction). The tablet product line has 34 features and 41 components. An SPL with k features and l components can result in a search space of 2^k specifications, and 2^l implementations. It is potentially possible to obtain 2^{k+l} products. Analysis of such a huge search space is a non-trivial task. The main objective of this paper is to provide a tool which answers the following kind of questions related to SPLs.

Q1. Is the given TPL valid?
The given TPL model is valid, because there exists a specification $F = \{Tablets,$ $Screen, Processor, Size, 5 - inches, Resolution, 800x600, Format, 4 - 3,$ $TouchTechnology, Capacitive, Type, A8, Speed, 1GHz, Memory, Internal\}$ and an implementation $C = \{TabletComp, ScreenComp, ProcessorComp,$ $SizeComp, 5InchScreen, ResolutionComp, 600RowLED, FormatComp, 4 -$ $3Ratio, \quad TouchTechnologyComp, \quad CapacitiveTouchPad, \quad ProcessorType,$ $A8Hwd, ProcessorSpeed, 1GHzHwd, HDD, 4GBHDD\}$. This we verified by using *valid* analysis operation.

Q2. Are the traceability and cost relations complete for TPL?
In the given TPL model, all the features have a traceability relation (see traceability table in [26]) with the components and all the components have a cost relation with cost factors (see cost relation table in [26]). Hence, the traceability and cost relations are complete.

Q3. Does TPL generate atleast a single product?
In the given TPL model, the implementation C given in *Q1* covers the specification F given in *Q1*. Hence, there exists a product in TPL. The analysis operation *void product model* hold false on the given TPL model.

Q4. What is the cost of feature 5 − inches?
In TPL, $cost(5 - inches)$ returns $\{\langle 5InchScreen, \langle 200, 7 \rangle \rangle\}$. A feature may be implemented by multiple sets of components. For example, $cost(Internal)$ returns $\{\langle 4GBHDD, \langle 150, 8 \rangle \rangle, \langle 8GBHDD, \langle 250, 7 \rangle \rangle\}$.

Q5. What is the cost of a given specification and implementation?
In TPL, $cost(C)$ will reutrn a tuple $\langle 2705, 6.8 \rangle$. $cost(F)$ will generate many implementation which covers F, but the implementation C $Q1$ was the with best cost i.e. $price = 2705$ and $rating = 6.8$.

Q6. Which is the cheapest and costliest products in TPL?
In TPL, $minCost()$ returns a product with minimum cost as $\langle 2155, 6.4 \rangle$. The $maxCost()$ returns a product with maximum cost as $\langle 6910, 7.25 \rangle$.

Q7. What is the homogeneity and heterogeneity of a given TPL model?
In TPL, $up = 22$ and $tp = 10368$ for feature diagram, so the homogeneity factor for specification was 0.9978.

Q8. What is the commonality percentage of a given product in a SPL?
In TPL, the specification F *Q.1* is present in 18 specification and the total number of possible specification are 10368. The commonality factor for specification F is 0.1736%.

Q9. What is the variability factor of the given SPL?
In TPL, for specification we found number of variation are 10368 and the total number of leaf features were 22. So the variability factor for the model was 0.0024.

4.2   QSAT Performance

All the above analyses were carried out using the QBF encoding of the previous section and application of the CirQit solver. After getting a SAT result from the CirQit solver, the costing related operations are handled in cost processing module of the SPLANE-CF.

5   Conclusion

In this paper, we stress the need to jointly analyze the specification and the implementation with cost factors of SPLs. Thus we have started from a formal definition of the notion of traceability and costing, and a set theoretical based framework. The analysis problems have been translated into Quantified Boolean Formulas and solved efficiently using a QBF solver. The cost related analysis operations are handled by cost processing module in our tool SPLANE-CF. Lastly, the approach is validated on industrial size case study tablet product line(TPL). The experiments shows that the benefit of using QBF solver instead of a SAT solver approach is far above the expectations in time but also in expressiveness. Further, as a future work we plan to extend the tool for providing the counter example and adding enough analysis operation based on cost factors.

References

1. Czarnecki, K., Wasowski, A.: Feature diagrams and logics: There and back again. In: SPLC 2007: Proceedings of the 11th International Software Product Line Conference, pp. 23–34. IEEE Computer Society, Washington, DC (2007)
2. Berg, K., Bishop, J., Muthig, D.: Tracing software product line variability: from problem to solution space. In: SAICSIT 2005: Proceedings of the 2005 Annual Research Conference of the South African Institute of Computer Scientists and Information Technologists on IT Research in Developing Countries, Republic of South Africa, South African Institute for Computer Scientists and Information Technologists, pp. 182–191 (2005)
3. Czarnecki, K., Eisenecker, U.: Generative Programming: Methods, Tools, and Applications. Addison-Wesley Professional (June 2000)
4. Pohl, K., Böckle, G., van der Linden, F.: Software Product Line Engineering: Foundations, Principles and Techniques. Springer-Verlag New York, Inc., Secaucus (2005)
5. Clements, P.C., Northrop, L.M.: Software product lines: practices and patterns. Addison-Wesley Longman Publishing Co., Inc., Boston (2001)
6. Benavides, D., Segura, S., Ruiz-Corts, A.: Automated analysis of feature models 20 years later: a literature review. Information Systems 35(6) (2010)
7. Pohl, K., Metzger, A.: Variability management in software product line engineering. In: Proceedings of the 28th International Conference on Software Engineering, ICSE 2006, pp. 1049–1050. ACM, New York (2006)
8. DeBaud, J.M., Schmid, K.: A systematic approach to derive the scope of software product lines. In: ICSE 1999: Proceedings of the 21st International Conference on Software Engineering, pp. 34–43. ACM, New York (1999)
9. Satyananda, T.K., Lee, D., Kang, S., Hashmi, S.I.: Identifying traceability between feature model and software architecture in software product line using formal concept analysis. In: International Conference on Computational Science and its Applications, pp. 380–388 (2007)
10. Anquetil, N., Grammel, B., da Silva, I.G.L., Noppen, J.A.R., Khan, S.S., Arboleda, H., Rashid, A., Garcia, A.: Traceability for model driven, software product line engineering. In: ECMDA Traceability Workshop Proceedings, Berlin, Germany, Norway, SINTEF, pp. 77–86 (June 2008)
11. Beuche, D., Papajewski, H., Schrder-Preikschat, W.: Variability management with feature models. Science of Computer Programming 53(3), 333–352 (2004); Software Variability Management.
12. Eisenbarth, T., Koschke, R., Simon, D.: A formal method for the analysis of product maps. In: Requirements Engineering for Product Lines Workshop, Essen, Germany (2002)
13. Zhu, C., Lee, Y., Zhao, W., Zhang, J.: A feature oriented approach to mapping from domain requirements to product line architecture. In: Arabnia, H.R., Reza, H. (eds.) Software Engineering Research and Practice, pp. 219–225. CSREA Press (2006)
14. Czarnecki, K., Antkiewicz, M.: Mapping features to models: A template approach based on superimposed variants. In: Glück, R., Lowry, M. (eds.) GPCE 2005. LNCS, vol. 3676, pp. 422–437. Springer, Heidelberg (2005)
15. Czarnecki, K., Pietroszek, K.: Verifying feature-based model templates against well-formedness ocl constraints. In: Proceedings of the 5th International Conference on Generative Programming and Component Engineering, GPCE 2006, pp. 211–220. ACM, New York (2006)

16. Cavalcanti, Y.A.C., do Carmo Machado, I., da Mota, P.A., Neto, S., Lobato, L.L., de Almeida, E.S., de Lemos Meira, S.R.: Towards metamodel support for variability and traceability in software product lines. In: Proceedings of the 5th Workshop on Variability Modeling of Software-Intensive Systems, VaMoS 2011, pp. 49–57. ACM, New York (2011)

17. Anquetil, N., Kulesza, U., Mitschke, R., Moreira, A., Royer, J.C., Rummler, A., Sousa, A.: A model-driven traceability framework for software product lines. In: Software and Systems Modeling [10]

18. Ghanam, Y., Maurer, F.: Extreme product line engineering: Managing variability and traceability via executable specifications. In: Agile Conference, AGILE 2009, pp. 41–48 (2009)

19. Riebisch, M., Brcina, R.: Optimizing design for variability using traceability links. In: ECBS 2008: Proceedings of the 15th Annual IEEE International Conference and Workshop on the Engineering of Computer Based Systems, pp. 235–244. IEEE Computer Society, Washington, DC (2008)

20. Metzger, A., Pohl, K., Heymans, P., Schobbens, P.Y., Saval, G.: Disambiguating the documentation of variability in software product lines: A separation of concerns, formalization and automated analysis. In: 15th IEEE Internationa Requirements Engineering Conference, RE 2007, pp. 243–253 (2007)

21. Goultiaeva, A., Bacchus, F.: (2013), http://www.cs.utoronto.ca/alexia/cirqit/

22. Mohalik, S., Ramesh, S., Millo, J.V., Krishna, S.N., Narwane, G.K.: Tracing spls precisely and efficiently. In: Proceedings of the 16th International Software Product Line Conference, SPLC 2012, pp. 186–195. ACM, New York (2012)

23. Benavides, D., Ruiz-Corts, A., Trinidad, P., Segura, S.: A survey on the automated analyses of feature models. In: Jornadas de Ingeniera del Software y Bases de Datos (JISBD 2006), Sitges, Spain (2006)

24. Goultiaeva, A., Bacchus, F.: (2013), http://www.cs.utoronto.ca/alexia/cirqit/

25. Peschiera, C., Pulina, L., Tacchella, A., Bubeck, U., Kullmann, O., Lynce, I.: The seventh QBF solvers evaluation (QBFEVAL'10). In: Strichman, O., Szeider, S. (eds.) SAT 2010. LNCS, vol. 6175, pp. 237–250. Springer, Heidelberg (2010)

26. Narwane, G.K., Krishna, S.N., Bhattacharjee, A.K.: Software product line analysis engine with cost factors, http://www.cse.iitb.ac.in/~krishnas/splane-cf.pdf

Fuzzy Logic Based Similarity Measure for Information Retrieval System Performance Improvement

Yogesh Gupta[1], Ashish Saini[1], A.K. Saxena[1], and Aditi Sharan[2]

[1] Dept. of Electrical Engg., Faculty of Engineering,
Dayalbagh Educational Institute, Agra-282110, Uttar Pradesh, India
ashish7119@gmail.com
[2] School of Computer and System Sciences,
Jawahar Lal Nehru University, New Delhi-110067, India

Abstract. The documents of any information retrieval system are ranked on the basis of similarity measure. Some similarity measures e.g. Cosine, Euclidean and Okapi etc. have been extensively used for retrieving relevant documents against the query. In present paper, a new fuzzy based similarity measure is proposed. Experiments have been performed on CACM data collection. The performance of proposed similarity measure is evaluated and compared with above mentioned similarity measures on the basis of Precision-Recall curves, average similarity value of documents for individual query and average number of retrieved relevant documents. The results show the marked improvement in performance of information retrieval system using proposed fuzzy logic based similarity as compare to other similarity measures.

Keywords: Information Retrieval, Similarity Measure, Precision, Recall.

1   Introduction

In last couple of decades, various methods have been suggested to improve the performance of Information Retrieval (IR) System. An IR system generally deals with retrieval of relevant documents against user defined queries. Baeza-Yates [1] defined a general Information Retrieval model as a quadruple [D, Q, F, R (q_i, d_j)], where D is a set composed of logical views for the documents in the collection, Q is a set composed of logical views for the user information needs expressed as queries, F is a framework for modeling document representations, queries and their relationships and R (q_i, d_j) is a similarity measure/ranking function which associates a real number with a query $q_i \in Q$ and a document representation $d_j \in D$. Such ranking defines an ordering among the documents with regard to the query q_i. Therefore similarity measure plays an important role to develop a quality IR system.

An IR system evaluates the relevancy using some representations of a document and a query. There are different models for representation documents and queries. Each model has its pros and cons. The Boolean model [2] was the first model which was adopted by most of the earlier systems and even today some of the commercial systems use this model, which makes use of the concepts of Boolean logic and set

R. Natarajan (Ed.): ICDCIT 2014, LNCS 8337, pp. 224–232, 2014.

theories. The documents and queries are a collection of terms and each term from the document is indexed. The presence and absence of a term in a document is represented by 1 and 0 respectively. For the term matching of document and query we maintain an inverted index of the terms i.e. for each term we must store a list of documents that contain the term. However, the Boolean model has some major limitations like binary decision criterion without any notion of grading scale and overloading of documents [3]. While some researchers have tried to overcome the weaknesses of the Boolean model by building refinements to the existing Boolean model, others have approached IR with a different search strategy called the Vector Space model [4]. The Vector Space Model, as the name implies, represents documents and queries internally in the form of vectors. In the vector space model all queries and documents are represented as vectors in |V|-dimensional space, where V is the set of all distinct terms in the collection (the vocabulary). Some of the advantages of the Vector Space Model are that it is simple and fast model, that it can handle weighted terms, that it produces a ranked list as output and that the indexing process is automated which means a significantly lighter workload for the administrator of the collection. Also, it is easy to modify individual vectors, which is essential for the query expansion technique [4] and logic based similarity measure. Therefore, vector space model is used as a base model in this paper.

An IR system needs to calculate the similarity of the query and the particular document in order to decide relevancy of that document with the query. When a document retrieval system is used to query a collection of documents with n terms, the system computes a vector D (d_{i1}, d_{i2}... d_{in}) of size n for each document. The vectors are filled with the weights and similarly, a vector Q (W_{q1}, W_{q2}... W_{qn}) is constructed for the terms found in the query. In recent years, some efforts have made to construct a effective similarity measure for enhancing the performance of IR System. In [5] Fan presented similarity functions as trees and a classical generational scheme. Pathak et al. [6] have proposed the idea of combined similarity measure in which they have proposed a linear combination of various similarity measures and then optimize the weight of each similarity measure using GA. Mehran Sahami [7] proposes a novel method for measuring the similarity between short text snippets by leveraging web search results to provide greater context for the short texts. Vincent Schickel-Zuber et al., [8] present a novel approach that allows similarities to be asymmetric while still using only information contained in the structure of the ontology. Torra et al. presented a method to calculate similarity between words based on dictionaries using Fuzzy graphs in reference [9]. Chen presented in reference [10] a new similarity measure based on the geometric mean averaging operator to handle the similarity problems of generalized fuzzy numbers. Usharani et al. [11] proposed a genetic algorithm based method for finding similarity of web document based on cosine similarity. In the past, most popular similarity measures used in IR Systems are Cosine, Euclidean, Jaccard and Okapi.

In the present paper, a Fuzzy Logic based Similarity Measure called as FLBSM, is proposed for vector space IR model. The performance of proposed similarity measure is evaluated and compared with above mentioned similarity measures on the basis of

Precision-Recall curves, average similarity value of documents for individual query and average number of retrieved relevant documents.

The rest of present paper is organized as follows: Section 2 describes proposed fuzzy logic based similarity measure. The details of evaluation of performance of Information Retrieval System are given in section 3. The experiments and results of FLBSM are presented in section 4. Finally, conclusion is drawn in section 5.

2   Proposed Fuzzy Logic Based Similarity Measure

The IR System retrieves documents based on a query given by the user. In most of the cases, both queries and documents are vague or imprecise and usually expressed in Natural Language (NL). Sometimes user may change his query during information retrieval process and/or he may not be conscious of his exact needs of information. Therefore, to handle this uncertainty, vagueness and impreciseness, Fuzzy Logic is very suitable. Fuzzy logic is based on Fuzzy Set theory and membership functions [12] [13].

In present paper, Fuzzy Logic is being used to develop a new similarity measure. Documents retrieved by a query are evaluated by the rules of Fuzzy Inference System (FIS). Vector Space Model is used as a base model due to its advantages over other models. In this FIS, we have used three input variables: term frequency (tf), inverse document frequency (idf), overlap and one output variable: relevance. These input variables are very useful to determine the relevancy of document against a particular query. TF indicates that the number of occurrences of a term in each document of the corpus. IDF can be given as log (N/n), where N is the total number of documents in corpus and n is the number of documents contains the term. Overlap reflects that many of the terms of the query are found in documents.

Mamdani type fuzzy inference system [14] is used in FLBSM with the help of Matlab Fuzzy Logic Toolbox. The range of input variables tf, idf and output variable relevance are represented by LOW, MEDIUM and HIGH, while the range of input variable overlap is represented by LOW and HIGH. In this paper, triangular membership function is being used to map input space to a degree of membership of fuzzy set. The details of the membership functions for input and output variables of FLBSM are shown in Fig. 1.

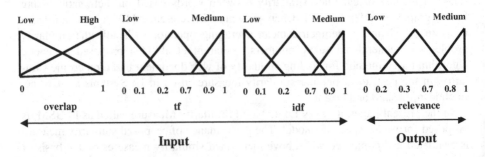

Fig. 1. Input and Output Membership functions

Fuzzy rules are derived from tf.idf weighting scheme i.e. if a query term has high tf and high idf in a document, then relevance is likely to be high. If many of the terms of the query are found in the document (overlap), then relevance is likely to be high. It is known that if the rules that penalize low features are added, the performance of the system is increased. So the following rules are constructed for each of the query term:

- If (tf is High) and (idf is High) then (relevance is High).
- If (tf is Medium) and (idf is Medium) then (relevance is Medium).
- If (tf is Low) and (idf is Low) then (relevance is Low).

Two fuzzy rules are also defined for overlap as follows:

- If (overlap is High) then (relevance is High).
- If (overlap is Low) then (relevance is Low).

Fig. 2-4 display the three dimensional surfaces to show the dependencies of two out three inputs variables to determine the output variable i.e. relevance.

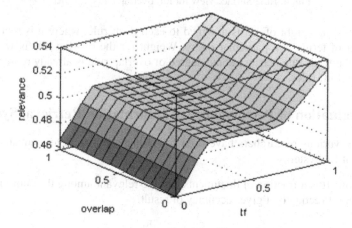

Fig. 2. Rule surface view for tf, overlap and relevance

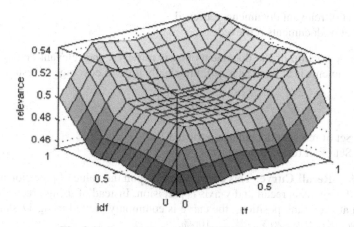

Fig. 3. Rule surface view for tf, idf and relevance

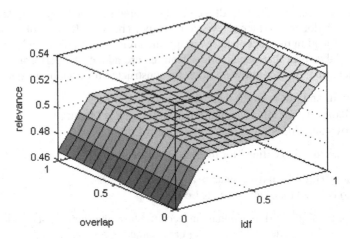

Fig. 4. Rule Surface view for idf, overlap and relevance

In FLBSM, a weight of 1/n is assigned to each tf.idf rule, where n is representing the number of terms in a particular query. Weight for the overlap rule is 1/10 of the weight of the tf.idf rule because some degree of overlap rule is already represented in each of the tf.idf rules.

3   Evaluation of Performance of Information Retrieval System

In the past, various researchers have used following parameters to evaluate the performance of IR Systems:

1. **Precision:** It is a fraction of documents that are relevant among the entire retrieved document. Practically it gives accuracy of result.

$$\text{Precision} = \frac{|R_a|}{|A|} \tag{1}$$

   R_a: Set of relevant documents retrieved
   A: Set of documents retrieved

2. **Recall:** A fraction of the documents that is retrieved and relevant among all relevant documents is defined as recall. Practically it gives coverage of result.

$$\text{Recall} = \frac{|R_a|}{|R|} \tag{2}$$

   R_a: Set of relevant documents retrieved
   R: Set of all relevant documents

3. **Precision-Recall Curve:** This curve is based upon the value of precision and recall where the x-axis is recall and y-axis is precision. Instead of using precision and recall on at each rank position , the curve is commonly plotted using 11 standard recall level 0%, 10%, 20% ....100%.

Moreover, average similarity value of documents for individual query and average number of retrieved relevant documents can also be used as parameters to check the performance of IR System. If the values for both of these parameters are high then the performance of IR System will be good.

4   Experiments and Results

Experiments have been performed on CACM data collection. The authors have selected randomly four queries from above data collection and the terms of those queries are shown in table 1 to perform all the experiments.

Table 1. Query terms used for experiments

Query	Terms
1	compute, system, operate, IBM, time
2	construct, language, compil, multi
3	problem, process, procedure, commun, possible, distribut, rather, example, call, mechan, descript, implement, between
4	paper, design, manage, essenti, human, implement, interpret, improv

Then the similarity value is evaluated by using proposed FLBSM and ranking done accordingly. After that we compared our results with extensively used similarity measures e.g. Cosine, Euclidean and Okapi.

4.1   Precision-Recall Curve

For experiments, top ranked twenty documents are taken and then precision and recall are calculated. FLBSM has given significantly better precision and recall values for all queries. Fig. 5 clearly shows the best Precision-Recall curve for query 3.

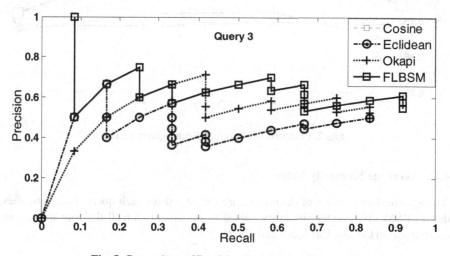

Fig. 5. Comparison of Precision-Recall curve for query 3

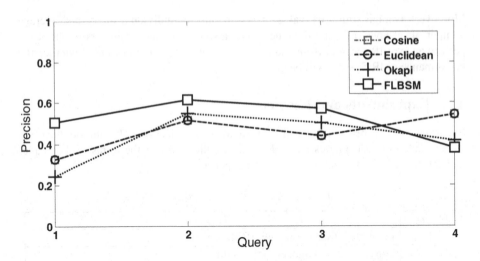

Fig. 6. Comparison of average Precision-Query curve

Fig. 6 and Fig. 7 illustrate that FLBSM gives better average precision and average recall values for all the four queries respectively as compared to other similarity measures.

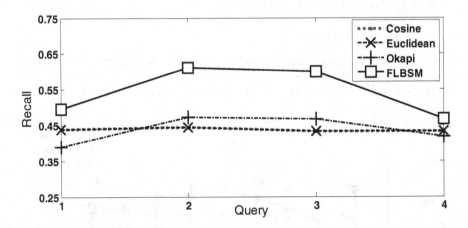

Fig. 7. Comparison of average Recall-Query curve

4.2   Average Similarity Value

Average similarity values of documents are calculated for each query. Fig. 8 justifies that FLBSM gives better similarity values of documents for all the four queries in comparison to Cosine, Euclidean and Okapi.

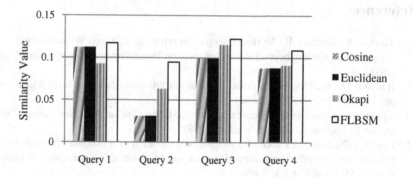

Fig. 8. Comparison of average Similarity Value for each query

4.3   Average Number of Retrieved Relevant Documents

In experiments, each similarity measure function retrieves some relevant documents. Average of retrieved relevant documents for all queries are considered and that clearly indicates that proposed FLBSM retrieves more relevant documents than any other similarity measure as shown in Fig. 9.

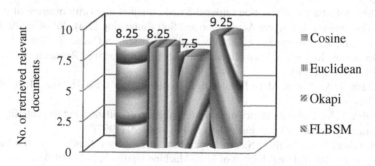

Fig. 9. Comparison of retrieved relevant documents

5   Conclusion

In this paper, a new fuzzy logic based similarity measure has been developed. This implementation returns an advantage in the form of improvement in IR system's performance. The performance of proposed similarity measure is compared with Cosine, Euclidean and Okapi similarity measures on CACM data collection. The results revealed the effectiveness of fuzzy logic to handle uncertainty and vagueness of queries and documents.

References

1. Yates, R.B., Berthier, R.: Modern Information retrieval. Addisson Wesley (1999)
2. Cooper, W.S.: Getting beyond Boole. Information Processing and Management 24, 243–248 (1988)
3. Harman, D.: Ranking Algorithms. Information retrieval: data structures and algorithms, pp. 363–392. Prentice-Hall (1992)
4. Salton, G.: Automatic text processing: the transformation, analysis, and retrieval of information by computer. Addison Wesley (1998)
5. Fan, W., Gordon, M., Pathak, P.: Automatic generation of a matching function by genetic programming for effective information retrieval. In: America's Conference on Information System, Milwaukee, USA (1999)
6. Pathak, P., Gordon, M., Fan, W.: Effective information retrieval using genetic algorithms based matching functions adaption. In: Proceedings of 33rd Hawaii International Conference on Science (HICS), Hawaii, USA (2000)
7. Sahami, M., Heilman, T.: A Web-based Kernel Function for Measuring the Similarity of Short Text Snippets. In: 15th International Conference on World Wide Web, pp. 377–386 (2006)
8. Schickel Zuber, V., Faltings, B.: OSS: A Semantic Similarity Function Based on Hierarchical Ontologies. In: International Joint Conference on Artificial Intelligence, pp. 551–556 (2007)
9. Torra, V., Narukawa, Y.: Word Similarity from dictionaries: Inferring Fuzzy measures and Fuzzy graphs. International Journal of Computational Intelligence Systems 1(1), 19–23 (2008)
10. Chen, S.J.: Fuzzy information retrieval based on a new similarity measure of generalized fuzzy numbers. Intelligent Automation and Soft Computing 17(4), 465–476 (2011)
11. Usharani, J., Iyakutti, K.: A Genetic Algorithm based on Cosine Similarity for Relevant Document Retrieval. International Journal of Engineering Research & Technology (IJERT) 2(2) (2013)
12. Zadeh, L.A.: Foreword to Fuzzy Logic Toolbox User's Guide. The Math Works Inc. (2004)
13. Zadeh, L.A.: Toward a theory of fuzzy information granulation and its centrality in human reasoning and fuzzy logic. Fuzzy Sets and Systems 90 (1997)
14. Mamdani, E.H., Assilian, S.: An Experiment in Linguistic Synthesis with a Fuzzy logic controller. International Journal of Man–Machine Studies 7, 1–13 (1975)

Maximizing Information or Influence Spread Using Flow Authority Model in Social Networks

Mohamed Mustafa Faisan and S. Durga Bhavani

School of Computer & Information Sciences,
University of Hyderabad, Hyderabad, India
sdbcs@uohyd.ernet.in

Abstract. Identifying a set of nodes of size k in a large social network graph which maximizes the information flow or influence spread is a classical subset selection problem which is NP-Hard. Recently Charu Agarwal et al. in paper [10] proposed a stochastic information flow model and two algorithms namely, RankedReplace and BayesTraceBack to retrieve influential nodes. Among the two, RankedReplace algorithm gives better information spread, but does not scale well for large data sets. The main objective of paper is to speed up the RankedReplace algorithm without compromising on the information spread. To achieve this we are using the idea of *degree discount heuristic* from [8] and *maximum degree heuristic*. As shown by our experimental results, the proposed modifications reduce the amount of time significantly, maintaining the influence spread almost equal and even marginally better at times as compared to RankReplace algorithm. We have also proposed *Willingness to send heuristic*(WS) and an algorithm based on this *WSRank* for directed social network graphs.

1 Introduction

Suppose we are given a social network graph $G = (V, E)$, and an integer k along with an information flow model. The problem here is to find a set S of k nodes at which if the information is released, the aggregate probability of information assimilation over all nodes in the graph is maximized. If $\pi(i)$ is the probability that node i contains the information, the problem can be expressed in the equation below.

$$\mathbf{S_k^*} = argmax_{\{S \subset V, |S|=k\}} \sum_{i \in V} \pi(i)$$

2 Related Work

Domingos and Richardson [1] used Bayes model of probability for calculating the network value of an individual in a social network and also proposed a hill climbing based greedy algorithm to incrementally find the set of nodes which would maximize the influence. Kleinberg et al. in [4,5] proved an approximation guarantee to the greedy algorithm. Even though we have an approximation guarantee, the greedy algorithm is not scalable to large graphs (graphs having a

R. Natarajan (Ed.): ICDCIT 2014, LNCS 8337, pp. 233–238, 2014.

few lakh nodes). Wei Chen et al. [8], presented an improvement to the greedy algorithm for both Independent Cascade Model and Linear Threshold Model and proposed a heuristic based algorithm called "Degree Discount Heuristic" for calculating the influential nodes. Charu Agarwal et al. in paper [10] proposed flow authority model, if $p_{i,j}$ be transmission probability along edge (i, j), $N(i)$ are neighbours of node i then $\pi(i)$ - probability that node i contains the information is given by

$$\pi(i) = 1 - \prod_{j \in N(i)} (1 - \pi(j) \cdot p_{ji}).$$

2.1   RankReplace Algorithm and Its Drawback

The *RankReplace* algorithm of [10] has mainly 3 steps
1. Run *steadyStateSpread* procedure on each node to find it's influence spread.
2. Sort nodes based on their influence spread.
3. Replacement step to increase influence spread. The total time of RankReplace algorithm is given by

$$|V| * Time_{steadyStateSpread} + Time_{Sort} + Time_{Replacements}$$

The *steadyStateSpread* procedure impacts the overall time of RankReplace algorithm. Consider a graph with 15000 nodes and 60000 edges. Suppose on average the *steadyStateSpread* procedure takes 0.5 seconds for each node, then the total time taken by first step would be $15000 * 0.5 = 7500$ seconds which is approximately equal to **2 hours**. Consider **1 second** for sorting. In replacement step after each replacement *steadyStateSpread* procedure is run, with 300 replacements this would take 300 * 0.5 = **5 minutes**. So the total time for RankReplace is **2 hours + 1 sec + 5 minutes**.

2.2   Degree Discount Heuristics

The standard MaxDegree heuristic, selection of top-k nodes having highest degree, can be used as initializing step for RankReplace algorithm. Chen et al. in[8] suggest that the edge (i, j) which has contributed to the degree of i should not be again used for degree calculation of j, if i has already been selected in seed set before j. This is the basic idea of degree discount heuristic called *singleDegreeDiscount*.

3   Proposed Algorithm

In this paper we claim that selecting top-k nodes having maximum degree nodes with degree discount heuristic can be used to speed up the initialization procedure without compromising on information spread. We propose that *RRDegreeDiscount* algorithm, selects the nodes in decreasing order of degree after the update of *singleDegreeDiscount* for replacements. We name the new algorithm as *RRDegreeDiscount*, the *RankedReplace* algorithm with degree discount heuristic. We also ran our experiments on *RRmaxDegree* algorithm. Note that *steadyStateSpread(S, P)* procedure is used only in replacement step.

Algorithm 1. RRDegreeDiscount(P:probMatrix, k:setsize, m:maxiterations)

1: Find *degree(i)* for each node i in the set V.
2: S = Initial set of k authority nodes with the highest value of *degree(i)*.
3: Arrange nodes in $(V - S)$ in descending order of *degree(i)*.
4: Update the degree of neighbors of set S using *singleDegreeDiscount(j, P)*.
5: **for** each node i in $(V - S)$ in descending order **do**
6:    sort the list S in ascending order of *singleDegreeDiscount(j, P)*.
7:    pick the first element of sorted list S which is such that replacing i with it increases value of *steadyStateSpread(S, P)*, update the degree of neighbors of selected node using *singleDegreeDiscount(j, P)*.
8:    if no replacement has occurred in the last m consecutive iterations, ***return(S)*** and terminate.
9: **end for**
10: **RETURN (S)**.

3.1 Willingness to Send Heuristic

The natural choice in a directed graph for selecting the initial set of nodes both in degree discount heuristic and max degree heuristic will be nodes having high out degree, but neighbors of a node with high out degree might be sink nodes i.e they might have very limited or no reachability. This will limit its influence on the other nodes in the graph. We formulate a new heuristic called *Willingness to send* (WSRank) to overcome this, it calculates rank of a node based on its reachability in the entire graph. Let $P_{i,j}$ be the influence propagation probability from node i to j, then rank of each node can be calculated using the formula given below.

$$WSRank(i) = \sum_{j \in Outneighbor(i)} P_{i,j} \cdot WSRank(j)$$

3.2 Algorithm Using Willingness to Send Heuristic

Input to $WSRank$ algorithm is k - number of influential nodes that are required and m -number of times the algorithm iterates before stopping. This important parameter should be carefully selected so that algorithm does not exit before the ranks have converged. And also it should not iterate unnecessarily even after ranks have stabilized.We choose $\log(n)$ as the value of m because the average path length in a scale free network is $\log(n)$.

Algorithm 2. $WSRank(P : probMatrix, k : setSize, m : maxIterations)$

1: V is the set of nodes;
2: **for** each node $i \in V$ **do**
3:    $WSRank(i) \leftarrow outdegree(i)$;
4: **end for**
5: **for** $i = 1 \rightarrow m$ **do**
6:    **for** $j = 1 \rightarrow N$ **do**
7:       $WSRank(i) \leftarrow \sum_{j \in Outneighbor(i)} P_{i,j} \cdot WSRank(j)$
8:    **end for**
9: **end for**
10: $TopNodes \leftarrow getTopkNodes(WSRank[], k)$;
11: **RETURN (TopNodes)**

---

4   Experimentation on Data Set

We ran our experiments on 3 data sets SIGIR, NetHEPTLT and NetHEPTWC all of them relating to publications in conferences in which an individual author represents a node and transmission probability of an edge is proportional to the number of times the two authors have co-published a paper and it is normalized.

4.1   Results

As can be seen from the graphs below there is significant reduction in time with negligible drop in influence spread. For example in NetHEPTWC dataset, for selecting 26 most influential nodes, the initialization step of RankReplace algorithm took 147 minutes (> **2 hours**) whereas RRMD and RRDD took only 0.71 and 0.96 seconds respectively. For the replacement step, RankReplace took 9.46 minutes whereas RRMD and RRDD took 4.29 and 3.99 minutes respectively. The number of replacements tried in RankReplace is 1812, and for RRMD, RRDD it is 810 and 774 respectively. From the above time break up, it is clear that most of time gained in both RRMD and RRDD algorithms is due the gain in initialization step.

As the target set increases the time taken by both RRDD and RRMD algorithms also increases. For instance for target size of 2, RRDD and RRMD take approximately 0.18 and 0.17 minutes respectively, whereas for target size of 44, they take 6 and 4 minutes. The RankReplace took 145.52 minutes for target size of 2 and 158.60 minutes for target size of 44. Generally the target size $\ll$ total nodes but one needs to be cautious about the time scalability in choosing the proposed modifications as the number of influential nodes to find increases. The last two graphs compare the time and information spread of $WSRank$ algorithm with other algorithms. Even though the time taken by $WSRank$ is least, but its information spread is also less among all the algorithms.

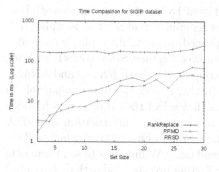

Fig. 1. Running Time SIGIR

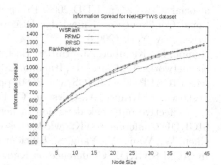

Fig. 2. Influence spread SIGIR

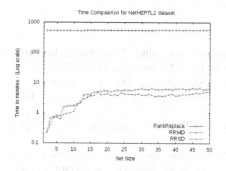

Fig. 3. Running Time NetHEPTLT

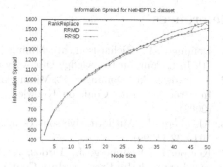

Fig. 4. Influence spread NetHEPTLT

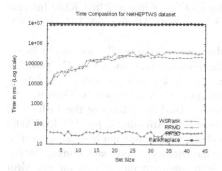

Fig. 5. WSRank time NetHEPTWC

Fig. 6. WSRank information spread

5 Conclusion

The proposed algorithms replaces *steadyStateSpread* procedure in the initialization step of *RankedReplace* algorithm with maximum degree and degree discount heuristics, the information spread has not dropped with these heuristics, because after selecting the initial set of nodes, other combinations from the remaining nodes are tried to improve the information spread iteratively; and once a node with better information spread is identified from the remaining nodes set, it is replaced in the selected nodes set S, and this iterative procedure gradually replaces the nodes with better information spread as done in *RankedReplace*. Since bayesTraceBack algorithm performs better in terms of time compared to both $RRDD$ and $RRMD$ algorithms, a reasonably good approach to further reduce the time comparable to bayesTraceBack, is to explore the heuristics that select the order in which nodes should be tried from the remaining nodes to increase the information spread. A good heuristic might significantly reduce the number of nodes tried which will directly reduce the time. The information spread using Willingness to send heuristic algorithm is not satisfactory and needs to be further investigated with real directed social network graphs.

References

1. Domingos, P., Richardson, M.: Mining the network value of customers. In: Proc. 7th Intl. Conf. on Knowledge Discovery and Data Mining, pp. 57–66 (2001)
2. Richardson, M., Domingos, P.: Mining knowledge-sharing sites for viral marketing. In: Proc. 8th Intl. Conf. on Knowledge Discovery and Data Mining, pp. 61–70 (2002)
3. Kleinberg, J.: Authoritative sources in a hyperlinked environment. JACM 46(5), 604–632 (1999)
4. Kempe, D., Kleinberg, J., Tardos, E.: Maximizing the spread of influence in a social network. In: Proc. 9th Intl. Conf. on Knowledge Discovery and Data Mining, pp. 137–146 (2003)
5. Kempe, D., Kleinberg, J., Tardos, E.: Maximizing the spread of influence through a social network. In: KDD 2003: Proceedings of the Ninth ACMSIGKDD International Conference on Knowledge Discovery and Data Mining, pp. 137–146. ACM Press, New York (2003)
6. Kempe, D., Kleinberg, J., Tardos, É.: Influential nodes in a diffusion model for social networks. In: Caires, L., Italiano, G.F., Monteiro, L., Palamidessi, C., Yung, M. (eds.) ICALP 2005. LNCS, vol. 3580, pp. 1127–1138. Springer, Heidelberg (2005)
7. Leskovec, J., Krause, A., Guestrin, C., Faloutsos, C., VanBriesen, J., Glance, N.S.: Cost-effective outbreak detection in networks. In: Proceedings of the 13th ACM SIGKDD Conference on Knowledge Discovery and Data Mining, pp. 420–429 (2007)
8. Chen, W., Wang, Y., Yang, S.: Efficient influence maximization in social networks. In: ACM SIGKDD Conference on Knowledge Discovery and Data Mining (2009)
9. Chen, W., Wang, C., Wang, Y.: Scalable influence maximization for prevalent viral marketing in large scale social networks. In: ACM KDD Conf., pp. 1029–1038 (2010)
10. Aggarwal, C.C., Khan, A., Yan, X.: On flow authority discovery in social networks. In: Proceedings of the Eleventh SIAM International Conference on Data Mining, SDM (2011)

A Second View on SecureString 2.0

Günter Fahrnberger

University of Hagen, Universitätsstraße 1, 58097 Hagen, Germany
guenter.fahrnberger@fernuni-hagen.de

Abstract. Many companies have thought about using external hosting solutions. Cloud computing as such a solution attracts prospective users who want to avoid initial costs and standing expenses with the underlying pay-as-you-use model. The outsourcing of sensitive information implies security risks, like eavesdropping and sabotage, for them as soon as they pass any unconfident area. If an outhouse hosting solution serves as data storage only, then an end-to-end cryptosystem without the necessity of having homomorphic properties comes up with the answer. Moreover, secure computations on the encrypted data need the use of more complex cryptosystems. SecureString 1.0 [3] and SecureString 2.0 [4] were proposed as such complex cryptosystems that focus on computing on encrypted character strings in untrustworthy environments (like clouds). While SecureString 1.0 offered a too inflexible approach, SecureString 2.0 as its improvement was introduced textually at a high level only so far. This paper contributes to foster the understanding of SecureString 2.0 by providing performance analysis for its supported operations plus formal definitions, theorems and proofs.

Keywords: blind computing, character string, character string function, character string operation, cloud, cloud computing, secure computing, string function, string operation.

1 Introduction

The outsourcing of own computing power to external places shifts (the responsibility of) the maintenance efforts of the outsourced facilities to a service provider and has been a valid strategy since the commercial use of computers. It began with central computations in mainframes and was supplemented with the hosting of foreign IT-hard- and software. The will to commercialize less utilized or even idle computing resources and the possibility of virtualized hardware has driven the emergence of the topical cloud computing with its three major service models Infrastructure as a service (IaaS), Platform as a service (PaaS) and Software as a service (Saas). Users of cloud computing save maintenance efforts. Furthermore, they also benefit of low or even no initial costs and standing expenses, because almost all cloud providers offer their resources by means of the pay-as-you-use model. The privacy level of outsourced digital data must be maintained somehow to give malicious forces neither the chance to obtain knowledge of sensitive information nor to endanger its integrity. Numeric or textual data intended just

R. Natarajan (Ed.): ICDCIT 2014, LNCS 8337, pp. 239–250, 2014.

to be stored in the cloud without any reading or writing computations on them can protected easily by employing one of the many available sorely approved as secure end-to-end cryptosystems. For (keyword) searches on encrypted character strings, there exist useful schemes in masses as well. The first big challenge are calculations with ciphered numeric operands and results that require either (fully) homomorphic cryptosystems [5,9] or disguising techniques [1]. The second field of research delves for modifying operations on ciphertext character strings. The use of trusted third parties [10], multiple parties [2,7] or cryptographic hardware [6] has led to appropriate solutions, but obviously all of them depend on substantial hardware efforts. Reasons, like the reduced or lost flexibility of clouds, higher costs or the unwillingness of integration by the cloud providers, make the use of additional hardware unattractive or even impossible.

SecureString 1.0 [3] was the first approach to overcome these extra hardware resources with a pure software solution. The detection of considerable limitations in this model ended up in the improved version 2.0 of SecureString [4] whose performance analysis for its supported operations plus its formal definitions, theorems and proofs are focus of interest in this publication.

Section 2 takes a formal look at the en- and decryption scheme of SecureString 2.0.

Section 3 contains the definitions of the three most important character string functions *querying*, *replacing* and *picking* that are supported by SecureString 2.0.

In Section 4 the probabilistic success of statistical attacks against SecureString 2.0 is proved by varying either the n-gram length or the character string length.

Section 5 deals with the time performance of the three character string functions *querying*, *replacing* and *picking*.

Section 6 summarizes and concludes the current document.

2   En- and Decryption Scheme

The en- and decryption scheme of SecureString 2.0 aims to protect the confidentiality of character strings on their way through a P2P-network or a distributed application comprising not only trustworthy nodes. While ciphertext character strings may occur in all nodes and transmission paths, plaintext character strings must not leave a trustworthy node. Therefore, en- and decryptions must be executed in confident environments only, which leads to the following encryption scheme steps in a trustworthy node.

1. Initially, the following input parameters must be chosen: the polygram length $n \in \mathbb{N}$, the number of concurrent coexisting encryption steps $a \in \mathbb{N}$, a filling character which never occurs in plaintext character strings at all and the underlying cryptosystem.
2. All confident nodes agree on a common secret key together.
3. A client repository with an amount of a encryption steps is created. Each of these a steps contains a set of all possible ciphertext n-grams (character strings of length n). Each encrypted n-gram of such a set is synthesized by

appending the same random character string (salt) to the end of the plaintext n-gram and encrypting the merged string with the chosen underlying cryptosystem and its secret key. Therefore, every set of encryption steps gets attached to its own unique salt respectively.

4. An unused encryption step of the client repository is exclusively chosen for each new plaintext character string v.
5. v is split it into its n-grams. If the string length $|v|$ is not dividable by n without having a remainder, then the last substring is be shorter than n characters and must be padded to length n with the defined filling character.
6. Each plaintext n-gram is sought in the client repository and exchanged for its encrypted pendant.
7. Just the ordered conglomeration of the ciphered n-grams represents the wanted ciphertext alternative as result of this encryption scheme.
8. If the number of unused encryption steps in the client repository has fallen below a critical threshold value, then the functionality of the client repository must be maintained by renewing it with maximum a new encryption steps.
9. Continuation with step 4

The previously described encryption scheme gains reversal with the following decryption scheme steps in a trustworthy node.

1. The decisions for the polygram length n, the filling character and the underlying cryptosystem are taken over from the encryption scheme.
2. All confident nodes have agreed on a common secret key together.
3. A new ciphertext character string is split into its ciphered n-grams.
4. Each gained ciphertext n-gram is decrypted separately with the selected underlying cryptosystem and its secret key.
5. Salts and filling characters in the results of the previous step are clipped to plaintext n-grams. The last portion can be shorter than length n of course.
6. Just the ordered sequence of the plaintext n-grams represents the wanted plaintext character string as result of this decryption scheme.
7. Continuation with step 3

While Figure 1 depicts the cryptosystem as output of the previously described en- and decryption scheme, Definition 2 expresses it formally. Definition 1 declares reoccurring notations (emphasized) and their explanations initially as reference in order to enhance the readability of all incident definitions, theorems and proofs.

Definition 1. *Let Σ denote an alphabet, let $\mathbf{D} \subseteq \Sigma^*$ denote a dictionary, let the floor function $\lfloor \mathbf{x} \rfloor = max\{y \in \mathbb{Z} | y \leq x\}$ output the largest integer less than or equal to x, let the ceiling function $\lceil \mathbf{x} \rceil = min\{y \in \mathbb{Z} | y \geq x\}$ output the smallest integer greater than or equal to x, let $\mathbf{m} \in \mathbb{N}$ denote the block size of the underlying cryptosystem, let the polygram length $\mathbf{n} \in \mathbb{N}$ denote the number of characters that are salted and encrypted together as a n-gram in ECB (Electronic CodeBook) mode, let $\mathbf{a} \in \mathbb{N} | 0 < a \leq |\Sigma^{m-n}|$ denote the number of concurrent coexisting encryption steps, let $\mathbf{v} \in \Sigma^*$ denote a plaintext character string, let $|\mathbf{v}| \in \mathbb{N}$ denote the length of a string v, let $\mathbf{w} \in \Sigma^{m*\lceil \frac{|v|}{n} \rceil}$ denote the arisen*

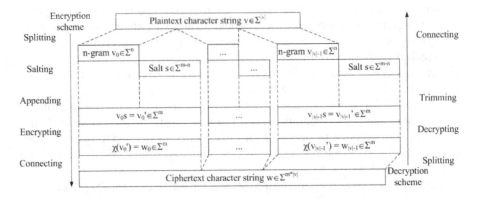

Fig. 1. En- and Decryption Scheme of SecureString 2.0 (n = 1)

ciphertext character string from splitting v into disjunctive n-grams before salting and encrypting them separately during the encryption scheme of SecureString 2.0, opposed to the decryption scheme that takes w, decrypts its ciphered n-grams and removes their salts in order to output v finally, let $\mathbf{C_z} = \frac{1}{z+1}\binom{2z}{z}|z \in$ $\mathbb{N}$ *the* z^{th} *Catalan number, let* $\mathbf{u} \in \Sigma^*$ *denote a plaintext matching pattern string and* $\mathbf{q_0}, \cdots, \mathbf{q_o}, \cdots, \mathbf{q_{a-1}} \in \Sigma^{m*\lceil \frac{|u|}{n} \rceil}$ *a set of a appropriate ciphertext alternatives, where* $\mathbf{o} \in \mathbb{N}|0 \leq o < a < |\Sigma^{m-n}|$ *denotes the* o^{th} *alternative, let* $\mathbf{q_{o0}}, \cdots, \mathbf{q_{op}}, \cdots, \mathbf{q_{o_{\lfloor \frac{|u|}{n} \rfloor}}} \in \Sigma^m$ *denote the encrypted n-grams of* q_o*, where* $\mathbf{p} \in \mathbb{N}|0 \leq p < \lceil \frac{|u|}{n} \rceil$ *denotes the index of the* p^{th} *n-gram, let* $\mathbf{t} \in \Sigma^*$ *denote a plaintext replacement string and* $\mathbf{r_0}, \cdots, \mathbf{r_o}, \cdots, \mathbf{r_{a-1}} \in \Sigma^{m*\lceil \frac{|t|}{n} \rceil}$ *a set of a appropriate ciphertext alternatives.*

Definition 2. *Let* Σ, m, n, v, w *denote according to Definition 1.*
Then SecureString 2.0 is a polyalphabetic, $|v|$*-graphic,* $(m*\frac{|v|}{n})$*-partite cryptosystem, which encrypts v with a bijective encryption step* $\chi : \Sigma^{|v|} \to \Sigma^{m*\frac{|v|}{n}}$ *and decrypts w with a bijective decryption step* $\chi^{-1} : \Sigma^{m*\frac{|v|}{n}} \to \Sigma^{|v|}$ *that are based on substitution and straddling.*

3   Character String Functions

This section comes along with the formal definitions for the three most important character string functions of SecureString 2.0: *querying*, *replacing* and *picking*.

3.1   Querying

A querying function tests the inclusion of any ciphertext alternative of the specified matching pattern string *u* in another, advisably longer encrypted string *w*. A tree or another suitable data structure feeds this operation with the *a* different ciphertext alternatives for u (see Definition 3). Topical programming languages mostly reserve the method name *contains* for this function.

Definition 3. *Let* $\Sigma, a, j, m, n, o, p, q_0, \cdots, q_o, \cdots, q_{a-1}$,
$q_{0_0}, \cdots, q_{0_p}, \cdots, q_{o_{\lfloor \frac{|u|}{n} \rfloor}}, u, v, w$ *denote according to Definition 1, and let*
$w_0, \cdots, w_j, \cdots, w_{\lfloor \frac{|v|}{n} \rfloor} \in \Sigma^m$ *denote the encrypted n-grams of* w*, where* $j \in$
$\mathbb{N} | 0 \leq j < \lceil \frac{|v|}{n} \rceil$ *denotes the index of the* j^{th} *n-gram, then* w *is queried by*

$$contains : \Sigma^{m*\lceil \frac{|v|}{n} \rceil} \times \Sigma^{m*\lceil \frac{|u|}{n} \rceil} \to \{false, true\},$$

$$(w, q_0, \cdots, q_{a-1}) \mapsto contains((w, q_0, \cdots, q_{a-1}))$$

$$:= \begin{cases} true & if (\exists o \in \mathbb{N})(\forall p \in \{0, \cdots, \lfloor \frac{|u|}{n} \rfloor\})(\exists j \in \{0, \cdots, \lfloor \frac{|v|}{n} \rfloor\})w_j = q_{0_p} \\ false & otherwise \end{cases}$$

3.2 Replacing

Initially, replacing does the same as querying a ciphered string w. Additionally, it exchanges occurring ciphertext alternatives of the specified matching pattern string u for ciphertext alternatives of the specified replacement string t (see Definition 4). A function, which replaces just the first occurrence of a ciphertext alternative of u with such one of t, is usually named *replaceFirst*. Such one, which replaces all occurrences of ciphertext alternatives of u with such ones of t, is commonly called *replaceAll*. Each replace function demands two trees or equally good data structures as arguments. The first one contains the a encrypted alternatives for u, and the second one possesses those ones for t. The replacement t can be the empty string ϵ as well, which ends in cutting out the first respectively all occurring ciphertext alternative(s) of u.

Definition 4. *Let* $\Sigma, a, j, m, n, o, p, q, q_0, \cdots, q_o, \cdots, q_{a-1}$,
$q_{0_0}, \cdots, q_{0_p}, \cdots, q_{o_{\lfloor \frac{|u|}{n} \rfloor}}, r_0, \cdots, r_o, \cdots, r_{a-1}, u, v, w$ *denote according to Definition 1, let* $w_0, \cdots, w_{j_0}, q_0, w_{j_0+\lceil \frac{|u|}{n} \rceil+1}, \cdots, w_{j_y}, q_0, w_{j_y+\lceil \frac{|u|}{n} \rceil+1}, \cdots, w_{\lfloor \frac{|v|}{n} \rfloor} \in \Sigma^m$
$|y \in \mathbb{N}$ *denote the encrypted n-grams of* w *that includes* $y + 1$ *occurrences of* q_0 *obviously, then the first occurrence of* q_0 *in* w *is exchanged for* r_0 *by*

$$replaceFirst : \Sigma^{m*\lceil \frac{|v|}{n} \rceil} \times \Sigma^{m*\lceil \frac{|u|}{n} \rceil} \times \Sigma^{m*\lceil \frac{|t|}{n} \rceil} \to \Sigma^{\{m*\lceil \frac{|v|}{n} \rceil, m*\lceil \frac{|v-u+t|}{n} \rceil\}},$$

$$(w, q_0, \cdots, q_{a-1}, r_0, \cdots, r_{a-1}) \mapsto replaceFirst((w, q_0, \cdots, q_{a-1}, r_0, \cdots, r_{a-1}))$$

$$:= \begin{cases} w & if\ contains(w, q_0, \cdots, q_{a-1}) = false \\ w_0 \cdots w_{j_0} r_0 w_{j_0+\lceil \frac{|u|}{n} \rceil+1} \cdots w_{j_y} q_0 w_{j_y+\lceil \frac{|u|}{n} \rceil+1} \cdots w_{\lfloor \frac{|v|}{n} \rfloor} & otherwise \end{cases}$$

or all occurrences of q_0 *in* w *are exchanged for* r_0 *by*

$$replaceAll : \Sigma^{m*\lceil \frac{|v|}{n} \rceil} \times \Sigma^{m*\lceil \frac{|u|}{n} \rceil} \times \Sigma^{m*\lceil \frac{|t|}{n} \rceil} \to \Sigma^*,$$

$$(w, q_0, \cdots, q_{a-1}, r_0, \cdots, r_{a-1}) \mapsto replaceAll((w, q_0, \cdots, q_{a-1}, r_0, \cdots, r_{a-1}))$$

$$:= \begin{cases} w & if\ contains(w, q_0, \cdots, q_{a-1}) = false \\ w_0 \cdots w_{j_0} r_0 w_{j_0+\lceil \frac{|u|}{n} \rceil+1} \cdots w_{j_y} r_0 w_{j_y+\lceil \frac{|u|}{n} \rceil+1} \cdots w_{\lfloor \frac{|v|}{n} \rfloor} & otherwise \end{cases}$$

3.3 Picking

A picking function, which is known under the name of *substring* generally, outputs a new string that is substring of an encrypted string w (see Definition 5). A substring function needs two arguments: the position of the first and of the last substring character in w. SecureString supports the second known kind of *substring* as well which is called with a start index only in order to use the last character of w as ending index implicitly.

Definition 5. *Let Σ, n, v, w denote according to Definition 1, let $d \in \mathbb{N}$ denote the beginning index, let $e \in \mathbb{N}$ denote the ending index, and let $w_0, \cdots, w_d, \cdots, w_e, \cdots, w_{\lfloor \frac{|v|}{n} \rfloor} \in \Sigma^m$ denote the encrypted n-grams of w, where $0 \leq d \leq e \leq \lfloor \frac{|v|}{n} \rfloor$, then a substring of w is picked out by*

$$ substring : \Sigma^{m*\lceil \frac{|v|}{n} \rceil} \times \mathbb{N} \times \mathbb{N} \to \Sigma^*, (w, d, e) \mapsto substring((w, d, e)) := $$

$$ w_d, \cdots, w_{e-1} $$

or by

$$ substring : \Sigma^{m*\lceil \frac{|v|}{n} \rceil} \times \mathbb{N} \to \Sigma^*, (w, d) \mapsto substring((w, d)) := w_d, \cdots, w_{\lfloor \frac{|v|}{n} \rfloor} $$

4 Threat Model

The initial publication of SecureString 2.0 [4] demonstrated the resistance of SecureString 2.0 against ciphertext-only-, known-plaintext-, (adaptive) chosen-plaintext-, (adaptive) chosen-ciphertext-attacks and a combination of the both latter ones as long as the secret key keeps concealed. This section addresses the evaluation of the success probability of two ciphertext-only attacks that are directed against cryptosystems based on substitution. Even if an opponent uncovered a single cloud repository or ciphertext character string, e.g. with one of these two ciphertext-only offenses, SecureString 2.0 would heal itself by using salts only once and exchanging its exhausted repositories. Hence the prudent design of SecureString 2.0 achieves forward and backward secrecy because compromised strings or repositories do not expose their predecessors or successors.

4.1 *n*-gram Repetition Pattern Attack

The first attack compares the n-gram repetition pattern of a ciphertext character string with all known n-gram repetition patterns of an appropriate dictionary D and the creation of a set of fitting plaintext character strings. A lack of reference repetition patterns would make this attack unworkable. While n is varying during the n-gram repetition pattern attack in Theorem 1, the character string length is changing in Theorem 2.

n-gram Repetition Pattern Attack with Variation of n

Theorem 1. *Let $\Sigma, D, m, n, o, q_o, r_o, t, u, v, w$ denote according to Definition 1. If n increases linearly, then the number of fitting plaintext character strings in D as result of a n-gram repetition pattern attack against w, q_o or r_o increases polynomially, and therefore the probability to reveal v, u or t decreases polynomially.*

The proof is done representatively for v/w-pairs by mathematical induction.

Basis ($n = 1$): The number of repetition patterns, to which all SecureString 2.0-ciphertext strings of length $m * \lceil \frac{|v|}{n} \rceil = m * \lceil \frac{|v|}{1} \rceil = m * |v|$ in D are distributed, is the $|v|^{th}$ Catalan number $C_{|v|} = \frac{(2*|v|)!}{(|v|+1)!*|v|!}$.

Induction step ($n \rightarrow n + 1$): The number of repetition patterns, to which all SecureString 2.0-ciphertext strings of length $m * \lceil \frac{|v|}{n+1} \rceil$ in D are distributed, is the $\lceil \frac{|v|}{n+1} \rceil^{th}$ Catalan number $C_{\lceil \frac{|v|}{n+1} \rceil} = \frac{(2*\lceil \frac{|v|}{n+1} \rceil)!}{(\lceil \frac{|v|}{n+1} \rceil+1)!*\lceil \frac{|v|}{n+1} \rceil!}$. $C_{\lceil \frac{|v|}{n+1} \rceil}$ is

$$\frac{C_{\lceil \frac{|v|}{n} \rceil}}{C_{\lceil \frac{|v|}{n+1} \rceil}} = \frac{\frac{(2*\lceil \frac{|v|}{n} \rceil)!}{(\lceil \frac{|v|}{n} \rceil+1)!*\lceil \frac{|v|}{n} \rceil!}}{\frac{(2*\lceil \frac{|v|}{n+1} \rceil)!}{(\lceil \frac{|v|}{n+1} \rceil+1)!*\lceil \frac{|v|}{n+1} \rceil!}} = \frac{(2*\lceil \frac{|v|}{n} \rceil)!*(\lceil \frac{|v|}{n+1} \rceil+1)!*\lceil \frac{|v|}{n+1} \rceil!}{(2*\lceil \frac{|v|}{n+1} \rceil)!*(\lceil \frac{|v|}{n} \rceil+1)!*\lceil \frac{|v|}{n} \rceil!} =$$

$$= \begin{cases} 1 & \text{if } \lceil \frac{|v|}{n+1} \rceil = \lceil \frac{|v|}{n} \rceil \\ \frac{2*(2*\lceil \frac{|v|}{n} \rceil-1)}{\lceil \frac{|v|}{n} \rceil+1} & \text{otherwise} \end{cases}$$

times lower than $C_{\lceil \frac{|v|}{n} \rceil}$.

Accordingly, the incidence probability per repetition pattern increases polynomially if n increases linearly. Therefore, the probability to reveal v decreases polynomially. □

n-gram Repetition Pattern Attack with Variation of Character String Length

Theorem 2. *Let $\Sigma, D, m, n, o, q_o, r_o, t, u, v, w$ denote according to Definition 1. If a length $|w|$, $|q_o|$ or $|r_o|$ increases linearly, then the number of fitting repetition patterns in D as result of a n-gram repetition pattern attack against w, q_o or r_o increases polynomially, and therefore the probability to reveal v, u or t decreases polynomially.*

The proof is done representatively for v/w-pairs by mathematical induction.

Basis ($|v| = 1$): The number of repetition patterns, to which all SecureString 2.0-ciphertext strings of length $m * \lceil \frac{|v|}{n} \rceil = m * \lceil \frac{1}{n} \rceil = m$ in D are distributed, is the $|v|^{th} = 1^{st}$ Catalan number $C_1 = \frac{(2*|v|)!}{(|v|+1)!*|v|!} = \frac{(2*1)!}{(1+1)!*1!} = \frac{2!}{2!} = 1$.

Induction step ($|v| \rightarrow |v| + 1$): The number of repetition patterns, to which all plaintext character strings of length $m * \lceil \frac{|v|+1}{n} \rceil$ in D are distributed, is the $\lceil \frac{|v|+1}{n} \rceil^{th}$ Catalan number $C_{\lceil \frac{|v|+1}{n} \rceil} = \frac{(2*\lceil \frac{|v|+1}{n} \rceil)!}{(\lceil \frac{|v|+1}{n} \rceil+1)!*\lceil \frac{|v|+1}{n} \rceil!}$.

$C_{\lceil \frac{|v|+1}{n} \rceil}$ is

$$\frac{C_{\lceil \frac{|v|+1}{n} \rceil}}{C_{\lceil \frac{|v|}{n} \rceil}} = \frac{\frac{(2*\lceil \frac{|v|+1}{n} \rceil)!}{(\lceil \frac{|v|+1}{n} \rceil+1)!*\lceil \frac{|v|+1}{n} \rceil!}}{\frac{(2*\lceil \frac{|v|}{n} \rceil)!}{(\lceil \frac{|v|}{n} \rceil+1)!*\lceil \frac{|v|}{n} \rceil!}} = \frac{(2 * \lceil \frac{|v|+1}{n} \rceil)! * (\lceil \frac{|v|}{n} \rceil + 1)! * \lceil \frac{|v|}{n} \rceil!}{(2 * \lceil \frac{|v|}{n} \rceil)! * (\lceil \frac{|v|+1}{n} \rceil + 1)! * \lceil \frac{|v|+1}{n} \rceil!} =$$

$$= \begin{cases} 1 & \text{if } \lceil \frac{|v|+1}{n} \rceil = \lceil \frac{|v|}{n} \rceil \\ \frac{2*(2*\lceil \frac{|v|+1}{n} \rceil-1)}{\lceil \frac{|v|+1}{n} \rceil+1} & \text{otherwise} \end{cases}$$

times higher than $C_{\lceil \frac{|v|}{n} \rceil}$.

Accordingly, the incidence probability per repetition pattern decreases polynomially if $|v|$ increases linearly, and therefore the probability to reveal v increases polynomially. This proof assumes the same number of dictionary words per character string length. In many dictionaries the number of character strings per length resembles almost normal distribution. Such a case opposes a decreasing number of words to an increasing number of repetition patterns for character string lengths larger than the median length. Thus the incidence probability per repetition pattern sinks respectively the probability to reveal v grows even faster than proved. $\qquad\square$

4.2 n-gram Distribution Attack

The second attack compares the n-gram distribution of a ciphertext character string with the overall n-gram distribution of an appropriate dictionary D statistically, e.g. with Fisher's exact test [8]. This attack becomes infeasible if the required reference n-gram distribution is unavailable. While n is varying during the n-gram distribution attack in Theorem 3, the character string length is changing in Theorem 4.

n-gram Distribution Attack with Variation of n

Theorem 3. *Let $\Sigma, D, m, n, o, q_o, r_o, t, u, v, w$ denote according to Definition 1. If n increases linearly, then the probability to reveal v, u or t statistically decreases.*

The proof is done representatively for v/w-pairs by mathematical induction.

Basis ($n = 1$): Each SecureString 2.0-ciphertext string of length $m * \lceil \frac{|v|}{n} \rceil = m * \lceil \frac{|v|}{1} \rceil = m * |v|$ in D consists of $\lceil \frac{|v|}{n} \rceil = \lceil \frac{|v|}{1} \rceil = |v|$ monograms (1-grams).

Induction step ($n \rightarrow n+1$): Each SecureString 2.0-ciphertext string of length $m * \lceil \frac{|v|}{n+1} \rceil$ in D consists of $\lceil \frac{|v|}{n+1} \rceil$ $(n+1)$-grams.

$\lceil \frac{|v|}{n+1} \rceil$ is

$$\frac{\lceil \frac{|v|}{n} \rceil}{\lceil \frac{|v|}{n+1} \rceil} = \begin{cases} 1 & \text{if } \lceil \frac{|v|}{n+1} \rceil = \lceil \frac{|v|}{n} \rceil \\ \frac{n+1}{n} = 1 + \frac{1}{n} & \text{otherwise} \end{cases}$$

times lower than $\lceil \frac{|v|}{n} \rceil$.

Accordingly, lowering the number of included grams per ciphertext string reduces the probability to reveal v statistically. □

n-gram Distribution Attack with Variation of Character String Length

Theorem 4. *Let* $\Sigma, D, m, n, o, q_o, r_o, t, u, v, w$ *denote according to Definition 1. If a length* $|w|$, $|q_o|$ *or* $|r_o|$ *increases linearly, then the probability to reveal* v, u *or* t *statistically increases.*

The proof is done representatively for v/w-pairs by mathematical induction.

Basis ($|v| = 1$): Each SecureString 2.0-ciphertext string of length $m * \lceil \frac{|v|}{n} \rceil = m * \lceil \frac{1}{n} \rceil = m$ in D consists of $\lceil \frac{|v|}{n} \rceil = \lceil \frac{1}{n} \rceil = 1$ n-gram.

Induction step ($|v| \to |v| + 1$): Each SecureString 2.0-ciphertext string of length $m * \lceil \frac{|v|+1}{n} \rceil$ in D consists of $\lceil \frac{|v|+1}{n} \rceil$ n-grams. $\lceil \frac{|v|+1}{n} \rceil$ is

$$\frac{\lceil \frac{|v|+1}{n} \rceil}{\lceil \frac{|v|}{n} \rceil} = \begin{cases} 1 & \text{if } \lceil \frac{|v|+1}{n} \rceil = \lceil \frac{|v|}{n} \rceil \\ \frac{|v|+1}{|v|} = 1 + \frac{1}{|v|} & \text{otherwise} \end{cases}$$

times higher than $\lceil \frac{|v|}{n} \rceil$.

Accordingly, a longer character string causes a higher number of grams in average and therefore abets the probability to reveal w statistically. □

5   Performance

This section evaluates the time performance of the three most important character string functions of SecureString 2.0: *querying*, *replacing* and *picking*. Additionally, the investigation confronts the obtained mean turnaround times of SecureString 2.0 with those ones of comparable cryptosystems, among them its predecessor SecureString 1.0 and AES (Advanced Encryption Standard) as bare transport cryptosystem. In contrast to the statistics of SecureString 1.0, those ones of SecureString 2.0 were drawn for $n = 1$ only, because queried, inserted or deleted substrings need not to follow the n-gram bounds if $n > 1$, and therefore they cause too time-consuming inter-n-gram-operations despite better privacy. For example let be $n = 2, u =$'bc', $v =$'abcd', then $q = \chi($'bc'$)$ must be found in $w = \chi($'ab'$)\chi($'cd'$)$, even if 'b' and 'c' are parts of different n-grams obviously. The memory consumptions of both SecureString-versions behave identically and thus require a citation of the performance analysis for SecureString 1.0 [3] only.

5.1   Querying Performance

Firstly, the querying performance of SecureString 2.0 is tested for character string lengths $1 \leq |v| \leq 64$ and all possible matching pattern string lengths $1 \leq$

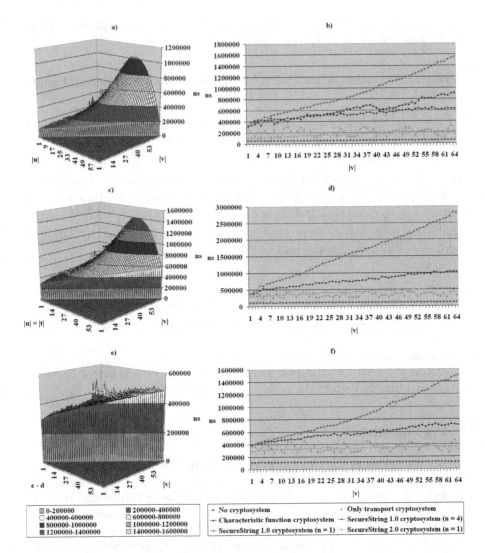

Fig. 2. Performance of Character String Functions

$|u| \leq |v|$. For each data value in Figure 2 a) the querying operation is conducted for 1.000.000 random ciphertext character string/matching pattern string-pair samples and the mean value shown in nanoseconds. As a result, the time complexity for querying functions turns out to be $O(|v| * \log(\min(|u|, |v| - |u|)))$.

Secondly, the inclusion of random matching pattern strings of length $|u| = \min(4, |v|)$ is tested in 1.000.000 random character string samples per length $1 \leq |v| \leq 64$. This is evaluated in nanoseconds per operation. It can be easily observed by means of Figure 2 b) that the performance of SecureString 2.0 behaves like that one of a transport cryptosystem and much more better than that one of SecureString 1.0.

5.2   Replacing Performance

Like for querying, the performance of replacing operations with SecureString 2.0 is measured for character string lengths $1 \leq |v| \leq 64$ and all possible matching pattern string lengths $1 \leq |u| \leq |v|$ firstly. Each found matching pattern string is replaced by a replacement string of equal length $|t| = |u|$. Each data value in Figure 2 c) represents the mean value of 1.000.000 random ciphertext character string/matching pattern string/replacement string-triplets in nanoseconds. The time complexity can be recognized with $O(|v| * \log(\min(|u|, |v| - |u|)))$ again.

In the second part of the performance analysis for the replacing operation, random matching patterns strings of length $|u| = \min(4, |v|)$ are replaced by random equally long replacement strings in 1.000.000 random character string samples per length $1 \leq |v| \leq 64$. Again, this is measured in nanoseconds per operation. Figure 2 d) displays that similar behavior as for the previous querying operation can be observed: SecureString 2.0 displays lower efforts than SecureString 1.0. Reference values for the characteristic function cryptosystem are omitted here because it lacks to support replacing functions.

5.3   Picking Performance

Initially, the performance of picking operations is examined by picking out substrings of all possible lengths $1 \leq e - d \leq |v|$, where d is a random left and e a random right border, out of character strings of length $1 \leq |v| \leq 64$. Each data mean value in Figure 2 e) consists of 1.000.000 samples and is scaled in nanoseconds. An approximate time complexity of $O(|v|)$ can be anticipated.

The comparison of the different cryptosystems for the picking operation is performed by cutting out substrings of length $\min(4, |v|)$ at random beginning indexes in 1.000.000 random character string samples per length $1 \leq |v| \leq 64$. Yet again, the measurement is taken in nanoseconds per operation. Figure 2 f) displays that SecureString 2.0 also surpasses the picking performance of SecureString 1.0. Of course, both SecureString versions perform worse than a transport cryptosystem, but provide privacy within the cloud application.

6   Conclusion

The cryptosystem SecureString 2.0 offers querying and modifying functions on encrypted character strings in untrustworthy environments (like clouds).

After defining the en- and decryption scheme and the three most important supported character string functions *querying*, *replacing* and *picking* formally, it was shown that the success probability to break an encrypted character string (with perceptible boundaries) by a n-gram distribution attack or a statistical n-gram distribution attack decreases with an increasing number of commonly ciphered characters n respectively increases with an increasing character string length. Inferred from these results, an implementer of SecureString 2.0 ought be firmly encouraged to use one salt only once and only to protect a single character string. Nevertheless, if a text of SecureStrings is conveyed or processed together, then each ciphered delimiter between two words or sentences, e.g. a blank or a full stop, can share the salt with its previously neighbored character string safely without risking detection of its meaning. Conducted analysis for three character string functions exposed improved time performance of SecureString 2.0 compared to SecureString 1.0.

In short, SecureString 2.0 offers a good trade-off between privacy and time performance. Nevertheless, better protection for the integrity of ciphertext character strings can be obtained, e.g. against cut and splice or replay attacks, by assembling a random nonce, a timestamp and an incrementing counter in each seeded salt.

References

1. Atallah, M.J., Pantazopoulos, K., Rice, J.R., Spafford, E.E.: Secure outsourcing of scientific computations. In: Zelkowitz, M.V. (ed.) Trends in Software Engineering. Advances in Computers, vol. 54, pp. 215–272. Elsevier (2002)
2. Brun, Y., Medvidovic, N.: Keeping data private while computing in the cloud. In: 2012 IEEE 5th International Conference on Cloud Computing (CLOUD), pp. 285–294 (2012)
3. Fahrnberger, G.: Computing on encrypted character strings in clouds. In: Hota, C., Srimani, P.K. (eds.) ICDCIT 2013. LNCS, vol. 7753, pp. 244–254. Springer, Heidelberg (2013)
4. Fahrnberger, G.: Securestring 2.0 - a cryptosystem for computing on encrypted character strings in clouds. In: Innovative Internet Community Systems, VDI Düsseldorf (2013)
5. Goluch, S.: The development of homomorphic cryptography - from rsa to gentrys privacy homomorphism. Master's thesis, Vienna University of Technology (2011)
6. Itani, W., Kayssi, A., Chehab, A.: Privacy as a service: Privacy-aware data storage and processing in cloud computing architectures. In: Eighth IEEE International Conference on Dependable, Autonomic and Secure Computing, DASC 2009, pp. 711–716 (2009)
7. Maheshwari, N., Kiyawat, K.: Structural framing of protocol for secure multiparty cloud computation. In: 2011 Fifth Asia Modelling Symposium (AMS), pp. 187–192 (2011)
8. Mehta, C.R., Patel, N.R.: A network algorithm for performing fisher's exact test in r x c contingency tables. Journal of the American Statistical Association 78(382), 427–434 (1983)
9. Rodríguez-Silva, D.A., González-Castaño, F.J., Adkinson-Orellana, L., Fernández-Cordeiro, A., Troncoso-Pastoriza, J.R., González-Martínez, D.: Encrypted domain processing for cloud privacy - concept and practical experience. In: CLOSER, pp. 591–596 (2011)
10. Wei, L., Zhu, H., Cao, Z., Jia, W., Vasilakos, A.: Seccloud: Bridging secure storage and computation in cloud. In: 2010 IEEE 30th International Conference on Distributed Computing Systems Workshops (ICDCSW), pp. 52–61 (2010)

Friend or Foe: Twitter Users under Magnification

Arjun Datt Sharma*, Ansuya Ahluwalia*, Shaleen Deep*, and Divya Bansal

PEC University of Technology, Chandigarh, India
arjun_datt@yahoo.in, ansuyaahluwalia@outlook.com, shaleen.deep@gmail.com,
divya@pec.ac.in

Abstract. In today's digital ecosystem, where people share vital information on a daily basis, it is imperative to identify security loopholes and vulnerability in social networks. Through identity resolution and disambiguation, information leakage and identity hijacking by malicious parties, can be reduced significantly. In this paper, we develop a simple model for successfully classifying Twitter users as suspicious and non-suspicious in their user activity. Our aim is to be able to find a concrete set of users that encompasses most users who misrepresent their identity on Twitter. Using user and tweet meta-data, we devised a mathematical model to tag users as listener, talker, hub, seed and absorber, and further conjugate the values generated by these equations, to identify suspicious and non-suspicious users in our 49,991-user dataset. This model of classification can be extended for integration with rigorous security mechanisms to identify true malicious users on Twitter and other online social platforms.

Keywords: classification, user meta data, suspiciousness, tweet score, user score.

1 Introduction

Social media has evolved the way people interact personally as well as professionally. Such media is easy to access and the size and the nature of the participants reveal vital information useful to third parties. With such large usage of social media, security and privacy risks have also increased manifolds. Fake profiles are being created to trick users into linking to these fake profiles and loading their own profiles with various forms of malicious software [12][10].

Twitter, among other social networking platforms is becoming a target of an increasing number of phishing and criminal activity [5]. In this paper, we delve deep into the changing role of identity management with application to Twitter. On Twitter, users' activity can be determined by the relationships they share (followers, following, lists) and the dynamics of those relationships (tweets, statuses, retweets). We study the characteristics of our crawled dataset by large scale, graphical analysis of user and tweet meta-data, which sheds light on the

---

* All authors contributed equally to the paper.

R. Natarajan (Ed.): ICDCIT 2014, LNCS 8337, pp. 251–262, 2014.

volatility of data characteristics on Twitter. Studying the salient behavioral pattern of such meta-data, we formulate mathematical equations for tagging users as listener, talker and hub based on the user scores, and seed and absorber based on the tweet scores. Subsequently, we analyze values of both the scores to classify users as suspicious or non-suspicious in their user activity.

The goal is to be able to identify users who could pose a threat to Twitter's security by misrepresenting themselves [2]. These users could be following other users but at the same time have minimal participation on Twitter . Such users probably have stolen identities and have created a duplicate profile for simply attracting friends belonging to the original user. Identifying them brings us one step closer towards finding true malicious users on Twitter [2]. Since we focus on a small section of Twitter users, it is an arduous task to be able to tag true malicious users accurately. However, we do succeed in identifying a superset (majority suspicious users) of the same (focused set of malicious users).

Our aim for designing such a model is to be able to quantify the number of users in a randomized set that intimate towards suspicious behavior on Twitter. Other research work in this area has focussed towards analyzing activity characteristics among users belonging to a network or clustered group, therefore those results are dependent on the kind of relationship for studying characteristics of suspicious and malicious users. We aim to identify suspicious users that belong to a randomly generated dataset, that has not been previously identified to share network relationship characteristics such as being bound by follower or following relationships with each other.

2   Related Work

A number of studies relevant to the current work involve techniques ranging from sentiment analysis of the immense amount of communication occurring on online social platforms, to machine learning techniques that identify spam. The goal of this family of literature is to study the behavioral dynamics of users through qualitative or quantitative analyses of online activities that point towards suspiciousness.

In contrast to the present study, a lot of work has gone into developing feature-specific suspiciousness detection models for online social platforms. In the study by Lee et al. [9], they proposed a suspicious URL detection system for Twitter, where they have correlated tweets via redirected chains of URLs. While chaining of tweets is a good method to identify suspiciousness, this is the sole metric used. Zhi Yang et al. [18] proposed a method to detect, characterize and understand Sybil account activity on Renren. They also focused on topological characteristics of malicious accounts. However, they too only focused on a section of user characteristics. Our work attempts to blend in both user and tweet related activity.

The study conducted by Benevenuto et al. [1] detected the percentage of spam and spammers out of the users who tweeted pertaining to certain famous trending topics. As compared to this study, our work aims at identifying a superset of malicious users that contain the set of spammers based on generic user and tweet activity. A spam detection prototype system has also been proposed to identify suspicious users on Twitter [17]. Using a directed social graph model the follower and friend relationships have been explored. In the current paper, instead of focusing on the friend-follower directed relationships, we have developed a social network independent model, by using generic meta-data as user suspiciousness indicators.

Other papers [16] [8] [15] that involve analysis of actual tweet content suffer from the drawback of language specifics. Even if the study tries to incorporate a few languages, it is not extensible to all dialects and languages. It also does not take into account quantitative analysis of user activity. However, the ideas presented do form a good basis for further study.

3   Data Characteristics

We successfully mined all meta-data pertaining to 49,991 users[12] in our dataset and around 10,00,000 tweets made by these users over 6 years spanning from mid 2006 to early 2012. The data was extracted randomly between September 2012 and March 2013, using Twitter4j API. Randomly choosing seeds, all data was extracted for the seed and propagated forward by randomly choosing his/her followers as seeds. Consequently, the data is completely random with people who speak and tweet in different types of languages (the notable ones being English, Spanish and Arabic) and who are located in different geographical locations. At the data extraction stage, no user activity metrics were considered to ensure we bring all kinds of users into our dataset, ranging from celebrities to organizations to common people. We studied the high-level data characteristics of the dataset to understand the overall site activity and how certain parameters can be conducive in our goal to classify users and tag suspicious ones[3].

Fig.1 shows the dynamics of user activity on Twitter. All the plots have a particular common behavior - all major activity on Twitter (i.e. the number of friends a user has, the number of users a user is following, the number of tweets a user posts or the number of public groups/lists a user is part of) is in small magnitudes for majority of Twitter users, but give us a good quantitative view of a user's activity on Twitter.

Other important meta-data such as *withheld_from_countries* and *withheld_scope* is very useful in narrowing down users, who due to inappropriate activity on Twitter have been granted restricted access. Our dataset does not contain users who had been banned from using Twitter or had any of their statuses censored. Another highly significant indicator that upholds the authenticity of a user's account is the verified parameter. This is a boolean parameter taking True or False values and is internally set by Twitter's administration, mostly for popular public entities. Our dataset also does not contain any user accounts that have been verified by Twitter, comprising of general public only.

---

[1] All figures and graphs have been plotted using this dataset of 49,991 users only.

[2] The users whose data is not public have been ignored for the purpose of this study.

[3] https://dev.twitter.com/docs/api/1/get/statuses/user_timeline

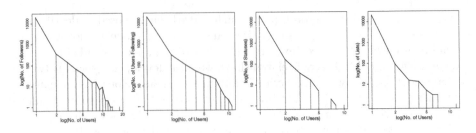

Fig. 1. Static plots for high level data characteristics

4   Investigating User Activity

In this paper, we study how to differentiate users given their activity, focusing only on user and tweet activity, ignoring the actual content of messages the user has exchanged or shared. Previous work in identity management has also employed sentiment analysis and other qualitative analysis techniques[16]. However, we look at the macroscopic view of user activity, trying to find behavioral patterns in suspicious and non-suspicious users. We further define the scope of these characteristics, that can be attributable to such users, on the basis of which further classification is done.

Intuitively, a user who is sluggish in tweeting and following other users, raises doubt as to his/her intentions of being on a social network such as Twitter. A user having very limited following count (i.e., a low number of followers) could be for a myriad of reasons depicted by the kind of his/her profile, like spam based profile, impersonated profile, fake profile, abandoned profile, profile that had once inflated number of following/followers using bots, etc., very few of which are genuine (nascent profile, genuinely shy person having few friends or profiles on Twitter for the sake of it). Similarly, very little tweet-based content (tweets, retweets, starred, likes, etc.) could be because of very limited content on a users home page to retweet or star from (which could be due to a number of reasons such as very low following/follower count, shyness on the part of the user, the use of Twitter primarily as an information source, etc.).

It has been found that 89% of fraudulent accounts created by spammers forgo participation in the social graph, instead relying on unsolicited mentions and trending topics to attract clicks. [14]

While analyzing a directed graph like that of Twitter, vertices with extremely high in-degree generally pertain to celebrities, politicians or news sources [19]. In our investigation, we have ignored all candidates with a very high follower count as they were found to be celebrities or organizations. Entities who draw suspicion in the user activity refer to vertices with a very high out-degree i.e. account holders who have an extremely low *follower/following* ratio, as depicted in Fig.2.

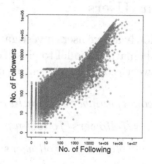

Fig. 2. Relationship between number of followers a user has and the number of users he is following

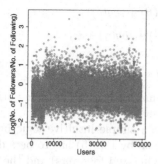

Fig. 3. Variation of the ratio *no. of followers : no. of followees*, for each user

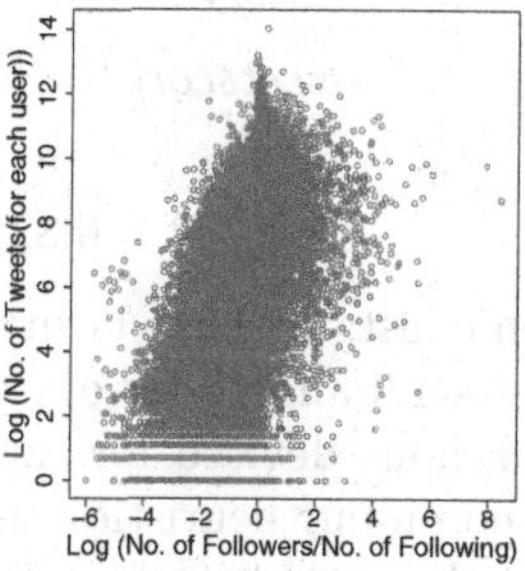

Fig. 4. Variation of tweeting activity of users with the ratio *no. of followers : no. of followees*

Suspicious users have very few followers (around 10 or less) and mainly seem to be following other users. The dispersed clustering of such users as shown in Fig.3 indicates that such users are less in number. However, they can be instrumental in performing malicious activities. Of course, they may also be users who aren't active on Twitter anymore due to legitimate reasons, but they surely arouse suspicion at a basic level.

Another factor indicating suspicion is the tweeting activity among users. People who tend to tweet a lot lesser may also be contributors to our suspicious group. Fig.4 also upholds our premise. As shown, users who fall on the extreme negative end of the x-axis depict a decreasing follower count in comparison to the following count and simultaneously also decrease in their tweeting activity. The dispersed low user activity members on Twitter, shown in Fig.4 , are also the users who have an extremely low tweet count as well. In totality, the low activity level on Twitter brings these chunk of users under the scanner for suspicion.

5   Tagging Suspicious Users

The anomalous behavior of lowly active users investigated in the previous section, was used for devising a mathematical model to classify users in our dataset. We computed user scores and tweet scores for the entire user domain.

Let

$$\alpha = tweet\,count/number\,of\,months\,on\,twitter \tag{1}$$

$$\beta = followers/following \tag{2}$$

$$\delta = following + followers \tag{3}$$

$$\gamma = tweet\,frequency\,per\,day \tag{4}$$

$$userscore^4 = (10/\phi) * (log(\beta) + log(\delta)) \tag{5}$$

$$tweetscore^4 = (10/\Omega) * (log(\alpha) + log(\gamma) + \psi) \tag{6}$$

where

$$\Omega = 6.82,\ \psi = 3.35\,and\,\phi = 9.02 \tag{7}$$

The chosen constants have been derived mathematically in order scale both the scores between 0 and 10 for our dataset.

The equations devised for these scores have a simple intuitive logic behind them. Based on our heuristics, user score as given by Eq. (5) has to be a direct function of the total friends in his circle (following and followers) and the ratio of *followers/following*. The heavy hand of the numerator or the denominator decides what category of the classification do the users fall under. Since logarithmic scales are used, a good friend count and a bad ratio balance out each other. However, a decent friend count and a decent ratio places the user in the Hub category.

Similarly, tweet score as given by Eq. (6) depends on both tweeting activity over a long period i.e. number of months the user has been tweeting and the tweet frequency per day, derived from the actual tweet timings. The latter part of the tweet score takes into account a user who may have a good tweet count but the bulk of which is concentrated in the past. Thus, making the user a likely suspect.

We assign user scores to each class of users [7] as follows:

- Listener : User having a user score *less than 1*. Such a user follows way more people than the number of his followers, in context to the magnitude of his followers and the users he is following. Thus, as shown in Fig.5a), till the local minima of user score equal to 1, an anomalous low user participation is detected in this region.
- Hub : User having a user score *between 1 and 7*. Such a user has comparable number of followers and the number of users he is following. A fairly large number of users fall in this region and thus do not seek attention as anomalous users.

---

[4] The equations have been normalized in the range 0-10.

- Talker : Similarly, an anomalous user region can be detected at $x > 7$ as shown in Fig.5b). We classify a talker as a user who has *user score greater than 7*. Such a user generally follows lesser people than the number of his followers, in context to their magnitudes.

Based on the tweet scores, we classify users as follows:

- Seed : A user who tweets very often. Such a user has a *tweetscore > 1* as shown in Fig.5a).
- Absorber : A user who does not tweet often and is "absorbing" the tweets from the people he follows. Such a user has a *tweetscore < 1* as shown in Fig.5b).

Evident from Fig.5, the demarcating value of 1 and 7 for user scores and 1 for tweet score is calculated by counting the rate of increase of users in the score range from *0 to x*, where *x* ranges from *0 to 10*.

Let $C(x)$ be the frequency of users having the score in range *0 to x*, then

$$\frac{C(x + dx) - C(x)}{dx} \tag{8}$$

Eq. (8) gives us $C'(x)$ which dips at the values mentioned above i.e. the local minima for the scores. The curves show a dip at 1 and 7 in the user score graph and at 1 for the tweet score graph.

$$\lim_{x \to 1} \int_{x+j}^{x+k} C(x)\, dx \tag{9}$$

Using Eq. (9) in Fig.5(a) we roughly represent a congregation of *Hubs* for *j=0 & k=6*. Whereas for *j=-1 & k=0* we roughly represent a congregation of *Listeners*.

Similarly, applying Eq. (9) to the curve represented by Fig.5(b) will give us a rough clustering of *Absorbers* for *j=-1 & k=0* and *Seeds* for *j=-1 & k=9*.

After examining the user and tweet scores through the subsequent plots, we were successfully able to tag users as suspicious or non-suspicious. This was the final aim of our work and reaped pertinent results shedding light on how a superset of the suspicious users leads to finding a concentrated subset of fake users on Twitter.

Fig.6a) clearly demarcates the anomalous user groups from the general hub category. The listeners are concentrated in user score regions less than 1 and also contribute significantly to our suspicious set. Their anomalous user activity is depicted by the low valued user scores. User score region at *x greater than 7* i.e. the talkers encompasses the big people (popular entities). Fig.6b) shows the clustering of users who fall in the tweet score region with *score less than 1* i.e. the absorbers. They are likely to be suspicious due to a cumulative low tweet frequency over their entire period of membership on Twitter.

Furthermore, our model also significantly points out that users who have low user and low tweet scores contribute to the suspiciousness of their intentions.

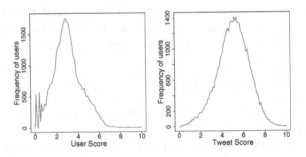

Fig. 5. Frequency distribution of users over scores calculated. a) Frequency of users for each user score x in the range 0-10. b) Frequency of users for each tweet score x in the range 0-10.

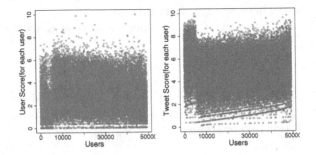

Fig. 6. Scores evaluated for each user. a) User score for each user. b) Tweet score for each user.

Fig.7 shows that a significant percentage of users having a low user score, also have a low tweet score, thereby pointing to the fact that overall lowly active users intimate towards suspiciousness.

There also exist a few anomalies in this scheme since we can find users with high tweet scores having low user scores and vice-versa. However, such examples are scattered exceptions which should also be under the suspicion radar in order to minimize the margin for error in detecting genuinely malicious users. For the present body of work, we have ignored such minor exceptions. We further manually verify our results as explained in the subsequent section.

6   Results

The objective of the current study is to identify a broad range of users who constitute a majority of suspicious users i.e., those users who have a profile with characteristics that are highly aberrant from an average user's profile. We analyzed user suspiciousness by studying the user scores and tweet scores. Based on our findings, we considered users who were listeners-absorbers, listeners-seeds

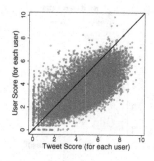

Fig. 7. Relationship between user score and tweet score

and absorbers to be suspicious. We found 1965 suspicious users based on the user scores alone, 2326 suspicious users based on the tweet scores alone and 794 suspicious users based on both user and tweet scores, all three being mutually exclusive sets as shown in Fig.8.

Most of the users who are suspicious based on user scores are also suspicious based on the tweet scores, but vice versa is not true, as reflected by the higher number of suspicious users based on tweet scores as compared to those based on user scores. Users having a low tweet score but a decent user score are those who have both followers and friends, and are only seeking information on Twitter rather than disseminating it. But it is also likely that such people are non-malicious and maintain a very good social network profile on platforms other than Twitter [13]. However, a bad user score and a good tweet score does not look ingenuous. Although there may be exceptions, but these users fall mostly under the category of spammers [1][17]. They could also be introverted and shy, who tweet for their self-contentment [6].

In order to study the effectiveness of our tagging, we manually screened the 5085 (1965+794+2326) suspicious users to find people who held fake profiles. In order to remove bias, all authors screened the results separately and the people identified as suspicious by both the authors were finally deemed to be suspicious.

Out of the 794 users who were found to be suspicious based on both scores, 115 users were actually fake, 301 users were shy i.e. sedentary in their user activity, 248 users kept a low profile on Twitter and 130 users were difficult to discern. Out of the 2326 users who were found to be suspicious based on tweet scores alone, 321 users were actually fake, 760 users were shy in their tweeting activity, 773 users kept a low profile and 472 users were difficult to discern. Lastly, out of the 1965 users who were found to be suspicious based on user scores alone, 350 users were actually fake, 649 were shy, 619 kept a low profile and 347 were unknown i.e. could not be discerned. The shy and low profile users are genuine users on Twitter. We cannot pass a definite judgement about the unknown users. Users who had locked tweets and information were unknown and could not be discerned. Looking at their tweets we identified users who are genuine. Most of them say,"My first tweet", "Joined twitter today", "feeling good" and "Hi twitter!". They also have followers who are genuine users. The results, as of

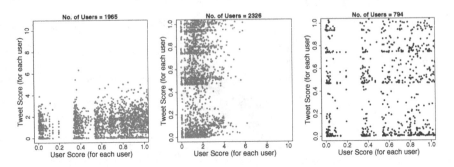

Fig. 8. Manually verified results. a) Users with a low tweet score but a moderate user score. b) Users with a low user score but a moderate tweet score. c) Users having an overall low score.

now, do not address the false negatives as a rigorously tested metric, partially because of scanning 44,915 remaining users is a daunting task. However, a manual screening of 500 random users from the remaining 44,915 users, did not produce any fake profiles.

Out of the 5085 suspicious users, we found 786 users to be fake, which tells us that about 15.41% of the users are malicious according to our model.

In order to obtain a better understanding of malicious users, we propose a generic methodology to identify a superset of users, that encompass a set of users that include malicious users and shy users who are not active on Twitter. Since the time we began working on our model, 357 (as of April 2013) out of 786 user accounts that have been identified as suspicious using our model, have been suspended from Twitter, which gives a success rate of 45.41%.

7   Discussion and Conclusion

Studying only the user and tweet activity, without going into the depth of the actual content of Tweets gives us a threefold advantage:

- It makes the whole process very simple and yet gives reliable results .
- Since malicious users are expected to maintain a very limited public presence on social networks, their status/tweet count is expected to be very low (especially over a reliable period of time). Therefore, qualitative analysis of content can not be the sole defining factor of user suspiciousness and will affect the statistical variation in the results marginally.
- Since most social networks have the same pattern of friends, followers and statuses, our study is extensible to other social networks as well. This can be done by incorporating some minor modifications in the parametric classifications and meta-data used in our mathematical model.

We have not aggregated the tweet and user scores in order to prevent masking of bad scores by good scores, since low tweet scores are a necessary but not a sufficient indicator of suspiciousness.

Our premise that listeners-absorbers, listeners-seeds and absorbers are suspicious users is well supported by the user and tweet scores computed and the anomaly in score trends depicted by user and tweet activity. The various scatter plots discussed depict saliency of such trends well. Although the model we propose is not the most rigorous treatment of statistical computations, but the benefit lies in the simple and yet robust scanning of suspicious users.

8 Future Scope

The next step in this work would be to successfully identify malicious users on Twitter. Using trust networks and social network footprint analysis techniques [11], it is possible to accurately identify and tag malicious users with a small error margin. Such an analysis is of huge benefit to investigation agencies and cyber crime cells that regularly need to find malicious users. We can also utilize the Twitter Counter API [5] to study profile growth more efficiently. We can incorporate several other aspects of user accounts such as analysis of URLs mentioned in the tweets, whether the URLs belong to malicious sites or not, to study suspiciousness. It is also known that malicious account holders also tend to use spam bots to increase their follower count [4].

We validate our results (set of suspicious users on Twitter) manually as the result set is of nominal size. However, bigger datasets may require an automated validation model. [3]. Such methods for verification do not produce 100% accuracy in results. Therefore, manual screening was the best option to produce utmost accuracy in verification.

Acknowledgements. We would like to thank Eshu Sharma[6] for his contribution towards materializing this paper.

References

[1] Benevenuto, F., Magno, G., Rodrigues, T., Almeida, V.: Detecting spammers on twitter. In: Collaboration, Electronic Messaging, Anti-Abuse and Spam Conference (CEAS), vol. 6 (2010)

[2] Bilge, L., Strufe, T., Balzarotti, D., Kirda, E.: All your contacts are belong to us: automated identity theft attacks on social networks. In: Proceedings of the 18th International Conference on World Wide Web, pp. 551–560. ACM (2009)

[3] Cao, Q., Sirivianos, M., Yang, X., Pregueiro, T.: Aiding the detection of fake accounts in large scale social online services. Technical report (2011), http://www.cs.duke.edu/~qiangcao/publications/sybilrank_tr.pdf

[4] Chu, Z., Gianvecchio, S., Wang, H., Jajodia, S.: Who is tweeting on twitter: human, bot, or cyborg? In: Proceedings of the 26th Annual Computer Security Applications Conference, pp. 21–30. ACM (2010)

[5] Gostev, A., Zaitsev, O., Golovanov, S., Kamluk, V.: Kaspersky security bulletin malware evolution 2008. Kaspersky Lab (April 2009)

---

[5] http://twittercounter.com/

[6] PEC University of Technology.

[6] Hauff, C., Houben, G.-J.: Deriving knowledge profiles from twitter. In: Kloos, C.D., Gillet, D., Crespo García, R.M., Wild, F., Wolpers, M. (eds.) EC-TEL 2011. LNCS, vol. 6964, pp. 139–152. Springer, Heidelberg (2011)

[7] Iskold, A.: 5 ways to have fun with twitter when you're bored (March 2008), http://readwrite.com (cited: May 11, 2013)

[8] Kouloumpis, E., Wilson, T., Moore, J.: Twitter sentiment analysis: The good the bad and the omg. In: Proceedings of the Fifth International AAAI Conference on Weblogs and Social Media (2011)

[9] Lee, S., Kim, J.: Warningbird: Detecting suspicious urls in twitter stream. In: Symposium on Network and Distributed System Security, NDSS (2012)

[10] Makridakis, A., Athanasopoulos, E., Antonatos, S., Antoniades, D., Ioannidis, S., Markatos, E.P.: Understanding the behavior of malicious applications in social networks. IEEE Network 24(5), 14–19 (2010)

[11] Mislove, A., Viswanath, B., Gummadi, K.P., Druschel, P.: You are who you know: inferring user profiles in online social networks. In: Proceedings of the Third ACM International Conference on Web Search and Data Mining, pp. 251–260. ACM (2010)

[12] Patsakis, C., Asthenidis, A., Chatzidimitriou, A.: Social networks as an attack platform: Facebook case study. In: Eighth International Conference on Networks, ICN 2009, pp. 245–247. IEEE (2009)

[13] Sankaranarayanan, J., Samet, H., Teitler, B.E., Lieberman, M.D., Sperling, J.: Twitterstand: news in tweets. In: Proceedings of the 17th ACM SIGSPA-TIAL International Conference on Advances in Geographic Information Systems, pp. 42–51. ACM (2009)

[14] Thomas, K., Grier, C., Paxson, V., Song, D.: Suspended accounts in retrospect: An analysis of twitter spam. In: Proc. of IMC (2011)

[15] Tumasjan, A., Sprenger, T.O., Sandner, P.G., Welpe, I.M.: Predicting elections with twitter: What 140 characters reveal about political sentiment. In: Proceedings of the Fourth International AAAI Conference on Weblogs and Social Media, pp. 178–185. AAAI Press (2010)

[16] Apoorv Agarwal Boyi Xie Ilia Vovsha and Owen Rambow Rebecca Passonneau. Sentiment analysis of twitter data. In: ACL HLT 2011, p. 30 (2011)

[17] Wang, A.H.: Don't follow me: Spam detection in twitter. In: Proceedings of the 2010 International Conference on Security and Cryptography (SECRYPT), pp. 1–10. IEEE (2010)

[18] Yang, Z., Wilson, C., Wang, X., Gao, T., Zhao, B.Y., Dai, Y.: Uncovering social network sybils in the wild. In: Proceedings of the 2011 ACM SIGCOMM Conference on Internet Measurement Conference, pp. 259–268. ACM (2011)

[19] Yardi, S., Boyd, D.: Tweeting from the town square: Measuring geographic local networks. In: Proceedings of the International Conference on Weblogs and Social Media, pp. 194–201 (2010)

Game Theoretic Attack Response Framework for Enterprise Networks

Arkadeep Kundu and Soumya K. Ghosh

School of Information Technology, Indian Institute of Technology, Kharagpur
arkadeep2687@gmail.com, skg@iitkgp.ac.in

Abstract. Choosing the right security measures and responses is an important and challenging part of designing an Intrusion Response System. This article proposes a stochastic game based approach to security and intrusion response in enterprise networks. To analyze the intrusion response scenario, this paper formally represents the real-time interaction of an attacker and network administrator as a two-player non-zero-sum stochastic game. The network configuration information and vulnerability scan results of an enterprise network are used to construct a network security state space, where a network security state changes as a result of actions taken by the attacker/administrator. Using the modeled stochastic game, a quantitative decision making framework has been proposed for enterprise network administrators to identify his optimal actions in case of network intrusion. Experimentations show that proposed model scales well with networks consisting of number of hosts in order of hundreds.

Keywords: Stochastic Game, Network Service Vulnerability, Network Intrusion, Attack Graph, Intrusion Response System, Nash Equilibrium.

1 Introduction

Present day security technologies include two major categories of risk management, namely, *proactive risk management* and *reactive risk management*. Proactive risk management consists of tasks like - (i) vulnerability scanning using Nessus, OpenVAS etc., (ii) use of firewalls, (iii) analysis of all possible network attack scenarios using *attack graphs, attack trees* etc. Proactive security measures are taken during network deployment phase to protect the network from future attacks. But still some security loopholes remain in the network to make way for unwanted security exploits. If the network administrator detects the malicious security exploit, reactive security measures are taken. Reactive risk management consists of tasks like - (i) deployment of IDS and IPS systems, (ii) deployment of *honeypots* , (iii) malware scanning etc. Reactive measures are taken to recover from the unwanted security incident.

Intrusion detection systems detects attacks, using signature-based or anomaly based methods. After detection of unwanted network behavior, recovery actions can be taken manually or in automated fashion. In literature, many investigations have been reported on automated intrusion response systems. In order

R. Natarajan (Ed.): ICDCIT 2014, LNCS 8337, pp. 263–274, 2014.

to construct a adaptive, cost-sensitive, automated intrusion response scheme, a huge amount of decision making is involved.

In order to facilitate automated decision making, a game-theoretic intrusion response framework has been proposed in this paper. Given a particular network configuration and vulnerability report, we model the possible interaction between *attacker-defender* as a two-player non-zero sum stochastic game [1]. Game is constructed prior to network security configuration deployment. At runtime, the administrator detects the state of the network or actions of the attacker by analyzing the network dynamically using *Intrusion Detection System* (IDS) or other monitors and responds according to pre-computed *Nash equilibrium* strategies. Contribution of this work lies in the decision making phase of intrusion response. Uncertainty and inaccuracy issues in IDSs are other existing challenges and those are not addressed here.

The rest of the paper is organized as follows. Section 2 mathematically defines stochastic games and discusses some related works. Stochastic game construction and intrusion response (IR) decision making procedures are discussed in Section 3. In Section 4, proposed framework is demonstrated with the help of a test network. Some of the implementation related issues is also addressed in this section. Computational complexity of the framework is shown in Section 5. Finally, Section 6 draws conclusion.

2   Preliminaries and Related Works

Formally, a two-player non-zero sum stochastic game, with discount factor zero, is a tuple $(S, A^1, A^2, Q, R^1, R^2)$ where,

- $S = \{s_1, ..., s_N\}$ is the *state set*, N is the number of states.
- $A^k = \{a_1^k, .., a_{M_k}^k\}; k = 1, 2; M^k = |A^k|$, is the set of *actions* for *Player$_k$*. The action set for *Player$_k$* at state s is a subset of A^k, i.e., $A_s^k \subseteq A^k$ and $\bigcup_{s=1}^{N} A_s^k = A^k$.
- $Q : S \times A^1 \times A^2 \times S \rightarrow [0, 1]$ is the *state transition function*.
- $R^k : S \times A^1 \times A^2 \rightarrow \Re$. $k = 1, 2$; is the *reward function* of *Player$_k$*. $\Re$ is the set of real numbers.

A stochastic game *state space* consists of the *state set* S and *action set* A^k along with a mapping function $F : A^k \rightarrow (S \times S)$. $F(a) = (s_{src}, s_{dest})$ denotes that action $a \in A^k$ is available at state s_{src} and if it is successfully executed, the resulting state is s_{dest}, where $s_{src}, s_{dest} \in S$.

You et al. [2] represented network security problem as a two-person zero-sum strategic game. Lye et. al. [3] have given a more specific example where the *attacker-administrator* interaction in an enterprise network is represented as a two-player general-sum stochastic game of complete and perfect information. Nguyen et. al. [4] considered the fact that each player (attacker/defender) has limited information about the other player. Bloem et al. [5] modeled intrusion response as a resource allocation problem based on *game theory*. Kantzavelou et al. [6] proposed a game based intrusion detection mechanism to monitor and control the behavior of *internal attackers* of an organization. Zonouz [7] proposed Response and Recovery Engine (RRE) for mitigation of intrusion incidents.

Many of the game-theoretic security approaches are based on either static game models [8] or games with perfect information [3] or games with complete information [4]. However, in a realistic scenario, the players take part in a dynamic game with incomplete and imperfect information.

In our work, we propose a stochastic game of complete and imperfect information. It is complete information game because reward function of the stochastic game has been estimated using available network related data. The model is of imperfect information because the administrator don't have to detect all exploits at all times in order to utilize the proposed model. The Administrator can estimate the network state at any moment using IDSs and decide optimal action using game-theoretic perspective.

3   Stochastic Game Based IR Model

Administrator has to construct the game prior to the deployment of the network. After the deployment, he will detect actual state of the network using IDSs and respond accordingly. The attacker does not have complete network configuration information and can not construct any game in his side. He gradually gathers network information as penetration proceeds. Only the administrator has the game and hence has an idea of all possible ways the attacker can penetrate the network. The block diagram of the proposed framework is shown in Figure 1.

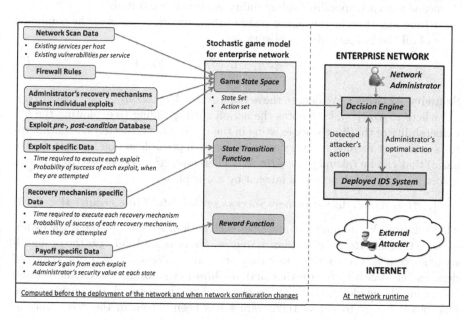

Fig. 1. Block diagram of the proposed framework

3.1 Construction of Stochastic Game - Given a Network Configuration

This section explains the construction of the stochastic game from relevant network information. The state set, action set, state transition function and reward function are derived from the data collected from enterprise LAN. It is assumed that the two *Players* in the current context are *Attacker* and network *Administrator* as $Player_1$ and $Player_2$ accordingly.

Network Security States : Information set (I) required on each host to construct the game -

- List of all running services in each host.
- List of vulnerabilities that exist for each of these services.

Administrator acquires this information using vulnerability scanning tools like Nessus[1], OpenVAS[2] etc. Only those vulnerabilities will be considered, for which patches are not available. The *Administrator* will apply the patches whenever they are available. Security state (S_{H_i}) for any host(i) is given as -

$$S_{H_i} = < \{w_1, \vec{v}_1\}, \{w_2, \vec{v}_2\}, \cdots, \{w_n, \vec{v}_n\} > \qquad (1)$$

where, w_i represents the ith service that runs on this host. w_i is '1' if the ith service is running or else '0' to denote that it has crashed. $\vec{v}_i$ is a vector containing binary values '0' or '1', which states which of the existing vulnerabilities are exploited by the *Attacker*(according to the sequence in information set I). '1' means the corresponding vulnerability is already exploited.

At time any time instance, the state of the network consists of the combined state of all the N hosts of the network -

$$S = \{S_{H_1}, S_{H_2}, S_{H_3}, \cdots, S_{H_N}\} \qquad (2)$$

Security Actions : We denote the actions of the *Attacker* by $A^1 = \{exploit(i, j, k)\}$ where $exploit(i, j, k)$ denotes the action corresponding to exploiting the kth vulnerability of the jth service existing in the ith host of the network. *Administrator*'s action set include recovery measure for each possible action (in a static scenario) that can be taken by the *Attacker*. Therefore, $A^2 = \{response\_to\_action(exploit(i, j, k))\}$. Each action is labeled by a 4-tuple -

$$\{Action\_name, Action\_owner, Success\_probability, Time\_required\} \qquad (3)$$

where *Action_Name* uniquely identifies each action. *Action_Owner* is the owner of the action i.e. *Attacker* or *Administrator*. *Success_probability* is the probability of success for each action, once they are taken *independently*. *Time_required* denotes the time to execute that action. *Administrator* has to estimate these values for the exploits, that can be executed on the network in consideration. One possible way to derive these values has been shown in the case study in Section 4.1.

Stochastic Game State Space Generation : In this section, we will construct the possible *state set* S that may occur in the network and state transition mapping function F from network configuration information.

For each exploit e, its preconditions and postconditions [9] are denoted by $Precon(e)$ and $Postcon(e)$ accordingly. Let s_0 be the initial network state, i.e. all services are running but no exploits are executed by the attacker, E be the set of all exploits that can be executed by the attacker, C_s be the set of conditions available to the attacker at state s and C_0 be the set of initial conditions. C_0 consists of the initial network configurations, connectivity information among the hosts of the network and the *Attacker*'s initial access to the network. Algorithm 1 describes how to generate the *Attacker*'s view of the stochastic game state space, i.e. all set of states and transition among them through *Attacker*'s actions. *generate_state(state s, exploit e)* function used in this algorithm returns a new state after marking e exploited in the passed state s. Algorithm 2 describes how to incorporate *Administrator*'s actions into the *Attacker*'s view of the *state space* generated by the previous algorithm. *response_to_action(e)* used in Algorithm 2 denotes the action administrator would have taken to mitigate exploit e (in a static scenario) when an attacker has already performed exploitation.

Algorithm 1. State space generation algorithm(Attacker's view)

---

    input : s_0, E, C_0
    output: Attacker's view of stochastic game *state space*(S, A^1, F)

1 $stateQueue = NULL$;
2 int $m = 0$;
3 $S = \{s_0\}$;
4 $A^1 = \{\phi\}$;
5 $stateQueue.\text{Enqueue}(s_0)$;
6 $C_{s_0} = C_0$;
7 **while** $stateQueue \mathrel{!=} NULL$ **do**
8     $s = stateQueue.\text{Dequeue}()$;
9   **for** *each* $e \in E$ **do**
10   **if** $\text{Precon}(e) \subseteq C_s$ AND $\text{Postcon}(e) \subsetneq C_s$ **then**
11          $m++$;
12          $s_m = \text{generate\_state}(s, e)$;
13          $S = S \cup s_m$;
14          $A^1 = A^1 \cup e$;
15          $F(e) = (s, s_m)$;
16          $C_{s_m} = C_s \cup \text{Postcon}(e)$;
17          $stateQueue.\text{Enqueue}(s_m)$;
18   **end**
19   **end**
20 **end**

Algorithm 2. State space generation algorithm(Both Attacker's and Administrator's view)

---

input : Attacker's view of stochastic game $state\ space(S, A^1, F)$
output: Full stochastic game $state\ space(S, A^k, F)$(k=1,2;)

1 **for** *each* $s \in S$ **do**
2     $path\_set$ = set of all paths from s_0 to s in form
      $(s_0, e_1, s_1, e_2, \ldots\ldots, e_n, s_n, e_{n+1}, s)$;
3   **for** *each* $path \in path\_set$ **do**
4   **for** *each exploit* e performed to reach state s **do**
5   /*According to construction, e must correspond to one and only one
          exploit in $path$*/
6   **if** $exploit == e_p$ and $e_p \in path$ **then**
7             $F(response\_to\_action(e)) = (s, s_p)$;
8   **end**
9   **end**
10   **end**
11 **end**

Computation of State Transition Probabilities : If any *independent* action by a single player is taken at any state, its probability of success is denoted by the *Success_probability* of that action. But in real life situations, state transition occurs due to the action of both the players taken together. Because action taken by the *Attacker* can be interrupted by the action taken by the *Administrator* and vice-versa. During the construction phase of the game, it is considered that at any stage when the players decide which actions to taken, they might have to take their actions multiple times before any of them succeeds.

Let the state of the game be s_j (where $s_j \in S$) at time t, *Attacker* takes action a_1^1 and *Administrator* takes action a_1^2. We have to estimate the probability that the game will move to s_k where $s_k \in S$ and $\sum_{s_k \in S} Prob(transition\ from\ s_j\ to\ s_k) = 1$. Let, *Attacker's* action a_1^1 has *Success_probability* $= p_1$ and *Time_required* $= t_1$. *Administrator's* action a_1^2 has *Success_probability* $= p_2$ and *Time_required* $= t_2$. *Attacker* can win only at the discrete time instances $t_1, 2t_1, 3t_1, \cdots, i.t_1, (i+1).t_1, \cdots$ because only in those instances, his action completes. In other instances, he is still in action and result cannot occur due to his action. Therefore,

$$Prob(Attacker\ wins) = \sum_{i=1}^{\infty} \{p_1 \times (1-p_1)^{i-1} \times (1-p_2)^{\lfloor i.t_1/t_2 \rfloor}\} \qquad (4)$$

Similarly, $Prob(Admin\ wins) = \sum_{i=1}^{\infty} \{p_2 \times (1-p_2)^{i-1} \times (1-p_1)^{\lfloor i.t_2/t_1 \rfloor}\}$ (5)

$$Prob(Both\ Player\ Wins\ Together)$$
$$= \sum_{i=1}^{\infty} \{(1-p_1)^{(i.LCM/t_1)-1} \times (1-p_2)^{(i.LCM/t_2)-1} \times p_1 \times p_2\} \qquad (6)$$

where LCM denotes the *least common multiple* value of t_1 and t_2. From the three equations above, the probabilities of state transition for each action pair can be computed at each state, one from the *Attacker* and one from the *Administrator*. Similarly, iterating over all the states, *state transition function* $Q : S \times A^1 \times A^2 \times S \to [0,1]$ is computed.

Computation of Expected Payoffs : A *state transition payoff matrix* M_{ij}^k is defined by the *Administrator* such that if the state moves from $State_i$ to $State_j$, then $Player_k$ receives the payoff value of M_{ij}^k. Let $s \in S$ = state of the game, $A_s^k \subseteq A^k$ = Actions available for $Player_k$ at state s. Then,

$$R^k(s, A_s^1, A_s^2) = Q(s, A_s^1, A_s^2, s_k) \times M_{s,s_k}^k + Q(s, A_s^1, A_s^2, s_{-k}) \times M_{s,s_{-k}}^k \quad (7)$$

where s_k is the state that occurs if $Player_k$ succeeds in his action and $Player_{-k}$ means the player(s) other than $Player_k$. Iterating over all states and all action pairs available at those states, *reward function* R^k is computed. Definition of M_{ij}^k is flexible and depends on the Administrator. Better estimation of M_{ij}^k will result in more accurate decision making by the whole framework.

3.2   Decision on Administrator's Optimal Action Using Nash Equilibrium

Constructed security game $G = (S, A^1, A^2, F, Q, R^1, R^2)$ can be solved to obtain the *Nash equilibrium strategies* for each player at each state of the game.

Using *Stage-game Payoff Matrix* : From the *reward functions* R^1 and R^2, the *Administrator* comes to know his expected payoffs for each action pair at each state. This information constructs a static game at each state of the game. For each *security state* s by using *Nash equilibrium strategies*, Administrator can maximize his *expected payoff* value. When the *Attacker* or the *Administrator* stick to their NE strategies, neither will gain a higher expected return if the other continues using his Nash strategy. Playing NE strategy will assure a fixed *expected payoff* value.

Other Solution Methods : Any existing method to solve stochastic games can be used to determine optimal actions for each state. Solution methods include - (i) $\epsilon-Nash equilibrium$, (ii) *strategy improvement method* by Hoffman-Karp [10], (iii) *successive approximation algorithm* by Nash [1], (iv) *nonlinear programming* by Filar and Vrieze etc.

The *Administrator* constructs the security game G using the information available on the network configuration and vulnerabilities. While constructing the game, the *Administrator* assumes the best possible capability of the *Attacker*. The *Administrator* can modify his strategies if he knows the limitations of the *Attacker*, rather than assuming best possible *Attacker* capabilities (discussed in Section 4.2).

4 Case Study

The proposed framework has been demonstrated on a test-network to show its practical utilization. Several implementation issues have come forward during the demonstration process. There are many parameters defined in the framework which needs to be assigned by the administrator. We have shown procedures to assign those values.

4.1 Stochastic-Game Construction for Test-Network

The *test-network* is shown in Figure 2. Vulnerability description of the running services are listed in Figure 3.

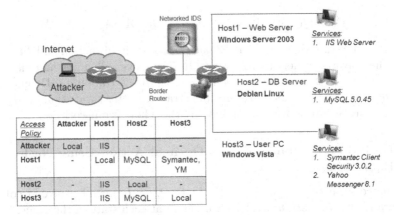

Fig. 2. Example test network and firewall configuration

Service	Vulnerability	Vulnerability type	CVE-ID	CVSS Base Score
Microsoft IIS 5.0	Microsoft IIS IDQ Path Overflow	Remote code execution	CVE-2001-0500	10
MySQL 5.0.45	MySQL yaSSL SSL Hello Message Buffer Overflow	Remote code execution	CVE-2008-0226	7.5
Symantec Client Security 3.0.2	Symantec Remote Management Buffer Overflow	Remote code execution	CVE-2006-2630	10
Yahoo Messenger 8.1	Yahoo! Messenger 8.1.0.249 ActiveX Control Buffer Overflow	Remote code execution	CVE-2007-3147	9.3

Fig. 3. Existing vulnerabilities in the network services

Enumeration of Attacker's/Administrator's Action Set A^k : As discussed in Section 3.1, the sets of all possible actions for the *Attacker/Admin* are -

$$A^{Attacker} = \{Exploit\_IIS\_BOF(Host_n), Exploit\_YM\_activex\_BOF(Host_n),$$
$$Exploit\_Symantec\_rtvscan(Host_n), Exploit\_MySQL\_YaSSL\_BOF(Host_n)\}$$

$$A^{Administrator} = \{Restart\_IIS(Host_n), Restart\_Symantec(Host_n),$$
$$Restart\_YM(Host_n), Restart\_MySQL\_Remove\_compromised\_Account(Host_n)\}$$

where $Host_n$ stands for corresponding host, in which the vulnerable service is running.

Computation of *Success_probability* Values : Exploits in this case study are available in *Metasploit framework v4.4.0* [11]. For each of the 841 exploits available in *Metasploit*, there are numbers of different configurations and payloads available. There is a total of 250 payloads available in *Metasploit*. For each exploit only few are compatible. We are assuming that the *Attacker* is selecting a payload randomly from the 250 available payloads. Therefore, *Success_probability* of exploit e_M is -

$$Success\_probability(e_M) = \frac{Number\ of\ payloads\ compatible\ with\ e_M}{Total\ number\ of\ payloads\ in\ Metasploit}$$

Success_probability value for the *Administrator*'s actions are mostly deterministic (i.e. Probability = 1). In this case study, *Success_probability* of *Administrator*'s actions are randomly assigned high values within 0.9 to 1.

Computation of *Time_required* Values : Each of the exploits in the case study are executed on test targets containing all the vulnerable services used in this case study. Exploits are executed from Metasploit framework. Time required to execute each exploit is computed. For *Administrator*'s actions, these values are assigned based on domain knowledge.

Construction of *state space* : The *network security state space* for the given network topology and configuration has been shown in Figure 4. Each oval represents a security state of the network. The *Attacker*'s actions are shown in *dotted arrows* and *Administrator*'s actions are shown in *continuous arrows*. The starting state of the network is the state where no vulnerability is exploited. Network administrator's goal is to keep the network in this state for as much duration as possible. The attacker starts from this state and might reach any security state of the network through a specific sequence of exploits. Network security states (according to definition in Section 3.1) shown in this figure are -
State 1 - [H1 {IIS(0)}, H2 {SQL(0)}, H3 {SYM(0), YM(0)}],
State 2 - [H1 {IIS(1)}, H2 {SQL(0)}, H3 {SYM(0), YM(0)}],
State 3 - [H1 {IIS(1)}, H2 {SQL(0)}, H3 {SYM(0), YM(1)}],
State 4 - [H1 {IIS(1)}, H2 {SQL(1)}, H3 {SYM(0), YM(0)}],
State 5 - [H1 {IIS(1)}, H2 {SQL(0)}, H3 {SYM(1), YM(0)}],
State 6 - [H1 {IIS(1)}, H2 {SQL(1)}, H3 {SYM(0), YM(1)}],
State 7 - [H1 {IIS(1)}, H2 {SQL(1)}, H3 {SYM(1), YM(0)}].

Enumerating *state transition payoff matrix* : Suppose, to reach state j, exploits $(e_1, e_2, \ldots, e_n)$ are executed. In this case study, *Administrator*'s security values at each state j (denoted by M_{1j}^2) is $(-) \sum_{i=1}^{n} CVSS\_Base\_Score(e_i) \times$ *criticality of the corresponding host*. *Criticality* value lies between 0 to 5. *Attacker*'s security values at each state j (denoted by M_{1j}^1) are estimated according to domain knowledge. M_{ij}^k, $(i \neq 1)$ is calculated from M_{1j}^k.

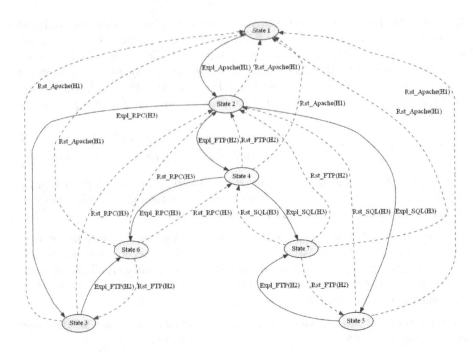

Fig. 4. Stochastic game State-Space for the example network

Computation of *Stage game payoff matrix* for each state : Computing the expected payoffs for all available action pairs at $State_3$, the *stage game payoff matrix* for $State_4$ of the game becomes as it is shown in Table 1. *Stage game payoff matrices* for other network states are not shown due to space limitation.

Table 1. Stage game payoff matrix for $State_4$ of stochastic game state space

Stage game for $State_4$	Restart_IIS(Host 1)	Restart_MySQL(Host 2)
Exploit_Symantec(Host 3)	-30.2, -10.65	25, 32.1
Exploit_YM(Host 3)	13, 0.56	-20.4, -9.58

4.2 Decision Making Using Nash Equilibrium

In the *stage game payoff matrix*, depicted in Table 1, the stationary mixed startegy $\{(0.19, 0.81),(0.51, 0.49)\}$ forms a *Nash Equilibrium*(NE) of the game. This means, for every 100 times the game comes in $State_4$, according to NE, the *Administrator* should take *Restart_IIS(Host1)* 51 out of 100 times *randomly* and take *Restart_MySQL (Host2)* 49 out of 100 times *randomly* if he has no prior information of the attacker's intents or objectives. If he has some prior information, he can modify his strategy accordingly.

The expected security payoff for playing NE is -1.59 for the *Administrator*. i.e. when the *Administrator* uses his NE strategies stated above, it will assure him the least expected security payoff of -1.59. This NE strategy can be considered as a *bullet-proof* strategy against the *Attacker* (provided that prior information on the *Attacker* is unavailable) where the minimum payoff *Administrator* receive is the *security value* -1.59. According to the definition of *Nash equilibrium*, he can achieve better, but not less.

5   Experimental Results

The proposed game theoretic framework has been implemented in *Java*. We used Boston university Representative Internet Topology gEnerator (BRITE) [12] to generate random topologies used for evaluation of our framework. Random vulnerabilities were injected into the topology. CVSS scores of vulnerabilities were also randomly assigned. For computing NE, a tool called *GAMBIT* [13] has been used. The experiments are carried on a PC with *Intel® Core i5-450M* Processor (3M cache, 2.40 GHz), 3.8 GB of usable memory and Windows®7 professional operating system. From the simulated environment, we have measured the time complexity of - (i) stochastic game construction, (ii) Nash equilibrium computation for all security states in a state space. The results are shown in Figure 5. Note that, the time requirements do not apply for each time an IDS sends an alert. Instead, both these processes are executed for a network only when the network is deployed or new services are added/removed from the network (may be once each week/month for real networks).

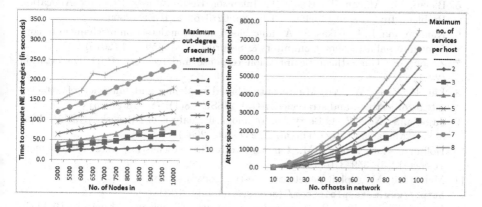

Fig. 5. Experimental results : (a) Time required for attack space construction, (b) Time required for computing Nash equilibriums

6   Conclusion

Optimal decision making while intrusion response has been modeled as a stochastic game between attacker and administrator. Administrator pre-calculated all possible attack scenarios. He determines the state of the network using IDSs and respond according to pre-computed Nash equilibrium strategies. Our model does not face *state space explosion problem*. The primary reason is we only construct those states of the network which can actually occur in the network, and not the combination of all possible states. Constructed attack space is free from cycles. We eliminate the occurrence of cycles during the construction of attack space. Experimentations show that proposed model scales well with networks consisting number of hosts in order of hundreds.

The present work can be extended in the following directions. First, proper formulation of *attackers' reward function* can be attempted, which is absent in our work. Second, in this model, we have assumed that administrator is able to identify the security state of network using IDSs. Proper correlation of IDS alerts with actual security state of the network can be incorporated in this stochastic model.

References

1. Shapley, L.: Stochastic games. Proceedings of the National Academy of Sciences of the United States of America 39(10) (1953)
2. You, X., Shiyong, Z.: A kind of network security behavior model based on game theory. In: Proceedings of PDCAT, pp. 950–954. IEEE (2003)
3. Lye, K., Wing, J.: Game strategies in network security. International Journal of Information Security 4(1), 71–86 (2005)
4. Nguyen, K., Alpcan, T., Basar, T.: Security games with incomplete information. In: Proc. of ICC 2009, pp. 1–6. IEEE (2009)
5. Bloem, M., Alpcan, T., Basar, T.: Intrusion Response as a Resource Allocation Problem. In: Proc. of the 45th CDC, pp. 6283–6288. IEEE (2006)
6. Kantzavelou, I., Katsikas, S.: A game-based intrusion detection mechanism to confront internal attackers. Computers & Security 29(8), 859–874 (2010)
7. Zonouz, S.: Game-theoretic intrusion response and recovery, PhD. Dissertation (2011)
8. Liu, P., Zang, W., Yu, M.: Incentive-based modeling and inference of attacker intent, objectives, and strategies. ACM TISSEC 8(1), 78–118 (2005)
9. Jajodia, S., Noel, S., O'Berry, B.: Topological Analysis of Network Attack Vulnerability. Managing Cyber Threats 5, 247–266 (2005)
10. Hoffman, A.J., Karp, R.M.: On nonterminating stochastic games. Management Science 12(5), 359–370 (1966)
11. Metasploit: Metasploit penetration testing software, http://www.metasploit.com/ (accessed on July 2013)
12. Boston university Representative Internet Topology gEnerator(BRITE), http://www.cs.bu.edu/brite/ (accessed on July 2013)
13. McKelvey, R., McLennan, A., Turocy, T.: Gambit: Software tools for game theory, version 13.1.0. Technical report, Gambit Project (2006)

Dynamic Ciphertext-Policy Attribute-Based Encryption for Expressive Access Policy

Y. Sreenivasa Rao and Ratna Dutta

Indian Institute of Technology Kharagpur, India
{ysrao,ratna}@maths.iitkgp.ernet.in

Abstract. In this paper, we address the problem of key update for attribute level dynamic operations in ciphertext-policy attribute-based encryption (CP-ABE). We present an efficient CP-ABE construction which features attribute addition to users with no cost and an attribute updation functionality at a cost proportional to ω, where ω is the maximum number of users hold each attribute. The proposed CP-ABE scheme resists collusion attacks, secure against chosen plaintext attacks in the generic bilinear group model, and work for any monotone access policy represented in a tree wherein internal nodes are threshold gates and leaf nodes are associated with attributes.

Keywords: attribute-based encryption, ciphertext-policy, attribute updation, generic bilinear group model.

1 Introduction

The notion of identity-based encryption (IBE) [1] solves the certificate management problem in public key encryption. However, IBE has two inherent drawbacks. First, the sender cannot encrypt a message without prior knowledge of the exact identity of a recipient. Second, IBE is not fine-grained in the sense that a sender cannot encrypt a message for a group of recipients even though the exact identities of recipients are known to sender. Sahai and Waters [2] proposed ABE that solves the aforementioned drawbacks of IBE. In ABE, each user is ascribed a set of descriptive attributes (or credentials), while secret key and ciphertext are associated with an access policy or a set of attributes. Decryption is then successful only when the attributes of ciphertext or secret key satisfy the access policy. ABE is classified as key-policy ABE (KP-ABE) [3] or ciphertext-policy ABE (CP-ABE) [4] according to whether the secret key or ciphertext is associated with an access policy, respectively. There is quite a number of ABE schemes that use a single trusted central authority (CA) to monitor attributes and secret key distribution [5–11].

Constructing ABE schemes for truly expressive access policies with acceptably low communication and computation cost, and featuring secure efficient dynamic operations (e.g., attribute addition/updation) has recently received much importance. Efficiency is a critical concern in designing such protocols for practical applications. In a dynamic setup, an attribute of a user can be added or

R. Natarajan (Ed.): ICDCIT 2014, LNCS 8337, pp. 275–286, 2014.

revoked at any time. Such schemes must ensure that key update is done upon every such membership change at attribute level, so that the subsequent cipher-texts are protected from revoked users and the previous ciphertexts are protected from joining users. The cost of updation associated with theses dynamic changes should be minimum.

The first CP-ABE scheme proposed by Bethencourt et al. [4] has received a lot of attention towards developing several secure authenticated access control primitives for different network scenarios. However, one limitation of their scheme is the lack of efficient attribute (secret key) update support. The scheme cannot update even single attribute key of a user without updating the other attribute keys related to the user. If every user has ℓ attributes and each attribute is held by maximum ω users, then $\mathcal{O}(\ell)$ attribute keys need to be updated to issue one additional attribute to a user and $\mathcal{O}(\ell \cdot \omega)$ attribute keys need to be re-computed to update a single attribute key of a user. Ibraimi et al. [11] suggested a CP-ABE scheme that is computationally efficient than Bethencourt et al. [4] CP-ABE scheme. However, their scheme exhibits the same foregoing drawback as well. The detailed comparison will be given in comparison section.

Our Contribution. In this paper, we study the key update problem of attribute level dynamic operations such as attribute addition/attribute updation. We design a CP-ABE scheme that supports efficient attribute (key) update mechanism. In this scheme, the CA can issue any number of attribute keys to users at any time in the system without accessing the attribute keys that have already been issued to users. A secret attribute key of a user can be updated with the cost of $\mathcal{O}(\omega)$ attribute key updates, where ω is the maximum number of users that can share each attribute. To this end, our scheme leverages the concept of global identifier, i.e., every user is identified with a unique global identity in the system and the attribute keys are issued based on the identity.

Our CP-ABE scheme supports any monotone access policy like [4, 11]. The proposed scheme is proven to be collusion-resistant and is secure against chosen plaintext attacks in the generic bilinear group model. We present comparisons between our scheme and some existing schemes in Table 1.

2   Background

In this section, we recall necessary background from [4, 11].

Definition 1. *Let* $\mathbb{G}$ *and* $\mathbb{G}_T$ *be multiplicative cyclic groups of prime order* p. *Let* g *be a generator of* $\mathbb{G}$. *A mapping* $e : \mathbb{G} \times \mathbb{G} \rightarrow \mathbb{G}_T$ *is said to be bilinear if* $e(u^a, v^b) = e(u, v)^{ab}$, *for all* $u, v \in \mathbb{G}$ *and* $a, b \in \mathbb{Z}_p$ *and non-degenerate if* $e(g, g) \neq 1_T$ *(where,* 1_T *is the unit element in* $\mathbb{G}_T$*). We say that* $\mathbb{G}$ *is a bilinear group if the group operation in* $\mathbb{G}$ *can be computed efficiently and there exists* $\mathbb{G}_T$ *for which the bilinear map* $e : \mathbb{G} \times \mathbb{G} \rightarrow \mathbb{G}_T$ *is efficiently computable.*

Definition 2 (Generic Bilinear Group Model). *Consider two injective maps* $\psi, \psi_T : \mathbb{Z}_p \rightarrow \{0, 1\}^{\lceil 3 \log(p) \rceil}$, *which we call random encoding maps. We write* $\mathbb{G} = \{\psi(x) | x \in \mathbb{Z}_p\}$ *and* $\mathbb{G}_T = \{\psi_T(x) | x \in \mathbb{Z}_p\}$ *which means the elements of* $\mathbb{G}$ *and* $\mathbb{G}_T$

are encoded as an arbitrary random strings. We are given two oracles that compute the group operations of $\mathbb{G}$ and $\mathbb{G}_T$ and an oracle to compute a bilinear pairing $e :$ $\mathbb{G} \times \mathbb{G} \to \mathbb{G}_T$. We refer to $\mathbb{G}$ as a generic bilinear group.

2.1 Access Policy Tree

Let T be a tree with root node root representing an access policy, which we call an *access policy tree*. Let num_v and t_v be the number of children and threshold value of a node v, respectively, where $1 \le t_v \le \text{num}_v$. Each non-leaf node v of T represents a t_v-of-num_v threshold gate. The threshold gate is an OR-gate if $t_v = 1$ and is an AND-gate if $t_v = \text{num}_v$. Each leaf node v of T is described by an attribute and the threshold value $t_v = 1$. The function $\text{parent}(v)$ denotes the parent of the node v and the function $\text{att}(v)$ denotes the attribute associated with the leaf node v. The children of each node v are numbered from 1 to num_v in an arbitrary manner and $\text{index}(c)$ of a child c is such a number (denoting its number for its parent node).

Let T_v be a subtree of T rooted at v. Then T is the same as T_{root}. For a set L of attributes, compute $T_v(L)$ recursively in a bottom-up manner as follows. If v is a leaf node, then $T_v(L) = 1$ if and only if $\text{att}(v) \in L$. If v is a non-leaf node, $T_v(L) = 1$ if and only if $T_c(L) = 1$ for at least t_v children c of the node v.

Definition 3 (Satisfiability of T). *A set of attributes L satisfies the access policy tree T with root node root if $T_{\text{root}}(L) = 1$.*

Definition 4 (Lagrange Coefficient). *The Lagrange coefficient $\triangle_{i,S}$ for $i \in \mathbb{Z}_p$ and a set, $S \subset \mathbb{Z}_p$, is defined as $\triangle_{i,S}(x) = \prod_{j \in S, j \neq i} \frac{x-j}{i-j}$.*

A couple of algorithms are in order.

1. Distribute(T, s)

Input: an access policy tree T and a random element $s \in \mathbb{Z}_p$
Output: {share$(v) : v \in Z$}, where Z is the set of all leaf nodes in T
1: **procedure** distribute_share(T, s, v)
2: $d_v \leftarrow (t_v - 1)$ /* d_v is degree of a polynomial q_v for node v */
3: **if** $v = \text{root}$ **then**
4:     $q_{\text{root}}(0) \leftarrow s$
5: **else**
6:     $q_v(0) = q_{\text{parent}(v)}(\text{index}(v))$
7: **end if**
8: choose d_v other points of q_v randomly to define it completely
9: **if** v is a leaf node of T **then**
10:    share$(v) \leftarrow q_v(0)$
11: **end if**
12: **for** each node $c \in$ T such that $\text{parent}(c) = v$ **do**
13:    call distribute_share(T, s, c)
14: **end for**
15: **end procedure**

2. Aggregate(T, $\{F_v : v \in Z\}$)

Input: an access policy tree T and $\{F_v : v \in Z\}$, where $F_v = e(g,g)^{r \cdot \text{share}(v)}$ or $\perp$, and Z is the set of all leaf nodes in T

Output: $e(g,g)^{r \cdot \text{share(root)}}$ or $\perp$

```
1: procedure aggregate_node(T, {F_v : v ∈ Z}, v)
2: if v is a leaf node of T then
3:    return F_v
4: else
5:    ct ← 0
6:    for each node c ∈ T such that parent(c) = v do
7:       res = aggregate_node(T, {F_v : v ∈ Z}, c)
8:       if res ≠ ⊥ then
9:          ct ← ct + 1
10:      end if
11:   end for
12:   if ct ≥ t_v then
13:      set S_v := an arbitrary t_v-sized set of child nodes c such that F_c ≠ ⊥
14:      compute F_v = ∏_{c∈S_v} F_c^{Δ_{i,S'_v}(0)} = e(g,g)^{r·q_v(0)} = e(g,g)^{r·share(v)}
             /* here i = index(c) and S'_v = {index(c) : c ∈ S_v} */
15:      return F_v
16:   else
17:      return ⊥
18:   end if
19: end if
20: end procedure
```

2.2 A CP-ABE Template

A CP-ABE scheme consists of the following four algorithms:

Setup($\kappa, \mathcal{A}$) → (PK, MK). This algorithm takes as input implicit security parameter κ and an attribute universe $\mathcal{A}$, and returns the public key PK and the master secret key MK.

KeyGen(PK, MK, L) → SK_L. This algorithm takes as input PK, MK and a set L of user attributes, and returns a secret key SK_L associated with L.

Encrypt(PK, M, T) → CT. This algorithm takes as input PK, a message M and an access policy tree T over the universe of attributes $\mathcal{A}$. It returns a ciphertext CT such that any user with a secret key SK_L satisfying T is able to decrypt the message M.

Decrypt(CT, SK_L) → M. This algorithm takes as input SK_L and a ciphertext CT which is encrypted under the access policy tree T. If the set L of attributes satisfies T, then this algorithm will return the message M.

We describe IND-CPA (ciphertext indistinguishability under chosen plaintext attacks) security model in terms of a game $\mathsf{Game}^{IND-CPA}$ which is carried out between a challenger and an adversary. The challenger executes the relevant CP-ABE algorithms in order to answer the queries from the adversary as follows:

Setup. The challenger executes the **Setup** algorithm and gives public key PK to the adversary.

Key Query Phase 1. The adversary is allowed to make secret key queries for the user identities coupled with attribute sets $(\mathsf{ID}_1, L_1), (\mathsf{ID}_2, L_2), \ldots, (\mathsf{ID}_{q_1}, L_{q_1})$. The challenger runs **KeyGen** algorithm and returns the corresponding secret keys $\mathsf{SK}_{L_1}, \mathsf{SK}_{L_2}, \ldots, \mathsf{SK}_{L_{q_1}}$ to the adversary.

Challenge. The adversary submits two equal length messages M_0, M_1 and an access policy tree T^*. This access policy tree cannot be satisfied by any of the queried attribute sets $L_1, L_2, \ldots, L_{q_1}$. The challenger flips a random coin $\mu \in \{0, 1\}$ and runs **Encrypt** algorithm in order to encrypt M_μ under T^*. The resulting challenge ciphertext CT^* is given to the adversary.

Key Query Phase 2. The adversary may receive secret keys $\mathsf{SK}_{L_{q_1+1}}, \ldots, \mathsf{SK}_{L_q}$ relate to the additional key queries for the pairs $(\mathsf{ID}_{q_1+1}, L_{q_1+1}), \ldots, (\mathsf{ID}_q, L_q)$, as long as they do not violate the restriction on the access policy tree T^* stated in Challenge phase.

Guess. The adversary outputs a guess bit $\mu' \in \{0, 1\}$ for the challenger's secret coin μ and wins if $\mu' = \mu$.

The advantage of an adversary Π in the IND-CPA game is defined to be $\mathsf{Adv}(\mathsf{Game}_\Pi^{IND-CPA}) = |\Pr[\mu' = \mu] - \frac{1}{2}|$, where the probability is taken over all random coin tosses of both adversary and challenger.

Definition 5. *The proposed CP-ABE scheme is said to be IND-CPA secure if for all polynomial time adversaries Π, there exists a negligible function* negl *such that* $\mathsf{Adv}(\mathsf{Game}_\Pi^{IND-CPA}) \leq \mathsf{negl}(\kappa)$, *where κ is a security parameter.*

Fig. 1. IND-CPA security model for CP-ABE

3 Proposed CP-ABE Construction

Let $\mathcal{A}$ be the attribute universe. Each user u is identified with a unique global identity $\mathsf{ID}_u \in \{0, 1\}^*$. A single trusted central authority (CA) manages all the attributes and its keys, and is responsible for issuing secret key to users. Our CP-ABE consists of the following four algorithms.

Setup$(\kappa, \mathcal{A}) \to (\mathsf{PK}, \mathsf{MK})$. On receiving the implicit security parameter κ, CA generates a prime number p, a bilinear group $\mathbb{G}$, a generator $g \in \mathbb{G}$ and a bilinear map $e : \mathbb{G} \times \mathbb{G} \to \mathbb{G}_T$, where $\mathbb{G}$ and $\mathbb{G}_T$ are multiplicative groups of same prime order p. Let $\mathcal{H} : \{0, 1\}^* \to \mathbb{G}$ be a collision resistant hash function. It then picks random exponents $\alpha, \beta, b, t_a \in \mathbb{Z}_p$ and computes $Y = e(g, g)^\alpha, h = g^\beta, g^b, T_a = g^{t_a}$, for $a \in \mathcal{A}$. The public key is $\mathsf{PK} = \langle p, \mathbb{G}, g, \mathbb{G}_T, e, \mathcal{H}, Y, g^b, h, \{T_a : a \in \mathcal{A}\} \rangle$ and the master secret key is $\mathsf{MK} = \langle \alpha, b, \beta, \{t_a : a \in \mathcal{A}\} \rangle$.

KeyGen$(\mathsf{PK}, \mathsf{MK}, L) \to \mathsf{SK}_L$. Let L be the set of attributes of a user u with identity $\mathsf{ID}_u \in \{0, 1\}^*$. CA selects a random exponent $r_u \in \mathbb{Z}_p$ and computes

$D_1 = g^{(\alpha + r_u)/\beta}, D_2 = g^{r_u}\mathcal{H}(\mathsf{ID}_u)^b, D_a = \mathcal{H}(\mathsf{ID}_u)^{t_a}$, for each $a \in L$. It then outputs the secret key $\mathsf{SK}_L = \langle D_1, D_2, \{D_a : a \in L\} \rangle$ associated with L.

Encrypt$(\mathsf{PK}, M, \mathsf{T}) \to \mathsf{CT}$. To encrypt a message $M \in \mathbb{G}_T$ under the access policy tree T, the encryptor first chooses a random secret $s \in \mathbb{Z}_p$ and then runs the algorithm $\mathtt{Distribute}(\mathsf{T}, s)$. Consequently, the encryptor will obtain a share set $\{\mathsf{share}(v_a) : v_a \in Z\}$ of the set, Z, of all leaf nodes in the tree T. Note that each leaf node v_a in Z is described by an attribute a. Finally, the ciphertext components are computed as follows. $C = MY^s, C_1 = h^s, C_{a,1} = g^{\mathsf{share}(v_a)}, C_{a,2} = (g^b T_a)^{\mathsf{share}(v_a)}$, for each $v_a \in Z$. The ciphertext is $\mathsf{CT} = \langle \mathsf{T}, C, C_1, \{C_{a,1}, C_{a,2} : v_a \in Z\} \rangle$.

Decrypt$(\mathsf{CT}, \mathsf{SK}_L) \to M$. When a user u with identity $\mathsf{ID}_u \in \{0,1\}^*$ receives a ciphertext CT, he first computes $\mathcal{H}(\mathsf{ID}_u)$. For each leaf node v_a in Z (the attribute associated with v_a is a), the following steps will be executed.

– If $a \in L$, then compute

$$F_{v_a} = \frac{e(C_{a,1}, D_2 D_a)}{e(\mathcal{H}(\mathsf{ID}_u), C_{a,2})} = \frac{e(g^{\mathsf{share}(v_a)}, g^{r_u}\mathcal{H}(\mathsf{ID}_u)^b \mathcal{H}(\mathsf{ID}_u)^{t_a})}{e(\mathcal{H}(\mathsf{ID}_u), (g^b T_a)^{\mathsf{share}(v_a)})}$$
$$= e(g,g)^{r_u \cdot \mathsf{share}(v_a)},$$

– If $a \notin L$, then set $F_{v_a} = \bot$.

After getting all F_{v_a} for all the leaf nodes in a tree T, invoke the algorithm $\mathtt{Aggregate}(\mathsf{T}, \{F_{v_a} : v_a \in Z\})$. This algorithm returns $e(g,g)^{r_u \cdot \mathsf{share}(\mathsf{root})} = e(g,g)^{r_u s}$ if the access policy tree T is satisfied by the set L of user attributes. Finally, the user computes $C/(e(C_1, D_1)/e(g,g)^{r_u s})$, which returns the message M.

4   Security Analysis

A crucial property in designing ABE schemes is *collusion-resistance*—no two or more recipients can combine their secret keys in order to decrypt a message that they are not entitled to decrypt alone. The encrypt algorithm blinds the message with another term $e(g,g)^{\alpha s}$. In order to recover $e(g,g)^{\alpha s}$, a user must pair the ciphertext component C_1 with its secret key component D_1. This will result in $e(g,g)^{\alpha s} \cdot e(g,g)^{r_u s}$. The additional term $e(g,g)^{r_u s}$ can be blinded out only if the user has enough secret key components to satisfy the secret sharing scheme embedded in the ciphertext. In sum, each user's secret key is randomized by a unique random value r_u, which is used to implicitly blind the term $e(g,g)^{\alpha s}$ so that collusion attacks will not work here like [4]. Thus, the proposed CP-ABE scheme preserves collusion-resistance property.

Theorem 1. *For any adversary Π having access to the oracles for the groups $\mathbb{G}$ and $\mathbb{G}_T$, the hash function $\mathcal{H}$ and the bilinear map e in the security game $\mathrm{Game}^{IND-CPA}$ given in Fig. 1 for the CP-ABE scheme, the advantage of the adversary $\mathrm{Adv}(\mathrm{Game}_{\Pi}^{IND-CPA}) = \mathcal{O}(q^2/p)$. Where, p is the order of $\mathbb{G}$ and q is the maximum number of oracle queries made by the adversary Π.*

Proof. Let Π_1 be an adversary who plays the original security game, say $\mathsf{GAME}_1 = \mathsf{Game}^{IND-CPA}$, described in Fig. 1. According to GAME_1, the challenge ciphertext has a component C which is either $M_0 \cdot e(g,g)^{\alpha s}$ or $M_1 \cdot e(g,g)^{\alpha s}$, and the adversary Π_1 has to distinguish them. Consequently, we define a modified game, say GAME_2, as follows. Setup, Key Query Phase 1 and Key Query Phase 2 are similar to GAME_1, but the challenge ciphertext component C in Challenge phase is computed as $C = e(g,g)^{\alpha s}$ if $\mu = 1$ and $C = e(g,g)^{\delta}$ if $\mu = 0$, where δ is selected uniformly at random from $\mathbb{Z}_p$, and other ciphertext components are computed in the same way analogous to Encrypt algorithm. Then we have the following claim.

Claim 1: If Π_1 has advantage ϵ to win GAME_1, then there is an adversary who wins GAME_2 with advantage at least $\epsilon/2$. (For proof we refer the reader to [12].)

This claim demonstrates that any adversary that has a non-negligible advantage in GAME_1 can have a non-negligible advantage in GAME_2. We shall prove that no adversary can have non-negligible advantage in GAME_2. From now on, we will discuss the advantage of the adversary in GAME_2, wherein the adversary must distinguish between $e(g,g)^{\alpha s}$ and $e(g,g)^{\delta}$.

Simulation in GAME_2: To simulate the modified security game GAME_2, we use the generic bilinear group model described in [4]. Consider two injective random maps $\psi, \psi_T : \mathbb{Z}_p \to \{0,1\}^{\lceil 3 \log(p) \rceil}$. In this model every element of $\mathbb{G}$ and $\mathbb{G}_T$ is encoded as an arbitrary random string from the adversary's point of view, i.e., $\mathbb{G} = \{\psi(x) : x \in \mathbb{Z}_p\}$ and $\mathbb{G}_T = \{\psi_T(x) : x \in \mathbb{Z}_p\}$. The adversary is given three oracles to compute group operations of $\mathbb{G}$, $\mathbb{G}_T$ and to compute the bilinear pairing e. The input of all oracles are string representations of group elements. The adversary is allowed to perform group operations and pairing computations by interacting with the corresponding oracles only. It is assumed that the adversary can make queries to the group oracles on input strings that were previously been obtained from the simulator or were given from the oracles in response to the previous queries. This event occurs with high probability. Since $|\psi(\mathbb{Z}_p)| > p^3$ and $|\psi_T(\mathbb{Z}_p)| > p^3$, the probability of the adversary being able to guess an element (which it has not previously obtained) in the ranges of ψ, ψ_T is negligible.

The notations $g^x := \psi(x)$ and $e(g,g)^x := \psi_T(x)$ are used in the rest of the proof. With this notation, g and $e(g,g)$ can be represented as $\psi(1)$ and $\psi_T(1)$, respectively.

Setup: The simulator chooses α, β, b from $\mathbb{Z}_p$. Note that if $\beta = 0$, which happens with probability $1/p$, then the setup is aborted as it would be in the original scheme. The simulator computes $g^{\beta}, g^{b}, e(g,g)^{\alpha}$ using respective group oracles and gives $\psi(\beta), \psi(b), \psi_T(\alpha)$ to the adversary. For each attribute $a \in \mathcal{A}$, the simulator chooses a random value $t_a \in \mathbb{Z}_p$, computes $g^{t_a} = \psi(t_a)$ and sends $\psi(t_a)$ to the adversary.

Query Phase 1: The adversary issues hash and secret key queries, and consequently the simulator responds as follows.

Hash queries: When the adversary requests $\mathcal{H}(\mathsf{ID})$ for some user identity ID for the first time, the simulator chooses a new, unique random value $h_{\mathsf{ID}} \in \mathbb{Z}_p$, computes $g^{h_{\mathsf{ID}}} = \psi(h_{\mathsf{ID}})$ using group oracle and gives $\psi(h_{\mathsf{ID}})$ to the adversary as $\mathcal{H}(\mathsf{ID})$. The association between values h_{ID} and the user identities ID is stored in Hlist so that it can reply consistently for subsequent queries in the future.

Secret key queries: If the adversary requests for a secret key of the set L_j of attributes for the same identity ID_j, the simulator chooses a new random value $r_u^{(j)} \in \mathbb{Z}_p$ and computes $g^{(\alpha + r_u^{(j)})/\beta}, g^{r_u^{(j)} + bh_{\mathsf{ID}_j}}, g^{t_a h_{\mathsf{ID}_j}}$, for each $a \in L_j$ by using group oracle, and returns as $D_1 = \psi((\alpha + r_u^{(j)})/\beta), D_2 = \psi(r_u^{(j)} + bh_{\mathsf{ID}_j}), D_a = \psi(t_a h_{\mathsf{ID}_j})$, for each $a \in L_j$, to the adversary. If $\mathcal{H}(\mathsf{ID}_j)$ has not been stored in Hlist, it is determined as above.

Challenge: In order to obtain a challenge ciphertext CT^*, the adversary specifies an access policy tree T^*. The simulator first chooses a random $s \in \mathbb{Z}_p$ and makes use of the linear secret sharing scheme (described in **Distribute** algorithm) associated with T^* to construct shares λ_a of s for all attributes a associated with the leaf nodes in T^*. As such, the choice of the λ_a's can perfectly be simulated by choosing some l random values $\tau_1, \ldots, \tau_l$ uniformly and independently from $\mathbb{Z}_p$, and then letting the λ_a be fixed public linear combination of the τ_k's and s. The simulator then flips a random coin $\mu \in \{0, 1\}$ and if $\mu = 1$, he sets $\delta = \alpha s$, otherwise δ is set to be a random value from $\mathbb{Z}_p$. The simulator finally computes the components of challenge ciphertext CT^* by using group oracles as follows. $C = \psi_T(\delta), C_1 = \psi(\beta s)$ and for each attribute a assigned to some leaf node of T^*, $C_{a,1} = \psi(\lambda_a), C_{a,2} = \psi((b + t_a)\lambda_a)$. The ciphertext $\mathsf{CT} = \langle \mathsf{T}^*, C, C_1, \{C_{a,1}, C_{a,2} : a$ is a leaf node$\}\rangle$ is sent to the adversary.

Query Phase 2: The adversary issues more hash and secret key queries. The simulator responds as in Query Phase 1. We note that if the adversary requests for secret keys of a set of attributes that satisfy the challenge access policy tree, then the simulator does not issue the key.

The adversary now can have in his hand, all values that consists of encodings of random values $\delta, 1, \alpha, \beta, b, h_{\mathsf{ID}_j}, t_a, r_u^{(j)}, s, \tau_k$ and combination of these values given by the simulator (e.g., $\psi((b + t_a)\lambda_a)$) or results of queries on combination of these values to the oracles. In turn, we can think of each query of the adversary as a multivariate polynomial in the variables $\delta, 1, \alpha, \beta, b, h_{\mathsf{ID}_j}, t_a, r_u^{(j)}, s, \tau_k$. We assume that any pair of the adversary's queries on two different polynomials result in two different answers. This assumption is false only when our choice of the random encodings of the variables ensures that the difference of two polynomial queries evaluates to zero. Following the security proof in [4], it can be claimed that the probability of any such collision is at most $\mathcal{O}(q^2/p)$, q being an upper bound on the number of oracle queries made by the adversary during the entire simulation. Therefore, the advantage of the adversary is at most $\mathcal{O}(q^2/p)$. We assume that no such random collisions occur while retain $1 - \mathcal{O}(q^2/p)$ probability mass.

Under this condition, we show that the view of the adversary in GAME_2 is identically distributed when $\delta = \alpha s$ if $\mu = 1$ and δ is random if $\mu = 0$, and hence the adversary cannot distinguish them in the generic bilinear group model. To prove this by contradiction, let us assume that the views are not identically distributed. The adversary's views can only differ when there exists two queries q_1 and q_2 in $\mathbb{G}_T$ such that $q_1 \neq q_2$ with $q_1|_{(\delta=\alpha s)} = q_2|_{(\delta=\alpha s)}$. Since δ only appears as $\psi_T(\delta)$ and elements of ψ_T cannot be used as input of pairing oracle, the adversary can only make queries of the following form involving δ: $q_1 = c_1\delta + q_1'$ and $q_2 = c_2\delta + q_2'$, for some q_1' and q_2' that do not contain δ, and for some constants c_1 and c_2. Since $q_1|_{(\delta=\alpha s)} = q_2|_{(\delta=\alpha s)}$, we have $c_1\alpha s + q_1' = c_2\alpha s + q_2'$ and it gives $q_2' - q_1' = (c_1 - c_2)\alpha s = c\alpha s$, for some constant $c \neq 0$. Therefore, the adversary can construct the query $\psi_T(c\alpha s)$, for some constant $c \neq 0$, yielding a contradiction to our Claim 2 given below.

Claim 2: The adversary cannot make a query of the form $\psi_T(c\alpha s)$ for any non-zero constant c. (Proof will be detailed in Appendix A.)

Hence the adversary's views in GAME$_2$ are identically distributed, i.e., the adversary has no non-negligible advantage in GAME$_2$, so in the original game GAME$_1$ by Claim 1. This proves the theorem. $\square$

5   Performance

In this section, we discuss the performance of our CP-ABE with the existing CP-ABE schemes [4, 11] in view of the basic attribute update strategy.

The following notations are used in Table 1: ℓ = number of attributes associated with secret key of a user, ϕ = number of attributes in the access policy tree, ω = maximum number of users that hold each attribute, $B_{\mathbb{G}}$ (resp. $B_{\mathbb{G}_T}$) = bit size of an element in $\mathbb{G}$ (resp. $\mathbb{G}_T$), ADD = number of secret attribute keys need to be recomputed to add one attribute to the user, UPD = number of secret attribute keys need to be recomputed to update one secret attribute key of a user, $E_{\mathbb{G}}$ (resp. $E_{\mathbb{G}_T}$) = number of exponentiations in a group $\mathbb{G}$ (resp. $\mathbb{G}_T$), P_e = number of pairing computations, σ = minimum number of attributes required to make decryption successful.

The comparison of computation and communication cost of our CP-ABE with the existing CP-ABE schemes [4, 11] are presented in Table 1.

With reference to the parameters used in Section 3, the secret key in [4] associated with a user attribute set L is $\langle D_1 = g^{(\alpha+r_u)/\beta}, \{D_{a,1} = g^{r_u}\mathcal{H}(a)^{t_a}, D_{a,2} = g^{t_a} : a \in L\}\rangle$ and the secret key in [11] of a user with an attribute set L is $\langle D_1 = g^{\alpha-r_u}, \{D_a = g^{r_u t_a^{-1}} : a \in L\}\rangle$. Note that all the attribute (secret) keys of the user u are randomized with the same random value r_u in both the schemes [4, 11]. Consequently, update of one attribute key affects all the attribute keys that the user possesses. Let $|L| = \ell$.

Adding one attribute to user. When a user is qualified for a new attribute a', the ℓ "old" attribute keys need to be updated in [4, 11] along with the new attribute key by executing the key generation algorithm for the set $L \cup \{a'\}$ of attributes, i.e., $\mathcal{O}(\ell)$ keys need to be recomputed to assign one new attribute key to the user.

Table 1. Comparative summary of our scheme against previous schemes

Scheme	KeyGen $E_{\mathbb{G}}$	Encrypt $E_{\mathbb{G}}$	$E_{\mathbb{G}_T}$	Decrypt $E_{\mathbb{G}_T}$	P_e	Secret Key Size	Ciphertext Size	ADD	UPD
[4]	$2\ell+2$	$2\phi+1$	1	$\mathcal{O}(\sigma)$	$\mathcal{O}(\sigma)$	$(2\ell+1)B_{\mathbb{G}}$	$(2\phi+1)B_{\mathbb{G}}+B_{\mathbb{G}_T}$	$\mathcal{O}(\ell)$	$\mathcal{O}(\ell\cdot\omega)$
[11]	$\ell+1$	$\phi+1$	1	$\mathcal{O}(\sigma)$	$\mathcal{O}(\sigma)$	$(\ell+1)B_{\mathbb{G}}$	$(\phi+1)B_{\mathbb{G}}+B_{\mathbb{G}_T}$	$\mathcal{O}(\ell)$	$\mathcal{O}(\ell\cdot\omega)$
Our	$\ell+3$	$2\phi+1$	1	$\mathcal{O}(\sigma)$	$\mathcal{O}(\sigma)$	$(\ell+2)B_{\mathbb{G}}$	$(2\phi+1)B_{\mathbb{G}}+B_{\mathbb{G}_T}$	1	$\mathcal{O}(\omega)$

Updating one attribute key of a user. If the secret key of an attribute a'' of one user is compromised, the attribute key is required to be updated. In this scenario, the other $\ell-1$ attribute keys of a user u who is holding the attribute a'' must be updated in [4, 11] with a new random value r'_u different from r_u in such a way that the attribute keys already generated with r_u are no longer considered as valid. If ω users are holding the attribute a'', then total $\mathcal{O}(\ell\cdot\omega)$ attribute keys need to be recomputed in order to update one attribute key.

In our CP-ABE scheme, secret key of a user with attribute set L is $\langle D_1 = g^{(\alpha+r_u)/\beta}, D_2 = g^{r_u}\mathcal{H}(\mathsf{ID}_u)^b, \{D_a = \mathcal{H}(\mathsf{ID}_u)^{t_a} : a \in L\}\rangle$, where $\langle D_1, D_2\rangle$ is the personalized secret key of a user, i.e., secret key components other than attribute keys. In order to alleviate the foregoing problems, we use the concept of global identifier for tying users' attribute secret keys in our construction and the unique random value r_u is only used to randomize the personalized secret key of a user. Therefore, the CA can efficiently issue additional attribute keys to users at any time without accessing the secret keys that have already been issued by recomputing $\mathcal{O}(\omega)$ keys for a group of ω users holding that attribute. Note that the other keys of users will not be affected here. The comparisons are given in Table 1.

6 Conclusion

We presented a new CP-ABE construction which can update user attribute keys dynamically. Our scheme supports any monotone access policy represented in a tree wherein internal nodes are threshold gates and leaf nodes are associated with attributes. The proposed scheme preserves collusion-resistance and is proven to be secure against chosen plaintext attacks in the generic bilinear group model.

References

1. Shamir, A.: Identity-Based Cryptosystems and Signature Schemes. In: Blakely, G.R., Chaum, D. (eds.) CRYPTO 1984. LNCS, vol. 196, pp. 47–53. Springer, Heidelberg (1985)
2. Sahai, A., Waters, B.: Fuzzy Identity-Based Encryption. In: Cramer, R. (ed.) EUROCRYPT 2005. LNCS, vol. 3494, pp. 457–473. Springer, Heidelberg (2005)
3. Goyal, V., Pandey, O., Sahai, A., Waters, B.: Attribute Based Encryption for Fine-Grained Access Control of Encrypted Data. In: ACM Conference on Computer and Communications Security, pp. 89–98 (2006)
4. Bethencourt, J., Sahai, A., Waters, B.: Ciphertext-Policy Attribute-Based Encryption. In: IEEE Symposium on Security and Privacy, pp. 321–334 (2007)

5. Ostrovsky, R., Sahai, A., Waters, B.: Attribute-Based Encryption with Nonmonotonic Access Structures. In: Proc. ACM Conference on Computer and Communications Security (CCS), pp. 195–203 (2007)
6. Cheung, L., Newport, C.: Provably Secure Ciphertext Policy ABE. In: CCS 2007: Proceedings of the 14th ACM Conference on Computer and Communications Security, pp. 456–465. ACM Press, New York (2007)
7. Goyal, V., Jain, A., Pandey, O., Sahai, A.: Bounded ciphertext policy attribute based encryption. In: Aceto, L., Damgård, I., Goldberg, L.A., Halldórsson, M.M., Ingólfsdóttir, A., Walukiewicz, I. (eds.) ICALP 2008, Part II. LNCS, vol. 5126, pp. 579–591. Springer, Heidelberg (2008)
8. Waters, B.: Ciphertext-Policy Attribute-Based Encryption: An Expressive, Efficient, and Provably Secure Realization. Cryptology ePrint report 2008/290 (2008)
9. Lewko, A., Okamoto, T., Sahai, A., Takashima, K., Waters, B.: Fully Secure Functional Encryption: Attribute-Based Encryption and (Hierarchical) Inner Product Encryption. Cryptology ePrint report 2010/110 (2010)
10. Waters, B.: Dual System Encryption: Realizing Fully Secure IBE and HIBE under Simple Assumptions. In: Halevi, S. (ed.) CRYPTO 2009. LNCS, vol. 5677, pp. 619–636. Springer, Heidelberg (2009)
11. Ibraimi, L., Tang, Q., Hartel, P., Jonker, W.: Efficient and Provable Secure Ciphertext-Policy Attribute-Based Encryption Schemes. In: Bao, F., Li, H., Wang, G. (eds.) ISPEC 2009. LNCS, vol. 5451, pp. 1–12. Springer, Heidelberg (2009)
12. Müller, S., Katzenbeisser, S., Eckert, C.: On Multi-Authority Ciphertext-Policy Attribute-Based Encryption. Bulletin of the Korean Mathematical Society 46(4), 803–817 (2009)

A Claim 2

The adversary cannot make a query of the form $\psi_T(c\alpha s)$ for any non-zero constant c.

Proof. To establish this claim, we examine the information given to the adversary during the entire simulation and perform case analysis based on that information.

In Table 2, we list all the possible adversary's query terms in $\mathbb{G}_T$ (except for those that involve β as β is not relevant to constructing αs) by means of the bilinear map and group elements given to the adversary during the simulation. Here the variables a, a' are possible attributes and j, j' are indices of secret key queries made by the adversary. The query terms are given in λ_a's rather than τ_k's. It can be seen that the adversary can query for an arbitrary linear combination of 1 (which is $\psi_T(1)$), δ and the terms given in Table 2. We will now show that no such linear combination can produce a term of the form $c\alpha s$ for any non-zero constant c.

We can see from Table 2 that the only way for the adversary to form a term containing αs is by pairing $(\alpha + r_u^{(j)})/\beta$ with $s\beta$ to get $\alpha s + s r_u^{(j)}$. Consequently, the adversary can create a query polynomial of the form $c\alpha s + \sum_{j \in J} c_j s r_u^{(j)}$, for some set J and non-zero constants c and c_j. In order to obtain a query polynomial of the form $c\alpha s$, the adversary should add other terms to cancel the terms of the form $\sum_{j \in J} c_j s r_u^{(j)}$. Since λ_a's are linear combinations of s and τ_k's, by refer to Table 2, the only terms of the form $s r_u^{(j)}$ that the adversary has

Table 2. Possible adversary's query terms in $\mathbb{G}_T$ (here, the variables a, a' are possible attributes and j, j' are indices of secret key queries made by the adversary)

h_{ID_j}	$b\lambda_a$	$t_{a'}(b+t_a)\lambda_a$	s
bh_{ID_j}	$b(b+t_a)\lambda_a$	$t_a h_{ID_j}$	λ_a
$h_{ID_j}h_{ID_{j'}}$	$r_u^{(j)}+bh_{ID_j}$	$t_a t_{a'} h_{ID_j} h_{ID_{j'}}$	$t_a t_{a'}$
$h_{ID_j}t_a$	$(r_u^{(j)}+bh_{ID_j})(r_u^{(j')}+bh_{ID_{j'}})$	$t_a h_{ID_j}\lambda_{a'}$	$bt_a h_{ID_j}$
$h_{ID_{j'}}(r_u^{(j)}+bh_{ID_j})$	$(r_u^{(j)}+bh_{ID_j})t_a h_{ID_{j'}}$	$t_{a'} h_{ID_j}(b+t_a)\lambda_a$	$t_a\lambda_{a'}$
$h_{ID_j}h_{ID_{j'}}t_a$	$(r_u^{(j)}+bh_{ID_j})\lambda_a$	$\alpha s+sr_u^{(j)}$	t_a
$h_{ID_j}\lambda_a$	$(r_u^{(j)}+bh_{ID_j})(b+t_a)\lambda_a$	$\alpha+r_u^{(j)}$	$t_a t_{a'} h_{ID_j}$
$h_{ID_j}(b+t_a)\lambda_a$	$(b+t_a)(b+t_{a'})\lambda_a\lambda_{a'}$	$b(r_u^{(j)}+bh_{ID_j})$	bt_a
$t_a(r_u^{(j)}+bh_{ID_j})$	$(b+t_a)\lambda_a$	$\lambda_a\lambda_{a'}(b+t_a)$	$\lambda_a\lambda_{a'}$

access to are obtained by pairing $r_u^{(j)} + bh_{ID_j}$ with some λ_a. To cancel the additional terms $bh_{ID_j}\lambda_a$, the adversary further has access to the terms $h_{ID_j}b\lambda_a + h_{ID_j}t_a\lambda_a$ and finally the adversary can construct a query polynomial of the following form:

$$
c\alpha s + \sum_{j\in J}\left(c_j sr_u^{(j)} + \sum_{a\in J_j} c_{(a,j)}\left(\lambda_a r_u^{(j)} + bh_{ID_j}\lambda_a\right) + \sum_{a\in J_j} c'_{(a,j)}\left(h_{ID_j}b\lambda_a + h_{ID_j}t_a\lambda_a\right)\right)
$$
(1)

for some sets J_j and non-zero constants $c_{(a,j)}$ and $c'_{(a,j)}$.

To conclude the proof of Claim 2, we will perform the following case analysis.
Case 1. Suppose there exists some $j^* \in J$ such that the set of secret shares $\{\lambda_a : a \in J_{j^*}\}$ do not allow for reconstruction of the secret s. Then, in this case, the term $sr_u^{(j^*)}$ will not be canceled and hence the adversary's query polynomial Eq.(1) cannot be of the form $c\alpha s$.
Case 2. For all $j \in J$, the set of secret shares $\{\lambda_a : a \in J_j\}$ allow for reconstruction of the secret s. Then the only terms left in the adversarys query polynomial other than $c\alpha s$ are of the form $h_{ID_j}t_a\lambda_a$ and the adversary must add other terms to cancel them. It can be seen from Table 2 that the only terms the adversary needs to access to cancel the terms of the form $h_{ID_j}t_a\lambda_a$ is $t_a h_{ID_j}\lambda_{a'}$ but only when $a = a'$. We now show that there is at least one such term $h_{ID_j}t_a\lambda_a$ with $a \neq a'$ in the adversary's query polynomial.

Fix any $j \in J$. Consider the set L_j of attributes corresponding to the j-th adversary secret key request. From the assumption stated in Challenge phase of the security model, no requested secret key should satisfy the challenge access policy tree and the properties of the secret sharing scheme. This in turn does not allow the set $\{\lambda_{a'} : a' \in L_j\}$ of secret shares to reconstruct the secret s. Hence, there exist at least one share λ_a in $\{\lambda_a : a \in J_j\}$ such that λ_a is linearly independent of $\{\lambda_{a'} : a' \in L_j\}$ when written in terms of s and τ_k's. Thus, there will be a term of the form $h_{ID_j}t_a\lambda_a$ ($a \neq a'$) left behind in the query for the adversary, thereby the adversary's query polynomial Eq.(1) cannot be of the form $c\alpha s$. This establishes Claim 2. $\qquad\square$

Improvisation of Biometrics Authentication and Identification through Keystrokes Pattern Analysis

Dwijen Rudrapal, Smita Das, and Swapan Debbarma

Dept. of Computer Sc. & Engineering
National Institute of Technology, Agartala
Jirania, Tripura (W). India
{dwijen.rudrapal,smitadas.nita}@gmail.com

Abstract. In this paper we presented one fresh approach where the authentic user's typing credentials are combined with the password to make authentication convincingly more secure than the usual password used in both offline and online transactions. With the help of empirical data and prototype implementation of the approach, we justified that our approach is ease of use, improved in security and performance. In normal approach different keystroke event timing is used for user profile creation. Keystroke latency and duration is inadequate for user authentication, which motivates exploring other matrices. In this paper we proposed combination of different matrices and calculation of degree of disorder on keystroke latency as well as duration to generate user profile. Statistical analysis on these matrices evaluates enhanced authentication process.

1 Introduction

Rapidly growing use of computer systems every day vast amounts of sensitive data is maintained by, and transmitted between computer systems. So, necessity of authentication and identification has increased accordingly. Recent studies revels that insider threats from employees and partners as the number one security threat and causing highest financial damage. So, adoption of two-factor authentication systems is most essential issue in the organizations where security is a top priority. Current security solutions have been conventionally categorized into the three factors like:

- Something the user has.
- Something the user knows.
- Something the user is.

The most widely implemented of these three has been password authentication systems [1]. However, passwords are plagued by several inadequacies and number of effective methods is available for attacking passwords. Last decade research shows that biometrics can be employed as 2nd factor of authentication in addition of 1st factor ID-password combination. Keystroke dynamics [2] [3] is one area where research has been showing positive results.

R. Natarajan (Ed.): ICDCIT 2014, LNCS 8337, pp. 287–292, 2014.

2   Motivation

Biometrics [4] offers a valuable approach to extending current security technologies that make it far harder for fraud to take place by preventing ready impersonation of the authorized user.Keystroke dynamics is the process of analyzing the way a user types on a keyboard and identify him based on his habitual typing rhythm. The features that are considered to be account on for authenticating purpose are: keystrokes latencies (fight), duration of a specific keystroke (dwell), pressure (Force of keystrokes), typing speed, frequency of error, overlapping of specific keys combinations, method of error correction.

Through this study we analysis the existing authentication mechanism using keystroke pattern. We also make an effort in using keystroke dynamic in the phases of authentication and verification of users. Due to the higher error rates and potential problems with physical and logical access control convergence till date keystroke dynamics could not fits popularly into the overall enterprise security strategy. To find out better keystroke credentials and matching result, in this paper we combined standard deviation of keystroke duration and degree of disorder for keystroke latency as well as disorder for keystroke duration.

3   Related Work

The pioneering research work done in keystroke dynamics dates back to the Rand report in 1980 inspired by individual unique rhythm when they sent telegraphs. After the Rand report, more experimental studies were conducted that establish the relevance of digraphs in identifying user typing signatures. In 1985, Umphress and Williams [5] conducted a more thorough experiment and gave more credence to the idea that keyboard dynamics was viable. These studies used statistics to compare a claimant typing sample against a reference profile in order to classify users [6]. Garcia's 1986 [7] patent described a scheme where users typed their names in order to authenticate. Three years later, a patent was granted to Young and Hammon [8] for their description of a keystroke authentication method. This patent mentions the use of keystroke latencies and keystroke pressures as important measurements of keystroke behavior. Brown and Rogers [9] also decided to take a more practical approach in their 1994 study on keystroke authentication. Their research was also the first to examine the use of neural networks as a method of classifying claimant vectors. Monrose and Rubin [10] recognized the shortcomings of both neural networks and statistical/mathematical strategies. Mathematical methods which require the storing of numerous reference profiles may suffer from long search times. Monrose and Rubin addressed this issue by clustering user profiles by typing speed. The two key contributions of their study were:

- The idea of using keystroke durations as an additional measurement of typing behave or and.
- The conclusion that certain people exhibited unique typing behaviors even when typing free text. Their overall results were average and they used implementations described in previous work.

4   Proposed Methodology

In this paper we subcategorized our proposed method into capturing keystroke features, calculation of degree of disorder, calculation of standard deviation then profile generation. One registration form has created for capturing keystroke data based on key pressed and release timing events.

4.1   Capturing Keystroke Features

When entering a character on a keyboard, a set of instructions is sent from the keyboard to the computer. Each time a key is pressed down or released, an event is triggered. This event (type according to key press or key release), will have a timestamp Viz. Key-pressed time stamp, Key released time stamp which consists of the number of microseconds (say 120 ms). The timestamp value is used for calculating the time from a key to be pressed down to it is released, and for calculating the time between the keys. In the below figure timestamp shown on three keys.

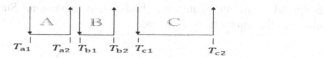

Fig. 1. Timing events of key pressed

4.2   Calculation of Degree of Disorder

A list of elements V of N elements, a simple measure of the degree of disorder [11] (or, simply, the disorder) of V with respect to its ordered complement V can be computed as the sum of the distances between the position of each element in V and the position of the same element in V.

The formula to calculate maximum disorder

$$do_{max} = \frac{|V|^2}{2} \text{ (if | V | is even)} \quad \text{Or } do_{max} = \frac{(|V|^2 - 1)}{2} \quad \text{(if |V| is odd)} \qquad (1)$$

After finding maximum disorder with the help of following formula we founf normalized disorder.

$$do_{nor} = \frac{do}{do \, max} \quad \text{(Where do is total disorder in array)} \qquad (2)$$

Through our experiments, we have taken both the disorder values for flight time and for keystroke duration to segregate user and validate with a suitable threshold value [12].

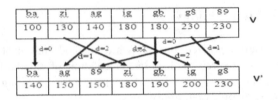

Fig. 2. Distance of the Disordered Element in Sorted Digraph Array

In above cited example array length is 7, so, do_{max}= 24 & do=(0+2+1+2+0+2+1) = 8. so

$$do_{nor} = \frac{do}{do\max} = \frac{8}{24} = 0.333$$

4.3   Calculation of Standard Deviation

Standard deviation is a measure of the dispersion of a set of data from its mean. The more spread apart the data, the higher the deviation. Standard deviation is calculated as the square root of variance.

$$\sqrt{\frac{1}{N}\sum_{i=1}^{N}\left(x_i - x'\right)^2} \text{ | where } x' = \frac{\sum_{i=1}^{N} x_i}{N} \tag{3}$$

In our experiment 8 character password 8 keys pressed durations are 70, 80, 50, 50, 90, 80, 40, and 60. So Standard deviation of key pressed duration is 16.583.

4.4   User Profile Generation

Based on the typing pattern every user will have own profile. A profile is in this work consists with calculated degree of disorder for keystroke duration and digraphs of logins from one user, userID, password, and standard deviation of keystroke deviation. The users underwent several independent login sessions, where 3 logins were attempted in a session (5 sessions).

4.5   Identification and Authentication

The identification step mainly consists, in computing the similarity between the template value (gallery) and real time keystroke capture value (probe) from the typing pattern of the user under controlled environment.

FAR and FRR values calculated based on user valid sample. Threshold value for degree of disorder on digraphs is 0.3 is taken for best result as per the experiments cited by Michal Choras and Piotr Mroczkowski [13]. Threshold value for degree of disorder on key pressed duration is 0.25 [12].

The point where the FAR and FRR in the following graphs cross, is the best possible outcome of the test and treated as Equal Error Rate (EER) [14] [15]. In fig 5 EER shows 10%, and in fig 6. EER result is 4% at threshold value of 0.25 for duration disorder.

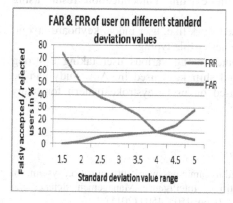

Fig. 3. EER graph on standard deviation

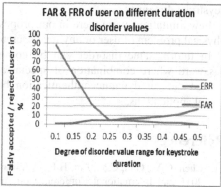

Fig. 4. EER graph on duration disorder

5   Simulation and Analysis of Result

Designing the layout and content of the login was done and tested carefully, making it very much standard without any confusing texts or extra features. Figure 8 shows registration screen along with calculation valued on same screen. At the time of new registration user will enter necessary information along with multiple entry of password. Entry of password must be done in natural rhythm as this gets recorded for future authentication and identification. Same rhythm must be followed at the time of login.

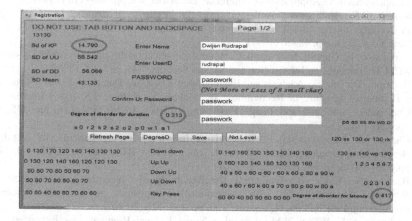

Fig. 5. Registration of user with calculation of key pressed disorder

6   Conclusion and Future Works

This study showed that degree of disorder on keystroke duration is also different for different human. Applying proposed method on collected data result shows FRR of 8% and FAR of 2%, which enhanced the existing authentication result using keystroke dynamics.

Few limitations were there in our proposed work like, user mode, keyboard layout, physical problem of user or any unconsciousness while typing.

In future, same disorder can be compute among various user taking a strong password where combination of special and shift keys used in. Any study can be carried out for dynamic authentication based on user keystroke pattern for many useful applications.

References

1. Chen, C.Y., Gun, C.Y., Lin, H.F.: A fair and dynamic password authentication system. In: 2011 2nd International Conference on Artificial Intelligence, Management Science and Electronic Commerce (AIMSEC), August 8-10, pp. 4505–4509 (2011)
2. Bishop, M.: Computer Security. Addison-Wesley, Boston (2003)
3. Joyce, R., Gupta, G.: Identity Authentication Based on Keystroke Latencies. Communications of the ACM 33(2), 168–176 (1990)
4. Jain, A.K.: Biometric Recognition: How Do I Know Who You Are? In: Roli, F., Vitulano, S. (eds.) ICIAP 2005. LNCS, vol. 3617, pp. 19–26. Springer, Heidelberg (2005)
5. Umphress, D., Williams, G.: Identity verification through keyboard characteristics. Int. J. Man Mach. Stud. 23(3), 263–274 (1985)
6. Obaidat, M.S., Sadoun, B.: Verification of computer users using keystroke dynamics. IEEE Transactions on Systems, Man and Cybernetics 27, 261–269 (1997)
7. Garcia, J.D.: Personal identification apparatus. US Patent 4,621,334 (November 4, 1986)
8. Young, J.R., Hammon, R.W.: Method and apparatus for verifying an individual's identity. US Patent 4,805,222 (February 14, 1989)
9. Brown, M., Rogers, S.J.: A practical approach to user authentication. In: 10th Annual Computer Security Applications Conference, December 5-9, pp. 108–116 (1994)
10. Monrose, F., Rubin, A.: Authentication via keystroke dynamics. In: CCS 1997: Proceedings of the 4th ACM Conference on Computer and Communications Security, New York, USA, pp. 48–56 (1997)
11. Bergadano, F., Gunetti, D., Picardi, C.: User Authentication through Keystroke Dynamics. ACM Transactions on Information and System Security 5(4), 367–397 (2002)
12. Rudrapal, D., Das, S.: Analysis and Evaluation of Keystroke Duration of User's Typing as a Distinctive Measure of Recognition. In: Mohan, S., Kumar, S.S. (eds.) International Conference on Signal and Image Processing (ICSIP). LNEE, vol. 221, pp. 375–385. Springer India (2013)
13. Choraś, M., Mroczkowski, P.: Recognizing Individual Typing Patterns. In: Martí, J., Benedí, J.M., Mendonça, A.M., Serrat, J. (eds.) IbPRIA 2007, Part II. LNCS, vol. 4478, pp. 323–330. Springer, Heidelberg (2007)
14. Bartlow, N., Cukic, B.: Evaluating the Reliability of Credential Hardening through Keystroke Dynamics. In: 17th International Symposium on Software Reliability Engineering, ISSRE 2006, November 7-10, pp. 117–126 (2006)
15. Grabham, N.J., White, N.M.: Use of a Novel Keypad Biometric for Enhanced User Identity Verification. In: IEEE Instrumentation and Measurement Technology Conference Proceedings, IMTC 2008, May 12-15, pp. 12–16 (2008)

Enhancing Privacy in Online Social Communities: Can Trust Help Mitigate Privacy Risks?

Venkata Swamy Martha[1], Nitin Agarwal[2], and Srini Ramaswamy[3]

[1] @WalmartLabs, California, USA
vmartha@walmartlabs.com
[2] University of Arkansas at Little Rock, AR, USA
nxagarwal@ualr.edu
[3] ABB Corporate Research, Bangalore, India
srini@ieee.org

Abstract. The context based privacy model (CBPM) has proved to be successful in strengthening privacy specifications in social media. It allows users to define their own contexts and specify fine-grained policies. Collective-CBPM learns the user policies from community. Our experiments on a sample collection of Facebook data demonstrated the models feasibility in real time systems. These experiments however, did not capture all of the user scenarios; in this paper we simulate users for all possible user scenarios in a social network. We operationalize the C-CBPM model and study its functional behavior. We conduct experiments on a simulated environment. Our results demonstrate that even the most conservative user never incurs risk greater than 20%. Moreover, the risk diminishes to 0 as the trust increases between donors and adopters. The model poses absolutely no risk to other liberal or semi-liberal users.

Keywords: context based privacy model, collective-CBPM, access control, trust, collective intelligence, social media.

1 Introduction

Though there exist privacy concerns, users are motivated to stay with online societies and participate in its user-friendly environment. Additionally, social media poses a challenging problem, i.e., privacy of Personally Identifiable Information (PII). Privacy aware systems address it by deciding "what" information to share. There is a significant body of work in studying security and privacy. However, there is a significant need for improving personal privacy especially in social media eco-systems.

In our previous work, we implemented a context based privacy model(CBPM)[1] that allows users to define their own contexts and specify fine-grained policies. Borrowing concepts from collective intelligence [2], the model further extended to recommend privacy policies for a user[3]. We performed experiments on a sample of real data collected from Facebook and presented the results in [4]. These experiments however, did not capture all of the user scenarios; in this paper we simulate users for various possible user scenarios in a social network.

R. Natarajan (Ed.): ICDCIT 2014, LNCS 8337, pp. 293–298, 2014.

Section 2 describes CBPM to illustrate C-CBPM model, Section 3 discusses the simulation details, Section 4 presents results and discussio, followed by Section 5 drawing conclusions from the results and ideas for further research.

2   Background

Context Based Privacy Model (CBPM): A context is defined as an abstract state of a subject and rich in expressing status of an entity compared to user or role identity. A privacy policy is defined as a rule to/not to share a data element from a given data set in a given context. The privacy policies for all the data sets and for all the contexts makes up a matrix called CBPM matrix. An entry in a CBPM matrix can be represented as:

$$(C_i, D_j) = 0 \ or \ 1 \tag{1}$$

where, C_i is a context, and D_j is a data set.

Collective- Context Based Privacy Model (C-CBPM): Donors, who are ready to donate, provide their CBPM matrices in C-CBPM donation pool. The donor could select parts (rows and columns) of his/her matrix to make a donation. Adoption of a matrix from C-CBPM involves three phases. 1: Requesting Donations, 2: Processing Requests, 3. Aggregation of donations. The aggregation matrix for an adopter 'X' is obtained using the following formula.

$$M_X = M_X +_{OR} [t(A, X)\mathcal{M}_A +_{OR} t(B, X)\mathcal{M}_B +_{OR} t(C, X)\mathcal{M}_C]_\mu \tag{2}$$

Where 'M_A' is a donation matrix from user 'A'.
'$\mathcal{M}_A$' is the masked matrix for the donation 'M_A' and is defined as,

$$\mathcal{M}_A(i, j) = M_A(i, j) \ if \ adopter \ accepts \ donation \ for \ the \ context \ 'i'$$
$$and \ dataset \ 'j'$$
$$= 0 \qquad otherwise$$

The matrix binarization operation '$[]_\mu$' on a matrix is defined as,

$$[t(A, X)M_A(i, j)]_\mu = 1 \quad if \ t(A, X) * M_A(i, j) > \mu,$$
$$= 0 \quad otherwise$$

'μ' is a binarization threshold. The threshold value ranges from '0' to '1'. And the matrix aggregation operator '$+_{OR}$' is defined as,

$$(M_A +_{OR} M_B)(i, j) = 0 \quad if \ M_A(i, j) = M_B(i, j) = 0,$$
$$= 1 \quad otherwise$$

It is trivial to show the $+_{OR}$ addition operation is commutative, associative, transitive, and closed. Each donation is associated with a trust value denoted as t(A,X). Trust values always lie in the range of [0,1]. Eq 2 gives us derived matrix for user 'X' from available donations. More detailed discussion of the C-CBPM model was presented in [3].

3   Simulation

Due to operational challenges with integration of the CCBPM in a real world social network (e.g., Facebook) at a large scale, in this section we simulate a social network of users with a synthetic privacy policies.

Simulation Parameters. There exists a set of users called user pool and corresponding CBPM matrices. Strength of the privacy policy of a user, is measured through "Privacy Index", which is defined as,

"Privacy Index (PI): Fraction of zeros in the CBPM matrix"[1]

Hence, a higher value of PI indicates the conservativeness of a user. Consider a user 'A' from the user pool as an adopter (learning privacy policies from community) and rest of the users are donors. Though the adopter 'A' embodies a CBPM matrix, we apply C-CBPM for the user 'A' to generate suggestion matrix derived from donations. We call the actual matrix of the adopter 'A' as "Expected Matrix (EM)" and the recommended matrix from C-CBPM model as "Observed Matrix (OM)". This strategy helps in two ways One, every user has a CBPM matrix (EM) which can serve as the ground truth for validation. Second, this allows us to quantify trust between adopter 'A' and donors. Though similarity may not always imply trust or vice versa, however research has shown strong evidence to counter this intuition [5]. We used EM of the adopter 'A' and CBPM matrix of a donor to calculate trust between the adopter 'A' and the donor, as defined below,

"Trust (t): Fraction of common entries in the matrix"

It must be noted that the model is adaptable to explicit trust scores. Trust values always lie in the range of [0,1]. Inducing acquired knowledge from trust scores, we classified the donors into several trust domains.

"Trust Domain (TD)[a,b]: Set of donors having trust scores with an adopter between 'a' and 'b' "'

We considered Trust Domain interval as 0.1 and each Trust Domain is represented by its upper limit. For example, TD=0.7 represents Trust Domain (0.6, 0.7][2] . To quantify a donation, we introduce a parameter called "Fraction of Donation (FoD)". FoD lies in [0,1]. The binarization parameter 'μ' in equ. 3, we call it threshold, ranges from '0' to '1'. We considered every 'μ' in (0,1] with an interval of '0.1. For an adopter 'A', C-CBPM exploits available donor matrices for a given FoD, TD, μ and generates "Observed Matrix (OM)". To address diverse real time scenarios, we apply C-CBPM for every FoD in (0,1], TD in (0.1,1], μ in (0,1] with an interval of 0.1.

---

[1] It is extremely challenging to quantify privacy as different attributes could have very different privacy sensitivity. The proposed Privacy Index measure is a very basic attempt toward this direction.

[2] The notation (a,b] denotes that the interval is open at a and closed at b. In other words, for any x, a$<$x$\leq$b.

Evaluation Metrics. Accuracy shows precision of the model for given parameters.

$$Accuracy = \frac{\sum_{i,j} (EM(i,j) \equiv OM(i,j))}{\sum_{i,j} 1} \tag{3}$$

Here the operator '$\equiv$' refers to boolean equivalence and is written as "$a \equiv b = \neg(a +_{XOR} b)$".

Next evaluation metric is "Risk Factor" that assesses the risk posed by a wrong recommendation. In other words, Risk Factor denotes the number of times an unshared data element is recommended to to share. This amounts to the risk incurred from the policies suggested by C-CBPM. Mathematically, Risk Factor is defined as,

$$Risk Factor RF = \frac{\sum_{i,j} (\neg(EM(i,j) \wedge OM(i,j)))}{\sum_{i,j} 1} \tag{4}$$

Likewise, we also calculate strength of privacy policy in OM by calculating Privacy Index (PI). The PI of observed matrix is represented by PI_{OM}.

3.1   Experimental Setup

The experiment is carried out in three phases: 1. Synthetic donation preparation, 2. Applying C-CBPM, 3. Evaluating the observations.

- Phase 1. Synthetic donation preparation: We can generate a matrix of size 1000x1000 with desired PI (desired number of zeros in a matrix) using Java's random number generation method. Here, we created a user pool of 100 users with PI values from 0 to 1 with an interval of 0.01.
- Phase 2. Applying C-CBPM: A user from the user pool is selected to name it adopter 'A' and its matrix is expected matrix (EM). Except the adopter, all the other users in user pool are donors. Therefore, we have 99 donors. With FoD=0, TD=0.1, and μ=0, the C-CBPM model generates OM for the adopter 'A'. The OM is evaluated with EM using the given metrics. This step (C-CBPM) is iterated by incrementing FoD, TD, and μ by 0.1 until 1.0. The whole phase is repeated by selecting other users in user pool as adopter, individually.
- Phase 3. Evaluation: The EM and OM are compared using "Accuracy", RF and PI metrics.

3.2   Simulation Results

We tabulated the results from each iteration. Each run in simulation is a row in the table. There are 100,000 rows in table (100 users * 10 TD * 10 FoD * 10). We then summarized the table for each user, i.e., for each EM having PI in (0,1]. For an EM and TD, we estimate average, minimum, and maximum of evaluation metrics i.e. Accuracy (A) and Risk Factor (RF). To demonstrate the models capability we chose users with $PI_{EM} = 1, 0.99, 0.5$ and 0.01 (from 'share nothing' to 'share all') and presented the plots from the table in Figure 1.

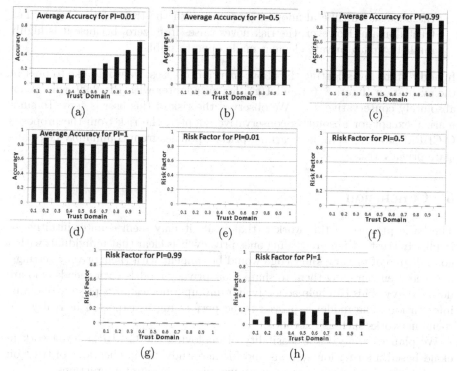

Fig. 1. Plots depicting behavior of C-CBPM for adopters with PI=0.01,0.5,0.99,1[3]

4 Discussion

Due to space constraints, we present detailed analysis for users with extreme characteristics, i.e., PI = 0, 0.5, and 1.

- Conservative user ($PI_{EM}=1$, i.e., 'share nothing'): From figure 1(d), the model always achieves high accuracy with the lowest value of 80%. Regardless of the trust values with the donors, a conservative user following the C-CBPM model will never incur risk more than 20% as shown in figure 1(h). Further the risk can also be reduced by adopting donations from highly trusted donors and less trusted donors.
- Semi-liberal user ($PI_{EM}=0.5$): The average accuracy for the semi-liberal adopter (figure 1(b)), i.e., $PI_{EM}=0.5$, is 50%. The model promises at least 50% accuracy irrespective of the other parameters. More importantly, figure 1(f) shows that the risk of adopting the recommended CBPM matrix is always zero to the adopter. Since the risk factor is zero, not even a single private element is made public.
- Liberal user ($PI_{EM}=0.01$, i.e., 'share all'): Here in all the instances, the adopter gets donations from more conservative user. This makes the model less accurate (figure 1(a)) compared to figures 1(b), 1(c) and 1(d). Though

the accuracy of liberal adopter increases with the trust of the donors, i.e., trust domain. However, the risk never raises from zero, because it is highly unlikely that a private element made open to public.

In addition to investigating the above-mentioned cases, we would like to present the evaluation (figures 1(c) and 1(g)) for an adopter with PI=0.99, who is not absolutely conservative user. We observed the risk of this user is zero. To summarize, except for absolutely conservative adopter, the risk from the proposed C-CBPM model is zero, i.e. learning pricacy policies from community help mitigate privacy risks.

5   Conclusion

The basic premise of this work is that while it may seem counter-intuitive to implicitly trust a friend regarding ones privacy, it is clear that individuals with a good degree of privacy knowledge would be diligent with their privacy settings, and hence encouraging them to share their privacy models with friends who are not as savvy. This can help collectively ramp up a novice users privacy of online information. The model is proved to be performing as expected in real world social networks such as Facebook.

We plan to analyze the feasibility of deploying the C-CBPM framework in cloud-based information systems and further study the implications of trust on user information privacy and security vis--vis service-level interactions.

Acknowledgment. This work was supported, in part, by grants from the NSF (under Grant Nos. CNS- 0619069, EPS-0701890, OISE 0729792, CNS-0855248, EPS-0918970, and IIS-1110868) and Office of Naval Research (Award number: N000141010091).

References

1. Venkata Swamy, M., Ramaswamy, S., Agarwal, N.: Cbpm: Context based privacy model. In: IEEE Social Computing (SocialCom), pp. 1050–1055 (2010)
2. Surowiecki, J.: The Wisdom of Crowds. Anchor Books (2005)
3. Venkata Swamy, M., Agarwal, N., Ramaswamy, S.: Collective context based privacy model. Journal of Ambient Intelligence and Humanized Computing (2012) (to appear)
4. Venkata Swamy, M., Agarwal, N., Ramaswamy, S.: Enhancing privacy using community driven recommendations: An investigation with facebook data. In: Proceedings of the 19th AMCIS Conference, AMCIS 2013. AIS (2013)
5. Einwiller, S., Geissler, U., Will, M.: Engendering trust in internet businesses using elements of corporate branding. In: Proceedings of the 16th AMCIS Conference, AMCIS 2000. AIS (2000)

Detection and Reduction of Impulse Noise in RGB Color Image Using Fuzzy Technique

Debashis Mishra[1], Isita Bose[1], Madhabananda Das[2], and B.S.P. Mishra[2]

[1] School of Computer Engineering, KIIT University
{debashis.engg,isitabose89}@gmail.com
[2] School of Computer Engineering, KIIT University
{mndas_prof,bsmishrafcs}@kiit.ac.in

Abstract. A concept of impulse noise reduction method for an RGB color image with a fuzzy detection phase is introduced and a fuzzy de-noising procedure is used to filter the color image. In this paper, each color component is correlated to the other two corresponding color components to overcome the color disorder on edge and texture pixel. Here the filtering technique is only applied to noisy pixel, detected by fuzzy technique, while preserving the color and edge sharpness. Experimental results show that the proposed method provides noteworthy improvement on other non-fuzzy and fuzzy filters.

Keywords: RGB color, fuzzy filter, image processing, impulse noise, fuzzy rule based system, membership function.

1 Introduction

Image processing is a technique to enhance raw images received from cameras/sensors placed on satellites, space probes and aircrafts or pictures taken in normal day-to-day life for various applications. Noise reduction from digital image is most important problem in image processing. Noise reduction is mostly helpful in case of satellite-taken photos, medical oriented photos like ultrasound photos etc. Over the last several years, number of fuzzy based and non-fuzzy filters have been developed for this purpose. e.g., Histogram Adaptive Fuzzy filter (HAF) [4], Adaptive Fuzzy Switching filter (ASFS) [1], the Fuzzy Similarity-based filter (FSF) [5], Fuzzy Impulse Noise Detection & Reduction method (FIDRM) [3], Fuzzy Random Impulse Noise Reduction Method (FRINRM) [7] etc. Generally grayscale images (2D images) are well suited for these filters, But we can apply these into different color component (red, green and blue) separately. This technique yields many disorder in specially edge and texture. So to minimize this type of disorder, different types of non-linear vector based approaches are developed.

A number of vector based impulse noise reduction methods have been introduced. Most of them follow the vector median filter(VMF) concept [11] [12] [13] . Classical vector filters successfully remove noise but in same time blur the image. All these filters have the following disadvantages.

1. The noise reduction capacity is inversely proportional to noise level .
2. The noises are clustered into large array.

R. Natarajan (Ed.): ICDCIT 2014, LNCS 8337, pp. 299–310, 2014.
© Springer International Publishing Switzerland 2014

The main reason of their disadvantages is the consideration of each pixel as a whole unit in vector based approach.

In many color image noise reduction techniques, generally color components are not compared and only the same grayscale noise reduction techniques are applied to each red, green and blue color spaces separately. But in the proposed method, each color component of a pixel is compared with other color components of the same pixel which overcomes such disadvantages. Unlike other methods, the de-noising technique which is applied to the detected noisy pixel only, is better in terms of algorithm time complexity.

In section 2 of this paper, background of this paper containing color model, impulse noise and fuzzy technique is explained elaborately. In section 3 the detection of impulse noise in color image is described elaborately. In section 4 the de-noising methodology of the noisy image is explained. In section 5 we describe the experimental results. Section 6 describes the motivation to present an image processing related paper in the conference   and finally the conclusion is drawn in section 7.

2   Background

2.1   Color Model

A color model is a mathematical model which explains the way colors can be represented as a vector of numbers, typically as three values of color component. The purpose of a color model is to facilitate the specification of colors in some standard acceptable manner. The RGB color model is basically used for sensing, representing and displaying images in electronic systems, such as televisions and computers, though it has also been used in conventional photography, where the three components of the image are Red, Green and Blue and all other colors are represented as three values of these three color components[14]. We propose a color image filtering method where Red-Green-Blue (RGB) color space is used as basic color space, shown in Fig.1.

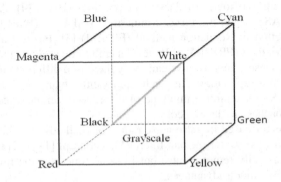

Fig. 1. R-G-B Color Model

2.2 Impulse Noise

Impulse noise is characterized in terms of impulsive sequences which occur in the form of short duration, high energy spikes attaining large amplitude with probability higher than that predicted by a Gaussian density model [10][6]. Generally the acquisition and transmission of image through communication channels causes this type of impulse noise [10][6]. It is generally recognized as salt & pepper noise. Impulse noise can be classified into 1) fixed valued impulse noise and 2) random valued impulse noise [3] [6] [10]. If P_i denotes the input noisy image and O_i denotes the original image at i^{th} pixel where η_i is the noise added with probability δ.

$$P_i^{col} = \begin{cases} O_i^{col}, & \text{with probability } 1\text{-}\delta \\ \eta_i^{col}, & \text{with probability } \delta \end{cases}$$

Here the index i the the 2-D pixel position and col is the color component, i.e., col=R or col=G or col=B as we use RGB color space.

2.3 Fuzzy Logic

Fuzzy Logic is the powerful tool, which deals with reasoning that is approximate rather fixed or exact. In traditional concept, variables may take on true (1) or false (0) values where as in Fuzzy logic variable may have a truth value that ranges in degree between 0 and 1[15]. When linguistic variables are used, these degrees may be managed by specific function named as membership function [15]. Human knowledge can be processed in terms of fuzzy if-then rules which can be represented using fuzzy set theory and fuzzy logic. In this paper, Fuzzy logic concept has been used to detect noise from image and it filters only noisy pixels without affecting the color and edge sharpness.

Image processing using fuzzy logic consists of the following vital stages 1)Fuzzification of image 2) Modification of Membership values and 3) De-fuzzification of image. Image Fuzzification and de-fuzzification are only the steps to represent the image data into fuzzy technique. The most important step among these three is the second step i.e. modification of membership values.

3 Detection of Impulse Noise in RGB Color Image

The main significant difference of the proposed method in the paper compared to other methods is to detect the noise using color components. The detection phase lies on the idea of finding the color components which are dissimilar 1) to the neighbor pixels in the same color component and 2) to the corresponding color component of the two other color band. Each pixel is processed with the proposed method which means that a fuzzy membership degree ranging from 0 and 1 in the fuzzy set "Noise-Free" will be assigned to each color component.

Here we are using R-G-B color space which means that each pixel of color image P_i contains three 2-D color components . So we can write

$$P_i = (P_i^R, P_i^G, P_i^B)$$

First we consider a sliding window of size n X n where n = 2m+1, m ϵ N where the acting pixel will be at center of the window and in total $k = (n^2-1)$ neighbors pixels will be there. If we consider a 3 X 3 sliding window then there will be 8 neighbors denoted as P_1 to P_8 shown in Fig.2.

	-1	0	1
-1	P_{1} (NW)	P_{2} (N)	P_{3} (NE)
0	P_{4} (W)	$(P_i)_{i=[0\ 0]}$	P_{5} (E)
1	P_{6} (SW)	P_{7} (S)	P_{8} (SE)

Fig. 2. A 3 X 3 sliding filter

The detection phase consists of five steps discussed elaborately below.

3.1   Calculation of Absolute Value Differences

In one n X n matrix, we first calculate the absolute differences of all k neighbor pixels from the P_0 pixel, where $k = 1$ to n^2-1 and P_0 is the processed pixel, as follows

$$\Delta P_k^R = | P_0^R - P_k^R |, \qquad \Delta P_k^G = | P_0^G - P_k^G |, \qquad \Delta P_k^B = | P_0^B - P_k^B | \qquad (1)$$

where ΔP_k^R, ΔP_k^G, ΔP_k^B are the absolute value differences with the neighbor pixels at position k in red, green and blue components respectively.

3.2   Computing Membership Degree

After computing the absolute value differences, we have to know that these differences are small or not. Small is one linguistic term or a fuzzy word which can be represented in fuzzy set with a membership degree. Before computing membership degree, we need to observe how these small values change according to different inputs of absolute differences. If differences are relatively small then membership degree will be high and it gradually decreases with increasing differences and after a certain value it decreases faster as compared to previous rate and finally becomes zero. So we can take a zmf (z-shaped membership function) which is defined as

$$zmf(x, [\alpha\ \beta]) = \begin{cases} 1, & \text{if } x \leq \alpha \\ 1 - 2\left(\frac{x-\alpha}{\beta-\alpha}\right)^2, & \text{if } \alpha \leq x \leq \frac{\alpha+\beta}{2} \\ 2\left(\frac{x-\alpha}{\beta-\alpha}\right)^2, & \text{if } \frac{\alpha+\beta}{2} \leq x \leq \beta \\ 0, & \text{if } x \geq \beta \end{cases} \tag{2}$$

where α and β are the parameters and it has been experimentally found that $\alpha = 20$ and $\beta = 75$ gives us better result, which means when the absolute difference is up to 20 then the membership degree is high (1), it decreases and after 75 it becomes low (0), the graphical presentation is shown in Fig.3.

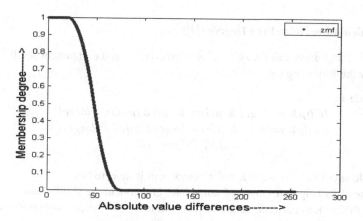

Fig. 3. Z-shaped membership function with params [20 75]

3.3 Degree of Similarity Calculation

After calculation of membership degrees, denoted as $Z_1(\Delta P_k^R)$, $Z_1(\Delta P_k^G)$ and $Z_1(\Delta P_k^B)$ for $k = 1,...., n^2-1$, these are used to find the similarity of processed pixel with other surrounding pixels of same color band. Here Fuzzy AND operation is used as Fuzzy conjunction operator and represented as T-norm [16]. The degree of similarity for Red component is given as

$$\mu^R = \prod_{j=1}^{k} Z_1(\Delta P_j^R) \tag{3}$$

and μ^G and μ^B will be calculated analogously, where μ^R, μ^G and μ^B are the degree of similarity for Red, Green and Blue components respectively.

3.4 Degree of Similarities among Different Color Components of Same Pixel

The core part of this paper to correlate the color component to preserve the color sharpness. So now we compare the other color components of the processed pixel to find out the similarities. we determine whether the local differences in one color component neighborhood correspond to the other color components. This joint similarity is given as

$$\mu_k^{RG} = Z_2\left(\left|Z_1\left(\Delta P_k^R\right) - Z_1\left(\Delta P_k^G\right)\right|\right) \tag{4}$$

and μ_k^{GB} and μ_k^{RB} will be calculated analogously, where Z_2 is the Z-shaped membership function (zmf) with $\alpha = 0.01$ and $\beta = 0.15$ which are experimentally illustrated. Now joint similarity is calculated as

$$\mu^{RG} = \prod_{j=1}^{k} \mu_j^{RG} \tag{5}$$

similarly μ^{RG}, μ^{GB} can be computed.

3.5   Calculating Noise Free Degree (Nf)

The membership degree in fuzzy set Noise-Free(Nf) in red component for P_0^R is calculated by the following rule.

Fuzzy Rule 1:
$$IF\ ((\mu R == large)\ \&(\mu G == large)\ \&(\mu RG == large))\ |$$
$$((\mu R == large)\&(\mu G == large)\ \&(\mu RG == large))$$
$$=> (Nf(P_0^R) = large)$$

The rule says that a Noise-free color component is detected as
1. Some of its neighbor values of same color component are similar and
2. The differences between neighbor pixels of other two color components are similar to the current one.

This rule contains four AND (&) i.e conjunctions and one OR (|) i.e. disjunction which can be replaced by triangular norm and conorm [1], respectively [16]. So Fuzzy rule 1 can be written as

$$Nf_{P_0^R} = \mu^R \mu^{RG} \mu^G + \mu^R \mu^{RB} \mu^B - (\mu^R)^2 \mu^G \mu^B \mu^{RB} \mu^{RG} \tag{6}$$

Same for green and blue components can be done analogously and the equations are given as

$$Nf_{P_0^G} = \mu^G \mu^{RG} \mu^R + \mu^G \mu^{GB} \mu^B - (\mu^G)^2 \mu^B \mu^R \mu^{GB} \mu^{RG} \tag{7}$$

$$Nf_{P_0^B} = \mu^B \mu^{RB} \mu^R + \mu^B \mu^{GB} \mu^G - (\mu^B)^2 \mu^R \mu^G \mu^{RB} \mu^{BG} \tag{8}$$

The fuzzy set *Noise(N)* for each color component can be derived by the help of standard negation i.e. $N = 1 - Nf$. we can also take Yager's complement [2] or Sugeno's complement [3] [16]. Examples of noise detection by the proposed method is shown in Fig.4 and Fig.5.

---

[1] Algebraic Product and Algebraic Sum are taken as T-norm and T-conorm or S-norm operators which are defined as $T(a,b) = ab$ and $S(a,b) = a+b-ab$ respectively. [16]

[2] Yager's Complement is given as $N_\omega = (1 - a^\omega)^{1/\omega}$, if $\omega = 1$ then $N_1 = (1 - a)$ [16].

[3] Sugeno's Complement is given as $N_s = (1-a)/(1+sa)$, if $s = 0$ then $N_0 = (1-a)$ [16].

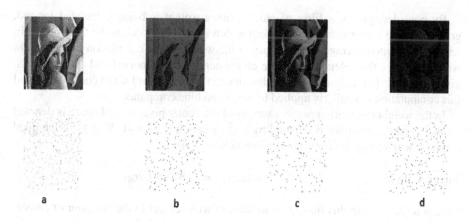

Fig. 4. First rows (a) lena image with 5% noise (b) R-component of noisy image (c) G-component of noisy image (d) B-component of noisy image; second row (a) Membership degree N_f (b) Membership degree N_f^R (c) Membership degree N_f^G (d) Membership degree N_f^B

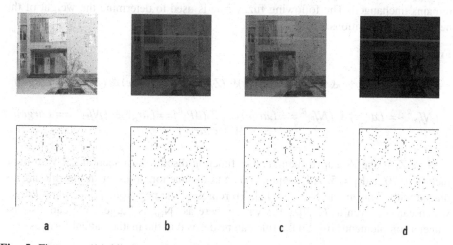

Fig. 5. First rows (a) kiit image with 10% noise (b) R-component of noisy image (c) G-component of noisy image (d) B-component of noisy image; second row (a) Membership degree N_f (b) Membership degree N_f^R (c) Membership degree N_f^G (d) Membership degree N_f^B

4   De-noising Method

The result of the fuzzy noise detection method is being used in the de-noising of the impulse noise in this paper. As discussed in the detection phase when some components of a color are found noisy, it is filtered in a proportional degree that is calculated by comparing with other color components which give the estimated values to evaluate the de-noising process.

By considering n X n filter window a fuzzy weight is being calculated for red, green and blue components of each pixel which is used to calculate the filter output in terms of weighted average of the values in the window. The calculation of the weight which involves the calculation of the component to be de-noised and its neighbors, gives the noise-free output. Here we describe the computation for red components and this computation is similarly applied to green and blue components.

In the weight calculation process weight of the center pixel for red space is denoted as W_0^R and the neighbor is denoted by W_k^R, where $k=1,.....n^2-1$. Weight of the pixel can be calculated by the fuzzy rules given below.

Fuzzy Rule 2:   *IF* ($N\!f_{P0}^R$ == *Large*) => (W_0^R = *Large*)

we can directly write this fuzzy rule as follows with respect to the behavior of antecedent and consequent[16].

$$N\!f_{P0}^R = W_0^R \qquad (9)$$

If the component to be de-noised, is noise-free, then no weighting assignment is performed i.e. the weight of the neighbor pixels are assigned zero   and value of pixel remains unchanged. The following fuzzy rule is used to determine the weight of the neighbors at k positions.

Fuzzy Rule 3:

IF (($N\!f_{P0}^R$ ~= *Large*)& ($N\!f_{Pk}^R$ == *Large*)& ($Z_1(\Delta P_k^G)$ == *Large*) & ($N\!f_{Pk}^G$ == *Large*))

|

($N\!f_{P0}^R$ ~= *Large*) & ($N\!f_{Pk}^R$ == *Large*) & ($Z_1(\Delta P_k^B)$==*Large*)& ($N\!f_{Pk}^B$ == *Large*)
=> (W_k^R = *large*)

Here Z_1 is the Z-shaped membership function discussed in section 2.2 with parameters $\alpha=20$ and $\beta=75$. All conjunctions and disjunctions present in the rule are replaced with T-norm and S-norm[1][16]. To represent the negation "$N\!f_{P0}^R$ is not Large" which can be given as $(1-N\!f_{P0}^R)$ is written here as "N_{P0}^R is Large". We can also use Yager's complement[2][16]. So the rule can be derived in the mathematical form as

$$W_k^R = N_{P0}^R \, N\!f_{Pk}^R Z_1(\Delta P_k^G) \, N\!f_{Pk}^G \quad + \quad N_{P0}^R N\!f_{Pk}^R Z_1(\Delta P_k^B) N\!f_{Pk}^B$$
$$- \quad N_{P0}^R N\!f_{Pk}^R \; Z_1(\Delta P_k^G) \, N\!f_{Pk}^G \cdot N_{P0}^R N\!f_{Pk}^R Z_1(\Delta P_k^B) N\!f_{Pk}^B \qquad (10)$$

The idea which is applied here is that if two colors have similar G and B components then it is found that R component is also similar with them. The value of P_0^R can be calculated applying the weighted average operation as :

$$P_0^R = \frac{\sum_{k=0}^{n^2-1} W_k^R P_k^R}{\sum_{k=0}^{n^2-1} W_k^R} \qquad (11)$$

For k={0, ... , n^2-1} this method gives good estimate values, but it generates some disordered values when W_k^R=0. It can be happened in two cases.

1) When $Nf_{P0}^R = Nf_{P0}^G = Nf_{P0}^B = 0$ i.e. when all color components are noisy which gives no similarities.

2) When $Z_1(\Delta P_k^G) = Z_1(\Delta P_k^B) = 0$. It can be happened in an extreme noisy case.

If these cases arise then we have to apply different methods of de-noising, where we can use Weighted Vector Median (WVM) method, in which it gives an output of P_{j*} from N size vector where $j^* = \arg_j ,\min \sum_{k=1}^N Wj||Pj - Pk||$ where W_j denotes weight of the color vector at position j and $||F_j-F_k||$ is the Euclidian norm[17]. The noise free degree Nf_{Pj} of each color vector P_j is computed as $Nf_{Pj} = Nf_{Pj}^R Nf_{Pj}^G Nf_{Pj}^B$ i.e. the conjunction of the noise free degree of each component. Here only those vectors which are noise-free are taken into account to avoid the noisy effect for calculation of the output, so it takes all vector for which Nf_{Pj}>0. If Nf_{Pj}=0 for j={0,....., n^2-1},we can't apply WVM and need to use other fuzzy and non-fuzzy filters in the case to de-noise the detected noisy pixel by the proposed method in section 2.

5   Experimental Results and Analysis

We have input different images to this filter with different proportion of impulse noise and yield the resultant de-noised image with their PSNR values which are listed in the Table 1 (comparisons are listed using Baboon image as input). PSNR results of other filter are taken from the reference papers related to those filters. We have placed the kiit and Baboon images in this paper with the input noisy and output de-noised images in Fig 6 and 7.

a   b

Fig. 6. (a) - kiit image impure with 10% impulse noise (b)- de-noised image

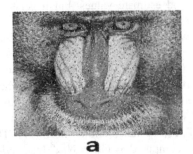 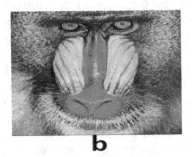

Fig. 7. Baboon impure with 5% impulse noise (b)- de-noised image

We have compared the proposed filtering method explain in this paper with other filters [1] [3] [5] [7][11]-[13] in terms of PSNR, considering the standard image as Baboon image shown in Fig 7, and the PSNR values are listed in Table 1.

Table 1. Comaprision of diiferent filters with the proposed filter considering Baboon image (255 X 255) introducing different percentage of impulse noise

Filters	5%	10%	15%	20%	25%	30%
Noisy Image	21.89	18.79	16.93	16.03	15.10	14.19
VMF	22.94	22.69	22.25	21.91	21.60	21.56
ASVMF	24.87	24.12	22.79	21.98	21.90	21.63
FISF	25.31	24.07	23.31	22.96	22.29	21.78
FIDRMC	26.03	25.32	24.67	23.88	23.32	22.76
Median	23.05	22.78	22.60	22.33	21.89	21.72
HAF	23.05	22.77	22.40	21.91	21.43	20.81
Proposed Method	**30.68**	**29.03**	**27.32**	**26.02**	**25.12**	**24.34**

After a fuzzy correlated noise detection method we can apply different filtering techniques to filter the noisy pixels, as the main focus is on detecting the noisy pixel in a real time application and to de-noise only those noisy pixels preserving the edge sharpness.

6   Motivation

Now-a-days image processing is in focus in almost every area of research though it itself is a very vast research field. Image is a source of information which is used in various fields like medical or health science (ultra sound etc.)[18], space science[19], environmental science[20], etc. Reduction of noise from an image is a very vital issue since all the systems used in the areas like IT infrastructures, environmental resources, and health applications etc. need accurate and relevant information for better results. Still images, videos, and animations etc. which are some of the components of multimedia are transmitted for information sharing. Here reduction of noise is always necessary for obtaining clear information. As image processing is almost present as a part of discussion in most of other research areas, we have been motivated to work on image processing and more specifically on detection and reduction of noise from digital color images as image is an imperative source of information and retrieval of correct information is essential.

7   Conclusion

In this paper, an advanced fuzzy filer is introduced for an R-G-B color image. The proposed method is different from the other methods on the basis of using the color information to detect the noise. We found that 1) the method reduces the impulse noise 2) it doesn't disorder color and edge sharpness. As future work, we will work on the proposed filter to reduce other different types of noise such as Gaussian noise, mixture of different types of noise etc.

References

1. Xu, H., Zhu, G., Peng, H., Wang, D.: Adaptive fuzzy switching filter for images corrupted by impulse noise. Pattern Recognit. Lett. 25, 1657–1663 (2004)
2. Nachtegael, M., Van der Weken, D., De Witte, V., Schulte, S., Melange, T., Kerre, E.E.: Color Image retrieval fuzzy similarity measures and fuzzy partitions. In: IEEE, ICIP, vol. VI (2007)
3. Schulte, S., Nachtegael, M., De Witte, V., Van der Weken, D., Kerre, E.E.: A fuzzy impulse noise detection and reduction method. IEEE Trans. Image Process. 15(5), 1153–1162 (2006)
4. Wang, J.H., Liu, W.J., Lin, L.D.: Histogram-Based fuzzy filter for image restoration. IEEE Trans. Syst., Man, Cybern. B, Cybern. 32(2), 230–238 (2002)
5. Kalaykov, L., Tolt, G.: Real-time image noise cancellation based on fuzzy similarity. In: Nachtegael, M., Van der Weken, D., Van De Ville, D., Kerre, E.E. (eds.) Fuzzy Filters for Image Processing, 1st edn., vol. 122, pp. 54–71. Physica Verlag, Heidelberg (2003)
6. Schulte, S., Morillas, S., Gregori, V., Kerre, E.E.: A New fuzzy color correlated impulse noise reduction method. IEEE Trans. on Image Processing 16(10) (October 2007)
7. Schulte, S., De Witte, V., Nachtegael, M., Van der Weken, D., Kerre, E.E.: Fuzzy random impulse noise reduction method. Fuzzy Sets Syst. 158(3), 270–283 (2007)
8. Schulte, S., Witte, V.D., Nachtegael, M., Weken, D.V.: Fuzzy Two-step Filter for Impulse Noise Reduction from Color Image. IEEE Trans. Image Processing 15(11), 3567–3578 (2006)
9. Rao, G.V., Somayajula, S.P.K., Mohan Rao, C.P.V.N.J.: Implementation of Impulse noise reduction method to color images using fuzzy logic. Global Journal of Computer Science and Technology 11(22), 72–75 (2011)
10. Plataniotis, K.N., Venetsanopouls, A.N.: Color image processing and Applications. Springer, Berlin (2000)
11. Lukac, R.: Adaptive vector median filter. Pattern Recognit. Lett. 24(12), 1889–1899 (2003)

12. Barni, M., Cappellini, V., Mecocci, A.: Fast Vector median filter based on Euclidean norm approximate. IEEE Signal Process. Lett. 1(6), 92–94 (1994)
13. Lukac, R., Plataniotis, K.N., Venetsanoloulos, A.N., Smolka, B.: A statistically-switched adaptive vector median filter. J. Intell. Robot. Syst. 42(4), 361–391 (2005)
14. Süsstrunk, S., Buckley, R., Swen, S.: Standard RGB Color space, Laboratory of Audio-visual Comm(EPFL), Xerox Architecture Center, Apple Computer Lausanne, Switzerland, Vebster
15. Morillas, S., Schulte, S., Kerre, E.E., Peris-Fajarnés, G.: A New Fuzzy Impulse Noise Detection Method for Colour Images. In: Ersbøll, B.K., Pedersen, K.S. (eds.) SCIA 2007. LNCS, vol. 4522, pp. 492–501. Springer, Heidelberg (2007)
16. Jang, J.-S.R., Sun, C.-T., Mizutani, E.: Neuro-Fuzzy and Soft Computing. PHI Learning Pvt., Ltd.
17. Nachbar, J.: Basic properties of Euclidean Norm. Economics 511 (2009)
18. Suapang, P., Dejhan, K., Yimmun, S.: Medical Image Processing and Analysis for Nuclear Medicine Diagnosis. In: International Conference on Control, Automation and Systems, KINTEX, Gyeonggi-do, Korea, October 27-30 (2010)
19. Laban, N., Nasr, A., ElSaban, M., Onsi, H.: Spatial Cloud Detection and Retrieval System for Satellite Images. International Journal of Advanced Computer Science and Applications 3(12) (2012)
20. Allen, M.P., Graham, E., Ahamadian, S., Ko, T., Yuen, E., Girod, L., Hamilton, M., Estrin, D.: Interactive Environmental Sensing: Signal and Image processing Challenges, Center for Embedded Network Sensing, University of California, Los Angeles

An Efficient Method for Speckle Reduction in Ultrasound Liver Images for e-Health Applications

Suganya Ramamoorthy[1,*], Rajaram Siva Subramanian[2], and Deebika Gandhi[1]

[1] Department of Computer Science and Engineering, Thiagarajar College of Engineering, Madurai-15, India
rsuganya@tce.edu, deebika@tce.edu
[2] Department of Electronics and Communication Engineering, Thiagarajar College of Engineering, Madurai-15, India
rajaram_siva@tce.edu

Abstract. There are seemingly an endless number of possible applications of information technology to health service management. The area of e-health is very broad, covers topics such as telemedicine, healthcare score cards, audits and information systems etc. In this paper, the focus is on identifying liver diseases at non invasive & low cost ultrasound modality. Our ultimate goal is to improve gray scale ultrasound images by removing speckles present in it. A new speckle noise reduction and image enhancement method, i.e. Laplacian pyramid nonlinear diffusion with Gaussian filter (Modified LPND), is proposed for medical ultrasound imaging. In the proposed Modified LPND, a coupled modified diffusivity function and gradient threshold is applied in laplacian pyramid domain of an image, to remove speckle and retains subtle features simultaneously. The performance of the modified LPND method is evaluated by both CNR and PSNR on a real ultrasound image dataset. In this work, we obtained an accuracy 95% and 12.34 in contrast-to-noise ratio and 13.32 in PSNR for liver cyst compared to the speckle reducing anisotropic diffusion (SRAD), nonlinear diffusion (ND) and LPND respectively. Also the proposed modified LPND showed clearer boundaries on both focal and diffuse ultrasound liver dataset. These preliminary results indicate that the proposed modified LPND can effectively reduce speckle noise while enhancing image edges for retaining subtle features like cyst and lesions.

Keywords: Laplacian pyramid, nonlinear diffusion, speckle noise, ultrasound liver images, diffusivity function.

1   Introduction

Through current technological developments are essentially limited to developed countries, e-Health is now a global topic. The term e-Health has been in use since the year 2000. E-Health encompasses much of medical informatics but tends to priorities

*Corresponding author.

R. Natarajan (Ed.): ICDCIT 2014, LNCS 8337, pp. 311–321, 2014.
© Springer International Publishing Switzerland 2014

the delivery of clinical information, care and services rather that the functions of technologies. Throughout many western national healthcare services, extensive e-Health infrastructures and systems are now viewed as central to the future provision of safe, efficient, high quality, and citizen-centered health care. Medical imaging technologies have provided physicians with powerful, non-invasive techniques to analyze the detailed structure, anatomical function and pathology of the human body. The acquisition of medical images in 2D or 3D has become a routine task for clinical research applications. The noninvasiveness, portability and relatively low cost make ultrasound imaging one of the most prevalent diagnostic techniques in a range of clinical applications. One particular challenge is related to the presence of speckle noise in ultrasound liver images, this is seen as a critical step for many clinical and research applications. Automatic interpretation of ultrasound images, however, is extremely difficult because of its low signal to noise ratio (SNR). One of the main reason for this low SNR is the presence of speckle noise. Speckle noise is a phenomenon inherent in any coherent imaging process. Speckle noise tends to obscure diagnostically important features and degrades the image quality significantly. The automated recognition of meaningful image components, anatomical structures, and other pathology bearing region, such as lesion, is typically achieved using some kind of speckle reduction techniques [1].

1.1   Speckle Reduction

Speckle noise is a granular noise that inherently exists in and degrades the quality of the active radar and synthetic aperture radar (SAR) images in e-Health applications. It increases the mean gray level of the homogeneous region. Speckle degrades the quality of ultrasound images and thereby reducing the ability of a human observer to discriminate intricate details of diagnostic examination. It may be due to one or more of the following reasons. (i) Physical nature of the system, (ii) Shortcomings of image acquisition devices, (iii) Due to environment and (iv) Image developing mechanism. Speckle is an important issue in Ultrasound images, and is modeled as multiplicative noise. The presence of speckle in a medical image would hide the necessary pathological information leading to improper results in diagnosis [2].

This work is based on the major issue in Ultrasound modality. This work provides the knowledge about adaptive and anisotropic diffusion techniques for speckle noise removal from various types of ultrasonic liver images. Speckle reduction makes an ultrasound image to enhance its edges and boundaries, and thus significantly improves the accuracy of automatic or semiautomatic image registration and classification techniques.

2   Related Works in Speckle Reduction

Several research works have been reported in the literature for analyzing the speckle reduction in ultrasound images. Perona et al [3] developed anisotropic diffusion to overcome the problems in standard scale space technique. It is observed that adaptive speckle reduction filter for log compressed B-scan images is suggested by Dutt [4]. But these spatial filtering methods have difficulty in removing speckle near or on image edges.

Pyramid transform has also been used for reducing speckle [5] and [6]. Sattar et al [4] adopted the Feavueau's pyramid transform. Considering the multiplicative nature of speckle, Aiazzi et al [6] introduced a ratio laplacian pyramid. In this method, the existing Kuan filter [7] is extended to multiscale domain by processing the interscale layers of the ratio laplacian pyramid, but it suffers noise variance in each interscale layer.

Alternatively, diffusion-based spatial filtering methods have been proposed. Yu and Acton [8] introduced an edge sensitive diffusion method [(i.e., speckle reducing anisotropic diffusion (SRAD)] to suppress speckle while preserving edge information. Abd-Elmoniem et al [9] presented a tensor-based anisotropic diffusion method i.e., nonlinear coherent diffusion (NCD)] for speckle reduction and coherence enhancement. Both of the above two diffusion method can preserve or even enhance prominent edges when removing speckles, but they have one common limitation in retaining subtle features, such as small cysts and lesions in ultrasound images.

Recently Zhang et al [10] presented a Laplacian pyramid-based nonlinear diffusion (LPND) method. In their work, laplacian pyramid was utilized as a multiscale analysis tool to decompose an image into different subbands, and then anisotropic diffusion with different diffusion flux is used to suppress noise in each sub band. But LPND works only on log compressed data and fails to retain small features like cyst. NLF (National Liver Foundation), a voluntary and non-profit organization reported that liver diseases are one of the most common diseases in India, causing lakhs of deaths every year [11].

Though much work has been done on the speckle reduction in ultrasound images in the literature, in most of the works, it is assumed that the Diffusion based spatial filter is to suppress the noise and preserve fine details of edges in ultrasound liver images. But it lack to diagnose small residual features like cyst and lesion which will lead to major problems like cirrhosis and cancer and finally lead to death. This drawback limits the applicability of ultrasound images for the purpose of e-Health applications. Since new e-Health applications are constantly emerging, so much care should be taken to identify small pathology bearing information which is hidden by means of speckles during pre-processing. Of the above mentioned filters the performance of LPND is good. In order to focus on subtle features like lesions, cyst and improve edge information for ultrasound liver images, this paper modifies diffusivity function & gradient threshold and proposed Modified Laplacian Pyramid Nonlinear Diffusion filter for speckle reduction.

3   Proposed Modified Laplacian Pyramid Nonlinear Diffusion for e-Health Applications

The proposed work is an extension of LPND (MLPND filters) that incorporates the favourable properties of multiscale analysis for improving noise suppression and edge preservation. It retains subtle features, such as small cysts and lesions in ultrasound liver images by calculating its new gradient values. The overall proposed MLPND system for speckle reduction is shown in the Figure 1.

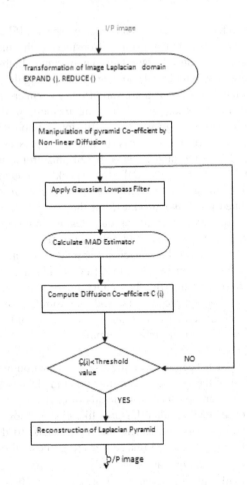

Fig. 1. Systematic Flow Diagram of MLPND for Speckle Reduction

The Modified LPND algorithm consists of following steps:

- Decomposition of a given input image into its Laplacian pyramid domain by using EXPAND and REDUCE operators.
- Calculation of pyramid coefficient values by modified diffusivity function for nonlinear diffusion in order to remove speckles from an image.
- Apply Gaussian low pass-filter to each sub band in laplacian pyramid to estimate new gradient threshold values ∇I.
- Reconstruction of the diffused laplacian pyramid by calculating modified gradient threshold value.
- Calculate Median Absolute Deviation (MAD) estimator and its new decision role based on the new gradient threshold λ for the proposed MLPND method.

3.1   Laplacian Pyramid Domain

Since the introduction of Laplacian pyramid by Burt and Adelson [12] a number of pyramid representations have been developed. A general structure of pyramid transforms consists of pyramid decomposition and pyramid reconstruction stages and can be described by approximation and interpolation filtering. However, the laplacian pyramid has one advantage compare to wavelet filter bank ie. Each pyramid level generates only one bandpass image which does not scrambled frequencies. In the decomposition stage, a signal is successively decomposed into a decimated approximation signal and a signal containing small information. This small signal is computed as the difference between the signals on a scale and the interpolated signal from a rough texture region. A smooth texture region corresponds to a lower pyramid layer. The lowest pyramid layer has the equal size as in the original image. A specific pyramid is determined by its particular decimation factor and approximation and interpolation filters which is shown in Figure 2.

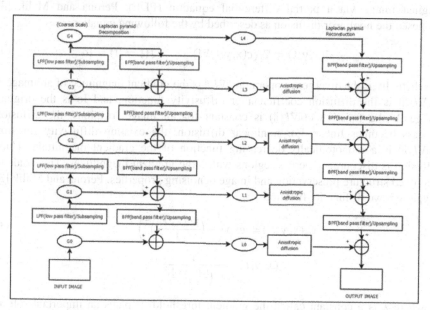

Fig. 2. Flow Diagram for construction and reconstruction of laplacian pyramid

In the Laplacian pyramid, two filters, REDUCE and EXPAND are commonly used. The REDUCE operator carry out a two-dimensional (2-D) lowpass filtering on ultrasound image followed by a sub-sampling by a factor of two in both directions. The EXPAND operator enlarges an ultrasound image to twice the size in both directions by up-sampling (i.e., insertion of zeros) and a lowpass filtering followed by a multiplication by a factor of four, which is in need to maintain the average intensity being reduced by the insertion of some cardinal number. For an input ultrasound liver image I, let its Gaussian pyramid at layer 1 be L1, where l=0, 1, 2... d-1 and d is the total decomposition layer. Then, the Gaussian and Laplacian pyramid can be defined as

$$G_0 = I \tag{1}$$

$$G_1 = \text{REDUCE } [G_{1-1}] \tag{2}$$

$$L_1 = G_1 - \text{EXPAND } [G_{1+1}] \tag{3}$$

The Gaussian pyramid consists of a set of lowpass filtered copies of the original image at different sizes, whereas the Laplacian pyramid break down the original image into a set of bandpass images and a final lowpass image. Reconstruction of an image from its Laplacian pyramid can be achieved by simply reversing the decomposition steps.

3.2   Nonlinear Diffusion

Diffusion filtering removes speckle noise from an ultrasound image by modifying the original image via a partial differential equation (PDE), Perona and Malik [3] proposed the nonlinear diffusion as described by the following equation:

$$\frac{\partial}{\partial t} I(x, y, t) = \nabla . (c(x, y, t) \nabla I) \qquad I(t = 0) = \text{Io} \tag{4}$$

where div is the divergence operator. $\| \nabla I \|$ is the gradient magnitude of an image I, $c(\|\nabla I \|)$ is the diffusion coefficient or diffusivity function, and Io is the original image. If the function $c(\|\nabla I \|)$ is constant for all image locations, the diffusion process becomes linear. For nonlinear diffusion, the existing diffusivity function $c(\|\nabla I \|)$ is a monotonically decreasing function of the gradient magnitude. Thus, diffusion is discouraged across regions with large gradient magnitudes. This leads to improved structure preservation and image denoising properties. Perona and Malik [3] suggested two diffusivity functions.

$$C_1(x, y, t) = \exp\left(-\left(\frac{|\nabla I(x,y,t)|}{\lambda}\right)^2\right) \tag{5}$$

$$C_2(x, y, t) = \frac{1}{1 + \left(\frac{|\nabla I(x,y,t)|}{\lambda}\right)^2} \tag{6}$$

where λ is a constant called the gradient threshold. It plays an important role in determining the degree of smoothing in the diffusion process.

3.3   Modified Diffusivity Function

The modified diffusivity function can be computed using (5) or (6). It has been found that a greater decay rate of the diffusivity function will create sharper edges that persist over longer time intervals in a narrower range of edge slopes, and that a more gradual decay rate will sharpen edges over a wider range of edge slopes. For the same valued of λ, the two diffusivity function in (5) and (6) will lead the diffusion process to significantly different results [12]. To make two diffusivity functions give similar results for the same value of λ, we have modified the diffusivity function $C2(\| \nabla I \|)$ in equation (6) to be

$$C_2(\|\nabla I\|) = \exp[1 - (\|\nabla I\|^2 / (2\lambda + 1))^2]$$

(7)

From equation (7), at each subbands in pyramid coefficients is improved, by multiplying the gradient threshold value by factor 2 and added by 1, For nonlinear diffusion, now the diffusivity function C2($\|\nabla I\|$) is gradually increasing function of the gradient magnitude. Thus, diffusion is encourages across regions with small gradient magnitudes. This leads to improved structure preservation and preserve small detailed structures present in ultrasound liver images compare to equation (6)

3.4   Gaussian Filter

After an image is breakdown into its pyramid structure of decreasing frequencies, the main noise and useful signal components of the image exist in different layers because of their different frequency in nature. Speckle noise has high frequency so that it mainly exists in low pyramid layers. On the other hand, in the highest pyramid layer, speckle noise is negligible. Thus, performing spatial adaptive filtering in each bandpass layer can effectively suppress speckle without degrading the image. The next step is the nonlinear diffusion filtering is to apply Gaussian filter in each bandpass layer of laplacian pyramid to suppress speckle while preserving edges. In the proposed MLPND, a Gaussian regularization strategy [13] which estimates the gradient ∇I on a Gaussian low pass filtered version of the image, is adopted. Based on this strategy, (4) becomes

$$\frac{\partial I}{\partial t} = div[c \parallel \nabla(G(\sigma) * I) \parallel)\nabla I]$$

(8)

where σ is the standard deviation of a Gaussian filter G and describes a level of uniform smoothing used to measure the image gradient, and * denotes convolution. The value of σ is chosen empirically based on the noise suppression and structure preservation.

3.5   Median Absolute Deviation (MAD) Estimator

The selection of the gradient threshold λ plays a major role in determining the small parts of an image that will be blued or enhance in the diffusion process. Before reconstruction of the diffused laplacian pyramid by applying Gaussian low pass filter. Calculate MAD estimator and its new decision role on the gradient threshold λ for the proposed MLPND method.

$$\lambda = \frac{MAD(\|\nabla I\|)}{0.6745}$$

(9)

where the constant is derived from the fact that the MAD of a zero mean normal distribution with unit variance is 0.6745.

$$\lambda(l) = \frac{1}{0.6745} MAD(\parallel \nabla I(\ell) \parallel)\sqrt{2log(1 + 1/2\ell)}$$

(10)

where l is the pyramid layer. This decision rule can help MLPND suppress noise more thoroughly and preserve important image features more effectively. If the value of λ is set very high, the diffusion will act as a smoothing filter and cyst information is hidden by speckle, if λ set too low, the diffusion will act as a sharpening filter and some big noise will be preserved. However, some automatic threshold selection mechanism requires a bipeak histogram, which is not common in medical ultrasound images. Currently, we proposed the modified gradient threshold λ in equation (9) is estimated using the median absolute deviation estimator.

4   Experimental Results

4.1   Liver Dataset

The experiment is carried out with 2D ultrasound liver dataset collected from GEM Hospital, Coimbatore for e-Healthy applications. The dataset include 60 cysts, 45 cavernous hemangioma, 66 normal livers and 41 hepatoma, 40 fatty liver and 48 Cirrhosis liver images. The modified Laplacian pyramid non-linear diffusion is tested with ultrasound liver images. In this paper, the performance of the MLPND is compared with other nonlinear diffusion filters like ND, SAD, and LPND respectively. The dataset used in this chapter of the work are authenticated dataset provided by doctors for e-Health applications The results at this phase have been evaluated with doctors in the relevant field. The size of the images is 512 x 512 pixels and images are saved at 12 bits per pixel gray level. The performance measure is evaluated based on contrast to noise ratio (CNR) and Peak Signal to Noise Ratio (PSNR). The MLPND works well because gradient threshold is automatically determined by a variation of median absolute deviation (MAD) estimator.

4.2   Performance Metrics

Contrast To Noise Ratio (CNR)
CNR is a measure for assessing the ability of an ultrasound imaging procedure to generate clinically useful image contrast.

$$CNR = \frac{|\mu_1 - \mu_2|}{\sqrt{\sigma_1^2 + \sigma_2^2}}$$

where $\mu1$ and $\sigma12$ are the mean and variance of intensities of pixels in a region of interest (ROI), and $\mu2$ and $\sigma22$ are the mean and variance of intensities of pixels in a background region that has the same size as the ROI to be compared with.

Peak Signal To Noise Ratio
Peak Signal to Noise Ratio is the ratio between highest power of the signal to the highest power of noise. Higher levels of PSNR indicate that the value of useful information is greater than noise. Therefore greater values of PSNR are preferable.

$$PSNR = 20 \log_{10}\left(\frac{MAX_f}{\sqrt{MSE}}\right)$$

In this section, we test the MLPND using both normal and diseased ultrasound liver image data. In this experiment, we compare the results of the MLPND with those of three existing systems, i.e., the Non-linear Diffusion (ND), Speckle Reducing Anisotropic Diffusion (SRAD) and Laplacian Pyramid Non-linear Diffusion (LPND) filter. We examine the Contrast to Noise Ratio (CNR) and Peak Signal to Noise Ratio (PSNR) to quantify the performance of algorithms in homogeneous regions.

4.3   Discussion

From the experiment above, it is noticed that modified laplacian pyramid nonlinear diffusion methods works directly on ultrasound raw image data. The result processed by the modified LPND is much sharper in terms of edge preservation and smoother in terms of speckle noise reduction than the other three filtered results. For quantitative quality evaluation, we provide two metrics namely – Contrast to Noise Ratio (CNR) and Peak Signal to Noise Ratio (PSNR). Table.1. and Table 2 shows evaluation results for the processed image. It explains about the comparison of CNR and PSNR values for liver images using MLPND with existing nonlinear diffusion filters. CNR values indicate that the proposed method gives a better processing result in terms of structure preservation and contrast enhancement for e-Health applications.

From table 2, it is inferred that the PSNR value indicates that the proposed method is better than other methods in terms of edge preserving ability. Due to its optimal noise reduction, Modified LPND provide better results compare to the other three methods, resulting in increased contrast and improved visibility of small structures (i.e., subtle features like lesion) in each image. These quantitative results show that the MLPND can eliminate speckle noise without distorting useful image information and without destroying the important image edges which is shown in figure 3. All the other three methods have limited noise reduction performance. SRAD broadens the boundaries of bright regions and shrinks those of dark regions. Although ND enhances the coherence of organ surfaces, LPND also causes blurring of small regions, and the contrast of its output image is not as good as that of MLPND. From Table 1 it can be inferred that e-Health applications for analyzing ultrasound images are easily recognized after that speckle is removed and the edge details are also restored effectively. The CNR value was able to provide conclusion that the image clarity is not affected.

Table 1. Comparision of CNR values for liver images using MLPND with existing Non-linear Diffusion filters

Liver Images / Filters	Normal	Cyst	Hemangioma	Hepatoma	Fatty	Cirrhosis
Noisy	4.45	5.34	5.90	4.40	6.12	6.23
ND	9.45	11.87	17.10	9.18	9.20	10.92
SRAD	9.41	11.36	18.57	14.18	15.23	16.01
LPND	9.46	10.89	19.01	14.63	15.61	16.94
Modified LPND	10.84	12.34	19.22	15.29	17.52	18.11

Table 2. Comparison of PSNR values for liver images using MLPND with existing Non-linear Diffusion Filters

Liver Images Filters	Normal	Cyst	Hemangioma	Hepatoma	Fatty	Cirrhosis
Noisy	5.49	4.99	5.89	5.72	7.13	8.29
ND	9.01	9.45	12.44	10.91	14.70	15.92
SRAD	9.25	8.11	12.56	13.44	14.71	14.98
LPND	10.11	11.89	13.15	14.99	15.74	17.36
Modified LPND	11.45	13.32	15.55	16.58	17.26	18.35

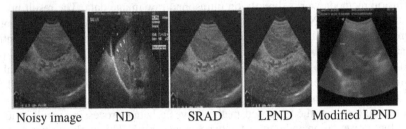

Noisy image   ND   SRAD   LPND   Modified LPND

Fig. 3. Comparison of various speckle reduction methods with modified LPND for Liver hepatoma

5   Conclusion

A modified nonlinear diffusion method in laplacian pyramid domain for ultrasonic speckle reduction has been investigated. The choice of the modified diffusivity function and gradient threshold plays an important role in determining the small parts like cyst and lesion of an image that will be blurred or enhanced in the diffusion process. The value of gradient threshold is estimated using the robust median absolute deviation (MAD) estimator. The proposed MLPND preserves edges and small structure while maximally removing speckle. Thus, it has the potential to improve the diagnostic capability of current ultrasound imaging and to enhance the performance of some high level image processing tasks in the ultrasound imaging systems. Thus the speckle reduction is completed by using MLPND method. The performance of this approach has been tested with 300 datasets. The result had an accuracy of 95%.

Provided experimental results and analysis prove that the proposed MLPND can be used as a practical solution to the problem of speckles in ultrasound images of e-Health applications. In future, we also investigate by combining different techniques and show that the best methods for e-Health applications have very high accuracy in ultrasound speckle reduction. It is important to highlight that the proposed solution is good and can also be applied for different stages of ultrasound liver diseases.

Acknowledgement. The authors convey their heartfelt thanks to Dr.R.Sambath, Radiologist and Dr.P.S.Rajan, M.S of GEM Hospital, Coimbatore, for providing the Medical image dataset used in this paper, and also Dr.Kasthurimohan, M.D of Malar

Hospital, Dindigul and Dr.Mahalakshmi, DGO, of Meenakshi Mission Hospital, Madurai for their motivation and support for conducting this work and valuable suggestions at different stages of the work.

References

1. Karaman, M., Kutay, M.A., Bozdagi, G.: An adaptive speckle suppression filter for medical ultrasonic imaging. IEEE Transactions on Medical Imaging 1(2) (1995)
2. Hwang, K.H., Lee, H., Choi, D.: Medical image retrieval: Past and present. Healthcare Research Information 18(1), 3–9 (2012)
3. Perona, P., Malik, J.: Scale-space and edge detection using anisotropic diffusion. IEEE Trans. Pattern Anal. Mach. Intell. 12(7), 629–639 (1990)
4. Dutt, V., Greenleaf, J.F.: Adaptive speckle reduction filter for log compressed B-scan images. IEEE Trans. Med. Imag. 14(6), 802–813 (1996)
5. Sattar, F., Floreby, L., Salomonsson, G., Lovstrom, B.: Image enhancement based on a nonlinear multiscale method. IEEE Trans. Image Process. 6(6), 888–895 (1997)
6. Aiazzi, B., Alparone, L., Baronti, S., Lotti, F.: Multiresolution local statistics speckle filtering based on a ratio Laplacian pyramid. IEEE Trans. Geosci. Remote Sens. 36(5), 1466–1476 (1998)
7. Kuan, D.T., Sawchuk, A.A., Strand, T.C., Chavel, P.: Adaptive noise smoothing filter for images with signal dependent noise. IEEE Trans. Pattern Anal. Mach. Intell. 7(2), 165–177 (1985)
8. Yu, Y.J., Acton, S.T.: Speckle reducing anisotropic diffusion. IEEE Transaction on Image Processing 11(11), 1260–1270 (2002)
9. Abd-Elmoniem, K.Z., Youssef, A.M., Kadah, Y.M.: Real-time speckle reduction and coherence enhancement in ultrasound imaging via nonlinear anisotropic diffusion. IEEE Transaction on Biomedical Engineering 49(9), 997–1014 (2002)
10. Zhang, F., Yoo, Y.M., Koh, L.M., Kim, Y.: Nonlinear diffusion in laplacian pyramid domain for ultrasonic speckle reduction. IEEE Transaction on Medical Imaging 26(2) (2007)
11. Assy, N., Nasser, G., Djibre, A., Beniashvili, Z., Elias, S., Zidan, J.: Characteristics of common solid liver lesions and recommendations for diagnostic workup. World Journal of Gastroenterology 15(26), 3217–3227 (2009)
12. Burt, P.J., Adelson, E.A.: The Laplacian pyramid as a compact image code. IEEE Trans. Commun. 31(4), 532–540 (1983)
13. Jin, J.S., Wang, Y., Hiler, J.: An adaptive nonlinear diffusion algorithm for filtering medical images. IEEE Trans. Inf. Tech. Biomed. 4(4), 298–305 (2000)

Comparative Improvement of Image Segmentation Performance with Graph Based Method over Watershed Transform Image Segmentation

Suman Deb and Subarna Sinha

National Institute of Technology Agartala,
Tripura, India
{sumandebcs,subarna.sinha9}@gmail.com

Abstract. Watershed transformation based segmentation which is a segmentation based on marker is a special tool used in image processing. Color based image segmentation has been considered an important area since its inception, due to its wide variety of applications in the field of weather forecasting to medical image analysis etc. Due to this color image segmentation is widely researched. This paper analyses the performance of two main algorithms used for image segmentation namely Watershed algorithm and graph based image segmentation. The performance analysis proves that graph based segmentation is better than watershed algorithm in cases where noise is maximum and also the over segmentation problem is removed. Color segmentation with graph based image segmentation gives satisfactory results unlike watershed algorithm.

Keywords: Watershed transformation, Graph based image segmentation, Marker, Over segmentation.

1 Introduction and Related Work

Image segmentation analyses and segments a particular image into meaningful segments. Generally segmentation is done on particular region of interest to detect the objects within it. The partitioned segments in an image can have same color or texture. The combination of segments produced by image segmentation is the entire image. Some particular feature like color, texture etc are used to determine the membership of a particular pixel in a particular image segment. Image segmentation has various applications like locating tumours [1], face recognition [2], and image retrieval[3].

The quality of result obtained by image segmentation is dependent on the segmentation algorithm chosen. Watershed algorithm which is based on morphology have been a major topic of discussion since it came into being.[4], [5], [6], [7]. Watershed algorithm is sensitive to noise, causing problems of over-segmentation. Whereas several modifications of watershed algorithm have been developed which claim to have solved the problems of watershed segmentation [5]. For example, the

R. Natarajan (Ed.): ICDCIT 2014, LNCS 8337, pp. 322–332, 2014.

long time consumption disadvantage of traditional watershed algorithm has been solved in few works [5], but the oversegmentation problem still remains to be a hurdle. The area of image segmentation is full of challenges and ideas. Even in case of human vision the perception segmentation plays an important role. Various recognition techniques and image indexing techniques make use of segmented image. This gives the importance of image segmentation in the field of image processing. Many low level image segmentation techniques like edge detection thresholding technique etc are there which provide output with minimal usability in other fields like recognition.

To obtain desired results, a segmentation method should work properly even in presence of noise by diminishing it or by performing any kind of preprocessing. The segmentation technique in case of watershed transform based method does not have efficient execution or processing time. Whereas an image segmentation technique should be time efficient. The graph based segmentation aims at solving this problem as well. Moreover the regions or segments formed by watershed algorithm do not give the desired output when compared to that of graph based segmentation. Image segmentation should result in extraction of semantically meaningful objects automatically from an image. Graph-based methods introduce a top-to-bottom approach, which models images as weighted graphs and provides segmentation by recursively partitioning the graph into sub-graphs. This approach is also seen in human perception, where a human interprets a whole perceptual view from top to bottom .

The organization of this paper is as follows. In the next Section we discuss Watershed algorithm, and the Efficient Graph-Based Image Segmentation by Pedro F. Felzenszwalb to implement graph based segmentation. [8]. In Section 4 the comparative analysis is done and then the sections following it consists of the implementation environment information and the results obtained when both the algorithms depicted in Section 2 and Section 3 are applied on the set of image provided in Section 4 .

2   Watershed Transform Image Segmentation

There are numerous types of image segmentation method like region based methods, thresholding technique, clustering etc. Watershed transform based image segmentation can be considered as a type of region based segmentation which uses mathematical morphology[9]. The concept of watershed algorithm is taken from geography, where a topographic relief is flooded by water. The watershed lines form the divide lines of the domains of attraction of rain falling over the region as in the figure shown below. Vincent and Soille [4] proposed an alternative technique, namely immersion simulations, based on a FIFO queue to implement the watershed segmentation. Watershed algorithm is an iterative adaptive threshold algorithm. It takes the gradient magnitude of the image as a topographic map, the gradient magnitude in correspond with altitude, the different gradient in correspond with the peak and basin in valley in the image. Marker is knowledge about the object based on application-oriented; it is selected by the operator manually or by automatic process. The watershed algorithm can transform and develop regional growth with the help of marker and then produce the required segmented image.

The advantages of Watershed algorithm are-[10]. The segmented image produced by application of this approach consists of connected segments unlike edge based detection which gives disconnected contours as result. Secondly, the region contours adhere well to the real object boundaries. Thirdly, the combination of regions produced by watershed segmentation is equal to the entire image. Like the advantages of Watershed algorithm, it also has some disadvantages. Watershed segmentation is sensitive to noise, the main reason leading to over-segmentation. Besides, it doesn't work well in detection of thin structures and significant areas with low contrast boundaries.

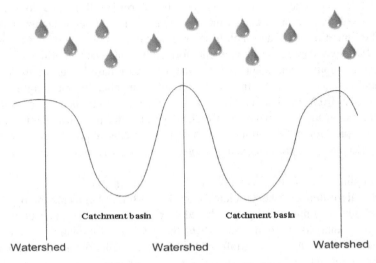

Fig. 1. Diagram of watershed algorithm

3   Graph Based Image Segmentation

The goal of Graph based image segmentation algorithm[8] described below is to develop computational approaches to image segmentation which can be used in various computer vision tasks like the widely used low level segmentation techniques(e.g.- edge based image segmentation). It is necessary that the segmentation technique should have two important properties. Firstly, the goal of an image segmentation method is to precisely understand the regions to be segmented perceptually. The important groupings or regions often reflect the global aspects of the image. The important aspects of the graph based segmentation method are to provide precise characterizations of what is perceptually important and produce the segments in the image accordingly. Secondly, the image segmentation techniques should be highly efficient, running in time nearly linear in the number of image pixels. In order to be of practical use, we believe that segmentation methods should run at speeds similar to edge detection or other low-level visual processing techniques [8]. For example, a segmentation technique that runs at several frames per second can be used in video processing applications.

Eigenvector-based image segmentation methods had been used extensively in the past few years [11]. These methods are too slow to be practical for many applications. The segmentation technique involving graph based approach satisfies both the properties mentioned above. It captures certain perceptually important non-local image characteristics and is computationally efficient, running in O(n log n) time for n image pixels.

Graph-based image segmentation requires the image to be represented in the form of a graph. [8] G = (V; E) is an undirected graph with vertices $v_i \in V$. The vertices together form the set of pixels to be and edges $(v_i, v_j) \in E$ represents the pairs of neighboring vertices representing neighboring pixels. Each edge $(v_i, v_j) \in E$ has a corresponding weight w $((v_i, v_j))$, which is a non-negative measure of the dissimilarity between neighboring elements v_i and v_j. In the case of image segmentation, the elements in V are pixels and the weight of an edge is some measure of the dissimilarity between the two pixels connected by that edge (e.g., the difference in intensity, color, motion, location or some other local attribute).

In the graph-based approach, a segmentation S is a partition of V into components such that each component (or region) $C \in S$ corresponds to a connected component in a graph G' = (V, E'), where $E' \subseteq E$. In other words, any segmentation is induced by a subset of the edges in E. There are different ways to measure the quality of a segmentation but in general we want the elements in a component to be similar, and elements in different components to be dissimilar. This means that edges between two vertices in the same component should have relatively low weights, and edges between vertices in different components should have higher weights.

3.1   Algorithm : Segmentation algorithm.

Input: Graph G = (V, E). It has p vertices and q edges.
Output: Segmentation of V into components S = $(C_1,...., C_p)$, where p denotes the number of components.

1. Edges E is sorted into a non-decreasing order by weight. Let O = $(o_1,..., o_q)$ be the order generated.

2. At the start each v_i is placed in its own component.

3. Repeat step 3 for m = 1,...,q.

4. S^{m-1} is generated from S^m in the following way.
Let v_i and v_j denote the vertices connected by the m-th edge in the ordering, i.e., o_m = (v_i, v_j). If v_i and v_j are in disjoint components of S^{m-1} and $w(o_m)$ is small compared to the internal difference of both those components, then merge the two components otherwise do nothing. More formally, let C_i^{m-1} be the component of S^{m-1} containing v_i and C_j^{m-1} the component containing v_j .

If $C_i^{m-1} \neq C_j^{m-1}$ and $w(o_m) \leq MInt(C_i^{m-1}, C_j^{m-1})$,(where $w(o_m)$ is the weight difference between two vertices and $MInt(C_i^{m-1}, C_j^{m-1})$ is the internal difference of two components C_i^{m-1} and C_j^{m-1}) then S^m is obtained from S^{m-1} by merging C_i^{m-1} and C_j^{m-1}. Otherwise $S^m = S^{m-1}$.

5. Return $S = S^q$

This algorithm[8] has been implemented to perform the segmentation based on graph concept.

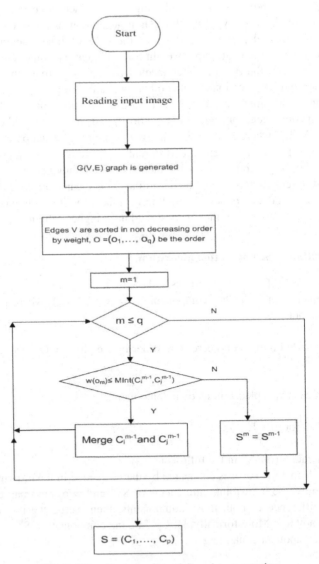

Fig. 2. Flow diagram of graph based segmentation

4   Analysis of Watershed Image Segmentation and Graph Based Image Segmentation

The comparative analysis of watershed algorithm and graph based algorithm for image segmentation can be made clear with the help of a set of images which we used for experiment purpose. The comparative study is done on the following set of images.

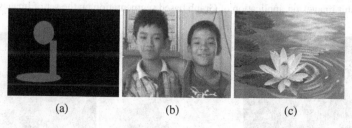

(a)   (b)   (c)

Fig. 3. Test images for segmentation

There are several aspects of watershed algorithm which fall under its disadvantages. The results obtained after applying the two algorithms on the set of images separately, show the flaws of watershed algorithm and prove that the graph based image segmentation is better for image segmentation. Watershed segmentation is sensitive to noise, the main reason leading to over-segmentation. Besides, it doesn't work well in detection of thin structures and significant areas with low contrast boundaries. Whereas graph based segmentation is not much effected by noise as in the case of watershed algorithm. So the segmentation results are better.

The graph based segmentation method has its own limitations as well. The method needs further research to be applied for automatic real time scenarios. Some important future explorations of research can be - incorporation of the fuzzy set theory into graph based frameworks to achieve enhanced segmentation performances, use of multi-criteria to partition a graph to achieve an efficient segmentation, constructing a graph using feature sets rather than pixel level information etc.

5   Implementation and Results

The performances of the two algorithms are evaluated in the following section. The algorithm is implemented in Microsoft Visual Studio with OpenCv in C++ environment and executed on a core i3 processor, 2.27 GHZ, 3 GB RAM computer.

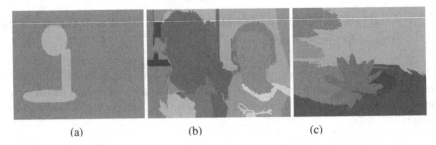

(a)   (b)   (c)

Fig. 4. Result images on application of Graph based segmentation on the set of images in Fig. 3

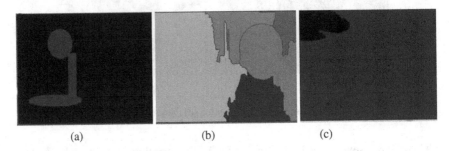

(a)   (b)   (c)

Fig. 5. Result images on application of Watershed based segmentation on the set of images in Fig. 3

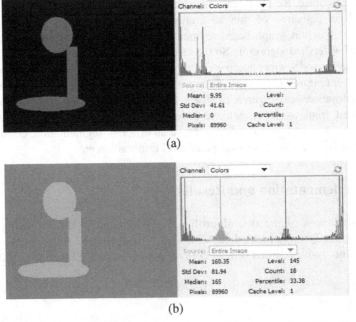

Fig. 6. (a) Original image histogram, (b) Histogram of image segmented by Graph based segmentation (c) Histogram of image segmented by Watershed algorithm

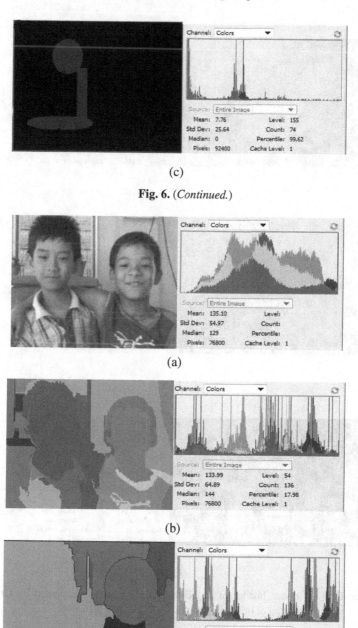

(c)

Fig. 6. (*Continued.*)

(a)

(b)

(c)

Fig. 7. (a) Original image histogram, (b) Histogram of image segmented by Graph based segmentation (c) Histogram of image segmented by Watershed algorithm

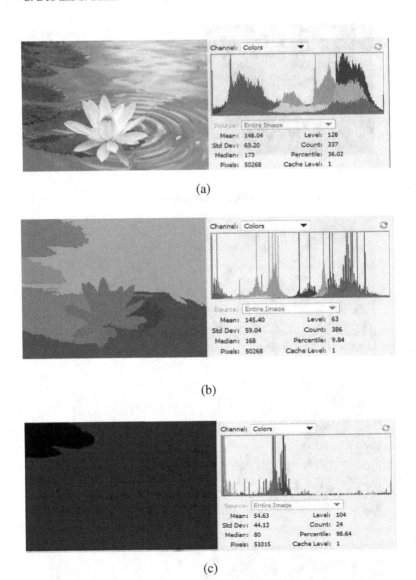

(a)

(b)

(c)

Fig. 8. (a) Original image histogram, (b) Histogram of image segmented by Graph based segmentation (c) Histogram of image segmented by Watershed algorithm

Table 1. Mathematical data obtained from histogram of the images under test

Images	Standard deviation	Mean	Median
Original Image 6 (a)	41.61	9.95	165
Graph segmented image 6(b)	81.94	160.35	0
Watershed algorithm segmented image 6(c)	25.64	7.76	0
Original Image 7 (a)	54.97	135.1	129
Graph segmented image 7(b)	64.89	133.99	144
Watershed algorithm segmented image 7(c)	83.42	137.84	179
Original Image 8 (a)	69.2	148.04	173
Graph segmented image 8(b)	59.04	145.4	168
Watershed algorithm segmented image 8(c)	44.13	54.63	80

The mathematical analysis on the histograms of all the three images and their respective outputs on application of watershed algorithm and graph based segmentation algorithm also prove that the graph segmentation method is better. The comparison of values of standard deviation calculated from the histograms of the three images in Fig.7 (a), Fig.7(b) and Fig.7(c) shows that the standard deviation obtained from the image segmented by graph based segmentation is close to the original one compared to Fig.7(c),which has been segmented by watershed algorithm. Similar kind of results is found in case of Fig.8 (a), Fig.8 (b) and Fig.8(c).

But if we notice the case of Fig.6 (a), Fig.6 (b) and Fig.6 (c), we can see that the value of standard deviation computed from the histogram of the image segmented from watershed transform algorithm is closer to that of original image unlike the cases in Fig.7 and Fig. 8. From that it can be concluded that the segmentation of image, (which is free from noise) in Fig.4 (a) is done nicely by the watershed based algorithm. And, thus it works for images without noise but does not work efficiently for images without noise.

Even if the results are viewed by someone having no knowledge to image processing methods, he/she can easily say that the segmentation performance is improved in case of graph based segmentation. Fig.3, Fig.4, Fig.5, proves this simple fact. In Fig.5 (a) we can see that watershed algorithm is producing as many segments as those produced by graph based segmentation in Fig.4 (a). But if we compare Fig 4(a) and Fig.5 (a) we can see that the segmentation in Fig.4 (b) is definitely better that Fig.5 (b). The same goes for Fig.4 (c) and Fig.5 (c). Fig.4 (a) and Fig.5 (a) is having similarity due to the absence of noise in the original image Fig.3 (a). But when we take some complex images like Fig.3 (b) and Fig.3 (c), the resultant images from graph based segmentation are definitely better.

6   Conclusion

Watershed transformation based segmentation and graph based image segmentation have been described and analyzed in this paper. Watershed algorithm which is based on geographical concept is a special tool used in image processing. Due to the wide range use of image segmentation in various fields of applications, it has become important to find out a proper image segmentation method from the various image segmentation techniques available. Color segmentation with graph based image segmentation gives satisfactory results unlike watershed algorithm. Graph based segmentation methods when used for image segmentation produce nicer results compared to that of Watershed based algorithm especially when noise is present in the image. Moreover the over segmentation problem in traditional watershed transform image segmentation is removed in the graph based segmentation of images. The segmentation results obtained from the later is having more resemblance when compared to the actual segments in the original image unlike the images segmented by watershed algorithm based segmentation.

References

1. Forghani, N., Forouzanfar, M., Forouzanfar, E.: MRI Fuzzy Segmentation of Brain Tissue using IFCM Algorithm with Particle Swarm Optimization. In: 22nd International Symposium on Computer and Information Sciences, pp. 1–4 (2007)
2. Azzawi, A.A.G., Al-saedi, M.A.H.: Face Recognition Based on Mixed between Selected Features by Multiwavelet and Particle swarm optimization. In: Development in E-system Engineering (DESE), pp. 199–204 (2010)
3. Younes, A.A., Truck, I., Akdaj, H.: Color Image Profiling using Fuzzy Sets. Turk. J. Elec. Engin. 13(3), 343–359 (2005)
4. Vincent, L., Soille, P.: Watersheds in digital spaces: an efficient algorithm based on immersion simulations. IEEE Transactions on PAMI 13(6), 583–598 (1991)
5. Kim, J.B., Kim, H.J.: A Wavelet-based Watershed Image Segmentation for VOP Generation. In: IEEE International Conference on Pattern Recognition, vol. 2(1), pp. 505–508 (2002)
6. O'Callaghan, R.J., Bull, D.R.: Combined Morphological Spectral Unsupervised Image Segmentation. IEEE Trans. on Image Processing 14(1), 49–62 (2005)
7. Chien, S.-Y., Huang, Y.-W., Chen, L.-G.: Predictivewatershed: a fast watershed algorithm for video segmentation. IEEE Transactions on Circuits and Systems for Video Technology 13(5), 453–461 (2003)
8. Felzenszwalb, P.F., Huttenlocher, D.P.: Efficient Graph-Based Image Segmentation. International Journal of Computer Vision 59(2), 167–181 (2004)
9. Tanygin, S.: Image dense stereo matching by technique of region growing. Journal of Guidance, Control, and Dynamics 20(4), 625–632 (1997)
10. Han, X., Fu, Y., Zhang, H.: A Fast Two-Step Marker-Controlled Watershed Image Segmentation Method. In: Proceedings of 2012 IEEE International Conference on Mechatronics and Automation, Chengdu, China, August 5-8 (2012)
11. Weiss, Y.: Segmentation using Eigenvectors: A Unifying View. In: Proceedings of the International Conference on Computer Vision, vol. (2), pp. 975–982 (1999)

Modeling Diffusion of Tabletop for Collaborative Learning Using Interactive Science Lab Simulations

Raghu Raman, Prema Nedungadi, and Maneesha Ramesh

School of Engineering, Amrita Vishwa Vidyapeetham,
Amritapuri, Kollam, Kerala, India - 690525
{raghu,prema,maneesha}@amrita.edu

Abstract. Within the context of Roger's Diffusion of Innovation theory we propose a pedagogical framework for attributes that can significantly affect student adoption of collaborative learning environment like multi-user, multi-touch tabletop. We investigated the learning outcomes of secondary school students in India collaboratively using OLabs on a tabletop (EG1 = 30) vs. individually using at desktops (EG2 = 92). We analyzed the nature of communication, touch and non-touch gesture actions, position around the tabletop, focus group interviews, and pre and post test scores. Using Bass model the study also accounts for the inter influence of related group of potential adopter teachers who are likely to exert positive influence on students. The results revealed that learning outcomes on tabletop are strongly associated with innovation attributes like Relative Advantage, Compatibility, Ease of Use, Perceived Enjoyment, Perceived usefulness and Teachers support. Overall students expressed much more positive attitude to adopt tabletop technology for learning vs. desktop. We find that the mean group performance gain is significant with collaboration using tabletop and significantly greater than the group using desktops. We also find that the group interactions with the tabletop area significant factor that contributes to the group's average performance gain. However, the total time spent in while using the tabletop is surprisingly not a significant factor in the performance gain. Our findings contribute to the design of new pedagogical models for science learning that maximizes the collaborative learning potential of tabletops.

Keywords: Laboratory, Diffusion, Innovation, Simulation, Collaboration, tabletop, experiments.

1 Introduction

The diffusion of innovative learning technologies like interactive multi touch tabletop, tablets etc. and associated pedagogies in school education continues to garner tremendous research interest. Rogers (2003) observed that innovations like Tabletop have five attributes that influence the rate of their adoption -Relative Advantage, Compatibility, Complexity, Trialability, and Observability. As the elements of the theory are discussed, the challenges to tabletop adoption will be

R. Natarajan (Ed.): ICDCIT 2014, LNCS 8337, pp. 333–340, 2014.

considered. Educational activities like science lab experimentation may benefit significantly from interactive tabletop technology because it combines the face-to-face interaction style of traditional small group work. More often students doing science lab experiments collaborate because of the need to share the equipment hence the tabletop provides an ideal virtual learning environment for our study. The purpose of our study is to investigate student perceptions of tabletop as a collaborative learning tool for performing science lab experiments. Additionally we also explored whether collaborative learning environment of tabletop differs from individual learning afforded by desktops. An interactive simulation application called OLabs (Prema Nedungadi, Raghu Raman, 2011) was modified so that it allowed multiple students to collaboratively perform the experiment on the tabletop.In the recent years Tabletops have found their ways into educational learning environments. SynergyNet (Hatch et al. 2009) is a classroom environment where several multi touch tables are connected into a large network that allows for sharing of multimedia objects. Then there are tabletop applications that focus on learning numbers and sorting (Khandelwal and Mazalek, 2007) and concept mapping (Son Do-Lenh et al., 2009). Quadratic (Rick, 2010) is another educational Tabletop application which allows learners to explore algebraic expressions on a tabletop. Bryce and Robertson (1985) observed that in majority of the schools the assessment of science lab work is non-hands in nature with much more focus on the report writing skills. What is needed is continuous formative assessment of lab work to assess procedural, manipulative, reporting and observational skills.

2   Case Study: Factors Affecting Diffusion of Tabletop Technologies for Collaborative Learning

Bass (1969) proposed a mathematical model as a nonlinear differential equation for diffusion of an innovation in a group of size M. According to Karmeshu and Pathria (1980), in such a scenario adoption of innovation is due to two influences viz. external influence (mass media) which is a linear mechanism and internal influence (word-of-mouth) which is a non-linear mechanism. The differential equation giving the diffusion is,

$$\frac{dN(t)}{dt} = \left(p + qN(t)\right)\left(M - N(t)\right) \tag{1}$$

Where, N(t) is the cumulative number of adopter-students who have already adopted by time t, M is total number of adopter-students who will eventually use the innovation, p is the coefficient of external influence and q is the coefficient of internal influence. This equation yields the S-shaped diffusion curve. It is assumed that the carrying capacity M of the adopter-students remains constant. Now we extend the Bass model to account for the influence of teachers on students (Table 1, Differential equations for Diffusion) by defining the following terms -m total number of adopters who will eventually adopt the innovation; μ relative importance students give to teachers for their support $(0 \leq \mu \leq 1)$; α proportion of teachers in the total population of potential adopters $(0 \leq \alpha \leq 1)$.

Table 1. Extended Bass model with influence factors

	Adopter-teachers	Adopter-students
External influence	p_1	p_2
Internal influence	q_1	q_2
Total number of Adopters who will eventually adopt the innovation	F	S
Cumulative number of Adopters who have already adopted by time t	f	s

Based on Table 1, we formulate diffusion differential equations for

Adopter-teacher f(t)

$$\frac{df}{dt} = f(t) = (p_1 + q_1 f)(F - f) \qquad (2)$$

Adopter-students with teacher influence s(t)

$$\frac{ds}{dt} = s(t) = (p_2 + q_2 s + \mu f)(S - s) \qquad (3)$$

Combined teacher-student population m(t)

$$\frac{dm}{dt} = m(t) = \alpha f(t) + (1 - \alpha)s(t) \qquad (4)$$

2.1   Research Model and Hypothesis

The tabletop's rate of adoption was investigated by assessing two groups of characteristics, which were the independent variables - innovation characteristics and environment characteristics. The most obvious advantage of tabletop is its large size, multi-user, multi-touch features that provides a rich immersive dynamic experience to the learners. We hypothesize that Tabletop's Relative advantage positively affects student's intention to adopt tabletop for learning (H1). Tabletop technology is compatible in its functionality with the preceding technology devices like desktop. We hypothesize that Tabletop's Compatibility positively affects student's intention to adopt tabletop for learning (H2). An important question is to what extent tabletop and related applications on them are perceived by users as complicated to use. We hypothesize that Tabletop's Ease of Use positively affects student's intention to adopt tabletop for learning (H3). Trialability is limited in the case of tabletop due to its initial high cost but users can still try the technology at electronic shops. We hypothesize that Tabletop's Trialability positively affects student's intention to adopt tabletop for learning (H4). We hypothesize that Tabletop's Observability positively affects student's intention to adopt tabletop for learning (H5). Upon adoption, individuals are more likely to use the tabletop that offer enjoyment more extensively than those which do not. We hypothesize that Tabletop's Perceived Enjoyment positively affects student's intention to adopt tabletop for learning (H6). We hypothesize that Tabletop's Perceived Usefulness positively affects student's intention to adopt tabletop for learning (H7). More often teachers and students are motivated to consider technology decisions that are sanctioned by the school management since those will have adequate support resources. We hypothesize that School Support for Tabletop positively affects student's intention to adopt tabletop for learning (H8). Teachers play a pivotal role in implementing innovations; their perception of the innovation will strongly influence their students thinking. We hypothesize that Teacher Support for Tabletop positively affects student's intention to adopt tabletop for learning (H9).

3   Research Methodology

3.1   Experimental Design

The study was conducted during a five day Science camp attended by over180 students. To ensure uniformity in performance levels and similar abilities selection of students was based on a minimum score of 90% in science in their grade 10 exams. None of the students had previous exposure to tabletop or OLabs but were exposed to using interactive educational content on desktops. A group of (EG1=30) students were randomly selected and divided into groups of 3 to participate in the collaborative tabletop study. To ensure diversity each group had members of both sexes and students in the group were from different schools to avoid any biases due to previous familiarity. Another group of (EG2=92) students were randomly selected for individual participation for the desktop study. The larger number of students in EG2 was solely due to the availability of large number of desktops. Both quantitative and qualitative measures were used to analyze the results. Pre and post lab assessment each consisted of 20 items, 5 each in the areas of procedural skills, conceptual skills, knowledge of equipment and reporting skills. Likert scaled questionnaire with 35 items was designed to evaluate student feedback. Qualitative measures consisted of analyzing the Video recordings for interaction among the students and a face to face interview with the students. All students were individually administered the pre and post-lab assessment. Next students filled out an online survey to capture their feedback.

4   Results Analysis and Discussion

4.1   Quantitative Analysis

Students had no difficulty in using the tabletop though none of them had prior exposure to working on a tabletop (based on the post-test questionnaire feedback). In terms of demographics both EG1, EG2 had about 50% split between males and females. The reliability of the nine factors had values ranging from 0.78 to 0.89 which according to Nunnally (1978) are acceptable. The discriminant validity for the factors confirms that the AVE (Average Variance Extracted) for each factor on the diagonal is higher than the correlations between the given factor and all other factors. The convergent validity was also good as AVE for each of the 9 factors were larger than 0.5Regression analysis was performed using all the 9 independent variables on the dependent variable intention to adopt tabletop. There is strong support for Hypothesis H1, H2, H3, H6, H7 and H9. The regression model was statistically significant (p < .0001) and accounting for 76% of the variation in intention to adopt (R^2= .76). Since student's perception of teacher support emerged as a significant factor for adoption of Tabletop for collaborative learning, we looked at the shape of the resulting diffusion curve using intergroup influence adoption diffusion equations. It is intuitive to assume that the proportion of teachers is much less than that of the students. To illustrate different types of diffusion patterns we plot the m(t) (Equation 4) along with its two parts αf(t) and (1 − α) (s(t) for different set of parameter values of p's, q's, αand μ (Table 2).

Table 2. Set of parameters for different diffusion patterns with varying levels of teachers support

Case	Teacher parameters	Student parameters	Level of Teacher support (μ)	Proportion of Teachers (α)
1	p_1= 0.02; q_1= 0.4	p_2 = 0.005; q_2 = 0.2	0.3 (high)	0.2
2	p_1= 0.02; q_1= 0.4	p_2 = 0.005; q_2 = 0.2	0.005 (very low)	0.2
3	p_1 = 0.02; q_1= 0.4	p_2 = 0.005; q_2 = 0.2	0.05 (low)	0.2

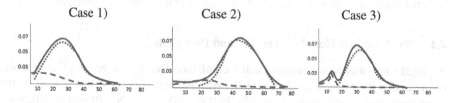

Fig. 1. Diffusion patterns based on students' perception of varying levels of teacher support

In Figure 1, Case 1) deals with the situation of high teacher support for students and results in a bell shaped diffusion curve. Case 2) deals with the situation of very low teacher support which results in delayed start of adoption by students but still results in a bell shaped diffusion curve. Case 3) where there is low teacher support, it results in a bimodal diffusion curve as teachers have reached their peak adoption levels before the students start adopting. It is easy to observe that low values of teachers support results in delay of diffusion among students.

4.2   Tabletop vs. Desktop

Students in EG1 expressed much more positive attitude to adopt tabletop technology with a mean score of 4.16 while the EG2 was slightly more than the middle of the range of scores (3.24).From the t-test, it is evident that the two experimental groups differed statistically significant in their intention to adopt tabletop and desktop for learning (p < 0.001, p < 0.001, respectively). Students in the EG1 perceived higher value for the tabletop based learning (t = 5.73, p < 0.001).

4.3   Video Analysis of EG1

To evaluate how the OLabs application on tabletop impacted collaboration among students we examined several measures like the number of touches on the tabletop (physical participation) and the number of times members in a group spoke while performing the experiment (verbal participation). Both individual and total touches and talk within a group where tracked. Successful completion of the experiment is another indicator of the group collaboration. It was observed that the students in a group focused mostly on the task and less on the interface. Frequent discussions were around "entering the values for the various configuration values" followed by touching the "the experiment procedure" tab and "theory tab". Though tabletop supported multiple concurrent touches we observed that they often choose to take turns interacting with the system and only sometimes worked concurrently.

Relevant research questions in this regard were

1. Does collaborative learning on a tabletop using interactive simulations like OLabs result in performance gain?
2. Are there significant differences in performance gains with collaboration using tabletop vs. individual learning of the same OLabs experiment with a desktop?
3. What are the collaboration metrics that contribute to the performance gain?

4.4   Performance Gain between Pre and Post Tests

A paired t-test was performed to see if the collaborative labs were effective in terms of increasing the average group scores between mean pre and posttests. For EG1, the mean percentage performance gain (M= 25.00%, SD=15.31, N=30) was significantly greater than zero (p < .001) providing evidence that the tabletop is effective in increasing the average group performance score. A 95% confidence interval about mean performance gain was (19.28%, 30.72%). For EG2, the mean percentage performance gain (Mean=19.78, SD=12.75, N=92) was also significantly greater than zero (p< .001). A 95% confidence interval about mean performance gain was (17.14%, 22.42%). In both cases the mean percentage is positive and the confidence interval does not contain zero and we infer that the mean difference is nonzero and positive. We conclude that collaborative learning of OLabs (EG1) with tabletop and individual learning of OLabs with desktops (EG2) were both effective in improving the performance of students. An independent-sample t-test scores assuming unequal variance shows a significant difference in performance gain (p < .05) and hence we conclude that performance gain was greater in EG1 than in EG2.

4.5   Regression Model for Collaborative Learning Using Tabletops

We analyzed the effect of both the number of touches performed by each student within a group and the total number of touches by the group on the performance gain. The number of individual touches by a student did not significantly contribute to the performance gain but the total number of touches (Total Touch) by the group was significant. The average total time spent by the group was also a significant factor in the performance gain ($p < .05$). This may be explained by the fact simulations in OLabs are highly interactive, the total number of touches would mean more interaction with the labs such as using additional variables, repeating the experiment etc. Though the group's total number of touch interactions was significant factor in both the group and the individual performance improvement, the individual touch interactions by a student was not a significant factor. This may be because the entire activity was done collaboratively with no part of the learning activity performed individually. Hence any student's interaction with the tabletop could contribute to learning for the other group members. From the audio recordings of each group session we found that groups spent an average 12.3% of the total session time talking among each other though the individual group talk time widely varied from 3.3% to 26.5% of the total session time. While analyzing the effect of amount of total talk time by each group to the average performance gain, we found that there was no significant effect on performance gain ($p > .05$) from the total talk time. Generally, we expect only the discussions about the subject to directly contribute to learning and hence to gain in performance. This may be a reason that the group's total talk time was not a significant factor in the regression analysis as it included both actual discussions that contributed to learning and also other items such as agreement, questions about using the tabletop etc. that may not contribute to learning.

5   Conclusions

Our study has provided a deeper investigation of multi touch tabletop for collaborative learning guided by the framework of Roger's theory of perceived attributes. Our empirical results show that DOI theory operationalized in this study was successful in predicting adoption of tabletop for learning. The results indicated that attributes like Relative advantage, Compatibility, Ease of Use, Perceived Enjoyment, Perceived Usefulness, Teacher support were positively related to acceptance of innovation while Trialability, Observability, and School support were not. Application developers for tabletop and tabletop designers seeking to increase the rate of adoption of tabletop by students will be better served adopting strategies that address the attributes of the tabletop found to be significant in this study. Our findings show that the collaboration using tabletop had a positive learning outcome with performance gain significantly larger than in the desktop. The significant factors are the groups' total touch interaction with the tabletop, the total time spent by a group and the interaction between total touch and time. Student interactions as observed in the video and feedback after the testing sessions validated that tabletop is both appropriate and motivating for students to learn.

Acknowledgements. This project derives direction and ideas from the Chancellor of Amrita University, Sri Mata Amritanandamayi Devi and is funded by Amrita University. The authors would like to acknowledge the contributions of faculty and staff at Amrita University whose feedback and guidance was invaluable.

References

1. Bass, F.M.: A new product growth for model consumer durables. Management Science 15, 215–227 (1969)
2. CBSE 2006 Assessment of Practical Skills in Science and Technology, Central Board of Secondary Education, India (2006)
3. Hatch, A., Higgins, S., Mercier, E.: SynergyNet: Supporting Collaborative Learning in an Immersive Environment. In: STELLAR Alpine Rendez-Vous Workshop 2009: "Tabletops for Education and Training", Garmisch–Partenkirchen (2009)
4. Karmeshu, Pathria, R.K.: Stochastic Evolution of a Nonlinear Model of Diffusion of Information. Journal of Mathematical Sociology 7, 59–71 (1980)
5. Khandelwal, M., Mazalek, A.: Teaching Table: A tangible mentor for pre-K math education. In: Proceedings of the First International Conference on Tangible and Embedded Interaction, pp. 191–194. ACM Press (2007)
6. Nedungadi, P., Raman, R.: Effectiveness of adaptive learning with interactive animations and simulations. In: 3rd International Conference on Advanced Computer Theory and Engineering (ICACTE), August 20-22, vol. 6, pp. V6-40–V6-44 (2010)
7. Nedungadi, P., Raman, R.: Learning-Enabled Computer Assessment of Science Labs with Scaffolds Methodology. The Technology Interface International Journal I 11(2) (Fall/Winter 2011)
8. Rick, J.: Quadratic: Manipulating algebraic expressions on an interactive tabletop. In: Proceedings of IDC 2010, pp. 304–307. ACM Press, New York (2010)
9. Rogers, E.M.: Diffusion of Innovations, 5th edn. Free Press, New York (2003)
10. Do-Lenh, S., Jermann, P., Cuendet, S., Zufferey, G., Dillenbourg, P.: Task Performance vs. Learning Outcomes: A Study of a Tangible User Interface in the Classroom. In: Wolpers, M., Kirschner, P.A., Scheffel, M., Lindstaedt, S., Dimitrova, V. (eds.) EC-TEL 2010. LNCS, vol. 6383, pp. 78–92. Springer, Heidelberg (2010)
11. Surry, D.W., Farquhar, J.D.: Diffusion theory and instructional technology. Journal of Instructional Science and Technology (1997)

A Binarization Feature Extraction Approach to OCR: MLP vs. RBF

Amit Choudhary[1], Savita Ahlawat[2], and Rahul Rishi[3]

[1] Maharaja Surajmal Institute, New Delhi, India
amit.choudhary69@gmail.com
[2] Maharaja Surajmal Institute of Technology, New Delhi, India
savita.ahlawat@gmail.com
[3] UIET, Maharshi Dayanand University, Rohtak, India
rahulrishi@rediffmail.com

Abstract. The aim of this work is to judge the efficiency of Multi Layer Perceptron (MLP) and Radial Basis Function (RBF) neural network classifiers for performing the task of cursive handwritten digit recognition. Binarization features are extracted from the preprocessed handwritten digit images. The features thus obtained are used to train MLP and RBF classifiers. A detailed investigation in the proposed experiment was done and it can be summarized that when binarization features of the digit images are extracted and used for training the neural network classifiers in the recognition experiment, RBF classifier outperforms the MLP classifier. The RBF Network delivers 98.40% recognition accuracy whereas the MLP classifier delivers 96.20% accuracy for the proposed experiment of cursive handwritten digit recognition.

Keywords: MLP, RBF, Binarization Feature Extraction, Character Recognition, OCR, Neural Networks.

1 Introduction

As far as the field of cursive off-line handwriting recognition is concerned, an artificial neural network is emerged as a quick and most consistent classifier tool resulting in brilliant recognition accuracy and is extensively being used in this domain for the last four decades [1,2,3]. The quality of features extracted and the choice of classification algorithm are the deciding factors for the accuracy of the OCR System used in recognizing the off-line handwritten digits [3]. The intention behind this work is to evaluate the efficiency of MLP and RBF neural network classifiers trained with binarization features. Both the networks work as universal approximators and are basically non-linear layered feed forward networks [5]. RBF network is also a type of MLP but with Radial Basis as the activation function for the hidden layer neurons [4]. For different types of pattern classification activities, one neural network as a classifier may be proved to be superior to the other. In this work, the superiority of the two classifiers is judged for the task of handwritten digit recognition.

R. Natarajan (Ed.): ICDCIT 2014, LNCS 8337, pp. 341–346, 2014.

2   Feature Extraction Using Binarization Technique

Feature extraction is a process of deriving useful information from the filtered input patterns. The derived information can be general features, which are evaluated to ease further processing. The selection of features is very important because there might be only one-two values, which are significant to recognize a particular pattern. Binarization can be defined as a process in which the pixel values are separated into two groups; white as background and black as foreground. Only two colors, white and black, can be present in a binary image. A grayscale image after binarization can be classified into Globally Thresholded and Adaptive (Locally) Thresholded images.

It has been found that the global thresholding approach gives excellent result when the text is written by a single pen with same intensity on a background of throughout uniform intensity but considerably different from the text intensity. In such type of grayscale images, only one threshold value is used for the whole image to classify it into two categories; text and background, and the thresholding is called Fixed Global Threshold. In the adaptive thresholding method, the document image is divided into small blocks and the threshold values are computed pixel by pixel or region by region.

In this work, as the background intensity remains almost uniform throughout the image and does not change drastically anywhere in the input image. Hence, in the proposed binarization technique, global intensity thresholding has been employed [5,6].

As the handwritten digit images have been resized to 14×9 (in order to make all the digit images of uniform size), the feature vector of each individual digit image is a column vector of size 126×1. The resized binary image of digit '3' and the feature vector of digit '3' are shown in Fig.1(a) and Fig.1(c) respectively.

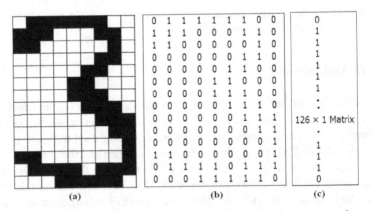

Fig. 1. (a) Resized Binary Image of Digit '3'; (b) Binary Matrix representation and (c) Reshaped Binary Matrix or Feature Vector of Digit '3'

3   Sample Preparation

For sample creation, 500 digit images were collected from 10 persons where each writer contributed 50 digits i.e. 5 samples of each of the digits (0-9). The feature vector of a single digit is a column vector of size 126 × 1. One such feature vector of digit '3' is shown in Fig.1(c). Similarly, the feature vectors of each of the 10 digits (0-9) are created in the form of binary column matrix of size 126 × 1 each. All these 10 feature vectors are combined to form a sample which is a binary matrix of size 126 × 10 as shown in Fig.2.

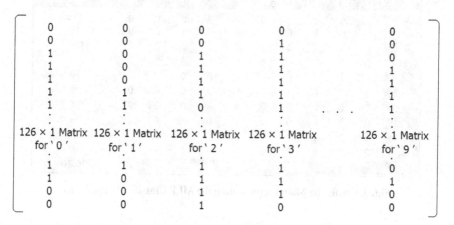

Fig. 2. Matrix representation of Input Sample

4   Implementation and Discussion of Results

Both the neural network classifiers have been trained with 50 sets of each digit i.e. 500 (50×10=500) digit image samples from the local database has been involved in the training process. Each digit at the input will put a '1' at that neuron in the output layer in which the maximum trust is shown and rest neuron's result into '0' status. The output of both the network classifiers is a binary matrix of size 10×10 each because there are 10 digits and every digit has 10×1 output vector. The first column stores the first digit's recognition output; the following column will be for next digit and so on for the complete sample of 10 digits.

The number of neurons in the input and output layers are fixed at 126 and 10 respectively. The 126 input neurons are equivalent to the input digit's feature vector size. The number of neurons in the output layer is 10 because there are 10 digits. The number of hidden neurons for the MLP classifier has been kept 30, by trial and error method, for optimal result.

The recognition results obtained when MLP and RBF network classifiers are used to recognize the handwritten digits using binarization features are shown the form of confusion matrices as shown in Fig.3 and Fig.5 respectively. The confusion matrix shows the confusion among the recognized characters while testing the neural network's recognition accuracy. The equivalent 3-D plots drawn in the 'MATLAB Environment' are also shown in Fig.4 and Fig.6 respectively.

During recognition using MLP, the confusion among the different digits is explained in Fig.3. Digit '0' is presented 50 times to the neural network and is classified 48 times correctly. It is miss-classified 2 times as '6'. Digit '1' is misclassified as '7' one time and is classified correctly 49 times. Digit '2' is classified 50 times correctly. The average recognition accuracy of 96.20% is very good for this handwritten digit recognition experiment using MLP as a classifier.

Digit	0	1	2	3	4	5	6	7	8	9	Accuracy (%)
0	48	0	0	0	0	0	2	0	0	0	96
1	0	49	0	0	0	0	0	1	0	0	98
2	0	0	50	0	0	0	0	0	0	0	100
3	0	0	0	47	0	0	0	0	3	0	94
4	0	1	0	0	48	0	0	0	0	1	96
5	0	0	0	1	0	49	0	0	0	0	98
6	0	0	0	0	0	0	48	0	2	0	96
7	0	0	0	0	2	0	0	47	0	1	94
8	0	0	0	0	0	0	0	0	50	0	100
9	0	0	0	0	0	0	0	1	4	45	90
Overall Recognition Accuracy =											96.20

Fig. 3. Confusion Matrix representing the MLP Classifier Performance

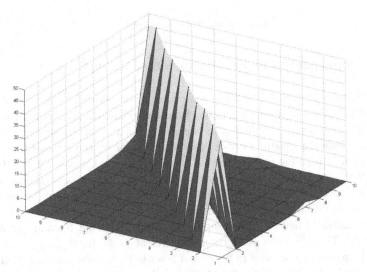

Fig. 4. Three-Dimensional Plot of Confusion Matrix representing the MLP Network Behavior

The RBF neural network has also been trained with 50 sets of each digit samples. Digit '0' is presented 50 times to the neural network and is classified correctly every time. Digit '4' is classified 48 times correctly and misidentified as digit '1' and digit '9' one time each out of a total of fifty trials. The recognition accuracy for each digit sample (0-9) as well as overall recognition accuracy is displayed in Fig.5. The average recognition accuracy of 98.40% is excellent for this handwritten digit recognition experiment using RBF as a classifier.

Digit	0	1	2	3	4	5	6	7	8	9	Accuracy (%)
0	50	0	0	0	0	0	0	0	0	0	100
1	0	50	0	0	0	0	0	0	0	0	100
2	0	0	50	0	0	0	0	0	0	0	100
3	0	0	0	49	0	0	0	0	1	0	98
4	0	1	0	0	48	0	0	0	0	1	96
5	0	0	0	1	0	49	0	0	0	0	98
6	0	0	0	0	0	0	50	0	0	0	100
7	0	0	0	0	2	0	0	48	0	0	96
8	0	0	0	0	0	0	0	0	50	0	100
9	0	0	0	0	0	0	0	0	2	48	96
Overall Recognition Accuracy =											98.40

Fig. 5. Confusion Matrix indicating the RBF Classifier Performance

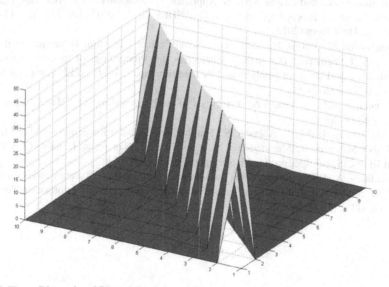

Fig. 6. Three-Dimensional Plot of Confusion Matrix representing the RBF Network Behavior

5   Conclusion and Future Scope

The choice of the classifier lies in the problem domain. In the field of cursive handwritten digit OCR using binarization features, the excellent recognition accuracy of 96.20% and 98.40% is achieved by using MLP and RBF classifiers respectively. It can be concluded that in the proposed experiment, by using RBF network as a classifier, higher digit recognition accuracy is achieved as compared to MLP network.

In future, a fusion of binarization features with some other type of features such as Projection Profile Features, can be investigated in the recognition experiment. Apart from MLP and RBF classifiers, other classifiers such as HMM, SVM etc. can also be examined in future.

Acknowledgement. The authors acknowledge their sincere thanks to the management and the director of Maharaja Surajmal Institute, C-4, Janakpuri, New Delhi, India, for providing infrastructure and financial assistance to carry out this research. The excellent cooperation of the fellow colleagues and library staff is highly appreciated. The authors gratefully acknowledge the contribution of the anonymous referee's comments in improving the clarity of the work.

References

1. Desai, A.A.: Gujarati Handwritten Numeral Optical Character Recognition through Neural Network. Pattern Recognition 43(7), 2582–2589 (2010)
2. Choudhary, A., Rishi, R., Ahlawat, S.: Unconstrained Handwritten Digit OCR Using Projection Profile and Neural Network Approach. In: Satapathy, S.C., Avadhani, P.S., Abraham, A. (eds.) Proceedings of the InConINDIA 2012. AISC, vol. 132, pp. 119–126. Springer, Heidelberg (2012)
3. Blumenstein, M., Verma, B., Basli, H.: A Novel Feature Extraction Technique for the Recognition of Segmented Handwritten Characters. In: Proceedings of the 7th International Conference on Document Analysis and Recognition, pp. 137–141. IEEE Computer Society Press, Edinburgh (2003)
4. Sivanandam, S.N., Deepa, S.N.: Principals of Soft Computing, pp. 71–83. Wiley-India, New Delhi (2008)
5. Choudhary, A., Rishi, R., Ahlawat, S.: Handwritten Numeral Recognition Using Modified BP ANN Structure. In: Meghanathan, N., Kaushik, B.K., Nagamalai, D. (eds.) CCSIT 2011, Part III. CCIS, vol. 133, pp. 56–65. Springer, Heidelberg (2011)
6. Choudhary, A., Rishi, R.: Improving the Character Recognition Efficiency of Feed Forward BP Neural Network. International Journal of Computer Science and Information Technology (IJCSIT) 3(1), 85–96 (2011)

Author Index

Agarwal, Nitin 293
Aggarwal, Pooja 79
Ahlawat, Savita 341
Ahluwalia, Ansuya 251
Amgoth, Tarachand 111
Anand, Deepa 176

Banerjee, Ansuman 200
Bansal, Divya 251
Berry, Gérard 1
Bhattacharjee, Anup Kumar 212
Bhattacharjee, Shrutilipi 68
Bhattacharya, Arani 200
Borkar, Vivek S. 14
Bose, Isita 299
Buchanan, Elizabeth A. 25

Casey, William 34
Choudhary, Amit 341

Das, Madhabananda 299
Das, Nabanita 134
Das, Smita 287
Datta, Anupam 43
Datta Banik, Abhijit 188
De, Sohini 86
De, Suddhasil 86
Deb, Suman 322
Debbarma, Swapan 287
Deep, Shaleen 251
Durga Bhavani, S. 233
Dutta, Ratna 275

Fages, François 50
Fahrnberger, Günter 239
Faisan Mohamed, Mustafa 233

Gandhi, Deebika 311
Ghosh, Nabin 111
Ghosh, Rabindranath 164
Ghosh, Soumya K. 68, 263
Ghosh, Souvik 188
Gopal, Krishna 146
Goswami, Veena 188

Guha, Dibyajyoti 188
Gupta, Yogesh 224

Jana, Prasanta K. 111

Khilar, Pabitra Mohan 98
Krishna, Shankara Narayanan 212
Kundu, Arkadeep 263

Mampilli, Bonson Sebastian 176
Martha, Venkata Swamy 293
Maskara, Shankar Lall 146
Mathkar, Adwaitvedant S. 14
Mishra, B.S.P. 299
Mishra, Bud 34
Mishra, Debashis 299
Misra, Alok 86
Mittal, Sangeeta 146
Mohapatra, Durga Prasad 98
Morales, Jose A. 34

Narwane, Ganesh Khandu 212
Nedungadi, Prema 333
Nguyen, Thomson 34

Pal, Shyamosree 134
Panda, Bhawani Sankar 122
Panda, Sanjaya Kumar 98
Patil, Sonal 68
Potluri, Anupama 105

Rajam, V. Mary Anita 92
Ramamoorthy, Suganya 311
Raman, Raghu 333
Ramaswamy, Srini 293
Ramesh, Maneesha 333
Rao, Y. Sreenivasa 275
Rishi, Rahul 341
Rudrapal, Dwijen 287

Saha, Dibakar 134
Saini, Ashish 224
Sarangi, Smruti R. 79
Sathyamoorthy, Sundararajan 92
Saxena, A.K. 224
Serrano, Manuel 1
Shankar, Rengaraj 92

Sharan, Aditi   224
Sharma, Arjun Datt   251
Sharma, Garvit   105
Shetty, D. Pushparaj   122
Shukla, Anupam   152
Sinha, Bhabani Prasad   164
Sinha, Koushik   164
Sinha, Subarna   322
Siva Subramanian, Rajaram   311

Spring, Jonathan   34
Sur, Chiranjib   152
Sur-Kolay, Susmita   200

Vignesh, Narayanan   92
Vutukuri, Krishna   105

Weaver, Rhiannon   34
Wright, Evan   34